T0340941

1971

1971

100 FILMS FROM CINEMA'S GREATEST YEAR

ROBERT SELLERS

The
History
Press

Front cover image: Malcolm McDowell as Alex DeLarge in Stanley Kubrick's 1971 film *A Clockwork Orange*. (Wikimedia Commons)

First published 2023

The History Press
97 St George's Place, Cheltenham,
Gloucestershire, GL50 3QB
www.thehistorypress.co.uk

British Library Cataloguing in Publication Data.
A catalogue record for this book is available from the British Library.

ISBN 978 0 7509 9999 1

Typesetting and origination by The History Press
Printed and bound in Great Britain by TJ Books Limited, Padstow, Cornwall.

CONTENTS

ACKNOWLEDGEMENTS

Vic Armstrong, Michael Attenborough, John Bailey, Derek Bell, Tony Lo Bianco, Erika Blanc, Michael Brandon, Timothy Burrill, Don Carmody, Kit Carson (2010 interview), Diane Sherry Case, Tom Chapin, Joan Churchill, John Cleese (2003 interview), Brian Clemens (2011 interview) Michael Deeley (2014 interview), Norman Eshley, David Foster (2010 interview), Clive Francis, Robert Fuest (2011 interview), Ellen Geer, Richard Gibson, Bruce Glover, Katherine Haber, Piers Haggard (2012 interview), John D. Hancock, Peter Hannan, Jo Ann Harris, Mike Higgins, Mike Hodges, Julian Holloway, Eric Idle (2003 interview), Henry Jaglom (2010 interview), Michael Jayston (2011 interview), Terry Jones (2003 interview), Tony Klinger, Hawk Koch, Harry Kümel, Valerie Leon, Mark Lester, Stephen Lighthill, Tom Mankiewicz (2010 interview), Michael Margotta, Kika Markham, Tom Marshall, Judy Matheson, Murray Melvin (2013 interview), John Milius (2004 interview), Donna Mills, Sofia Moran, David Muir, Danielle Ouimet, Tony Palmer, Anne Raitt, Alvin Rakoff, Angharad Rees (2011 interview), Anthony B. Richmond, Christian Roberts, Ken Russell (2005 interview), Ilya Salkind, Peter Samuelson, Christopher Sandford, Peter Sasdy (2011 interview), Jerry Schatzberg, Julio Sempere, Carolyn Seymour, Ralph S. Singleton, Mel Stuart (2011 interview), Michael Tarn, Damien Thomas, Beverly Todd, Patrick Wayne, Stephen Weeks, Michael Winner (2010 interview), Deborah Winters.

INTRODUCTION

What is the greatest year in movies? I guess there will never be a definitive answer. It's all subjective of course. There's no single greatest anything really – no greatest film, no greatest song, no greatest painter, no greatest football player. It's always going to be a question of personal taste and opinion. But, as I'm the one writing the book, I guess my opinion holds sway, and in my opinion 1971 is pretty hard to beat.

Just take a look at some of the filmmakers plying their trade in 1971 – Roman Polanski, Woody Allen, Steven Spielberg, Stanley Kubrick, Sam Peckinpah, Luchino Visconti, Sergio Leone, Peter Bogdanovich, Rainer Werner Fassbinder, Robert Altman, George Lucas, Dario Argento, John Schlesinger, Pier Paolo Pasolini, Nagisa Ōshima, Ken Loach, François Truffaut, Miloš Forman, William Friedkin, Joseph Losey, Mike Nichols, Mario Bava, Nicolas Roeg, Louis Malle, Ken Russell, Satyajit Ray, Jacques Tati, Mike Leigh and Ingmar Bergman. Can any other year match that amount of creative talent on display?

And if it's stars you want, how about John Wayne, Marlon Brando, Clint Eastwood, Steve McQueen, Paul Newman, Jack Nicholson, Jane Fonda, Dustin Hoffman, Warren Beatty, Al Pacino, Gene Hackman, Bruce Lee, Sean Connery, Michael Caine, Richard Burton, Peter O'Toole, Richard Harris, Julie Christie, Faye Dunaway, Dirk Bogarde, Anthony Hopkins, Goldie Hawn, Robert De Niro, Albert Finney, Burt Lancaster, Charlton Heston, Robert Mitchum, Kirk Douglas, Raquel Welch, Oliver Reed and Vanessa Redgrave?

What was the state of play in 1971? Well, it was all change. As usual the British film industry was in a state of flux, but this time it faced falling off a precipice. The American studio money that had been pumped into British films during the heyday of the 1960s had virtually dried up. It was always a dangerous situation to have one's indigenous industry dependent upon outside finance. At one time during the 1960s Hollywood was contributing over 80 per cent of the finance for British film production. This was never sustainable – and so it proved. Film producers now faced finding finance from new sources and the scarce few independent British companies around. Luckily, there was enough product already in the pipeline to make 1971 a healthy-looking year for British movies; but this really was the last hurrah. The rest of the decade resembled something of a wasteland until the industry picked itself up again in the 1980s.

Hollywood was changing too. It was the last embers of the studio system. The studios still wielded enormous power, but they were like dinosaurs, out of date and out of time. Some faced bankruptcy and had to sell off their backlots to property developers to stay afloat or sell out to non-media companies. Michael Margotta was a young actor under contract then to Columbia:

> You could still feel the ghosts of the past. There was an executive dining room and if you went up to have lunch there you could still feel the atmosphere of what it was like before, when Harry Cohen ran the place and the executives couldn't sit down until he sat down.[1]

This old guard was fading away and a new breed was on the march. The old guard knew it too. With a decline in box office attendances, along with an inability to recognise what audiences wanted to see, studio heads gave unprecedented freedom to younger writers and directors to make the kinds of film they wanted to make. This was really the start of the 'New Hollywood' that was to result in a decade of remarkable filmmaking. But it's perhaps in 1971 that we see it at its freshest, that the transfer of power can be felt most exhilaratingly.

Much of the richness of the films of 1971 is due to the political and social situation of a USA still coming to terms with the political assassinations of the Kennedy brothers and Martin Luther King, along with the continuation of the Vietnam War that had led to unrest and riots on college campuses around the country. A lot of films tapped into this mood and embraced the spirit of the counterculture, while others clung desperately onto the tenets of the past.

It also helped that this movement coincided with the continuing decline in censorship, which had stifled the industry for decades, ushering in an explosive age of sex and violence on screen. The British censor perhaps suffered its most contentious and controversial period during 1971, dealing with such hot potatoes as *A Clockwork Orange*, *Straw Dogs*, *Get Carter* and *The Devils*.

What may be most striking about 1971 is just how many firsts there were. Steven Spielberg made his first feature-length film, *Duel*, which aired as an ABC TV Movie of the Week in America and received a theatrical release in Europe. George Lucas made his feature debut too, with *THX 1138*, a chilly dystopian vision of the future that is worlds away from *Star Wars*.

Clint Eastwood made his directing debut with *Play Misty for Me*. The year 1971 must rank as Eastwood's busiest and most significant year, as it also saw the release of *The Beguiled*, and the iconic *Dirty Harry*. As San Francisco police detective Harry Callahan, *Dirty Harry* spawned a five-film franchise, and gave birth to some of the most quotable movie lines in history: 'Do you feel lucky, punk?' and 'Go ahead, make my day.' His arrival on screens came just two months after the introduction of another iconic cop, Gene Hackman's Jimmy 'Popeye' Doyle in *The French Connection*.

In Melvin Van Peebles's landmark independent movie *Sweet Sweetback's Baadasssss Song*, the police are painted as a force of oppressive white supremacist power. The extraordinary success of *Baadasssss Song*, combined with Gordon Parks's *Shaft*, with Richard Roundtree as a Black private eye, initiated the blaxploitation genre that would flourish over the course of the next half decade. There was a boom in martial arts pictures too, starting in 1971 after the financial success of Bruce Lee's first starring role in *The Big Boss*. Meanwhile, Mario Bava's *A Bay of Blood* laid down the ground rules for every '80s slasher movie to come.

1971 really has everything, from Godzilla to spaghetti westerns, Monty Python to Hammer horror, *Carry On* to Giallo. That's why, for me, it stands out from any other year in movie history, just by virtue of the sheer variety of films on offer. What other year could possibly serve up both *Harold and Maude* and *Willy Wonka and the Chocolate Factory*?

Notes
Release dates pertain to the movie's country of origin. For example, if it's a British film, the release date in Britain is the one given. If the film is a co-production, then it's usually the earliest release date that is noted. Release dates are courtesy of the American Film Institute and the Internet Movie Database.

100 FILMS

This is a film that straddles two decades and two different worlds. Made in 1968, it's very much a comment on what was happening as the 1960s began to draw to a close. It was a swansong to that most brilliant decade, and an introduction to the 1970s. Shelved by Warner Brothers, scared and repulsed in equal measure by its contents, it finally opened in the summer of 1970 in the USA, but British audiences didn't get the chance to see it until the start of 1971. Launching the career of its co-director Nicolas Roeg, *Performance* pushed the boundaries of British cinema in terms of explicit sex and drug use, and made a studio executive's wife vomit into her handbag.

The whole thing began as a star vehicle for Mick Jagger. The man chosen to bring it to life was painter-turned-filmmaker Donald Cammell. His story idea was, 'what would happen if a London gangster stepped into the very different world of a rock star?' This was the Kray twins meets the Rolling Stones. By the 1960s the East End thug had become almost a celebrity in his own right; the likes of the Krays hung around the fringes of showbiz, owned clubs and nightspots, and cultivated the friendship of stars. In *Performance*, Chas is a particularly vicious London gangster who is forced to go on the run when he murders one of his own. He finds refuge in a vast townhouse occupied by a reclusive and faded pop star called Turner, played by Jagger in his first film role. Slowly Chas's identity is broken down, as he is subjected to psychedelic drugs and mind games.

Cammell wanted Marlon Brando to play Chas, but in the end cast James Fox. As part of his research Fox visited Ronnie Kray in Brixton prison. However, it was the participation of Jagger and the prospect of tapping into the youth market that enticed Warners into supplying the £400,000 budget. Roeg, an acclaimed cinematographer, joined Cammell as co-director when shooting began in August 1968. The exterior of Turner's mansion was shot in Notting Hill, while the interiors were in an altogether different house that was found by the production team. This house was in the process of being renovated, which made it perfect to create the claustrophobic and bohemian rooms that Turner inhabited. According to Peter Hannan, who was on the camera unit as focus puller, this house was situated just off Sloane Square. Hannan has fond memories of the shoot. Roeg had personally asked him to do it and the two later became good friends. Hannan would later shoot Roeg's *Insignificance* (1985), along with films like *Withnail & I* (1987). At close quarters Hannan observed how Roeg and Cammell complemented each other in the unusual dual role of director: 'Donald would rehearse the actors in the green room or any room he could find, but the visuals were Nic. They worked really well together.'[1]

As for working with Jagger, who had no previous acting experience, Roeg told Hannan, 'If they're a star, they're an actor.' This was something he said about David Bowie too, when he cast him in *The Man Who Fell to Earth* (1976). Initially, Jagger had no discipline. Hannan says:

He'd say his lines and walk off the set, still saying his lines. He didn't know where the shot started or where it finished. But he was very good. Between set-ups, quite often he would just be sitting on a chair or a stool singing beautiful blues. He was an amazing blues singer.[2]

Hannan noticed a lot of hangers-on all over the set, girls that Jagger knew. There was also 'super groupie' Anita Pallenberg, who had previously dated Brian Jones, was currently going out with Keith Richards and reportedly had an affair with Jagger during the shoot. Then 26, Cammell asked her to appear as the strong-willed girlfriend of the washed-up Turner. Jagger's real-life girlfriend, Marianne Faithfull, had been approached to play the role, but she was pregnant at the time.

Performance conveys a vivid sense of the criminal underworld of London, probably because there were actual bona fide villains involved, like John Bindon. He'd fallen into the acting game when director Ken Loach spotted him holding court one night in a Fulham pub and cast him in his working-class drama *Poor Cow* (1967). Hannan recalls:

I became quite close to John Bindon. Quite often we'd meet for a drink. Sometimes we'd go to a pub in Fulham, his home manor: 'Let me introduce you to the lads,' he'd say and point, 'This one's carrying, carrying, not carrying, cop, cop, carrying', and when he said 'carrying' it meant he had a gun on him.[3]

Another pub Bindon frequented was the *Star Tavern* in Belgravia. Hannan says:

> There was an upstairs bar, and they'd all be crooks up there. But as long as you were with Johnny you weren't in any trouble. He was well respected by the lords and ladies of this world, people like Princess Margaret.[4]

Famously, when *Performance* was unveiled at a test screening for Warner executives it was a disaster. They hated it. 'At those executive screenings, once somebody doesn't like it, no one likes it,' claims Hannan. 'They all agree with each other. They're all yes people.'[5] Shocked by the more permissive elements in the picture, its dense storyline and the decadent behaviour of the characters, Warners refused to release the film in its present state. Cammell took off to Los Angeles to recut it, changing things around a bit, reducing the violence and sex and the insinuation of a relationship between Turner and Chas. At another test screening the alleged throwing-up incident took place, forcing it to be halted. It would take Warner Bros another eighteen months to gather up the courage to release it to the American public and then finally to the UK.

Performance did find a loyal audience, but it was never a commercial success. Only later did it build a reputation and the kind of cult status that few films manage to acquire. Numerous books have been written about it, along with academic theses. It certainly left its mark on a few of the participants. Fox would later admit that it had been a traumatic film to make. In a way, he felt like the character Chas, this straight actor thrown into a maelstrom of personal anguish and extreme drug-taking. He'd be sitting there on the set with the script every morning, studying his lines, while his co-stars deliberately walked around smoking joints to piss him off. Shortly afterwards, Fox left acting altogether to become a Christian evangelist. He didn't make another film until 1978. Others affected were Pallenberg, who emerged from it all a heroin addict, and Cammell, who took his own life in 1996. 'He was a very interesting man,' says Hannan.[6] His was a unique talent, although he only managed to make three further feature films. One of his personal projects was a historical epic about Nelson and Lady Hamilton that would have recreated some of Nelson's great sea battles. 'But no studio was prepared to pay for it,' says Hannan, who was going to work on it. 'The script was a million pounds a page, really.'[7]

(UK/US: London opening 7 January)

2 MURPHY'S WAR

By the early 1970s such was Peter O'Toole's reputation as a hellraiser that, when director Peter Yates and producer Michael Deeley cast him in *Murphy's War*, they came up with a cunning plan to keep him under control. Deeley relates:

> Because of one's fear that Peter might be unreliable, pissed out of his mind or something, we decided to cast his wife Siân Phillips to play opposite him. Of course, she's a great actress, but stuck in the jungles of Venezuela, we thought she would be our insurance. In the event it was totally unnecessary, because Peter behaved with absolute perfection in every way. Actually, he was the glue that held that film together.[8]

Murphy's War was based on a 1969 novel by Max Catto, who served in the RAF during the Second World War. It takes place during the last dregs of the conflict, when a British merchant ship is sunk by a German U-boat and the survivors are machine-gunned to death in the water. One of the sailors, Murphy, makes it ashore to a missionary settlement on the Orinoco in Venezuela. Looked after by a nurse, the only female role in the film, he learns that the submarine has taken shelter somewhere up river, and sets about obsessively plotting to sink it by any means.

Peter Yates was a 'name' in Hollywood after helming the Steve McQueen crime hit *Bullitt* (1968), and Deeley's previous picture was the classic *The Italian Job* (1969). With such a pedigree Paramount agreed to provide most of the finance. Deeley and Yates were handed a list of ten actors by the studio, and told to make their choice; Paramount's preference was for Robert Redford. Among the 'usual suspects' were a couple of left-field choices, chief among them O'Toole. A Connery or a Lee Marvin would have given a perfectly fine bravura performance, but Yates was aiming for something quirkier than your regular war movie. In that regard O'Toole was the perfect fit.

The movie's title, *Murphy's War*, was a play on the old adage 'Murphy's Law,' which says that anything that can go wrong will go wrong. That certainly summed up the making of the picture. For Deeley, who went on to produce *The Deer Hunter* (1978) and *Blade Runner* (1982), *Murphy's War* was fun but an enormous challenge, and the toughest film he ever worked on. The location was an absolute killer. Shooting on the Orinoco River, the unit were miles from any kind of civilisation and surrounded by hazards: piranha fish in the shallows and poisonous snakes just about everywhere else. 'It was a dangerous location because if you fell into the water, you'd be dead. It was that serious.'[9] Tracks were cut through the rainforest to location sites only to be impassable again within a week, reclaimed by the vegetation. One night the river rose 15ft, totally submerging one of the sets.

To make matters worse, an old, converted ferry that was going to accommodate the crew got stuck on a sand bank as it approached the mouth of the Orinoco, a mile from the location, demanding the use of small flat-bottomed boats to move everyone back and forth. One morning a party that included O'Toole and Phillips, along with Deeley and his wife, were halfway across when the weather turned bad and the sea began to cut up rough. As Deeley recalls:

> The fella who was driving the boat suddenly had hysterics and got down on his knees and started praying. The boat was now completely out of control. Luckily, our stunt arranger Bob Simmons knocked the guy out, seized the wheel and took over. But it was very nasty for a moment.[10]

O'Toole flourished in the hostile surroundings, living it like some kind of adventure. 'Peter was the absolute soul of the picture,' confirms Deeley. 'And I've never seen this with an actor before.'[11]

Up river, the crew came across a compound owned by a former German officer, who'd clearly decided not to hang around after the war was over for fear of his record emerging. Inevitably, this compound became a frequent destination for drinking and socialising. 'It was amazing,' says Deeley. 'My wife and I were walking down to his hut one night when a huge anaconda wound its way out of a tree into one's path.'[12] It was that kind of place. The officer himself was a genial host, despite being eaten away by leprosy.

After a couple of weeks O'Toole and Phillips were rehoused in a hotel in the nearby town of Puerto Ordaz; a helicopter ferried them into the rainforest for filming. The chopper was manned by a French stunt pilot called Gilbert Chomat, and on weekends O'Toole and Phillips were taken on jaunts round the area, landing on mud banks to search for pre-Columbian artefacts or visiting some of the local tribes.

The scenes involving the burning and sinking of the merchant ship were done later in Malta, at one of the world's largest exterior water tanks. After his experiences on *Lawrence of Arabia* (1962), where he had suffered countless injuries, O'Toole decided never again to handle his own stunts: 'Films employ stunt men, for a reason!' This changed on *Murphy's War*, where in Malta he swam through water filled with burning oil and explosives going off around him and in Venezuela took the controls of a seaplane; his terror-struck face on-camera was not acting.

The gruelling circumstances in which *Murphy's War* was made certainly paid dividends on screen, as this offbeat war film is wholly authentic, stunningly shot by Oscar-winning cameraman Douglas Slocombe. O'Toole delivers a whimsical and hard-edged performance, as his obsession to avenge his shipmates turns to madness. Even the discovery that the war is over and the German nation has surrendered doesn't stop him: 'Their war … not mine!'

Murphy's War didn't fare particularly well with the public or the critics on release. Deeley himself feels the film is flawed due to Yates's insistence that Murphy be killed off at the end. He survives in the book:

> Yates had this passion to make a picture which mattered, but this was not a film which mattered, it was a film which was meant to be a lot of fun, an adventure movie. So, Yates wanted to have this great sad ending, this anti-war message or something, which is such shit, and I think that's why the picture didn't do as well as it could have done.[13]

(US/UK: London release date 13 January)

3   *THE MUSIC LOVERS*

When Michael Caine wanted Ken Russell to direct the third Harry Palmer feature, *Billion Dollar Brain* (1967), producer Harry Saltzman wasn't so sure. A bold talent, to be sure, winning plaudits for his BBC art programmes, Russell had made only the one feature, a black and white comedy called *French Dressing* (1964). Caine was adamant, however, so Saltzman made a deal that he would bankroll any film of Russell's choosing if he agreed to make *Billion Dollar Brain*. Russell accepted and, after the work on it was finished, he turned up at Saltzman's office to remind him of his promise. 'Yeah, yeah,' said Saltzman, asking what Russell wanted to do. 'I'd like to do a film on Tchaikovsky.' Russell saw Saltzman grimace. 'Come back in a week,' the producer said.

A week elapsed and Russell duly returned. 'Ok, what about the Tchaikovsky film?' Saltzman's face was beaming this time. 'The Soviets are doing one already,' he gleefully reported, 'with Dimitri Tiomkin and he's already started putting together the score!'[14]

Russell did finally get to make his Tchaikovsky picture, but not for Harry Saltzman. After the critical and commercial success of his adaptation of the D.H. Lawrence novel *Women in Love*, United Artists (UA) were keen for Russell to do another picture with them. 'I said, "Yes, a film on Tchaikovsky." Their faces fell. They asked what the story was about and I said, "It's about a homosexual who falls in love with a nymphomaniac." They gave me the money instantly.'[15]

Russell's first choice to play Tchaikovsky was Alan Bates, with whom he'd just worked on *Women in Love*. 'But when he read the script, he got cold feet. He didn't want to play two sexual deviants one after the other.'[16] It was Russell's agent who suggested Richard Chamberlain, then still best known for his role in the hit US television series *Dr Kildare*. 'He was the romantic figure everybody expects Tchaikovsky to be who knows nothing about him,' according to Russell. 'And I thought he was very good in the film. He played it with just the right touch, the closet homosexual beneath the surface.'[17] For Chamberlain it was the biggest challenge of his career to date. As a closeted gay man himself, not coming out publicly until much later in his life, the actor could certainly relate to the need for duplicity and tortured aspect of the composer's private life.

Melvyn Bragg's screenplay remains fairly faithful to many of the known details of Tchaikovsky's extraordinary life, such as his dealings with Nadezhda von Meck, a Russian businesswoman and patron of the arts whose regular financial allowance freed Tchaikovsky to dedicate himself wholly to composition. Most notorious of all was his marriage to Antonina Milyukova. This was no marriage of love, rather one of convenience; for her it was status and money, for him an attempt to both hide and perhaps subdue his homosexuality. As related in the film, the marriage was an immediate disaster, causing Tchaikovsky to have a nervous breakdown and even attempt suicide. Although the couple separated after a few weeks, they remained married, with Antonina continuing to believe in the possibility of some kind of future reconciliation.

For the role of Antonina, Russell cast Glenda Jackson, despite the fact the two of them did not end up on the best of terms after finishing work on *Women in Love*. By far Jackson's toughest scene was set in a railway compartment, where she writhes around naked on the floor, bringing herself to ecstasy, as her husband, unable to perform sexually, looks upon her white, lanky flesh with disgust. As Russell cried 'action', crew hands rocked the set violently and a champagne bucket, followed by glasses and some cutlery, fell on Jackson, cutting her skin. 'Wipe the blood off,' roared Russell, 'it will never show.' Next, she was bombarded by heavy luggage. 'Never mind, get on with it,' said Russell. 'The bruising doesn't show.' To cap it all, the renowned cameraman Douglas Slocombe, fell right into her lap, managing to splutter, as a way of apology, 'It's alright, I'm a married man.'[18]

Chamberlain found there to be a certain sadism in the way Russell directed this sequence, filming it over and over again. Indeed, he gave serious thought to giving up acting after finishing the film, confessing to the American film critic Rex Reed that he'd never been so depressed and that it took him many weeks to get over it. He admitted to liking Russell, but found him to be excessively demanding in his working methods. 'It was no fun. That picture nearly put me in a looney bin. But I loved the film.'[19]

The Music Lovers is typical Ken Russell: controversial, flamboyant, excessive and, in places, quite bonkers. Of all his features on the lives of composers, which also included Gustav Mahler and Franz Liszt, it's by far the best, and is one of Russell's most satisfying films. It ends darkly with Tchaikovsky's death from cholera, after drinking a glass of unboiled water. Was this an error of judgement or, as some have suggested, suicide? As for Milyukova, she spent twenty years of her life in an asylum, diagnosed with chronic paranoia.

(UK/US: New York opening 25 January)

 ## 4 THE LAST VALLEY

James Clavell was an interesting figure in cinema. He'd been responsible for the screenplays of such diverse films as *The Fly* (1958) and *The Great Escape* (1963). On the strength of his successful adventure novel *Tai-Pan*, and the film *To Sir, with Love* (1967), which he both wrote and directed, Clavell had the means to forge ahead with a very personal project, a screen adaptation of J.B. Pick's historical novel *The Last Valley*. 'That was a project he had wanted to do for a long time,' says actor Christian Roberts. 'The success of *To Sir* gave him the opportunity.'[20]

With its seventeenth-century setting requiring vast warring armies, this wasn't going to come cheap; it ended up costing almost $7 million. A package was put together by Clavell's agent, Martin Baum, who also happened to be the head of ABC Pictures, the film division of the US television network ABC. A decision was also made to shoot the picture in the expensive Todd-AO process, becoming the last film to be shot in this process for twenty years.

As befits this kind of historical drama, marquee names were essential and Clavell chose Michael Caine and Omar Sharif. The two met for the first time in a Paris hotel and it didn't take long for the conversation to turn to the thorny question of billing. Sharif suggested that top billing go to whoever had the fattest pay cheque. Caine agreed. Back in London, Caine discovered Sharif was getting $600,000. Immediately he rang his agent and instructed him to hold out for $750,000. He got it, his biggest fee for a movie up to that time, and grabbed top billing too.

Using a German accent that he later recycled for *The Eagle Has Landed* (1976), in *The Last Valley* Caine plays the hard-bitten leader of a band of mercenaries during the Thirty Years' War, a religious conflict fought in Europe and one of the longest and most brutal wars in history. The mercenaries lay waste to any village they encounter, until they come upon a fertile, idyllic valley, seemingly untouched by the devastation surrounding it. Sharif, as a teacher on the run, has also taken refuge there and aids Caine's captain in arranging a truce with the local inhabitants, pledging to protect them from invasion in return for food and shelter.

Caine took on the role because it was a million miles away from the cockney strut of Alfie and Harry Palmer. It also said something about war and religion, especially prescient at the time with the troubles in Northern Ireland. For Clavell, the story's depiction of soldiers pillaging and destroying brought to mind America's current involvement in Vietnam. Clavell knew something about war. He served as a captain in the Royal Artillery during the Second World War. Captured by the Japanese in 1941, he spent three years as a prisoner of war in the notorious Changi Prison in Singapore, an experience that inspired his first novel, *King Rat*, in 1962.

For his supporting cast, Clavell brought in an interesting bunch: Florinda Bolkan, Nigel Davenport, Michael Gothard and Brian Blessed. Christian Roberts was just 27 and had played one of the juvenile leads in *To Sir, with Love*. 'James was very much a father figure to me as he knew *To Sir* had changed my life. He was always giving me friendly advice.'[21]

Filming took place in Austria and the cast were based in a hotel in Innsbruck. Most nights the cast played poker. 'After winning a few hands Sharif said he would not play anymore as he was a professional Bridge player and it would be unfair,' recalls Roberts. 'Caine continued to play.'[22] Sometimes the cast would go out to a local club for dinner. 'On arrival, when they saw Sharif, the band would play the theme song from *Dr Zhivago*,' says Roberts. 'Caine used to say, "Why don't they ever play *Alfie*?"'[23]

Filming was long but enjoyable, except for one terrible incident when the veteran Czech character actor Martin Miller, who had complained that morning about having to shoot in high altitude up in the mountains, suffered a fatal heart attack and died. Work was suspended for the day.

Most of the actors were required to ride a horse, something Caine never cared for. Having stipulated that his horse be small and docile, Caine was more than a bit put out to be presented with the biggest damn horse he'd seen in his life. Despite its fearsome appearance, this, Caine was told, was the calmest out of all the horses. Caine took it for a gentle trot, and all seemed well. On the first day of shooting, he mounted his steed in full costume, only this time it bolted, with the actor barely hanging on to its mane. A jeep followed and finally caught up with them 3 miles distance. Back at the set Caine let rip. 'I have a filthy temper sometimes, bordering on the psychotic, and on this occasion, I ranted and raved for about ten minutes.'[24] It turned out that his character's sword was slapping against the horse's side, urging it to go faster.

With an intelligent script and expert direction, stunning photography and one of John Barry's most majestic scores, *The Last Valley* did quite good business in Britain. America was a different story, where it was a box office disaster par excellence and no doubt contributed to ABC Pictures ceasing production in 1972 with millions in losses, having never turned a profit.

For Caine, the failure of *The Last Valley* was one of his bitterest disappointments. He'd given what he thought to be one of his best performances, 'and all to no avail,' he wrote in his autobiography. 'I knew the day we finished it that it was not going to work.' As for Clavell, he would not direct another feature film. Instead, he returned to writing books, just to see if he still had it. The result was the bestseller *Shogun*.

(US/UK: New York opening 28 January)

5 *10 RILLINGTON PLACE*

The infamous serial killer John Christie, who was estimated to have murdered at least eight women, including his own wife, was a role that Richard Attenborough had no real appetite to play when he was first approached about it. And yet he accepted it at once without seeing the script. His friend, the actor and producer Leslie Linder, had been told that an MP was trying to introduce a private member's bill into the House of Commons to reintroduce capital punishment to Britain, which had been abolished in 1965. Both Linder and Attenborough were firm advocates against capital punishment. Attenborough had been opposed to it all his life, according to his son Michael:

> Famously his hero Mahatma Gandhi said, an eye for an eye turns the whole world blind. And that's what my father believed, that as an act of revenge what you're doing is stooping to the level of the killer himself. On a purely moral ground he thought it was abhorrent.[25]

Of all the arguments against capital punishment it was the argument that if you get it wrong there's no going back that Attenborough found the most convincing. 'I remember dad saying that you can argue the moral case endlessly, but nobody surely can come up with an argument that justifies hanging the wrong man. And Timothy Evans was the classic case in point.'[26]

Timothy Evans was hanged in 1950 for the murder of his wife Beryl and baby daughter. The young couple were living at Christie's squalid tenement at 10 Rillington Place, Notting Hill. Only much later did it emerge that Christie was guilty of the crime and had framed Evans in a bid to cover up what was a killing spree that went back to the 1940s. It was in March 1953, after Christie had moved out of the ground floor flat that he rented, that a new tenant discovered a number of hidden bodies. Christie was caught, tried and executed.

The wrongful conviction of Evans is viewed as one of the great miscarriages of British justice and a factor in the subsequent abolition of the death penalty. In 1961 journalist Ludovic Kennedy wrote his successful book *10 Rillington Place*, which subsequently led to a posthumous pardon for Evans. Now it was Linder and Attenborough's hope that a film of Kennedy's book might act as a warning against the failings of capital punishment and drown out the voices of those who wished to bring it back.

Having committed to playing Christie, Attenborough carried out extensive research. He read all the reports about the trial, along with pieces written about Christie himself. He met the policeman who arrested Christie, and even visited Madame Tussauds Chamber of Horrors exhibit. All this, and a gruelling daily make-up routine, helped build up a picture of who Christie was, and Attenborough was later to say that never before or since did he become so totally immersed in a role. This had a deeply troubling effect. During shooting he didn't really speak to anybody and, at lunch, would often sit alone in his dressing room. At the end of the day, he felt uncomfortable going back home to his wife and family, feeling almost 'unclean', in his words. Michael recalls:

> It's no coincidence that I visited the set very late on in the shooting. I think my dad felt quite apprehensive about any of the family coming. But having lunch with a man looking and sounding like John Christie was bloody spooky.[27]

Attenborough had brilliantly perfected Christie's accent and soft-spoken voice and even off the set continued to use it. This was not unusual; almost with any part Attenborough played the physical or vocal characteristics of the character would often stay with him. Michael reports:

> He did a film called *Guns at Batasi*, in which he was playing a regimental sergeant major, and he used to rehearse all his parade ground shouting and yelling in the cellar. Then when he'd come up and you'd sit down for lunch with him he'd still talk in the manner of a sergeant major.[28]

Director Richard Fleischer brought the same kind of realism and non-sensationalism to the horrific crimes of Christie that he did with his dramatisation of the life of the Boston Strangler, Albert DeSalvo, a few years earlier in a film starring Tony Curtis. His approach is especially potent in the hanging scene of poor Evans, played brilliantly by John Hurt. This was the first time a British film had recreated an actual hanging, and real-life retired executioner Albert Pierrepoint, who had hanged both Evans and Christie, served as technical advisor to ensure complete authenticity.

10 Rillington Place is a deeply unsettling experience. The fact that the film was shot on the real location adds immeasurably to the pervading atmosphere of evil. The entire street was due for demolition, but the council agreed to pause until filming had been completed. Attenborough would recall how the commotion of a film unit brought so many sight-seers and souvenir hunters, taking bricks from the house, that the police were called in. Then, after Fleischer's crew were finished, the demolition crews arrived, and the area redeveloped beyond all recognition.

It was an unpleasant feeling working inside No. 10, standing on the same floorboards beneath which some of Christie's victims had lain. However, the bulk of interior shots were completed at No. 7, along with some work at Shepperton Studios. One thing Fleischer does well is to convey the squalor of the area and period. 'The social and physical conditions of the time were so important to the movie and so important to dad,' says Michael.[29] Despite his fervid anti-capital punishment views, Michael recalls his dad jokingly saying to him one day, 'I have a feeling I'd hang those who forced people to live in houses like that.'[30]

Despite the critical favour in which Attenborough was held as an actor, he didn't like watching himself, so whenever there was a press show he would ask Michael to go in his place and afterwards pass judgement. Attenborough had recently made a film called *Loot*, based on the Joe Orton play, which came out at the end of 1970. It just so happened that the press shows for *Loot* and *10 Rillington Place* fell within a short space of time of each other. Michael saw *Loot* first and met his father for lunch afterwards. 'Look, I'm not going to beat about the bush, you are way over the top. I'm sure you had a great time making it, but it's an out-rageous performance.'[31] About ten days later Michael saw *Rillington Place* and talked to his father as usual afterwards. 'And I kicked off by saying, "I'm so glad I was honest with you about *Loot* because I can honestly tell you, and you will be able to believe me, that you were wonderful, extraordinary, terrifying as Christie."'[32]

Attenborough always ranked *10 Rillington Place* and his own perfor-mance among his career highlights, although, according to Michael, it wasn't a film he liked to talk about. Perhaps he didn't want to dredge up all those awful feelings he'd had inhabiting Christie. It's a performance that one is surprised to learn didn't gain him either an Oscar or BAFTA nomination, although that kind of thing never bothered him. As Michael says, 'He was never somebody who cared hugely about awards.'[33]

(UK/US: London opening 29 January)

6 ▌ LITTLE MURDERS

Author and celebrated cartoonist Jules Feiffer's play *Little Murders* opened on Broadway in April 1967 and, just five days later, closed after a barrage of brutal notices. At one performance there were fewer than fourteen people sat in the audience. The play was inspired by the assassination of John F. Kennedy and, mere days later, the slaying, live on television, of Lee Harvey Oswald. Feiffer viewed this as nothing less than a total breakdown of all forms of authority. The country had descended into madness: it was no longer the place he had been raised in, the rules had changed, something had gone wrong. These feelings were merely heightened when the Vietnam War kicked in. At the time Feiffer felt that no one was really talking about these issues in the way they should have been. At the time he was a cartoonist at *The Village Voice*, a news and culture paper published in New York. This was far too heavy and complex a subject for a mere six panels of satiric art, and so Feiffer began to write it as a novel. When it dawned on him that he wasn't a novelist he began to adapt it into a theatre piece and, to his delight, discovered that he was a pretty good playwright.

Feiffer's comment on the malaise and horror of contemporary America is interpreted through a mismatched New York couple, eccentric photographer Alfred Chamberlain, whose art is photographing piles of dog poo, and idealistic interior designer Patsy Newquist. When she saves Alfred from being mugged outside her apartment, Patsy finds herself attracted to him and tries to find ways to turn him into a suitable husband.

Following its Broadway debacle, *Little Murders* fared much better on the London stage, where it was the first American play produced by the Royal Shakespeare Company. In 1969, Alan Arkin directed an off-Broadway revival, and this time the play was a success. Maybe the timing was now right. In the face of the recent assassinations of Robert Kennedy and Martin Luther King, the shootings at Kent State University and a climate of anti-war demonstrations, Feiffer's satire rang a bit truer. Arkin was also to give the play the right kind of satiric insanity that the original Broadway production lacked.

On the back of this new-found success, Elliott Gould, who had appeared in the ill-fated 1967 production, obtained the screen rights and tried to interest Jean-Luc Godard into directing. This would have marked Godard's first American production. Feiffer had seen Godard's surreal road trip film *Weekend* (1967) and suggested to Gould they try to get him. Godard flew to New York for some meetings, but Feiffer was to recall that it was obvious right from the start that the French filmmaker was there just for a payday from backers UA. Nor did he do much to hide his disdain for the whole lot of them. It was suggested that the screenplay be written by the team of David Newman and Robert Benton, of *Bonnie and Clyde* fame. According to Godard, UA reneged on the deal he had with them; the studio wanted to keep the Newman/Benton screenplay but ditch him. Maybe the reason was that Godard had totally turned the project upside down and wanted the film instead to be about a French director who comes to New York to make a film called *Little Murders* but finds he is unable to do it. Goodbye Godard, hello Alan Arkin, despite Arkin never having directed a feature film before. He was also persuaded to play a scene-stealing supporting role as a manic and paranoid detective trying to solve 345 motiveless homicides.

Little Murders is a surreal satire of urban alienation and is among a group of outsider-type movies that came out in 1971, such as *Carnal Knowledge*, *Harold and Maude*, *Minnie and Moskowitz* and *A New Leaf*. Alfred and Patsy's relationship plays out against a backdrop of a New York that often resembles an urban battlefield, with random muggings, sniper shootings, garbage strikes and blackouts. There's a scene where Anthony takes the subway, his shirt covered in blood, and his fellow passengers blithely ignore him, which anyone who has lived in New York can certainly relate to. Several contemporary reviewers commented that Feiffer's view of urban violence had become more relevant than ever, with noted critic Roger Ebert calling the film 'a definitive reflection of America's darker moods'.

Elliott Gould reprised his role of Anthony in the film and, for a while, considered Jane Fonda for the role of Patsy, before casting noted stage actress Marcia Rodd to reprise her role from the off-Broadway revival. *Little Murders* also reunited Gould with his *MASH* co-star Donald Sutherland, who agreed to do one day's work on the film as a favour to his friend. Sutherland plays a New Age reverend that performs Alfred and Patsy's wedding ceremony.

This is an edgy, risky and frightening comedy. After seeing it, Jean Renoir wrote to Alan Arkin telling him, 'This film will never be forgotten.' Unfortunately, largely, it has been. It deserves far more notice.

(US: New York opening 9 February)

7 THE HOUSE THAT DRIPPED BLOOD

In British horror, Amicus were really the only rivals to Hammer's crown. The company's headquarters was in a small purpose-built hut on the back lot at Shepperton Studios. It was run by two American producers/screenwriters, Max Rosenberg and Milton Subotsky. Generally, Rosenberg was the least visible of the two, usually away somewhere raising money; it was Subotsky that was more involved on the creative level. Generally, people liked working for them, despite the fact that things were done as cheaply as possible. 'I would much rather have worked for Amicus than I would for Hammer,' admits assistant director Mike Higgins. 'They had a nice production team there; it was a family kind of situation. And it was fun.'[34]

Ever since the enormous success of *Dr Terror's House of Horrors* in 1965, Amicus specialised in the portmanteau film. These typically featured four or sometimes five short self-contained tales linked by a framing device, and their popularity has given them a special place in British horror movie history. *Torture Garden* followed *Dr Terror* into cinemas in 1967, and garnered such a lukewarm reception that Amicus didn't return to the format until *The House That Dripped Blood*, whose surprise success, especially in America, resulted in a production line of anthologies over the next three years: *Tales from the Crypt* (1972), *Asylum* (1972), *Vault of Horror* (1973) and *From Beyond the Grave* (1974).

For *Dripped Blood* Amicus followed the same pattern that was used on *Torture Garden*: a selection of four short stories from the acclaimed American writer Robert Bloch, the author of *Psycho*. The framing device is simple yet effective, a Scotland Yard inspector's investigation into a disappearance leads him to an old house where numerous strange occurrences have taken place.

Another trademark of the portmanteau horror film is its generous use of stars and familiar faces. *The House That Dripped Blood* is no exception, featuring as it does Britain's two great horror icons in Christopher Lee and Peter Cushing. The cast also includes Ingrid Pitt, Denholm Elliott and Jon Pertwee, then starring in the title role in television's Doctor Who. While the film itself took something like five weeks to shoot, actors were only needed for about a week to film their individual episode.

New Zealand-born actress Nyree Dawn Porter, who had recently starred in the BBC's hugely popular drama serial *The Forsyte Saga*, appeared in one of the stories. At the time she was suffering from the recent tragedy of her husband dying from an accidental drug overdose. 'She was a lovely lady,' remembers Higgins. 'But she was still trying to get over what had happened and was taking sleeping pills in order to sleep. I was particularly attentive to making sure that she was ok.'[35]

The most fondly remembered episode is probably the one featuring Pertwee as a horror movie star who buys a cloak for his vampire costume from a mysterious shop, only to discover it belonged to a real blood sucker. This story was a personal favourite of Subotsky. Unlike the rest of the film, this was deliberately played for laughs. Pertwee's pompous horror star was actually a send-up of Lee. After the premiere Lee, who had enjoyed the segment enormously, approached Pertwee asking who he'd based the character on, totally oblivious that it was him!

During the shooting of the segment, Higgins played a practical joke on the production office when he phoned up Subotsky's secretary pretending to be from Chipperfield Circus and discussing the possibility of lending them a vampire bat:

> I said I was in charge of the bats and before we let it go, we wanted to make sure that they had the correct environment to keep the bat safe. I could hear her getting more anxious as I went on. Then I said, 'These are rare and delicate creatures from the upper reaches of the Amazon – and they only eat blooooood.' At which point she ran out of the office in hysterics.[36]

There are a few neat in-jokes in this segment. One of the vampire cloaks has a label declaring it to be the property of Shepperton Studios, where the film was actually made, and Pertwee's dressing room is littered with publicity photos, including one of him with Bessie, the famous old car from *Doctor Who*. Other neat references litter the film, including Lee's character reading *Lord of the Rings*, the actor's favourite book, and the estate agent handling the sale of the doom-laden house is called A.J. Stoker.

As for the house itself, this was actually real and situated in the grounds of Shepperton, although only the exterior was used. The house was later demolished to make way for a housing estate. There was very little location shooting to speak of. A second unit crew were sent out to Weybridge high street, where one of the buildings was mocked up to look like a wax museum for the Peter Cushing story. For one shot the crew wanted to capture normal passers-by and so hid a camera across the street. They began rolling, all seemed fine, until this one woman stopped and began to peek inside the window of the fake wax museum. The first assistant director was stood next to Higgins, picked up a loud hailer and blasted, 'Heh, lady in the red hat.' Of course, everybody in the street started looking round. 'And the lady in question was terrified,' recalls Higgins.[37] The ideal course of action would have been to just let things go; the lady would have got bored and walked on. But no, this bloke blasted out more orders. Higgins says:

> Then everybody was rushing about to see where the camera was, and of course it caused absolute chaos and there was the first AD yelling, 'Don't move, go away from the window, don't look at the camera.' It was chaotic.[38]

The House That Dripped Blood may not be the best of the Amicus portmanteau films, but it's a solid example. One of the strangest aspects about it is the virtual lack of any blood or gore. Indeed, the British film censor was all for bestowing it with an A certificate, only for Subotsky and Rosenberg to demand they be given an X (suitable for over-14s), since that guaranteed the usual horror crowd. Subotsky's stated desire to make a horror picture for younger audiences had perhaps succeeded a little too well.

(UK/US: London opening 21 February)

DEATH IN VENICE (MORTE A VENEZIA)

For a long time, Luchino Visconti used to carry around with him a copy of Thomas Mann's novella *Death in Venice* and it was his ambition to one day bring it to the screen. For him, it wasn't really a tale about death but, as he called it, 'intellectual death', an artist's search all his life for absolute beauty, which he finds in a young boy. This man, who knows he has not long to live, goes to Venice for the last summer of his life and sees in this child the essence of everything that is beautiful and pure; 'a young god,' in Mann's words.

Unfortunately, Visconti could raise only a small portion of finance from Italian sources; the rest of the money he sought in America. This came from Warner Brothers despite them making no secret of the fact that they would have preferred the story to be about a little girl being lusted after, rather than a little boy. Or, as Visconti heard one studio executive say, 'A dirty old man chasing a kid's ass.'

For his star, Visconti only wanted Dirk Bogarde; the two of them had recently worked together on *The Damned* (1969). Visconti likened Bogarde to a dead pheasant, hung from the neck, whose body is ripe. In other words, he was exactly ripe for this role. Bogarde was under no illusion that this would be the biggest challenge of his career. When the script finally arrived four days before filming was due to start, he declared himself to be genuinely 'scared'.

The film was almost scuppered when Visconti failed to reveal that he didn't actually own the rights to Mann's novella. They lay with the actor José Ferrer, who had bought them from the Mann estate back in 1963 with the intention of directing rather than starring, only for him to relinquish the director's chair to Franco Zeffirelli. Stars like Burt Lancaster, John Gielgud and Alec Guinness all turned the role down, Guinness later admitting it to be among his biggest career mistakes. A deal was finally made for the rights, after several days of anguished phone calls between lawyers, and Visconti's film was back on.

Bogarde was under no illusion that he was in fact playing composer Gustav Mahler. Others say that the character of Aschenbach is modelled more on Mann himself, who took a similar vacation to Italy in 1911, and there saw a young Polish boy who became the inspiration for Tadzio. Bogarde was made to resemble both Mann and Mahler, with a little moustache and pair of vintage spectacles. His famous white silk suit was also vintage. They were going to put a false nose on him too, but due to the heat it kept falling off. Mann's protagonist, Aschenbach, is a poet, but Visconti changed him to a composer. This gave him the excuse to memorably fill the screen with Mahler's lush third and fifth symphonies. When the film came to be screened in Los Angeles, the reception was icy cold. Bogarde and Visconti knew it had fallen flat in the room. There was complete silence. Suddenly one of the Warner executives asked who wrote the music. Visconti told them it was Mahler. Impressed at least with that aspect of the film, the executive pondered whether it was worth putting this Mahler fellow under contract. This story sounds apocryphal, but Bogarde always insisted it happened.

Visconti's European trek to find the right boy to play Tadzio concluded in Stockholm where he discovered 15-year-old Björn Andrésen. Tadzio is the object of Aschenbach's yearning, not lust or any other feelings. Bogarde would admonish any reporter who suggested his character was gay. Visconti, too, stated that the love Aschenbach feels for Tadzio was not homosexual, but love without sexuality. *Death in Venice* would turn Andrésen not into a mere star but an instant icon, his face became the embodiment of youthful beauty. The role completely eclipsed his life. This is a boy who never really wanted to act in the first place; he was much more interested in chewing gum, girls and playing the guitar. Fifty years later he would describe his troubled life in the documentary *The Most Beautiful Boy in the World*.

Bogarde admired Visconti greatly; best of all Visconti left him alone. They never once discussed the film or the part. Visconti merely told him to read the book. Bogarde did, something like thirty times, but still wanted to discuss it with Visconti, who told him to read the book again. During filming Visconti gave Bogarde just one piece of direction. It was when he was in a boat and Visconti screamed down a megaphone for him to stand up when the sun hit his face. This was because Visconti had already edited the sequence in his head and where the music was going to go. It wasn't until he saw the finished film that Bogarde realised his movements were being orchestrated in large measure to fit with certain passages of Mahler's music.

As for the famous death scene, Bogarde knew Aschenbach's tragic end and was dreading it. It was never scheduled; Visconti merely came up to Bogarde one morning on the set and said casually, 'Today you die.' Bogarde sat in the make-up chair for almost four hours while he was plastered with this unknown white substance that came to resemble a death mask. It stung so badly that Bogarde implored the make-up artist to be careful not to put it in his eyes, fearing it could blind him. Sat on a canvas chair on his own on the Lido beach, it was then that Bogarde saw Visconti had brought over all his friends and the world's press to watch. They sat in the shade beneath umbrellas drinking champagne while Bogarde roasted in the sun.

Death in Venice was lavished with praise and garnered with prizes at festivals throughout the world. Bogarde's performance was much lauded and he received a BAFTA nomination for Best Actor. It is the performance for which he is best remembered. Bogarde knew at the time it was both the peak of his career and the end of it, that he would never again give a better performance in a better film. On the last day of shooting, after inhabiting the role for three months, he saw the wardrobe mistress bundle up his character's clothes into a bag. He was no longer

Aschenbach. Good riddance, he thought to himself, then gave a great sigh of relief and wept all the way home in his car.

(Italy/US: Rome opening 4 March)

9 THE EMIGRANTS (UTVANDRARNA)

Widely considered to be among the finest Swedish films ever made, *The Emigrants* is a mammoth, and yet at the same time intimate, epic set in the mid-nineteenth century about a Swedish farming family's voyage to America and their efforts to put down roots. Max von Sydow and Liv Ullmann, who had already played couples in three Ingmar Bergman pictures, play Karl Oskar and Kristina, a couple who face numerous physical and emotional trials. There's a wonderful, celebratory moment when Karl tramples through dense woodland to reach and stake his claim for what will be his family's new home and farm. He chips his name and nationality into the bark of a tree; only then does he allow himself to sit and rest, quietly satisfied.

The film was based on a series of four books by acclaimed Swedish writer Vilhelm Moberg, which he started in 1948 and took twelve years to complete. Travelling across the Swedish countryside to acquaint himself with the subject, looking through library archives, Moberg also spent four years in America, starting in Minnesota, where he followed and studied the emigrants' paths. Moberg had been a newspaper man and brought that journalist's zeal for facts and details to his fiction – he liked to describe his *Emigrants* books as 'documentary novels'. His efforts were well rewarded; the books are hailed as one of Sweden's greatest literary achievements and have sold close to two million copies in Sweden alone.

It was inevitable that a movie would eventually be made, although for many years Moberg resisted overtures from filmmakers, including John Ford. Swedish director Jan Troell was Moberg's personal choice, having admired the naturalistic and poetic approach he brought to his subjects. Troell was a very hands-on director, acting as editor and cameraman on his films. *The Emigrants* was only his third feature, having previously worked on shorts and documentaries. Troell also co-wrote the screenplay, with producer Bengt Forslund.

The decision was taken to adapt all four books but to split them into two films. *The Emigrants* covers the opening two books while *The New Land*, which was released in 1972, follows Kristina and Karl Oskar's struggles to make a life for themselves. Though each film is over three hours long, it makes sense to view them both as one long film, in the same way that Moberg considered his four volumes as one single work. It's no surprise to learn that this project was up to that time the most expensive undertaking in Swedish film history.

Both films were shot in Sweden and America and made back to back, which meant the cast and crew worked for almost a year. It was particularly tough on the two leads. As Kristina, Ullmann ages from 17 to an old 45 when she dies after a life of physical burden. At the time Ullmann was in her early 30s and, as a Norwegian, was a highly contentious choice for such an important Swedish fictional heroine, but Moberg was adamant she played it. Often in interviews Ullmann described Kristina as the favourite of all the roles she played on film. Her performance earned her an Oscar nomination for Best Actress.

The Emigrants is presented with brutal realism and authenticity and, at times, a lyrical beauty, and it won international acclaim. It was only the third film not in the English language to be nominated for Best Picture in the history of the Academy Awards.

Stanley Kubrick was a huge admirer of both films and put a call through to Troell to discuss them with him. Troell thought it was a prank call and hung up. This was a regular occurrence; most people didn't believe it was Stanley Kubrick when he called them. Kubrick particularly loved the costumes, and went on to hire *The Emigrants'* costume designer Ulla-Britt Söderlund to work on *Barry Lyndon* (1975).

Although the running times were heavily cut, the movies were popular enough in the USA to spawn a network television series on ABC, *The New Land*, starring a young Kurt Russell. Described as a Swedish *Waltons*, the show received critical plaudits but poor ratings and was taken off the air after just six episodes. In the mid-1990s there was even a musical based on the films, called *Kristina från Duvemåla*, written by Benny Andersson and Björn Ulvaeus of ABBA. Running for a bladder-pulverising four hours, the musical played in Stockholm for four years. Testament to the enduring appeal of Moberg's saga, *The Emigrants* was remade in 2021 by Norwegian director Erik Poppe.

Tragically, in 1973 Moberg drowned in a lake near his home in Roslagen, north of Stockholm. He left a note: 'It's twenty past seven, I'm going to search in the lake, sleep without end.'

(Sweden/US: Swedish opening 8 March)

10   *WHEN EIGHT BELLS TOLL/*
PUPPET ON A CHAIN

1971 saw the release of a pair of thrillers based on Alistair MacLean novels and, while not in the same ball park as, say, *Where Eagles Dare* (1968) or *Guns of Navarone* (1961), they are engaging entertainments and were paired together on the same double bill a few years later.

Elliot Kastner, a maverick American producer based in Britain, had already scored a major success with *Where Eagles Dare*. After that, he'd commissioned two original movie ideas from MacLean, including a western, but felt more drawn to his latest novel, *When Eight Bells Toll*. It was an exciting sub-Bond thriller about gold smugglers but, more than that, Kastner liked the central character of dour agent Philip Calvert and sensed the potential for a series. Like the Bond producers when they cast the relatively unknown Sean Connery, Kastner didn't want a star; not just that, he wanted an actor with a classically trained background. After briefly considering Michael Jayston, Kastner fixed on Anthony Hopkins. Making his breakthrough at the National Theatre, Hopkins had grown tired of stage work and yearned for a career in movies. He wanted what his Celtic compatriots Richard Burton and Richard Harris had – stardom. Kastner had seen Hopkins on stage, but it was a private screening of the 1968 *The Lion in Winter*, in which Hopkins made his film debut, that clinched it.

Hopkins was invited to see Kastner at his office at Pinewood. Yes, they were interested in him playing this James Bond-type spy, but frankly he was overweight and needed to lose a few pounds first. Hopkins submitted to spending ten days in a health farm, munching lettuce leaves and knocking back carrot juice. For his first leading role in a movie Hopkins' fee was £8,000.

Filmed on location on the Isle of Mull, just off the Scottish mainland, Hopkins spent many a boozy night with fellow actors Maurice Roëves and Leon Collins in the local hostelry; it was an open secret that Hopkins had a drink problem. Ironically, it was booze that led to him meeting the woman that would be his wife for almost thirty years. Along with Collins, Hopkins had been drinking in a bar and missed the flight back to London to start work on interiors at Pinewood Studios. Production assistant Jennifer Lynton was given the task of collecting an aggressive and argumentative Hopkins when he finally showed up at

Heathrow Airport. It wasn't an auspicious start to their romance but, before the film was in the can, Hopkins had left his wife and young child and he and Lynton began dating. They married in 1973.

When Eight Bells Toll was a modest hit, but Kastner decided against making a second film, for which Hopkins had an option. Despite its relative failure, Hopkins enjoyed much of the filming, particularly the physical stuff, running and throwing himself around like a kid playing cowboys and Indians. He also did bits of stunt work, including some of the underwater scenes, such as when a helicopter ditches into the sea and he has to scramble out.

While *Eight Bells* concerned itself with *Boy's Own* heroics, *Puppet on a Chain*, which opened later that year, focused on the heroin trade, and was an altogether more vicious and nasty film. MacLean had made the acquaintance of Geoffrey Reeve, a former maker of television commercials who was keen to get into movies. During a business trip to Amsterdam, they passed a warehouse on the docks and noticed a puppet hanging by its neck from a chain. This stirred MacLean's imagination and, out of that, came his latest bestseller about an Interpol narcotics agent set on breaking up a smuggling operation out of the Netherlands that uses souvenir dolls to hide drugs. The gang also despatch their enemies by hanging them on the end of a chain.

MacLean all but gave Reeve the film rights to the book, with the intention of him making his feature film directorial debut. Producer Kurt Unger put together the money. Swedish singer and actor Sven-Bertil Taube was cast in the lead and ex-Bond baddie Vladek Sheybal brought his usual menace to a villainous role.

A decent thriller in its own right, *Puppet* is best remembered today for an extraordinary boat chase through the canals of Amsterdam, a scene that undoubtedly influenced a very similar action set piece two years later in the 007 film *Live and Let Die*. Australian Don Sharp, who had directed a few Hammer horrors, was brought over exclusively to shoot the sequence, and several boats were wrecked performing outrageous stunts and hurtling about at reckless speeds.

There had been some trepidation on the part of the money people regarding putting the inexperienced Reeve at the helm – and so it proved. The film wasn't working, and serious discussions took place about scrapping it altogether and cutting their losses. Instead, impressed by Sharp's work on the boat chase, Reeve was fired, and the Australian brought in to undertake several weeks of reshoots. 'It was literally a film of two halves,' claims Higgins, who worked as second assistant director. 'It was basically Don that remade that whole movie.'[39]

(UK: London opening 9 March)

11 *GET CARTER*

One morning early in January 1970 Mike Hodges received a parcel in the post. It was a book, *Jack's Return Home* by Ted Lewis, along with a letter from a producer called Michael Klinger asking if he was interested in adapting and directing it. 'I didn't hesitate,' says Hodges.[40]

At first sight Klinger was a caricature of the movie producer: big cigar, bigger personality. But as Hodges was to find out he was anything but a caricature. 'In my experience he was unique. Having chosen a director, he left him alone to do his job – no room for megalomania. As a consequence, the *Get Carter* project came together easily like pieces in a child's jigsaw.'[41]

Jack's Return Home immediately leapt off the page for Klinger. The central character of Jack Carter, a London mob enforcer who returns to his home town to investigate the mysterious death of his estranged brother, was an interesting anti-hero. It helped that Klinger was a Raymond Chandler fan and connected with the story's *crime noir* ingredients.

Klinger had been dealing with an agent called Robert Littman, who called up out of the blue saying he was now head of MGM's European division and was looking for product, 'Have you got anything?' Klinger had just bought the rights to Lewis's novel. Littman said to get a director attached and then they could talk.

By the age of 18, Klinger's son Tony was already developing scripts and producing documentaries and small professional films. His agent had another up-and-coming director on their books, Hodges. Starting his career in the 1960s, producing and directing hard-hitting documentaries for ITV's *World in Action*, Hodges had moved into television drama and directed two standalone thrillers. Tony's agent suggested he check them out: 'They were both fantastically well directed and stylistically outstanding.'[42] At home, Tony watched one of them with his dad. 'As we were watching, we made the call to the agent and said, we want him. And we made the deal on the phone.'[43] It was a gamble; this would be Hodges's first feature, but Klinger liked working with first-time directors, 'because he could influence them,' says Tony.[44]

The biggest difficulty facing Hodges was adapting the book. He admired it so much that he was initially reluctant to change a word. Reading it conjured up vivid images from his National Service in the Royal Navy working on the lower deck of a minesweeper:

> It was in the 1950s when we sailed into every fishing port on the East coast, witnessing poverty and degradation the like of which I'd never seen before or since. In many ways it replicated the same territory as the author's.[45]

In the novel, Jack Carter changes trains at Doncaster and it was here that Hodges uncoupled the film from its literary source.

> Instead of going to an unnamed steel town I had Jack travel North to Newcastle. The great iron bridges straddling the Tyne, the towering cargo ships docked along its banks, the ferries criss-crossing were visually arresting. More importantly these images reveal a hard unforgiving environment in which a psychopath like Carter might well have been rooted.[46]

Certainly, Hodges's background in documentary and TV current affairs greatly informed *Get Carter*. 'For me background research is part of the immersive process when starting a new project. Real events often trigger the creative juices; lending the fiction believability and providing the building bricks on which to build your imaginary world.'[47] While carrying out his research in Newcastle a hazy memory kept nagging at Hodges. It concerned a sensational local murder in the late 1960s committed close to a nightclub called *La Dolce Vita* and revealed corruption at every level of society, involving pornography, working men's clubs, fruit machine rackets, many of the elements Lewis had weaved into his novel. It even had a hit man from London, who was found guilty of the killing.

> My research into this crime led me to locations and characters that gave our fictional story a certain veracity. The most important was locating the home of the racketeer behind the crime, one Vince Landa. I found that it was still on the market after he'd done a moonlight flit two years earlier. Entering it was like boarding the *Mary Celeste*, everything was still in place from the time of his hurried getaway. This now

became the home of Cyril Kinnear, our fictional racketeer. Towards the end of the film there's a long tracking shot of extraordinary faces in a police line-up. These extras were real participants in the parties Landa threw most weekends.[48]

The casting of Michael Caine was a masterstroke. His icy, steely, ruthless performance became iconic. However, Hodges didn't cast him in the role. Caine was Klinger's first choice. Tony had other ideas, though, and thought the whole project should be switched and set in America and star Steve McQueen. 'I met Steve McQueen once and told him my idea,' recalls Tony. 'He looked at me and said, "It would have worked."'[49] At that stage in his life, Caine would in effect do one film a year that he really wanted to do, one film for the money, and one film that was just a chance. 'And that was his working-class roots,' says Tony. 'People who have grown up poor, they're looking for security and even years and years later, when he was worth millions of pounds, Michael still felt that way.'[50]

Although he hadn't chosen Caine, Hodges got on extremely well with the star and they'd make another film together, 1972's *Pulp*:

I was lucky with Michael; at no point did he pull rank on me. If I designed a scene that excluded his close-up he never complained. Stars tend to expect close-ups. Each day he came to the set fully prepared. His movements and delivery had the precision of an expensive watch.[51]

In a key supporting role was Ian Hendry, playing a particularly reptilian-like gangster. There have been stories that Hendry was up for the role of Carter, but Tony dismisses those, although no doubt Hendry would have loved to have played it. 'And he was really resentful that he didn't have that part.'[52] Battling alcoholism and a faltering career, Hodges used Hendry's animosity towards Caine to create extra tension in their scenes together. For main villain Kinnear, Hodges hired noted playwright John Osborne. 'I'd always found casting villains difficult,' says Hodges, 'avoiding the cliches of Bond films. These characters should be subtle.'[53] MGM were pushing Klinger to use Edward G. Robinson. Klinger refused and went with Hodges's choice of Osborne.

Shooting began in July 1970 and, despite this being Hodges's first film, there were scarcely any nerves.

Looking back, I was scarily confident. I shot it in a white heat, composing each shot only when all the ingredients (actors, location, props) were in place. I'd already learnt that staying awake all night planning the next day's shoot was pointless. You arrived on the set exhausted, only to find your plans were unachievable.[54]

Something else he'd learnt, from fellow director Richard Lester, was to stay in a different hotel from the cast and crew. It turned out to be a wise move. 'Entering the foyer of their hotel was like being devoured by a shoal of piranha, each one wanting answers to their (often petty) production problems.'[55]

Filming passed off relatively smoothly and the Newcastle locals made the unit feel at home. 'Geordies are warm wonderful people,' says Hodges. 'They welcomed us with open arms.'[56] The film's opening scene, where a bunch of gangsters are watching a porn film, was not shot in Newcastle but in a flat in London. Tony's girlfriend at the time invited him back one night to this very expensively furnished flat in Lancaster Gate. It turned out to belong to her uncle. Tony asked if they could do a deal to use it in the film as a gangster's flat, at which point she burst out laughing. It turned out her uncle was Tony Schneider, a notorious loan shark who had links to organised crime. Schneider agreed to his flat being used, on one condition – that Caine came over to have dinner with him.

In post-production Klinger pulled off another masterstroke by suggesting Roy Budd as composer. Klinger and Budd's agent were friends. Hodges knew of Budd's work and was more than happy to go with Klinger's choice. 'Glad I did.'[57] Budd's minimalist, jazz-oriented score has since become almost as iconic as the film.

Get Carter received mixed reviews on release, with some critics condemning its violence and misogyny. It was certainly Hodges's intention to create the most realistic portrait of violence and criminality yet seen in a British film, showing the brutal consequences of what criminals do. 'My father and Caine both came from parts of London where they had seen and experienced that,' says Tony.[58]

After a solid start at the UK box office the film faded away, spasmodically turning up on television. In America it fared even worse, going out as a second feature. 'They completely screwed it up,' says Tony.[59] The irony was that MGM remade the film just nine months later as a blaxploitation picture called *Hit Man*.

Things started to change when the British Film Institute (BFI) decided to release *Get Carter* to cinemas again in 1999, 'and it was taken seriously and reassessed,' says Hodges.[60] Today *Get Carter* sits, alongside *Brighton Rock* and *The Long Good Friday*, as the best British crime films ever made.

(UK/US: London opening 10 March)

12 *THX 1138*

When George Lucas was a graduate student at the University of Southern California's film school his short film *Electronic Labyrinth: THX 1138 4EB*, about a dystopian near future, won first prize at the National Student Film Festival in 1968. It got Lucas noticed. Even better, Francis Ford Coppola said he wanted to help Lucas make it as a feature for American Zoetrope. This was a San Francisco-based filmmaking 'commune', founded and funded by Coppola, which encouraged talented young filmmakers to operate outside the influence of the Hollywood studio system. *THX* became one of at least five projects on Zoetrope's books, and Coppola managed to acquire significant funds from Warner Brothers to bring them all to the screen. The first to get the green light was *THX*. Coppola would be executive producer.

Lucas approached *THX* as a kind of *cinéma-vérité* film of the future. He wanted it to look like a documentary crew had jumped forward a few years and made a film. To achieve his aim, he hired not one but two cinematographers, both of them new to cinema features. Albert Kihn had worked as a TV newsreel cameraman, while David Meyers was a respected documentary cameraman who'd shot *Woodstock* (1970).

Lucas must have talked to every cameraman in San Francisco. One of these was Stephen Lighthill, who began his career shooting for news shows, such as *60 Minutes*, before moving into documentaries. Lighthill ended up on the camera team as an assistant. 'George wanted a very naturalistic look,' explains Lighthill:

And he set up every shot. George is a classic non-collaborator in a collaborative medium. Everything that was done on set was run by him, which to a great extent is common. But he never said to anyone that I'm aware of, 'Heh, what do you think of this? Am I off-base here? Should I do this or that?' He made his own choices and he stuck with them, right or wrong. The whole film was in his head.[61]

If Lucas explained his ideas to anyone it was usually to his two directors of photography. There did appear to be a lack of communication with the actors. 'Donald Pleasence would say to me, "What does George want me to do?"' Lighthill recalls. 'George never has been an actor's director. He was very much to himself.'[62] Lucas had cast two quality actors in the leads, Pleasence and Robert Duvall. Lighthill recalls:

> Donald was a lot of fun. He knew his craft like crazy. He was one of those actors that cinematographers love. You're loathe to tell people where to stand, but with Donald, he didn't give a shit, you could tell him anything and he would get in character and be the character. He was very smart, but he was very confused about the nature of the film itself.[63]

As for Duvall, Lighthill found him to be highly dedicated. 'He was one of those actors where you didn't approach them unless they approached you because you didn't want to fuck with them, you wanted them to have their concentration.'[64]

While futuristic, *THX* was a direct comment on where America was circa 1970. Duvall, in his first lead film role, plays THX 1138 (names are replaced by numbers), an unquestioning citizen living in a homogenous world where conformity is the rule, and where silver-faced robot guards are the law. When he stops taking his mandatory drugs, his perception begins to change. When he falls in love he decides to go on the run.

Duvall's escape is thrilling, when he commandeers a car and is chased by police motorbikes through lengthy tunnels, in reality a not-yet completed rail transit tunnel in the San Francisco Bay Area. Two working tunnels were also used at night and blocked off from traffic. The car Duvall drove was the futuristic-looking Lola T70 Mk III race car. At one point Duvall crashes into some building works and one of the bikes behind hits a piece of debris and the rider comes off. This stunt had been meticulously planned, but when stuntman Duffy Hambleton hit a hidden ramp he flew over the handlebars and landed some distance away on his back and crashed into the parked Lola. Lighthill saw the whole thing unfold; he'd volunteered to turn on the camera that was in the Lola, which was sitting in the middle of the tunnel.

> And so, I was in the car when Duffy crashed and slid under the Lola, and as soon as they called 'cut' everyone came running over. I popped

open the door and the first thing George did was come up to me and say, 'Did you get it?'[65]

He did and the remarkable stunt is in the film. As for Hambleton, he was miraculously unhurt.

Lucas shot the bulk of *THX* in the San Francisco area with a relatively small crew of primarily young technicians new to movies, as indeed was Lucas. Post-production was handled over at Zoetrope. When an early print of the film was screened to Warner execs, it didn't go well. 'They were basically like, what the fuck is this?' says Lighthill. 'They did not see a diamond in the rough by any means.'[66] All Zoetrope projects with Warners were scrapped. 'One I think was *Apocalypse Now*,' claims Lighthill.[67] Worse, Coppola had to pay back their advance, landing him in a big financial hole. 'In those days we always knew Francis was on the edge of a financial precipice,' says Lighthill.[68] He was ploughing his money into Zoetrope and had a large building in San Francisco decked out with all manner of equipment. 'Francis and George talked a lot in those days about how San Francisco was cool, and LA wasn't and they were going to start a film company together,' says Lighthill.[69]

Coppola and Lucas were an odd combination. 'They were completely different,' says Lighthill. 'Francis was approachable. He was busy as hell but if you interrupted him, he would say, "Ok, what do you want?", and you could talk to him. He'd won an Oscar for *Patton*, so we all considered him a hero.'[70] As it turned out, it was Lucas who had the business brain. Lighthill later worked for Lucas at his Skywalker Ranch, 'that was absolutely gorgeous.'[71] It was what Coppola had wanted to create with Zoetrope, but the dream was fulfilled by Lucas, paid for by *Star Wars*.

THX 1138, although unsuccessful at the time, launched Lucas and today stands as a flawed but fascinating debut. And highly prophetic. 'If you look at China, you're seeing *THX*,' says Lighthill,[72] who went on to become a director of photography in his own right and president of the American Society of Cinematographers.

(US: New York and Los Angeles openings 11 March)

13 *LAWMAN*

By the early 1970s Michael Winner was seen as a director who largely specialised in comedies or lightweight dramas. Certainly not westerns.

Except he'd been handed a western script that he desperately wanted to do. The money was there provided he got a star in the lead, and that star had to be Burt Lancaster. Winner flew to Los Angeles to meet Lancaster and for two days the actor went through the script with Winner, querying every piece of direction and every line. Towards the end of the story Lancaster's character shoots a man in the back. 'Why?' Lancaster wanted to know. 'Because your character's a total arsehole, Burt,' said Winner. Lancaster agreed to do the movie.

Lawman was Winner's first picture in America. He also had a reverence for the Old West and was determined to make his western as authentic as possible, bringing in two senior professors of western history to check the sets in Durango, Mexico, a favourite destination for Hollywood filmmakers, where Winner planned to shoot. On arrival he found out Howard Hawks wanted the place for a John Wayne picture and managed to beat the veteran director to signing the contract by just one hour. Growing up watching westerns, Winner found himself living it for real, in a western town that was rough and tough and where the two biggest causes of death in the area were scorpion bites and gunshot wounds.

Lancaster plays a US marshal, a dark and troubled avenger, determined to bring a group of rowdy cowboys, who are in the employ of a rich cattle baron, to justice for the accidental killing of an elderly citizen during a drunken rampage. One scene called for him to burst through the usual saloon swing doors towards the camera. At the end of the take Lancaster asked how it was. 'Well, all I can say, sir,' said Winner, 'is that it scared the shit out of me.'[73]

Winner put together a fine supporting cast – Robert Ryan, Lee J. Cobb and Robert Duvall – in a tale where there are no obvious good guys or bad guys. For the most part Winner and Lancaster got on well and afterwards remained great friends. Lancaster, though, was known for blowing his top on sets, and when it happened on *Lawman* it was a terrible sight to behold. It all came about thanks to a scene where Lancaster has to shoot his injured horse. It was a question of continuity; Winner was adamant he'd used a Colt 45 in the previous shot and Lancaster was adamant it was a Winchester 73 and wasn't having a 'limey prick' tell him how to make a western. Lancaster's wrath reached its peak when he grabbed Winner by the lapels and dragged him to the edge of a cliff with a perilous drop and threatened to let go unless he admitted the weapon in question was a Winchester 73. Winner obliged.

Months later in a London dubbing theatre the scene in question played and there was Lancaster shooting his horse with a Colt 45 and in the next shot, with a Winchester 73. 'That's very careless of you, Michael,' said Lancaster. 'Why did you do that?' A surprised Winner replied, 'Because you threatened to kill me unless you used the Winchester 73.' Lancaster shook his head, 'I don't remember that, Michael.' A bit of clever editing saved the scene.[74]

Lawman is a good solid western, and Lancaster had another decent western open in 1971, *Valdez is Coming*. Based on a novel by the renowned American author Elmore Leonard, which tries to say something about racial prejudice and bigotry, Lancaster plays a grizzled and ageing Mexican and former US cavalry scout, now the sheriff of a small town, who sets out on revenge when he is forced by a cruel rancher to execute an innocent man. Originally to have been made by Sydney Pollack, with Marlon Brando as Valdez and Lancaster playing the rancher, the picture was postponed to allow Lancaster to do *Airport* (1970). When he came back to the project Lancaster wanted to play the title role and hired rookie movie director Edwin Sherin. Filmed in Almeria, Spain, Lancaster had such a miserable time working on it he threatened to retire.

(US/UK: London opening 11 March)

14 *DAD'S ARMY*

It was a trend in the early to mid-1970s to regularly churn out film versions of popular British TV sitcoms. This made perfect sense, really; they cost little to make and were usually popular with audiences. *Dad's Army* is arguably the most cherished sitcom Britain has ever produced. It was the brainchild of Jimmy Perry, who drew upon his own experiences serving with the Home Guard during the war as a 16-year-old before being called up to the regular army. He gave the idea to BBC producer David Croft, another war veteran, serving in the Royal Artillery. Against the advice of some senior BBC executives, worried about potential negative effects of a series mocking the British war effort, the series was a big hit when it began in 1968 and made a star of Arthur Lowe as the boorish Captain Mainwaring.

The idea to bring *Dad's Army* to the big screen came from Irish film director Norman Cohen, who had already made a cinema version out of another BBC sitcom *Till Death Us Do Part* (1968). He asked Croft and

Perry to write a script and then to help him pitch it to some film producers. The first port of call was the Boulting Brothers, famous for their
comedies with Peter Sellers such as *I'm All Right Jack* (1959). For Perry it
was a sobering introduction to film people as his script was poked about
as if it were some diseased object. 'What would you call this?' is how
the conversation started.

'It's a film script of *Dad's Army*,' answered Perry.

'Oh no it's not,' came the reply from one of the brothers, who
admitted to watching a few episodes and not liking them. 'They are
quite appallingly directed. Are they directed?'[75] They were, by Croft,
Perry's partner and friend, and he felt right then like punching the
Boulting brother hard on the nose. Eventually it was left to Columbia
to put up the cash. Even more strange, when Cohen first met the *Dad's
Army* cast at BBC Television Centre, he freely admitted never having
seen a single episode of the show. 'I don't know if he was winding
us up or not,' recalled Ian Lavender, who played Pike. 'But we all
thought – what?!'[76]

In an attempt to expand the story and make it more cinematic, Cohen
rewrote much of the screenplay. Feeling marginalised, Croft did not
involve himself any further with the production; Perry stayed on as an
adviser. Columbia also began to make all manner of arbitrary changes,
notably moving the outdoor scenes to Chalfont St Giles rather than
Thetford, the Norfolk market town that was the fictional Walmington-
on-Sea in the television series. The decision was also made to cast the
more 'high profile' Liz Fraser as Pike's mother instead of Janet Davies,
who played the role on television. These changes did not find favour
with the writers nor the cast. The cosy familiarity and pleasant working
atmosphere created for the TV show was largely absent, too, on the film
version. Columbia wanted the whole thing shot in just six weeks and
badgered Cohen almost daily about how much footage he'd shot and
then complain it wasn't enough.

Arthur Lowe was put out for another reason, namely an authentic
revolver he'd been told to use. It was decommissioned, of course, but a
little too heavy to be practicable. Preferring a plastic replica, when the
prop department said they didn't have one the actor took matters into
his own hands. With actor Paul Dawkins, who was playing a German
general, Lowe took a unit car to the nearest high street Woolworths. The
staff were more than surprised to be confronted by Captain Mainwaring
and a Nazi asking for a plastic revolver. Unfortunately, the store could

not oblige, and Lowe left disillusioned, muttering, 'You could always buy a sixpenny pistol in Woolworths when I was a lad.'[77]

For many of the regular cast, the screen version of *Dad's Army* was a disappointment – it had lost the spirit of the original series. Perry was so angry how it turned out he couldn't bear to watch it for years. Over time, however, he and others associated with the show came to appreciate the film more. Like many sitcoms turned into movies, it does feel like two or three episodes rather crudely stuck together. In *Dad's Army* we retread familiar ground with the creation of the platoon, before we see them go on manoeuvres and then finally encounter the enemy as they rescue hostages from a church hall held captive by the crew of a downed German aircraft.

A popular success at the British box office, a sequel was discussed. Croft and Perry's plot had the war office concerned about the sinking of war ships off the coast and the possibility of there being a clandestine U-boat base in the area. Mainwaring and his troops are sent to investigate. Nothing came of the idea, a shame since Laurence Olivier, a big fan of the show, had voiced interest in playing the German U-boat leader, who was passing himself off as the local lord of the manor.

Dad's Army was not the only sitcom to make the transition from the small to big screen in 1971. The film version of Frankie Howerd's *Up Pompeii* proved so popular it was followed by two sequels, variations of Howerd's Lurcio character through history, not dissimilar to what *Blackadder* later did: *Up the Chastity Belt* (also 1971) was set in medieval times, while *Up the Front* (1972) took place during the First World War. All three films were directed by Bob Kellett, with Ned Sherrin acting as producer.

Then there was *Please Sir!* Written by Bob Larbey and John Esmonde and set in an unruly school in south London, it was one of ITV's biggest hits and made a star out of John Alderton as a young, naïve teacher. But by far the most successful sitcom movie of 1971, and the most popular ever made, was *On the Buses*. According to the *Daily Express* it broke eighty-eight box office records in its opening week and, within five days, had already covered its production cost of £98,000. The plot sees bus driver Stan, played by Reg Varney, scheming to put a stop to a new company policy that allows the employment of, perish the thought, female drivers. The prevailing snobbish attitude towards the show was clearly evidenced when an examiner at the British Board of Film Classification referred to the picture as 'simple, good-hearted dirt for the working chap'. *Mutiny on the Buses* and *Holiday on the Buses* followed in quick succession.

(UK: London opening 12 March)

 ## 15 *VANISHING POINT*

For what is widely regarded to be one of the best road movies ever made, it's interesting to note that its literary source came courtesy of a former supporter of Fidel Castro. Guillermo Cabrera Infante was a Cuban novelist, screenwriter and critic. When Castro swept into power in Cuba, Infante became editor of an important cultural weekly paper, after that cultural attaché to Brussels. Critical of Castro's rule, Infante went into exile to London in 1965 where he lived for the remainder of his life.

It was while working in England that the American director Richard C. Sarafian came across Infante's screenplay. Written under a pseudonym, Infante was supposedly inspired by reading Jack Kerouac's classic novel *On the Road*, along with a newspaper piece about the high-speed pursuit of a driver who refused to stop and was killed when he crashed into a police roadblock. Infante's protagonist is Kowalski, a man who seeks freedom in speed and is hired with the task of transporting a white 1970 Dodge Challenger from Denver to San Francisco. Tanked up with amphetamines, Kowalski makes a bet with his drug dealer that he can conquer the distance in only fifteen hours. Not surprisingly he ends up in a dangerous pursuit with police across several states.

For Sarafian what interested him about the script was the challenge of bringing to the screen the pure essence of speed, to physicalise speed. He pitched the idea to Richard Zanuck at 20th Century Fox. The studio chief had just the one question: does Kowalski die at the end? Sarafian, being Catholic, lent on the side of him making it. 'No,' said, Zanuck. 'He's got to die.' Zanuck also insisted on Barry Newman playing Kowalski over Sarafian's original choice of Gene Hackman. Sarafian was disappointed, but he was going to make the car the star anyway. And it worked; the white Dodge Challenger became one of the most revered vehicles in cinematic history.

Filming began in the summer of 1970 with a planned schedule of sixty days, but this was almost halved on the orders of Zanuck, faced with making stringent cost-cutting measures at a studio haemorrhaging money. Sarafian's small crew, including cameraman John A. Alonzo, spent hours driving, sometimes several hundred miles in one day, to different locations as everyone made their way through Colorado, Utah, Nevada and into California. The pulsating driving sequences and stunts were handled by Carey Loftin, one of the film industry's most accomplished stunt drivers. Barry Newman learnt from Loftin and was encouraged to try some of his own stunts. He once crashed the car, equipped with three cameras, into some bushes on the side of the road in order to avoid a head-on collision when a 'civilian' driver ignored the traffic blocks installed to ensure the safety of the crew. By the end of the shoot only one out of the eight Dodge Challengers used in the film was returned intact to Chrysler.

As Kowalski drives through arid desert landscapes his back story is told in a series of flashbacks. An ex-marine and ex-cop, Kowalski is disillusioned by America's Vietnam experience. Sarafian's film is a statement about the end of the 1960s, the disillusionment of the Woodstock hippie generation and a harsh introduction into the 1970s. Along the way, Kowalski encounters an old prospector, a nude woman on a motorcycle and a blind radio DJ called Super Soul (played by Cleavon Little) who champions his cause and turns him into something of a hero.

Vanishing Point was the victim of scathing reviews and scant audiences when it opened in the USA, so bad that Fox pulled it after a few weeks. However, it was a critical and commercial success in the UK and Europe which prompted the studio to rerelease it in the USA. The film has since achieved huge cult status with fans like Spielberg, Chris Cornell and Edgar Wright. Scottish rock band Primal Scream named their 1997 album after it.

The film's ending has provoked much debate. Kowalski heads straight towards two bulldozers, placed in the road by police to stop him. Before impact, a smile sweeps across Kowalski's face. Is this a man who would rather be free and die trying than surrender to authorities? Far from accepting his fate, Newman believed Kowalski thinks he can get through a gap in the two bulldozers when he sees a blinding light. In Infante's original script, Kowalski, who struggles more internally between the contradictory impulses to survive or self-destruct, swerves his car at the last minute to avoid hitting the roadblock.

For Sarafian the blinding light meant something else, that the road Kowalski is travelling on is endless and that his death is not the end; it goes on in terms of him moving on to another astral plane. This is alluded to earlier in the picture in a scene when Kowalski picks up a young hitch-hiker, played by Charlotte Rampling. They smoke pot together and Kowalski pulls to the kerb, stoned, and they stay there all night. She won't tell him her name, instead saying she has been 'waiting for him, everywhere and since forever'. In the morning, when Kowalski wakes, she's gone. Sarafian spoke about the hitchhiker being an allegorical figure representing death. This scene was cut from the US theatrical release because the studio felt it was too esoteric and that audiences would be baffled by it.

(US: Los Angeles opening 18 March)

16 THE ANDROMEDA STRAIN

Michael Crichton was still a medical student when he began writing the novel that was to establish his credentials as a bestselling novelist. As a way of paying his way through medical school, Crichton wrote several novels using a variety of pseudonyms. He didn't want to use his real name, worried that when he became a practising doctor patients might think they'd end up as characters in one of his books. *The Andromeda Strain*, published in 1969, was his first novel published under his own name and was an immediate success.

Crichton never liked to label himself as a writer of science fiction; rather, his novels were based on science fact, pushed one step beyond. *The Andromeda Strain* certainly set the pattern for some of his other works such as *Coma*, *Westworld* and, of course, *Jurassic Park*. It also led to fellow author Tom Clancy referring to Crichton as the father of the techno-thriller, a term that stuck. In *Andromeda* he tapped into societal concerns about the moon landings and the chances of astronauts returning to Earth with some kind of alien bacteria. Crichton merely took what was a genuine fear voiced by microbiologists at the time and imagined a worst-case scenario.

Universal Studios were sent the galley proofs of the novel prior to publication and contacted the director Robert Wise to see if he was interested. Wise read it and was intrigued by the potential to make a cautionary tale about the dangers of biological research. In the novel, a returning NASA probe carrying an alien disease crashes in the New Mexico desert, killing practically the entire inhabitants of a small town. A team of scientists, brought to a top secret, state-of-the-art laboratory, have just days to identify the strain, contain it and find a cure before it possibly spreads around the world. When Wise wanted to add a new plot point, that the probe was seeking out micro-organisms in space that could potentially be used as biological weapons, Crichton readily agreed. As they stand, the novel and film were the first popular works to alert the public to the growing power of biological science. Those hazmat-suits worn by scientists in the movie looked very sci-fi back in 1971, but today are all too common.

By the early 1970s Wise was one of Hollywood's most respected film-makers. Starting his career as an editor, working with Orson Welles on *Citizen Kane* (1941), Wise graduated to directing classics like *The Day the Earth Stood Still* (1951), *The Sound of Music* (1965) and *The Haunting* (1963). Nelson Gidding, who had so brilliantly adapted the Shirley Jackson novel *The Haunting of Hill House*, was brought in by Wise to do a similarly fine job with the Crichton story. One of the first things he did was identify that the team of scientists in the novel were all men – and that in the film one of them should be female. At first Wise wasn't convinced, imagining a scenario of a Raquel Welch type in a skimpy outfit. The studio required a lot of convincing too. But Gidding argued that a woman would add an interesting dynamic to the group as well as a nod to female empowerment. He got his way. Wise cast the character actress Kate Reid in the role. Although well respected, Reid was not a big name, and this was typical of Wise's approach to the casting. He didn't want instantly recognisable stars to take away from the almost documentary realism that he was after. The other scientists were played by James Olson, Arthur Hill and David Wayne.

The film was shot at Universal Studios, and Crichton paid several visits. He was once given a studio tour by a young, upcoming director by the name of Steven Spielberg. Wise allowed Crichton to hang around the set and the writer plays a cameo role as a surgeon. This was Crichton's first exposure to the filmmaking process, and he was able to pick up moviemaking tips that helped when he became a director himself. Crichton saw breaking into Hollywood the natural next step after being a bestselling author.

Although it's a cold, austere film, the acting is uniformly excellent, and the suspense is well built up to a truly nail-biting 'ticking clock finale', where Olson has to dodge laser guns to shut down the lab's self-destruct mechanism. These were actually real lasers, and Olson and the crew were told never to look directly into the beam.

Another impressive element is the production design of the laboratory complex, augmented by the use of something like $3 million worth of computers and technical equipment provided by several companies, along with special advisers. The design highlight is the central core of the complex. Such was its height that Wise had to use the largest stage at Universal, and even then they had to dig out the concrete floor. Special photographic effects came courtesy of Douglas Trumbull, who had worked on *2001: A Space Odyssey* (1968). Working on Trumbull's team was someone just starting out in the effects business called John Dykstra, who would later make his name working on *Star Wars*. Wise also shot in CinemaScope and makes clever use of split-screen techniques.

The Andromeda Strain did well at the box office but wasn't the smash hit everyone hoped for. Wise was to direct just one more sci-fi film, the 1979 *Star Trek: The Motion Picture*.

(US: New York opening 21 March)

17 | THE BEGUILED

By 1971 Clint Eastwood was one of the biggest stars in the world, making highly commercial pictures, westerns, war movies and cop thrillers. *The Beguiled* was a radical departure for the actor, and audiences didn't really know what to make of it. Eastwood knew it was a risk when he first read the novel by Thomas Cullinan while out in Mexico shooting *Two Mules for Sister Sara* (1970) with Don Siegel. It's a strange tale, almost a gothic horror, set during the American Civil War about a wounded Union soldier who seeks refuge in an isolated girls' school. As he recuperates, he takes advantage of the young women's sexual fantasies about him, which lead to tragic consequences. After reading the book Eastwood showed it to Siegel and by the next morning both were already hatching plans for a film adaptation as part of the star's deal with Universal.

Turning down an offer to shoot at the Disney Studio's Southern plantation lot, Siegel found an authentic Civil War mansion in Baton Rouge, Louisiana. 'That house was literally just a shell,' recalls Jo Ann Harris, who played Carol, one of the girls seduced by Eastwood's soldier:

> The outside of it was intact. The inside was gutted. The set designers built all the sets we used, the staircase, the class room. That house was

pretty secluded, but it really created a mood, all that Spanish moss in the garden. It was quite beautiful.[78]

One of the things Siegel was most conscious about was giving the picture an authentic look. 'When we were on the plantation everything was natural light,' recalls Harris. 'And in the house some scenes were literally lit by candle light.'[79] To achieve this brooding atmosphere Siegel worked closely with cinematographer Bruce Surtees. Having worked as a camera operator on both *Coogan's Bluff* (1968) and *Two Mules for Sister Sara*, Surtees made his debut as director of photography on *The Beguiled*. He worked in that capacity on a further eleven Eastwood movies.

Harris liked working with Eastwood:

He was a lovely guy. He was shy. He told me that when he started his career, they used to call him 'little coop', after Gary Cooper, because he was that kind of shy, soft-spoken, laid-back guy. He was also very practical. He realised that Universal wanted him to do what he was known for, shoot 'em up westerns. And so, his deal with them was, one for me, one for you. And *The Beguiled* was for him.[80]

Harris liked Siegel too; there was no messing about with him. 'He was an interesting guy. He was demanding but he knew what he wanted. Don could get hot sometimes and easily frustrated, but he had a good sense of humour.'[81] Harris doesn't recall Eastwood ever getting heated on the set, or raising his voice. 'That wasn't his style. He didn't have that ego. He didn't have a lot of patience for silliness or tantrums or drama though. When you were on the set, you were there to work.'[82]

Having already collaborated on two pictures, Eastwood and Siegel were very much attuned to how the other worked. 'They got on very well,' says Harris. 'Their temperaments were good together. I remember on the set Clint was watching Don. He was learning. They worked very closely on that film. And Clint trusted Don. Don was quite the mentor to him.'[83]

Eastwood was the only leading male in a predominantly female cast. 'We all got on,' says Harris. 'When you have a bunch of teenage girls it's like herding cats, poor Don Siegel. I think it must have been challenging for him to have us all.'[84] The patriarch of the school and headmistress is Martha. After his first choice, Jeanne Moreau, proved unavailable, Siegel cast Broadway actress Geraldine Page. Harris found Page quite distant and ethereal, she didn't socialise or interact much with the others.

Martha doesn't take kindly to Eastwood's soldier sleeping with her students, she wants him for herself. When her advances are resisted, she plots revenge. Along with its gothic trappings, *The Beguiled* is a highly charged psychological drama. The school could almost be a nunnery or some religious order, with Martha as Mother Superior; Eastwood is the rooster in the hen house among these sexually repressed women.

The fact that Eastwood ultimately dies in the film did not go down well with Universal chief Jennings Lang. The star hadn't died before in any of his films and Lang worried how his fans might react. Siegel and Eastwood fought hard to keep the ending as it was. What they couldn't do anything about was the way the film was marketed. 'When the poster came out,' recalls Harris, 'and it showed him holding up a gun Clint was furious, because this wasn't that kind of film and to sell it that way really drove him crazy.'[85] Universal also gave the film a blanket release, while Eastwood and Siegel's preference was to open first in key cities so it could gradually build an audience. Harris confirms:

> Clint was very smart about his image and how to sell himself. He knew that was the wrong strategy and they didn't listen to him. They didn't know how to market *The Beguiled* because it didn't fall into the typical Clint Eastwood film. And that was the point for him. He wanted a new challenge.[86]

As a result, despite some excellent reviews, *The Beguiled* failed to find an audience in America – a shame, since Eastwood had given the best performance of his career so far. The picture fared much better in Europe, where its art house pretensions found a more appreciative audience. Today, *The Beguiled* is rightly regarded as one of Eastwood's most rewarding movies. It was remade by Sofia Coppola in 2017, with Colin Farrell in the Eastwood role and Nicole Kidman as Martha.

(US: New York opening 31 March)

 18 *JUST BEFORE NIGHTFALL*

(JUSTE AVANT LA NUIT)

Often referred to as 'the French Hitchcock', Claude Chabrol rose to prominence alongside the likes of François Truffaut and Jean-Luc

Godard, all young critics on the influential magazine *Cahiers du Cinéma*, and who rebelled against the more traditional films of the past. They went on to spearhead the *Nouvelle Vague* or the French New Wave. Unlike his contemporaries, who were seen to operate more as auteurs, Chabrol immersed himself in mainstream cinema, with sometimes trashy and pulp material. He was also the most prolific, making more than sixty features over fifty years.

Alfred Hitchcock was a touchstone for all of the French New Wave filmmakers; Truffaut wrote a book on his interviews with the master; Chabrol, too, produced a literary tribute. It was Hitchcock's black humour and fascination with murder and guilt that was to pervade a lot of Chabrol's suspense thrillers, many of which scrutinised French middle-class hypocrisy. The bourgeoisie was often the target for his work, partly because he himself came from a comfortably-off Parisian middle-class family.

Just Before Nightfall is a delicious study of bourgeoisie conscience and morality, and ends the cycle of films Chabrol made in the late 1960s and beginning of the 1970s that explored similar themes. All starred his wife Stéphane Audran and playing a character called Hélène. The series began with *La Femme infidèle* about a man who murders his wife's lover. In *Le Boucher*, a village butcher falls in love with the school mistress, but he turns out to be a Ripper-style killer. And in *La Rupture*, a woman is fighting to gain custody of her child from her drug addict husband.

In *Just Before Nightfall* Charles Masson is a Parisian advertising executive who is having an affair with the wife of his best friend and he strangles her in an S&M game gone wrong. Masson is a typical Chabrol protagonist, comfortably off, living in a smart home, he presents a facade of total respectability to the outside world. But underneath there are dark passions and something rotten. In a dazed condition Masson flees the scene of the crime and returns to his wife Hélène and their two children as if nothing has happened. Although he appears to have got away with murder, as the police scramble around with no clues, his guilt soon begins to overwhelm him and finally he reveals the truth to his wife. Interestingly, it's Hélène who tries to dissuade her husband from going to the police for the sake of the children. Masson, however, remains determined to do the right thing, so Hélène solves matters by giving him a fatal dose of laudanum.

Just Before Nightfall is yet another meticulously crafted psychological drama at which Chabrol seems to excel. Like Hitchcock, Chabrol always looked to bring elements of humour into his films, although *Nightfall* was something he viewed as an outright comedy:

> It's really vaudeville material transformed into tragedy. It's about a character who wants to confess, and people say: 'Shut up! Shut up!' It's subject matter that could have very well been used in a comedy. But the film is funnier if comic material is treated in an austere way.[87]

Chabrol's other 1971 picture was a very different proposition. *Ten Days Wonder* was based on an Ellery Queen mystery and starred Anthony Perkins and Orson Welles. Although it was his most ambitious project to date, boasting a $2 million budget, the biggest of his career until then, Chabrol dismissed it as a failure. At least he got to work with Welles. 'Far from being dominating, he was very sweet,' Chabrol later recalled, 'except for one day when his wife was away all day, and he became more drunk than a man is entitled to be.'[88]

(France/Italy: French opening 31 March)

19 TAKING OFF

In August 1968 Russian tanks rolled into Czechoslovakia to crack down on reformist trends in Prague. On the night of 9 January 1969, Czech filmmaker Ivan Passer called his friend Miloš Forman, telling him they were getting out of the country and to quickly pack a few essentials. The two of them drove to the Austrian border in Passer's car. At a checkpoint, a guard with a Kalashnikov enquired where they were going. 'Vienna,' they lied. Examining their passports, the guard wanted to know where their exit visas were. They didn't have one. Just then, the guard recognised Forman; he'd seen all his movies and was a big admirer. He waved them through. Passer and Forman had managed to escape a regime that would surely have meant the end of their careers.

Forman was one of the key architects of the New Wave of Czech cinema with his films *Loves of a Blonde* (1965) and *The Firemen's Ball* (1967), which brought a new vitality with their sharply observed portraits of working-class life. After arriving in America, Forman intended to make films in exactly the same way he would have done back in Czechoslovakia, looking at life and its quirks. In this way

Taking Off is often viewed as a bridge between Forman's former work in Czechoslovakia and his subsequent American productions.

A group of people that fascinated Forman were hippies. He didn't dare become a hippie himself, but he wanted to learn about their lifestyle and why they'd checked out of normal society. While carrying out research and talking to a lot of these kids and also their parents, Forman realised that the kids were on the whole a dull bunch; it was their parents who were going through all the dramas. Forman decided to explore the cultural and generational divide between parents and their children, while at the same time observe contemporary American life through the lens of a foreigner. His story is about a well-to-do suburban couple whose teenage daughter Jeannie runs away from home to become a singer and meets up with a community of hippies and bohemians in New York. In one of the film's most famous scenes Jeannie's parents join a group, eager to understand and gain insight into the youth culture, where they are initiated into the etiquette of pot-smoking by their teacher.

As part of his research, Forman would go every weekend, with the photographer Mary Ellen Mark, to the Bethesda Fountain in Central Park, where a lot of hippies hung out. Mark took pictures, while Forman looked for faces that he might cast in his film. It was here one day that he came across Linnea Heacock and cast her as Jeannie in what turned out to be her only film.

As the parents Forman cast the actor and screenwriter Buck Henry (he wrote *The Graduate*) and Lynn Carlin. There was also a screen debut for Vincent Schiavelli, whom Forman was to frequently cast in his films. In one scene at a record company audition for female singers there are a host of now familiar faces. We see Jessica Harper, a pre-fame Carly Simon and a young Kathy Bates in her film debut. The scene plays out like a counterculture version of *The X Factor*. Included is a sincere folk song satire called 'Ode to a Screw' that included the word 'fuck' multiple times. The critic for *Life* magazine mused that this was perhaps the reason for the film's R-rating.

In the wake of the massive low-budget high-return success of 1969's *Easy Rider*, Universal ran a scheme that gave filmmakers complete artistic freedom as long as their budgets came in under $1 million. Forman was able to take advantage of this deal, and *Taking Off* cost just $810,000. To keep costs low Forman deferred his fee, as did the producer Michael Hausman. All the actors worked for scale. Transportation to each location was Hausman driving his own car, with Forman and his director of photography, Miroslav Ondricek in the front seat, and room for Buck Henry, Lynn Carlin and one other actor in the back seat.

Taking Off was warmly received by American critics, although some took offence at a foreign filmmaker critiquing American culture. It numbered among the 1971 Ten Best lists of *The Washington Post*, *Newsweek* and the *Chicago Sun-Times*. At Cannes Forman won the Grand Prize of the Jury and was nominated for the Palme d'Or. In addition, he earned six BAFTA nominations, including Best Film and Best Director. Financially, though, the film was a flop. As part of the Universal deal, directors only got paid if their film turned a profit, so Forman didn't earn a cent out of it. Remaining enormously proud of the film, Forman moved into the Chelsea Hotel, feeling depressed and wondering where his career was going next, as he was determined not to return to Czechoslovakia. His unlikely saviour turned out to be Royal Crown Cola, who saw *Taking Off* and liked it so much they asked Forman to direct a commercial based on the montage of singing auditions. The budget for the TV spot was $1 million, more than his whole movie. This was Forman's education in capitalism. He didn't have to wait too long, though, for his next film, when Michael Douglas sent him a copy of Ken Kesey's book *One Flew Over the Cuckoo's Nest*.

(US: Los Angeles opening 7 April)

20 ┃ *MELODY*

Alan Parker was a copywriter for a top advertising agency in London. He enjoyed his job, saw his future in advertising and had absolutely no ambitions whatsoever to go into movies. That all changed one afternoon when he was invited to lunch by Charles Saatchi and David Puttnam, who had recently left the agency and decided to make films. The idea was for Parker and Saatchi to each write a script, then Puttnam would fly to America and try to raise finance to make them. Parker's first effort was, in his own view, dreadful – a depressing thing based on The Beatles' song 'Eleanor Rigby'. He was politely asked to try again. This time Puttnam gave him a brief; it should be about two school kids falling in love and involve seven Bee Gees' songs to which he had just acquired the rights. Using some of his own experiences growing up in a working-class area in Islington, north London, along with some of Puttnam's childhood memories, Parker came up with *Melody*.

Off went Puttnam to New York and, with nerve and tenacity, managed to raise some money for Parker's script. As for Saatchi's, there were no takers. Almost instantly he lost interest in the film industry and announced that he was going to start an advertising agency with his brother Maurice. Within just a few months Saatchi & Saatchi was launched.

In a brilliant piece of casting, the decision was taken to reunite the child stars of *Oliver!* Mark Lester and Jack Wild. They play two school mates, Daniel and Tom, whose friendship is fractured when Daniel falls in love with a classmate, Melody. Since the colossal success of *Oliver!* Mark and Jack had kept in touch with each other, but they weren't friends as such; the age gap between them was something like five years. 'Jack was like an older brother to me, really,' says Lester. 'A bit of a wayward older brother.'[89]

There's a knack to directing children, and when Waris Hussein was first approached to direct *Melody* this was one of the considerations he had to think about. There are tricks you can employ. 'On *Oliver!* Carol Reed was very clever,' Lester recalls, 'he'd bring clowns and magicians to the set, in order to get reactions from the kids.'[90] You can do that with very young children, but older kids can't be fooled. 'Waris was very much a hands-off sort of director,' confirms Lester. 'Although he gave direction, he stood back a lot and watched the dynamics of it.'[91]

As much as anything else Hussein, who was predominantly a television director (he directed the very first *Doctor Who* story), was after spontaneity and naturalism. 'He pointed the camera at us and we just learnt our lines and got on with it,' says Lester.[92] That didn't mean talking down to the children or patronising them. 'We were treated just the same as the adult members of the cast,' says Lester.[93] In this way Hussein managed to get an enchanting performance from Tracy Hyde, who'd never acted in front of a camera before and was chosen out of many hopefuls to play the role of Melody.

Filmed mostly around south London, Lester recalls that Alan Parker visited the set maybe two or three times. Significantly, one of those occasions was during the filming of the school's sports day. Handed a camera, Parker was asked to shoot a bit of second unit. At the agency Parker had played around with cameras and would go on to direct commercials, but this was the first time he'd operated on an actual film set. *Melody* would also influence his directorial debut, *Bugsy Malone* (1976), another film that revolved around children. 'Alan was such a down-to-earth bloke,' says Lester, 'the kind you could go down the pub and have a pint with.'[94] In contrast, Puttnam, producing his first film, was on the set the whole time. He would go on to become one of the leading figures of the British film industry.

Melody was only a modest success in the UK and didn't do anything in the USA; however, it found an extraordinary life in South America and in Japan, where it was a phenomenal success. Over time the film has increased in popularity in Britain and is now highly regarded and much loved. One of the reasons is undoubtedly the fact that it's set in a school, something we can all relate to. There's a sweet innocence to the whole thing, too, especially in the relationship between Daniel and Melody. 'It wasn't a sexual thing,' says Lester. 'It was two young kids who fell in love and just wanted to be together.'[95]

That sense of innocence is perhaps the key to the film's appeal. When the Mexican filmmaker Alfonso Cuarón contacted Hussein about obtaining the rights to remake *Melody*, he wondered how the innocence of the film and those characters could be replicated in today's world where kids operate in such a different way, especially with social media. Hussein was, however, pleased when Cuarón told him that *Melody* was one of the films he watched as a child that prompted him to be a director. Wes Anderson is another admirer and *Melody* had a great influence on his 2012 film *Moonrise Kingdom*.

One should mention, too, the wonderful songs of the Bee Gees. It wasn't until years later that Lester eventually got to meet Barry Gibb:

> He was a friend of Michael Jackson's and Michael took me over to see him once in Florida and we spent most of the time talking about *Melody*. Michael kept looking at me going, 'I didn't know you guys knew each other'. We didn't, but we had this connection.[96]

In the end though, *Melody* owes most of its charm to the wonderful double act of Mark Lester and Jack Wild. As people they were chalk and cheese, polar opposites, but their on-screen chemistry was undeniable. And there's no sense of the almost five-year age gap in the way their characters interact with each other. Off-set things were a little different. 'Jack was doing things like smoking, openly, and probably going out with girls,' says Lester. 'I didn't hang out with him during the film. I was more interested in climbing trees and playing football than girls.'[97]

There's a nicely observed class divide between the two boys too, with Daniel coming from a comfortable middle-class home, while Tom lives in a house he's ashamed to bring his friends back to. This was very much an echo of the lives of the two men who created *Melody*: Daniel was Puttnam, really, and Tom was Alan Parker.

(UK: London opening 8 April)

21 | *TRAFIC*

One of the all-time great comedy characters of cinema is the amiable and accident-prone Mr Hulot, the alter ego of its creator, French actor, writer and director Jacques Tati. Immediately recognisable by his tall, gangly demeanour, short mac, hat and perpetual pipe, Mr Hulot's quixotic and childlike struggle with a relentlessly mechanised modern world matched Tati's own concerns.

The character made his debut in 1953's *Mr Hulot's Holiday*, a satirical look at middle-class life in a seaside resort. *Mon Oncle* followed in 1958, parodying post-war France's obsession with modernity and American-style consumerism; it won the Academy Award for Best Foreign Language Film. *PlayTime* (1967), Tati's masterpiece, focused on the dehumanising effects of modern living. Shot over two years, its box-office failure was catastrophic for Tati. By the time he came to *Trafic*, he was bankrupt. Old friends and business colleagues shunned him.

With a background in music hall and mime, Tati had raised sight gag comedy to the level of high art. He was lauded around the world. And yet there was no money to make his new film. Enter Dutch filmmaker Bert Haanstra. The two men were friends and admirers of each other's work, and the plan was for Haanstra to direct and Tati to star in and write the screenplay. With a little bit of funding, along with his own resources, Haanstra began shooting in the spring of 1969.

The idea for *Trafic* dated back to 1960 when Tati observed car after car whizzing past on the motorway, anonymous people inside what he called 'moving cages', having no contact with the outside world, whether it be nature or their fellow drivers. When work began on the film there was no script, just a six-page outline that Tati hastily wrote to appease the nervous backers. Tati saw the film purely in visual terms, and commissioned a series of cartoons displaying the action. Its story is simple. Employed as a design director at a Paris auto company, Mr Hulot must transport his latest product, an all-purpose 'camping car' outfitted with all the latest mod cons, to an auto show in Amsterdam. He's accompanied by a truck driver and an American public relations officer. Predictably they encounter numerous mishaps along the way.

As shooting continued in Amsterdam, Haanstra grew exasperated with Tati, whose promise of a shooting script never materialised; he was also prone to disappearing at short notice. Having put his own money into the project, Haanstra decided to cut his losses and walk away, followed by some of the backers. It was a mess. By the end of the year, with the film only half completed, it was temporarily abandoned. Tati managed to raise some more funding and production restarted in the summer of 1970. Still there was no script, with Tati partly improvising as he went along. Early in 1971 the money ran out again. The producer ordered the cameraman to return to Paris with all the equipment. Luckily, a Swedish television crew were following Tati around for a documentary. Desperate, and with only three days left of the schedule, Tati asked the documentary camera team to take over. Included in their number was Lasse Hallström, later the acclaimed director of *My Life as a Dog* (1985), *The Cider House Rules* (1999) and *Chocolat* (2000).

Just a month later *Trafic* opened in Paris. The critical view was that this was minor Tati, and it is an assessment that hasn't really changed over the years. Tati himself saw it as a step back after the accomplished *Playtime*. Yes, it's still fun and clever, just not as consistent as his previous work. There are some amusing jokes, a woman's sumptuous cleavage turns out to be a baby's bottom and Hulot desperately tries to prove that the squashed shape under his wheel is not a dead dog but a woolly jacket. And there's an elegantly choreographed motorway pile-up, a personal act of purging for Tati who suffered a horrific crash in 1955 when a coach slammed into the side of his car at a crossroads leaving him with substantial injuries.

Trafic is by no means an anti-car film, maybe anti-car noise as the soundtrack is filled with interminable screeching, car horns and engine chatter. Tati's statement is that, in the modern world, the inevitable environment of the car is gridlock. We see cars bumper to bumper, unable to advance more than a few inches at a time. At one point a television is showing news coverage of the moon landing, as if to say it's easier to get to the moon than it is for Hulot to get his camping car from Paris to Amsterdam.

Trafic is notable, however, in that it marked the final film appearance of the Mr Hulot character and was the very last feature directed by Tati.

Then in his mid-60s, and suffering bad health, he worked on a couple of TV projects before retiring altogether.

(France/Italy: Paris opening 16 April)

22 *SUMMER OF '42*

This is one of the all-time classic coming-of-age dramas, the story of three teenage boys who, during one unforgettable summer, experience first love and loss of innocence. It was based on screenwriter Herman Raucher's own magical summer of 1942, when he was 14 years old, spending a long family vacation on Nantucket, a tiny, isolated island off Cape Cod, Massachusetts. He met and befriended a young woman, recently married, whose husband had been called up to fight in the war. Her name was Dorothy, and the young Raucher was smitten. Then one evening he paid her a visit; she was drinking and crying after receiving news that her husband had been killed. As he tried to comfort her, she kept calling Raucher by her husband's name and they ended up spending the night together. Dorothy was a woman Raucher never forgot and never saw again. The following morning, she left the island, leaving behind a note wishing him good fortune – the same note read out at the end of the film.

Afterwards Raucher didn't quite know what to make of the incident. One odd psychological side effect was that for years he only dated girls called Dorothy. When he became a writer for television Raucher began to assemble his memories of that summer and wrote a screenplay. No one was interested in it; Raucher got something like forty-nine rejections over a seven-year period. Years later he met Robert Mulligan, best known for directing *To Kill a Mockingbird* (1962). Mulligan fell in love with the screenplay, took it to Warner Brothers and said he could make the film for under $1 million. They said go ahead without even reading the script.

Raucher's screen alter ego is Hermie, a character made 15 years old by Warners, who thought 14 was just a little too young. He and his friends Oscy and Benjie have to deal with the dilemmas of adolescence, along with the fear of war with America's recent entry into the conflict after the Japanese attack on Pearl Harbor. They get up to the sort of things most teenage boys do, the difficulty of buying that first packet of condoms at the chemist and trying to get to first base with a girl. Back in the 1940s there was no sex education to speak of, and everything was learnt 'on the job', as it were. In the roles, Mulligan decided to cast young actors with little or no previous film or television experience; Gary Grimes, who played Hermie, had just done a few TV appearances, while for Jerry Houser and Oliver Conant this was their first acting job.

When it came to casting Dorothy, Mulligan didn't want to see any actress under the age of 30. Jennifer O'Neill was 22 and had been a high fashion model since the age of 15, and played small roles in a couple of movies including the John Wayne western *Rio Lobo* (1970). Her agent loved the script for *Summer of '42* and fought hard to get his client an audition, finally persuading Mulligan that there was enough difference in age for O'Neill to be convincing as the older woman. She won the role. Cleverly, during the shoot, Mulligan deliberately kept O'Neill apart from the three young actors so they would feel awkward and have a very natural unease around her.

Still unsure about the film's potential, Warners asked Raucher to adapt his script into a book for publication prior to the opening in the hope of garnering some interest. Raucher had never written a book before, but decided to have a go, taking just three weeks. The novel became such a huge success that when the ads for the movie came out, they declared it was 'based on the national bestseller'.

Much to everyone's surprise, *Summer of '42* turned into one of the box office hits of the year. Mulligan had taken huge care to accurately depict the right period atmosphere and the film did much to create a new-found nostalgia for everything 1940s. Michel Legrand's Oscar-winning score is also fondly remembered, notably the theme song 'The Summer Knows', which has since become a pop standard sung by the likes of Frank Sinatra and Barbra Streisand.

Stanley Kubrick was evidently an admirer of the film. In his horror classic *The Shining* (1980) the young boy and his mother are watching it on television in the common room of the deserted Overlook Hotel.

The inevitable sequel, *Class of '44*, arrived in 1973, and reunites Hermie, Oscy and Benjie as they graduate from high school. Benjie departs shortly to war while Hermie and Oscy go on to college. O'Neill did not appear. Written By Raucher, *Class of '44* was something of a disappointment.

After the success of *Summer of '42* Raucher began to receive several letters from women claiming to be 'his' Dorothy. One of the letters looked familiar – he recognised the handwriting from the note left so many years before. It turned out to be her. She had remarried and had lived for years with the guilt of what had happened that night and that it might have traumatised him psychologically. Back in the 1940s sexual relations between adults and those much younger was viewed in a far more serious light. Touched by the fact she'd reached out to him, unfortunately the letter had no address on it, so he was unable to write back. He never heard from her again.

(US: New York opening 18 April)

23 | *SWEET SWEETBACK'S BAADASSSSS SONG*

This landmark of Black and American independent cinema sent shock waves through the industry and popular culture. Credited by *Variety* as leading to the creation of the blaxploitation genre, so incredible was the story behind the film that the director's own son was to turn the making of it into a movie.

Following the success of Melvin Van Peeble's first outing as a director, the racially charged comedy *Watermelon Man* (1970), which poked fun at white liberals, he was offered a three-picture deal at Columbia. While still deciding whether to accept the lucrative contract, Van Peebles began to develop what became *Sweet Sweetback's Baadasssss Song*, the story of a man who prevents the savage beating of a young Black suspect by the LA police, only to find himself framed for a crime he didn't commit. Going on the run, Sweetback makes his way through the city's disenfranchised communities of pimps and hustlers, Puerto Rican nationalists and Mexican illegals, hippies and female bikers.

When no studio was prepared to back him, Van Peebles walked away from the Columbia deal, determined to make the film on his own terms. Money was the first hurdle. Some of the finance came courtesy of Van Peebles's earnings from *Watermelon Man* and some from comedian Bill Cosby by way of a personal loan. To get around having to employ expensive union members, and bring in non-union people, Van Peebles 'pretended' he was making a porno. At that time 'skin flicks' were conveniently allowed to operate outside union rules. Another reason for using non-union labour was Van Peebles's desire to employ mostly African American crew members, who were then underrepresented in Hollywood unions.

Problem No. 2 was who was going to play his hero. In the end no established Black actor would work for the poor wages on offer; there was also the fact that the character had only a few lines of dialogue, so Van Peebles opted to play Sweetback himself. Van Peebles ended up doing a lot of things himself. Unable to pay for a stunt man, he ended up handling the stunts, including having to jump off a bridge no less than nine times before the cameraman Bob Maxwell was happy with it.

Sweet Sweetback's Baadasssss Song was finished in a blistering nineteen days on a budget of $500,000. Most of the cast were non-professionals and Van Peebles often had to think on his feet and adapt during shooting in the face of dwindling funds. As a result, *Sweetback* is pretty crude and messy to watch today, enhanced by some avant-garde flourishes. Money was so tight there weren't sufficient funds for a traditional advertising campaign. Van Peebles came up with the idea of releasing a soundtrack record first to generate publicity. Because he had no money to hire a composer, Van Peebles wrote the music. It so happened that his secretary was dating a musician from a rising new funk ensemble called Earth, Wind & Fire. She convinced her boss to bring them in, and they went on to perform on every track. The soundtrack was released on the legendary Stax label and reached No. 13 on the Billboard Top R&B Album chart.

Before it even opened *Sweet Sweetback's Baadasssss Song* caused issues, mainly its profusion of sex and nudity. The film opens with the 13-year-old Sweetback (played by Van Peebles's son Mario, later an actor and director in his own right) getting seduced by a prostitute. We learn that Sweetback has grown up in a brothel, where he was expected to service the female clientele. This opening scene was later censored on British editions of the DVD for breaching the Child Protection Act. Back when the film originally opened it was given the severest rating possible, an X, 'by an all-white jury,' blasted Van Peebles defiantly. Even then, some theatre owners cut several minutes out of the sex scenes before allowing it to be shown. It has been reported in several articles about the film that some of these sex scenes were done for real and that Van Peebles contracted gonorrhoea. Ironically, he successfully applied to the Directors Guild to get workers' compensation because he was 'hurt on the job'. Van Peebles used the money to purchase more film stock.

Only two theatres in America were interested in screening the film at first, one in Atlanta and the other in Detroit. But from the opening day the film attracted sell-out crowds and its success grew and grew. By 1972 some industry analysts predicted that it would become the most lucrative independent production of all time. There were also reports that Van Peebles was planning a sequel, although this did not come to fruition.

Reaction to the film was interesting to say the least. Huey P. Newton, the founder of the Black Panther movement, devoted an entire issue of *The Black Panther*, his party's newsletter, in June 1971 to welcoming the film as 'the first truly revolutionary Black film made … by a Black man', and decreed it 'required viewing' by all active members. Van Peebles was to call the film 'the first Black Power movie'. Some critics hailed the director for creating, in the words of the *New York Times* review, 'a viable, sexual, assertive, arrogant black male hero'. Others criticised Van Peebles for pushing the racist stereotype of the Black stud. Whatever the view, there is no denying the film's impact on Black audiences and for helping open the door for other Black filmmakers such as Spike Lee.

Van Peebles desire to make 'a victorious film', where Black members of the audience could walk out of the theatre 'standing tall', had been achieved. As the opening titles boldly state: 'This film is dedicated to all the Brothers and Sisters who had enough of the Man.'

(US: New York opening 23 April)

24 BANANAS

On the strength of his 1969 comedy *Take the Money and Run*, Woody Allen struck a three-picture deal with UA. Of all the Hollywood studios Allen could have landed at, UA was far and away the most suitable due to its reputation, once filming got underway, of leaving the filmmaker to their own devices. All Allen had to do was pitch a story idea to company boss David Picker and, if he liked it enough, it was greenlit.

Allen's first pitch was for a heavy piece about a touring jazz musician. Picker hated it, telling Allen, 'I really thought we were going to do some comedies together. That's why we made the deal.' Allen later reworked his jazz story into 1999's *Sweet and Lowdown*. Allen left Picker's office, promising to be back in touch. Two days later he called with another idea. 'The title is *Bananas*.'

'It's approved,' was all Picker said.[98]

With one film already under his belt as a director, Allen came into *Bananas* with a lot more confidence. He plays Fielding Mellish, a product tester for a major corporation and another of his neurotic, sexually frustrated outsiders; he can't even get to first base with the office nymphomaniac. Mellish meets and falls in love with a political activist student, played by Allen's real-life ex-wife Louise Lasser – the couple had only recently divorced. When she dumps him, Mellish tries to prove his activist credentials by visiting the fictitious South American country of San Marcos, where he becomes embroiled in a revolution.

While not overtly political – Allen himself called it 'coincidentally political' – *Bananas* (the title is a pun on the term 'banana republic') is a satire on the uprisings and regime changes that seemed to plague Latin American politics in the 1960s and early 1970s. Allen also takes aim at US institutions like the CIA, the FBI and television; a mock TV ad where a priest extolls the virtues of New Testament cigarettes ('I smoke them,' pause and a glance heavenwards. 'He smokes them') earned the movie a 'Condemned' rating by the Catholic Church. Even Howard Cosell, famed sports commentator for ABC TV, makes a guest appearance, covering a 'live, on the spot' presidential assassination as if it were a sporting event.

As with *Take the Money and Run, Bananas* served merely as a vehicle on which to hang as many jokes and madcap situations as possible. '*Bananas* was still a film where I only cared about being funny,' commented Allen.[99] During the editing process, he ruthlessly threw out material he felt didn't work. 'Woody packed *Bananas* so full of jokes that another movie could have been made from its outtakes,' recalled the film's editor Ralph Rosenblum.[100]

This scattergun approach of one gag after another harked back to the comedies of the Marx brothers, and also looked towards the future style of filmmakers like the Zucker brothers and their *Airplane* and *Naked Gun* films. At times Allen's comedy in *Bananas* is almost cartoon-like, such as when he is being taught guerrilla warfare and how to use a grenade. He throws the pin and the grenade explodes in his hand. At his next attempt he throws the grenade only for the pin to explode this time. Unlike, say, Monty Python, who would have had Peckinpah-like jets of blood, all we see is a modest bandage wrapped round Mellish's hand. Allen wanted no blood at all in the film (even during executions or assassinations) lest it take away from the comedic tone.

Some of *Bananas* was shot out in Puerto Rico. Louise Lasser was slightly put out when Allen's new girlfriend Diane Keaton arrived on location. The rest took place in Allen's beloved New York, the setting for most of his subsequent films. In one scene Mellish sits on a subway train, his head nervously buried in a magazine, as an elderly lady next to him is menaced by thugs, including a young but unmistakable Sylvester Stallone. A jobbing actor at the time, with just a couple of walk-on parts in films, Stallone turned up at the audition with another actor, only for Allen to turn the pair away for not looking dangerous enough. The actors begged to be given another chance – they'd change their clothes, their hair, anything. Allen agreed. Five minutes later they came back looking completely different. It taught Allen a valuable lesson – not to pre-judge an actor merely on appearance. When Stallone became famous, Allen recalled seeing the film playing in a small town; the cinema marquee read: '*Bananas* with Woody Allen and Sylvester Stallone'.

The film ends with Mellish, now inexplicably the dictator of San Marcos, travelling back to America to raise funds for his impoverished people, only to be picked out as a subversive threat by the US Government. The final scene was to have seen Mellish targeted on a university campus by Black militants. After an explosion, he emerges from the rubble with a sooty face, causing the activists to mistake him for one of their own. This idea was wisely dropped.

Bananas received positive reviews and was a modest success – a good start to Allen's career at UA, an affiliation that continued into the late 1980s.

(US: New York opening 28 April)

 ## 25   *MURMUR OF THE HEART*

(LE SOUFFLE AU COEUR)

When director Louis Malle was 13 years old, he suffered a heart murmur that impinged upon his life for almost two years. He was taken out of boarding school and studied at home. At one point his doctor suggested he convalesce for a few weeks at a spa in the country. This being the height of the season, rooms were at a premium, so the teenage Louis ended up sharing a room with his mother.

For years Malle had been in denial about his own past and his own bourgeoisie background; he was born into a wealthy industrialist family. This wasn't a cool thing to confess to in the 1960s, when so many left-wing, pro-socialist European filmmakers were savagely attacking the establishment. Returning to France from a trip to India, where he had submerged himself in the culture, Malle found an inner peace and an acceptance of where he came from and how he'd become the man he was.

For his new project, Malle began to adapt a novel by Georges Bataille called *Ma Mère* (*My Mother*) that followed the incestuous relationship between a 17-year-old boy and his attractive, promiscuous 43-year-old mother. After writing something like fifty pages Malle suddenly ditched the idea, realising that he was not speaking with his voice, but somebody else's. It was no accident, however, that Malle had been drawn to this particular story, seeing how it resonated so much with some of the childhood memories now flooding back to him. He began making notes about what happened back when he had his heart murmur. 'I suddenly admitted to myself, maybe for the first time, that I'd had this strange and very passionate relationship with my mother.'[101] In just a week Malle churned out a treatment that was pretty much a finished product. The incident of incest that occurs in the film never happened in reality, but Malle used his feelings for his mother and the trip to the spa as a springboard for his imagination and what he termed 'partly invented autobiography' to create what American critic Pauline Kael was to call 'one of the cinematic masterpieces of the early '70s'.

Murmur of the Heart is a delightful, poignant and provocative coming-of-age drama that focuses on a precocious teenage boy, Laurent. To find the right person to play the role, ads were placed in newspapers and magazines across France. Out of something like 500 applicants Malle personally tested or interviewed over 100, without success. Benoît Ferreux arrived one day, interested in being an extra – he'd never been in a film before – and landed the role of Laurent.

Laurent grows up in a bourgeoisie family in the mid-1950s during the French downfall in Indochina. His passion for jazz (Dizzy Gillespie and Charlie Parker tunes feature throughout), curiosity about literature and the tyranny of his elder brothers and how they introduced him to sex (taking him to a brothel and drunkenly barging in at the most intimate moment) are shaped by Malle's past. The mother of the film is not Malle's own, however; she was ultra-devout and conservative. As played by Lea Massari, Laurent's mother is sensuous and Italian, and she dotes on her son.

The incest scene was the last to be shot. This moment is neither vulgar or exploitative, but handled with sensitivity by Malle as an expression of love gone too far between a mother and her son. In the script, after the encounter, the mother lays asleep as Laurent goes into the bathroom and contemplates taking his own life. Malle shot this scene but removed it during the edit. Instead, Laurent seeks out a girl he's become friendly with at the spa, and they spend the night together.

In the early 1970s, when so many barriers were being broken in terms of how violence and sex were depicted on the screen, Malle found that incest was still a big no-no. Predictably the film provoked a storm of controversy in the more traditional quarters of France. Some critics demanded the film be banned and voiced concern that young Ferreux might wind up emotionally scarred by the experience. For the most part the critical reaction was positive, and it ended up a big box-office success in France.

In many ways *Murmur of the Heart* was a breakthrough film for Malle, both in his use of child actors and in the way he was able to translate his personal experience into screen drama. In his very next film, he discovered a 17-year-old French farm boy called Pierre Blaise and cast him in his film *Lacombe, Lucien* (1974). In 1978, he directed *Pretty Baby*, starring 13-year-old Brooke Shields as a prostitute in New Orleans, and in 1987's *Au Revoir Les Enfants* he again used untrained children to play the leads. The huge international success of *Au Revoir Les Enfants* led in 1989 to its distributor Orion rereleasing *Murmur of the Heart* back into cinemas in the USA, where it originally only had a limited release.

(France/Italy/West Germany: French opening 28 April)

26 BILLY JACK

This small, low-budget movie about a half-Native American Green Beret Vietnam veteran became one of the most profitable independent movies of the 1970s. Billy Jack was a counterculture superhero who spoke not just to those with an anti-war sentiment, but to disaffected youth and to the fight for Native American rights.

The character's origins go back to 1967, when Tom Laughlin starred and directed an American International Pictures (AIP) biker exploitation movie called *The Born Losers*, which pitted Laughlin's Billy Jack against a bunch of marauding Hells Angels. Laughlin was an ex-football player turned movie maker, a sort of low-rent Orson Welles, in that he invariably wrote, directed and starred in his movies.

The success of *Born Losers* resulted in Laughlin being able to raise the funds to make a sequel, *Billy Jack*, which explored issues that were very personal to him. For years Laughlin had wanted to raise awareness about discrimination against American Indians after witnessing first hand the degrading conditions at a reservation in South Dakota, where some Indians lived all year round in abandoned cars. One shocking incident he learnt about, when a local store owner refused to serve a Native American family and doused them in flour to make them look 'white', is recreated in the film.

Laughlin's wife Delores Taylor plays the headmistress of a Freedom School on an Indian reservation that's under threat from a politically corrupt town boss and his henchmen. Interestingly, since *Born Losers*, the character of Billy Jack has taken on a mythical, almost supernatural presence. He seems always to be around when someone is in trouble or needs his help. He has also become an expert in martial arts, thanks to the Hapkido master Bong Soo Han, who was the fight choreographer and Laughlin's personal trainer. One suspects the Indian theme, combined with the martial art fight scenes, is why Elvis Presley was such a big fan. According to Laughlin, Elvis watched *Billy Jack* nine times in one sitting.

Shot on location in Arizona and New Mexico, the film ran into trouble, and assistant director Hawk Koch was asked to get on a plane and go help out. He arrived in the morning and by 1 p.m. was running the set. Koch was told for tomorrow's shoot they needed a nude double for Delores Taylor, who was 5ft 3in, flat-chested, kind of skinny, with light brown hair. Koch recalls:

> They had about fifteen different women. I picked one that was about 5ft 4in, light brown hair, not particularly buxom and skinny. I said to Tom, 'This woman most resembles your wife.' And he said, 'What the hell are you talking about?!' Some of the women were still hanging around and he looked and there was a blonde woman, 5ft 10in, with big tits, and he said, 'What about her?' And I learnt very quickly, this was early in my career, I was 24 years old, I said, 'Yes sir,' and that was the woman that doubled for his wife. The next day the whole crew were laughing going – what the hell is this?'[102]

Laughlin had made a deal with 20th Century Fox to act as distributor, but studio head Richard Zanuck disliked the film and intended to make cuts. Laughlin stole the negative, leaving Zanuck with no choice but to sell the rights back to him. After previewing the film in twenty cities, Laughlin sent the enthusiastic preview cards to studio heads, and it was Warner

Brothers that stepped in. Only, Laughlin fell out with them too, claiming they botched the marketing campaign and put the film on in porno houses and drive-ins. Frustrated, Laughlin sued the studio and fought hard to get the film reissued. This time it was a monster hit. It even prompted AIP to rerelease *Born Losers* with the tagline: 'The film that introduced Billy Jack.'

The inevitable sequel, *The Trial of Billy Jack*, arrived in 1974 and was a runaway success. However, *Billy Jack Goes to Washington* (1977) was a box office disappointment. Laughlin himself was to seek the office of president of the USA on no less than three occasions in the 1990s and 2000s.

Laughlin resurrected the character for *The Return of Billy Jack* in 1985, but after money issues it was never completed. But the legacy survives and is fondly remembered by many, especially for its pacifist message – although for someone preaching the merits of peace, Billy Jack karate-chops an awful lot of butt!

Jump ahead to around 2018 and Brad Pitt is playing a stunt man in the latest Quentin Tarantino movie *Once Upon a Time in Hollywood*. Pitt arrived at Tarantino's house with a DVD copy of *Billy Jack*. He thought perhaps Laughlin's cult character could be a good starting off point for his stunt man and wanted the director to watch it. Unbeknown to Pitt, Tarantino already had a 35mm print of *Billy Jack* threaded up on his projector ready to go.

(US: opening 1 May)

27 | *WR: MYSTERIES OF THE ORGANISM*

Dušan Makavejev's *WR: Mysteries of the Organism* was something of a cause célèbre and an art house smash when it opened. Ruminating about the state of socialism in the director's home country, it's a surreal mash-up of documentary and fiction that starts as an examination into the life and work of controversial Austrian psychologist and philosopher Wilhelm Reich, before turning into a free-form narrative of a young Serbian girl's sexual liberation. A leading figure in the Yugoslav New Wave cinema movement of the 1960s, Makavejev's film, made at the height of Marshall Tito's power as the Yugoslav leader, was banned in his homeland, and the director was forced to flee to the West.

Blending themes of politics and sexuality, Makavejev employs real and faked documentaries, old newsreel footage, clips from vintage porno films, beat poetry, scenes from a Soviet propaganda film featuring Stalin and on-camera interviews. One of these interviews was with Betty Dodson, the painter of erotica who went on to become a feminist sexologist and taught generations of women in workshops, books and videos how to masturbate, viewing the act as a liberating social force, as did Reich.

Then we have some very strange New York street theatre and performance art. Tuli Kupferberg, co-founder of the underground rock band The Fugs and a key figure in the US 1960s counterculture, dresses in an orange jumpsuit, of the kind worn by convicted criminals in the USA, topped off by a military helmet and a phony machine gun; an irony seeing that in real life he was a pacifist. He then runs around the financial district of Manhattan, much to the amused bafflement of the public, all to the strains of The Fugs' song 'Kill for Peace'. Literally the 'climax' of the sequence is Kupferberg masturbating his toy rifle, alluding to Reich's ideas that sexual frustration and violence are connected.

We also have the Andy Warhol superstar, the cross-dressing Jackie Curtis, playing herself, wandering down 4th Street in Manhattan sharing an ice cream cone with her boyfriend and getting quite a few odd looks. However, the film's most infamous sequence involves New York artist Nancy Godfrey, who numbered among a loose group called Plaster Casters, which became well known for taking plaster casts of rock star's penises. In the film Nancy takes a cast of the erect penis of Jim Buckley, co-founder/editor of the underground porn magazine *Screw*. When *WR* was shown at the Academy Cinema in Oxford Street, at that time the premier art house in Britain, the censor objected to the brief view of Mr Buckley's erect penis, albeit covered in stiffening plaster. The manager of the Academy refused to show the film unless it was in its entirety. It was allowed to proceed, although on future UK video prints Buckley's penis was obscured by *Top of the Pops*-style psychedelic colours. The film also shows behind-the-scenes footage at the *Screw* offices, where Buckley casually interacts with his nude models.

These New York sequences are meant to be a comment by Makavejev on what he saw as the perversions of sexuality in the capitalist system – just as the Stalin newsreel satirises the perversions of sexuality under communism.

The film actually begins as a documentary on Wilhelm Reich. A respected disciple of Sigmund Freud, Reich's ideas grew more and more extreme as he got older. A reformed Marxist, Reich believed sexual repression was at the root of all neuroses, and claimed that better orgasms could cure both psychological and social ills. He came to believe in a mystical energy called 'orgone'. This led to the promotion of bizarre orgone accumulators, essentially wooden boxes lined with metal. These were wonderfully parodied by Woody Allen as the 'Orgasmatron' in his comedy *Sleeper* (1973).

After he had come to live in the USA, in 1956 Reich's books were incinerated by order of the government, and he was imprisoned for contempt after continuing to promote his orgone accumulators without proof that they actually worked – in other words, fraud. He died in prison. Makavejev interviews Reich's daughter and some of his former associates. The director first encountered and became interested in Reich while studying psychology at university before he went to film school.

Closing the picture, we have a story about a pretty Belgrade beautician called Milena, played by Milena Dravić, who follows the theories of Reich and tries to seduce Vladimir, a sexually repressed Soviet ice skater by helping him to achieve the perfect orgasm. He's reluctant, more interested in discussing the finer points of Marxist ideology. Milena eventually gets her way, but unleashes a sexual power Vladimir can't handle, which ultimately leads to her getting decapitated with one of his ice skates. As her head sits on a tray in the morgue, she continues to talk about the need for social, political and sexual revolution.

WR (which stands for Wilhelm Reich) remained banned in Yugoslavia until 1986, and Makavejev's exile from his home country lasted until the end of the communist regime. Heavily censored in many other countries, *WR* has to be seen to be believed, but is perhaps merely just a product of its time rather than anything else.

(Yugoslavia: opening 10 May)

28 *BLUE WATER, WHITE DEATH*

This acclaimed documentary follows the adventures of a group of top divers travelling the world determined to find and film the great white shark. Featuring underwater footage that still astonishes today, it also inspired a young journalist by the name of Peter Benchley to write a novel called *Jaws*.

Tom Chapin was in his early 20s and holding down a teaching post when he heard that his brother Harry, at the time a documentary filmmaker, was being scouted for a film job. He asked to come along and meet with James Lipscomb, a documentary producer, who was putting together a crew to sail around the Indian Ocean looking for sharks. It all sounded incredibly exciting, so when Harry said he couldn't do it, Tom asked if he could take his brother's place. Tom got hired as a general do-everything guy, like a roadie, and took some diving lessons.

The man behind *Blue Water, White Death* was underwater photojournalist Peter Gimbel. 'He was the engine that started the whole thing,' says Tom.[103] Work began in the spring of 1969 and the team's first destination was Durban, South Africa, where they chartered a boat and headed out for the whaling grounds, where big sharks were known to follow the fleet. They were killing sperm whales with a giant cannon that fired a harpoon with an exploding head. 'It was horrible stuff,' says Tom.[104] Sharks duly appeared but when the ships returned to shore Gimbel bought a dead whale from them and tied it to the side of the boat where it attracted whitetip sharks, dusky sharks and blue sharks. But no great white. Still, the divers got into their frail aluminium cages and managed to grab some exciting footage.

This sort of epitomised the almost *cinéma-vérité* style that Lipscomb employed on the film. Tom says:

> That was his background. That was the world that he brought. And Gimbel and the divers brought the underwater *cinéma vérité*, and I think that combination made the film so special because you really got to know the divers and you got to know the people on the boat too, and then you've got this phenomenal underwater footage.[105]

Life on board was tough but interesting. It was a South African crew; the captain was Norwegian. The boat was a big old whale catcher hired for six months, and they'd maybe spend two or three days on it at a time. Tom had ended up as the sound guy for all the on-board shots, and it was very much a case of learning on the job. With this being one of the very few documentaries shot in the widescreen format, the camera weighed something like 55lb and Lipscomb had it strapped to his shoulder and would wander round the ship, with Tom behind doing the sound, capturing the divers coming back aboard, asking them what they'd found and seen.

The divers were a skilled bunch, some of the best in the business. There was Ron and Valerie Taylor, an acclaimed husband-and-wife team from Australia with a background in marine research and filmmaking. 'They kept telling Peter Gimbel that he had to go to the Great Barrier

Reef. That's where the great whites are,' recalls Tom. 'But Gimbel kept to his original plan.'[106] There was Stan Waterman, an Emmy award-winning cinematographer, and a diver by the name of Rodney Fox, who had been bitten by a great white. This was during a spear-fishing competition in Australia, when he was holding a bag of dead fish. Tom has never forgotten Fox telling him what happened:

> All of a sudden, the ocean went silent and then – boom – it was like a piano hit me and I realise it's a shark, so I poked it in the eye and the shark let me go and I got to the surface. Then it came back up at me, but he went for the bag of fish.[107]

Luckily there was a boat nearby and Fox was pulled out. 'He was probably held together by his wet suit,' says Tom. 'It's astonishing he survived.'[108] These were the kind of men aboard, real pros.

One time, when the divers were in the water, a huge wave came bearing down on them. Scrambling back to the boat there were no crew around, just Tom and Lipscomb. Valerie was screaming for help. 'I start to move forward,' recalls Tom, 'but Jim grabs me and says, "Take sound." Finally, some of the crew come over and pulled them up.'[109] The divers were not happy, but at the start of the whole thing Lipscomb had sat everyone down and told them:

> I'm going to take pictures, that's my job. If something happens and we don't get the pictures, then what are we doing here? So, I just want to let you know, if you get bitten, I'm going to be filming, if you're in trouble, I'll be filming.[110]

With no luck finding any great whites, the team headed to the Seychelles and then Sri Lanka. After six months it was time to head back home. No great whites had been sighted so Gimbel suspended the project until January 1970, when he decided to take the Taylors' advice and head to Australia and the Reef. 'They had three quarters of a movie but no ending,' says Tom.[111]

Lipscomb wanted Tom to join them, especially if he wanted a career in documentaries. But Tom wasn't sure anymore. He wanted to pursue music. On the boat he brought his guitar and was often singing songs on deck in footage that ended up in the film. 'I was 24, didn't quite know what I wanted to do, and I watched these divers who'd made really strong decisions to live the life they wanted to live.'[112] Back in America, Tom forged a successful career as a singer/songwriter, as did his brother Harry.

The team headed to the Reef and found their great white, managing to get some incredible footage from inside the cages. Earlier in the expedition the divers had swum free with feeding sharks, but no one suggested doing the same with the great whites. Just as well: one of the team was almost killed when a great white grabbed a huge chunk of bait hanging on the cage and wouldn't let go. Realising the shark was never going to give up on its prize, the diver cut the bait loose before the whole cage was smashed to pieces.

In an interview Peter Benchley revealed that it was this scene that inspired him to write *Jaws*. According to Tom, however, Benchley lived in the same town as diver Stan Waterman, and they used to play tennis together. Benchley knew all about the trip and was privy to some of the early footage as well. Certainly, Waterman would have talked with Benchley about the film. 'It just fired up his imagination,' says Tom.[113] Ironically a documentary that hoped to promote an understanding of sharks gave birth to a novel that stigmatised the creatures for decades.

(US: New York opening 11 May)

29 | THE ABOMINABLE DR. PHIBES

Director Robert Fuest was relaxing on holiday in Greece. He'd been given a script to read by AIP, with whom he had recently worked on a screen adaptation of *Wuthering Heights*. It was a strange-looking thing, housed in a black leather folder and enormously thick, about twice the size of a normal script. On the front it said 'The Curse of Dr. Phibes'. He began to go through it. 'And it was unlike any other script I've ever read.'[114] It was full of oddities and a bit on the overwrought side:

> When I'd finished, I thought, this is terrible. It's awful. But it did have some wonderful ideas, which shone through, the idea of this maniac taking revenge on the doctors he blames for his wife's death. And I said to myself, if I could rewrite this, play around with it, we might make quite an offbeat, interesting movie.[115]

From the start Fuest recognised the need to inject a sense of humour into the story, a knowing twinkle in the eye, rather like TV's spy series *The Avengers*, for which Fuest directed seven episodes. As it stood, the script was all terribly serious. Phibes, horribly disfigured in a car accident and presumed to be dead, lives in a typical horror-movie castle and, at the end of the story, strangles his beautiful assistant and throws her off the tower before setting the place on fire. 'It really was very heavy Victorian rubbish.'[116] He's inspired to kill the doctors one by one using the Ten Plagues of Egypt. One murder was death by a rat on a boat, which Fuest thought a bit feeble – all you had to do to escape was jump over the side. This was later reworked to take place inside the cockpit of an airplane.

Fuest said he'd do the film on the condition that he be allowed to rewrite the script. It was all progressing nicely until he hit an impasse; he couldn't come up with an ending. Working at Elstree Studios, Fuest had an office just two doors down from Brian Clemens, with whom he'd worked on *The Avengers* and the thriller *And Soon the Darkness* (1970). Over lunch one day Fuest explained his problem. Clemens said to leave it with him. The next day Clemens came in with three neatly typed pages. He'd concocted a brilliant climax to the film. Phibes has kidnapped the son of Vesalius, the last remaining doctor alive. The boy has been strapped to an operating table and the doctor must surgically remove a key near the boy's heart that will unlock his restraints before a slowly descending container of acid is released. The doctor is given just six minutes, the same amount of time that Phibes's wife was on the operating table. 'Everything was incapsulated in those pages,' says Fuest. 'And it was so much in tone with the rest of the film. Brian takes all the credit for that.'[117]

As AIP's in-house horror star, there was really no other actor other than Vincent Price who was going to play Phibes. Fuest's first meeting with Price was in his London hotel:

I knew he was a great gourmet and we were having lunch and I wondered what he was going to order. He came downstairs looking extraordinarily grand. He was a very elegant and charismatic man. And he had shepherd's pie and rhubarb and custard.[118]

During the shoot Fuest had no problems with Price at all. 'We laughed a lot. And he was so easy to direct.'[119]

Because Price had to wear a mask to replicate Phibe's disfigurement, the character speaks out of a voice box in his neck; all the actor's dialogue was pre-recorded. This was a bit disconcerting for Joseph Cotton, playing Vesalius, who heard all of Price's replies to his lines coming back from a tape machine. 'But he was wonderful about it,' says Fuest, 'and the whole experience was one of the happiest times of my life.'[120] It was a very enjoyable set. On one of the other stages at Elstree they were shooting a Frankie Howerd comedy, 'and they all used to come on our set and have a laugh.'[121]

Fuest brought in Terry-Thomas and Hugh Griffith to play cameo parts. 'They were both sweet to work with.'[122] Griffith was known to fancy a tipple and quite often his wife would be asked to accompany him to the studio to make sure he could work at least before lunch. As for Terry-Thomas, he rather did have just the one performance. 'When you booked Terry-Thomas, you booked the act,' says Fuest. 'So, you couldn't really "direct" him because you've got him already. He did his thing and that was it.'[123] In the film, Thomas is strapped to a chair and ghoulishly slowly drained of his blood. 'He dried, literally,' recalls Fuest. 'There were two or three lines in that scene which he didn't give; he wasn't in too great shape health wise. I thought the scene held up without them.'[124]

Dr. Phibes has an unusual look, quite unlike any other horror picture. This was down to the set designer Brian Eatwell, who was a huge art deco fan, as was Fuest – 'both of our houses were loaded with the stuff'[125] – and, as the film is set in the 1920s, the style seemed to lend itself to the overall tone Fuest was after. Then there is Phibe's clockwork orchestra, which is made up of animatronic musicians. 'I wanted people to think, "What on earth is this film going to be about? What am I watching?" I liked the idea of wrong-footing everybody.'[126]

The success of *Dr. Phibes* inevitably led to a sequel, *Dr. Phibes Rises Again* (1972), which Fuest directed. But he ended up being somewhat disappointed by it. It lacked the originality and structure of the first film, and wasn't as fun to make. 'I think in retrospect we were very silly to try and make a second Phibes on such a low budget, and it showed.'[127] More instalments were planned, but nothing materialised. Fuest was also offered the chance to direct *Theatre of Blood* (1973), with Price again starring as a manic thought to be dead who seeks revenge, this time on drama critics. Fuest declined the offer, something he later regretted.

(US/UK: Los Angeles opening 20 May)

30 *ESCAPE FROM THE PLANET OF THE APES*

The huge success of *Planet of the Apes* (1968) rather demanded a sequel, but at the close of *Beneath the Planet of the Apes* (1970) Earth was seen to be destroyed, which rather put the kibosh on any future instalments. In reality, screenwriter Paul Dehn was under strict orders from 20th Century Fox not to leave the door open for any sequels, hence the slaughter of the lead characters and the end-of-the-world scenario. However, when *Beneath* performed much better than expected at the box office, Dehn received a telegram from the studio: 'Apes exist, sequel required.'

The problem for Dehn was how to move the saga forward after it had so resolutely reached a natural conclusion. Dehn was an interesting man. Born in Manchester in 1912, he was a journalist, poet and film critic and, during the war, became involved in military intelligence, an experience that came in handy when he wrote the screenplays for *Goldfinger* (1964) and *The Spy Who Came in from the Cold* (1965).

Dehn's masterful solution to his problem was to be far-reaching, turning *Escape* into an origin story, a prequel and a reboot all in one. Cornelius and Zira, the two apes we encountered in the first film, again played by Roddy McDowall and Kim Hunter, manage to salvage the spaceship flown by astronaut Taylor (Charlton Heston). With the help of an ape scientist called Milo, they leave Earth prior to its destruction and are sent back in time to modern-day Los Angeles. The original idea was to open with the apes witnessing the destruction of Earth from inside the spacecraft. Instead, the film starts brilliantly with the capsule retrieved from the water and, in front of a host of dignitaries and military, the three astronauts remove their helmets to reveal their astonishing identities.

The idea of a contemporary setting was largely forced on Dehn, given that the budget was less than the first two pictures. There was simply no way the production could afford futuristic ape cities or large numbers of ape characters requiring elaborate make-ups. Dehn also cleverly takes the original movie and flips it upside down. Now it's the apes, not the humans, that are the objects of curiosity and fear. At first, they are treated well, even becoming media celebrities, until it's discovered Zira is pregnant and the government comes to see them as a threat. Here the film dramatically shifts gear into darker terrain and a truly bleak conclusion.

Escape was directed by former actor Don Taylor, who does a fine job given that he had to complete filming in a brisk thirty-five days. Taylor would go on to make further genre pictures, *The Island of Dr Moreau* (1977) and *Damien: Omen II* (1978). Taylor saw the film first and foremost as a love story, and Zira and Cornelius's relationship is at the core of the film; thanks to a script that gives them ample opportunity for humour, the two actors bounce off each other wonderfully. McDowall was to continue with the *Apes* film series, also starring in a 1974 TV spin-off, but *Escape* was Hunter's swansong. A celebrated stage actress, Hunter had needed persuading to return as Zira in *Beneath*, but *Escape* was a different proposition – she liked the script much more. Still, she was glad to leave the series, having never truly come to terms with the intrusive make-up, the awful feeling of claustrophobia and the hours putting it on and taking it off. Once in make-up, the actors stayed like that until the end of the day's work.

Sal Mineo, cast as Milo, had real problems under the make-up, suffering terrible panic attacks that necessitated Hunter hugging him until he calmed down. It didn't get any better and, as a result, his character was killed off early in the film. Mineo had risen to fame alongside James Dean in *Rebel Without a Cause* (1955), but his career had faltered in recent years. It was his friend, McDowall, who knew he needed the money and a job, who got him the role in *Escape*. It proved to be Mineo's last theatrical feature.

Supporting the 'apes', Don Taylor put together a nice complement of 'humans'. Bradford Dillman, and Natalie Trundy, who was producer Arthur P. Jacob's wife and had appeared as a mutant in *Beneath*, play two young animal psychiatrists the apes befriend. Eric Braeden is memorable as the government's scientific adviser, who is suspicious from the start about the apes and their potential threat to mankind. And Ricardo Montalban is a friendly circus owner who shelters the apes when they go on the run. A genre favourite, Montalban portrayed the iconic villain Khan in the *Star Trek* episode 'Space Seed' and the 1982 movie *Star Trek II: The Wrath of Khan*.

Escape from the Planet of the Apes ranks as the best of the original sequels. Not only did Dehn find a way to extend the story, but he turned the *Apes* series into a fully developed cinematic saga, paving the way for two more films that follow the story of Zira and Cornelius's son Caesar and the apes' rise to power.

(US: Los Angeles opening 26 May)

31 *BIG JAKE*

This western was a real family affair for John Wayne; his son Patrick co-starred, his other adult son Michael was producer, and it marked the acting debut of his 8-year-old son Ethan. A sizeable chunk of Wayne's cowboy stock company also appears, the likes of Bruce Cabot, Harry Carey Jr and Richard Boone as a particularly vicious baddie.

Big Jake also marked the last of five films in which Maureen O'Hara appeared opposite the Duke. Wayne had huge respect for the actress, and O'Hara only agreed to play what was quite a brief role because he'd asked for her personally. Afterwards, she retired from film acting, returning twenty years later to play John Candy's mother in *Only the Lonely*. O'Hara plays the tough matriarch of the McCandles. When her ranch is attacked by a group of desperados and a young grandchild is kidnapped and held to ransom, she calls on her estranged husband for help. Made by Wayne's own production company Batjac, shooting began in Durango, Mexico, without Wayne's participation. 'On the third day when my father showed up there was a whole different atmosphere amongst the cast and crew,' remembers Patrick. 'People jumped to attention, became much more focused in their work; the world just took on a different order.'[128]

Big Jake was the tenth and final occasion Patrick worked with his dad on film, but the first time they played father and son. Patrick first appeared with his dad in *Rio Grande* (1950) when he was 11 years old, and it was always something special:

> And it was special for so many reasons: first and foremost, at an early age I found that my other brothers and sisters had no interest in working on films, so for a while I had my dad all to myself. When we went out on location there was no competition with the siblings. There was also a comfort level knowing you were in a secure place and you were free to perform without fear of rejection or negative criticism.[129]

Jeff Bridges was the original choice to play Jake's other son but, after several interviews and tests, he turned the offer down. Chris Mitchum was cast instead, having played a small role in the Duke's previous film *Rio Lobo*. Mitchum had idolised Wayne growing up and felt intimidated by him at first, only for the star's easy-going manner on the set to quickly put him at ease. On the *Jake* set they spent a lot of time playing chess.

Wayne started off cheating, until Mitchum plucked up the courage to admonish him for it. 'I was wondering when you were going to say something,' said Wayne. It had been a test. Jake's third son in the film was played by 'Blue Velvet' recording star Bobby Vinton.

There was another reunion for Wayne on the picture, with director George Sherman. Back in the late 1930s the pair of them made a batch of B-movie westerns together for Republic Studios. Sherman hadn't worked for a while and was ill during the shoot. On the days when he couldn't come on set, Wayne took over. 'But when he was feeling well George handled the helm quite admirably,' says Patrick.[130]

It proved a trouble-free shoot and, as usual, Wayne attempted to do as many of his own stunts as possible – tough for a man who had trouble breathing and required an oxygen tank off-set. Naturally, the cast were on horseback most of the time, including riding bareback, something Patrick didn't have a whole lot of experience with. To get prepared, he worked with a stunt man for several weeks prior to filming. Patrick's first bareback scene was with his dad and Cabot, up a hill of uneven ground:

> My horse stumbled and started to slip. I didn't have any stirrups to put my feet in, so I gripped the horse tightly with my legs. Unfortunately, I was wearing spurs and the tighter I gripped the faster the horse went. I shot by Bruce and my dad like they were standing still and a few feet later I fell off. I was waiting for the roof to fall in on me when my dad rode up, but he was cool and asked how I was. 'Nothing hurt but my pride,' I replied. But all of that work I did was for nought, because it didn't matter what I did for the rest of the film, people were going to say, the guy can't ride bareback.[131]

There's another scene where Wayne throws Patrick off his horse into a muddy puddle for sarcastically calling him daddy. 'It seems like whatever film we were on he was knocking me on my butt literally or figuratively,' says Patrick. 'And he even went to the extent of shooting me on the movie *McLintock*. It was all in good fun.'[132]

One of the more popular of Wayne's late westerns, *Big Jake* is probably the most violent he ever made. This is probably because it was written by the husband-and-wife team of Harry Julian and Rita Fink, who that year also wrote *Dirty Harry*. The Finks injected a much harsher tone to proceedings, perhaps catering to audiences that wanted more blood and violence in these kinds of films. One assumes Wayne wasn't entirely happy with this direction, since he insisted on balancing the violence with a lot of humour. Interestingly, Wayne turned down the chance to play Dirty Harry, and in *Big Jake* the Finks give him a variation of the famous 'Do you feel lucky?' speech.

Big Jake was a sizeable hit and Wayne ended the year as America's No. 1 box office attraction, beating Clint Eastwood into second place. It was the last time the Duke would command that position.

(US: New York opening week of 27 May)

32 *DAUGHTERS OF DARKNESS*

Belgian filmmaker Harry Kümel made his directorial debut with *Monsieur Hawarden* in 1968, a drama based on the true story of a nineteenth-century aristocrat who disguised herself as a man to avoid prosecution for murdering her lover. 'Some young Belgian producers who liked that film asked me to do an exploitation movie with lots of sex, blood and violence – but in the style of that first film.'[133]

Kümel had no idea what to make until he came across, quite by chance, an article about the historical Elizabeth Báthory, aka the Blood Countess, a Hungarian noblewoman who supposedly bathed in the blood of virgins in a perverse bid to stay young. Kümel reports:

> When I proposed to do that, they couldn't accept this, because a period film in costumes would be too costly for their tight budget possibilities. So, I proposed a storyline in which the countess was still alive thanks to all that virgin blood, and still roamed the world with her henchwoman Ilona.[134]

Together with one of the producers, Kümel wrote a sixty-page treatment in three days and nights, and gave it to a French producer who sold the idea to various backers at the film festival in Cannes. A screenplay was quickly put together by French writer Jean Ferry, who'd worked with the likes of Luis Buñuel and script-doctored Marcel Carné's *Les Enfants du paradis* (1944).

Getting finance from several international sources did present problems. 'The US financiers did not want to stress the vampire aspect of the plot,' reveals Kümel. 'They wanted in fact a detective story.'[135] This is how the character of a retired policeman became integrated into the

storyline. The financiers also impinged on casting choices. 'Each par-
ticipating country wanted to have at least one actor of their country
involved,' reveals Kümel.[136] This resulted in Andrea Rau from Germany
playing Ilona, while Kümel brought in France's Delphine Seyrig as the
countess. Seyrig first came to prominence in Alain Resnais's *Last Year in
Marienbad* (1961). Kümel knew Resnais. 'And he told Delphine to accept
the part because in his view the film would be a grandiose comic-strip.
Alain was a great fan of comic strips.'[137]

Playing a honeymoon couple, Stefan and Valerie, who encounter
the countess at an eerily deserted grand hotel, was the American actor
John Karlen, best known for the US horror TV serial *Dark Shadows*, and
Canadian Danielle Ouimet. Ouimet had starred in the sexually charged
Valérie (1969), which caused a sensation as the first Quebec film to show
nudity. *Daughters of Darkness* was just Ouimet's third film, and she found
Seyrig a willing collaborator:

> She could see that I didn't have a lot of film experience and decided
> to help me, and she helped me in a wonderful way. One day I had a
> problem with a scene, and she was sitting looking at me, knowing
> that I was panicking, and she came up to me and said, 'Danielle I have
> a problem with my text. I'm afraid of forgetting the words. Can you
> please help me rehearse.' And I know perfectly well it was for me, not
> for her. And she did that so many times.[138]

The two remained friends after the film. 'She was quite a secretive
person, though. But on the film, she imposed herself on the whole set.
When she was around, we the actors followed her lead, we responded
to her.'[139]

Ouimet got on well with Karlen too. 'He protected me and looked
out for me. We had a lot of fun. We laughed a lot.'[140] Even so, it was a
little unnerving being naked in front of a total stranger, and a film crew,
for the first time. Ouimet reveals:

> Very few people can understand why being on a set naked can be
> traumatising on the first day, but then afterwards it's just business. It's
> funny, when I did *Valérie*, I was 20 and living with my parents. I shared
> a bedroom with my sister, and I was getting dressed and undressed in
> my wardrobe, then they went to see the film and saw me naked and
> said – what happened?![141]

Eroticism plays an important role in the film, as the countess courts and then actively seduces the young couple, deciding that Valerie should be her new companion. Seyrig's presence in the film is striking; dressed either in red, furs or a tight-fitting silver lamé dress, she is one of the screen's great vampires, exuding mystery. The hotel porter is adamant that the countess stayed at the hotel forty years before, but is puzzled that her appearance is unchanged. When quizzed about this she puts it down to diet and lots of sleep.

Kümel shot his film in Belgium in a breathless five weeks, largely in an out-of-season grand hotel on the Ostend seafront and another in Brussels. It was autumn and the inclement weather added to the atmosphere of the piece. Often the sunlight was shut out in order to create the right mood, which gave the actors a sense of being cooped up. 'At midday when we ate,' says Ouimet, 'we always opened the windows to make sure that we had a little bit of sun otherwise it was very hard on the emotions.'[142] As it was, there was some tension and frayed nerves.

Not wholly appreciated on its initial run, *Daughters of Darkness* is now a recognised horror classic, the ultimate lesbian vampire movie. It's a personal favourite of uber horror fan Mark Gatiss, and the Criterion channel calls it 'one of the most exquisitely mesmerising adult horror films ever made'. The reverence with which the film is held today is, in Kümel's words:

> An astonishing mystery to me. It was truly planned as a pure exploitation film, and I did my best to stick to my assignment. The initial idea of the young producers who wanted me to make a trash movie 'in my style' was a good one, akin to having an intellectual actress with a great theatrical reputation like Delphine in a movie of that genre – a kind of cinema that is better accepted now. Mind, I would be lying in saying that I'm not happy that the film still 'holds' after so many years – with all kinds of audiences. Still, it remains a mystery.[143]

(Belgium/France/West Germany/US: New York opening 28 May)

 ## 33 *CARRY ON HENRY*

By the early 1970s the *Carry On* franchise, started back in 1958 by the producing/directing team of Peter Rogers and Gerald Thomas, was already a British institution. However, the saucy seaside postcard humour beloved by homegrown audiences did rather restrict their scope of appeal; there was very little market for the series in Europe and none at all in the USA. It was possible back then to recoup production costs and turn a reasonable profit just from UK showings but, even so, producer Peter Rogers kept a tight rein on spending. 'He was unrelentingly cheap,' recalls *Carry On* regular Julian Holloway. 'If you did two takes that was a lot.'[144]

This philosophy extended most bitterly to the actors, who were poorly paid and never given any residuals for TV showings etc. 'Woe betide anyone who asked for more money,' says Holloway. 'Charlie Hawtrey did at one point and was given a tremendous bollocking and a threat that he would never work for Rogers again, which he took seriously.'[145] Kenneth Williams was always complaining how badly he and the rest of the cast were treated, but always came back and did more. Like many of his colleagues, Williams was so typecast by the films that non-*Carry On* work was getting harder to come by.

Home to the *Carry On* films was Pinewood Studios, from where the film unit rarely strayed – and even then only to a nearby housing estate, a local high street or stretch of countryside. Holloway recalls:

The first rumblings of a location were on *Carry On Follow That Camel*. It was rumoured that they were going to shoot it in Morocco, whereupon Sid James had a heart attack, probably from that information, and Phil Silvers was drafted in at £30,000, which was six times more than Sid got. And so, four weeks in Morocco became three days on Camber Sands.[146]

Follow That Camel (1967) was Holloway's first *Carry On* and he went on to appear in several others. In *Carry On Henry* Holloway shares all his scenes with Sid James:

I'd known Sid since I was a little boy. He'd done a couple of movies with my dad [Stanley Holloway], *The Lavender Hill Mob* and *The Titfield Thunderbolt*, so I was 6 or 7 when I first met him. He was extremely welcoming and nice and we got on very well. He was a dyed-in-the-wool gambler, loved a bet on the gee-gees. Sid was not a particularly successful gambler, but did it none the less. And he always had a poker school going all the time on the *Carry Ons*.[147]

Sid James was born to play King Henry VIII, but it very nearly didn't happen. At the time stage commitments ruled him out and ex-Goon Harry Secombe was considered for the role. In the end schedules were altered and Sid turned up on the second day of shooting, wearing the same cloak that Richard Burton had recently worn playing the king in *Anne of the Thousand Days* (1969).

The idea to spoof the dysfunctional court of England's most colourful ruler and his marriage difficulties was one Rogers first envisaged back in the mid-1960s. Filming went well. Holloway recalls:

> It was like a big nursery. Kenneth [Williams] would throw his toys out of the pram every now and again, but you knew you were going to have fun. It was like a big family, and you looked forward to going in every day. Not because of the work, it was very much the companionship.[148]

Holloway got on with most of the actors. 'I was very fond of Kenneth. He was a very complex personality, but a sweet and interesting man. Once you got through all the bullshit and the campery he was a very different proposition.'[149] In contrast, Holloway was not alone in finding someone like Terry Scott Julian unappealing: 'I think there was something slightly barmy about him.'[150] Holloway recalls an occasion during the shooting of *Carry On Camping* (1969) when the team were all having lunch in the restaurant at Pinewood, and there was Gregory Peck eating alone:

> Terry suddenly went over to Peck and said, 'You don't know me, I'm part of a humble group of English comics, but why are Americans so nasty?' And instead of Peck saying, 'Why don't you fuck off,' he started to indulge Terry Scott. And Dilys Laye was so incensed that she wrote Peck a letter to say that she was apologising on behalf of her colleagues and I said to Dilys, 'I don't regard him as a colleague!'[151]

Carry On Henry was the twenty-first in the series, and is a particular favourite among the fans. The *Carry On* team seemed always to be at their best doing period comedy where the bawdy humour didn't come across as too gratuitous. For *Henry*, Holloway remembers a lot of riding was involved. He had ridden as a child, but it wasn't something he had kept up. On his first day of filming in Windsor Great Park he was handed a horse that went by the name of 'Marvel' and, upon reaching a semi-gallop, was thrown:

Well, the difference between steeplechase jockeys who fall off is they're expecting to fall off; I wasn't, so landed in a heap and was terribly winded. I'm lying on the floor, panting for breath, and Gerald Thomas said, 'Will you be alright for the first take?' So, I said, 'Will you leave – the first take – out of that sentence and ask me how I am!' That was the attitude.[152]

Thomas was actually perceived as the gentler personality of the producing/directing team; he had risen from the cutting rooms as an editor to become a director. His partnership with Rogers was very much a case of good cop/bad cop, with Rogers as enforcer, a position many felt he enjoyed a little too much. Holloway recalls:

On one of the films Barbara Windsor was bitching and moaning to Kenneth, 'that fucking Peter Rogers', forgetting that she had a radio mic on. Of course, the sound engineer left it running and the following day at rushes, that was all shown, and Rogers was not amused and Barbara thought she would never work for them again.[153]

By the end of filming Holloway had begun to count himself as a rather reticent Carry On regular:

I always felt that the quality of the work was very poor, the writing was very poor and I remember Kenny telling me, 'You've got to get out, don't let the stigma surround you, we're all tainted.' And to a certain extent that was absolutely true.[154]

Holloway did have a 'blink or you'll miss it' cameo in the next in the series, Carry On at Your Convenience, which also came out in 1971, then bowed out. There was an offer to do another, Carry On Girls (1973), but:

I said no, I don't want to do it, and the casting director called my agent and he said, 'This is a message from Peter Rogers that if Julian doesn't do Carry On Girls he will never work for Peter Rogers again.' And I said, 'Can I have that in writing?'[155]

(UK: London opening 3 June)

34 · *THE CEREMONY (GISHIKI)*

Undoubtedly the most controversial of all Japanese filmmakers was Nagisa Ōshima, responsible for the infamous and sexually explicit 1976 film *In the Realm of the Senses*, which caused outrage in his home country and was refused a screening at the New York Film Festival. Born into privilege in the ancient capital city of Kyoto, the son of a government worker reportedly of Samurai ancestry, Ōshima studied law and political history at Kyoto University, where he was a student leader involved in left-wing activities. He then became a film critic, before learning his craft as an assistant director at the Shochiku Studios, the oldest and one of the biggest film studios in Japan.

Ōshima started directing his first features at the time of the French New Wave, and was particularly influenced by Jean-Luc Godard. As he established himself as a filmmaker, Ōshima would often be cited as 'the Godard of Japan'. He was also a founding figure of the Japanese New Wave, a loosely connected group of filmmakers that represented a full and complete break from the likes of Yasujirō Ozu and Akira Kurosawa. They focused on such formerly taboo subjects as racism, sexual violence and the devastating aftermath on the Japanese psyche of the Second World War. Ōshima was the most radical figure among this pack; it was his films that were usually more highly politicised, openly challenging and critical of Japanese cultural and social values, along with the conventions of Japanese cinema, which he despised. The country of his birth was Ōshima's greatest subject, the one he returned to again and again. He once said that the goal of his films was 'to force the Japanese to look in the mirror'. Nowhere is this theme better developed than in *The Ceremony*.

This is perhaps Ōshima's most ambitious film, dealing as it does with the whole post-war history of Japan as shown through the gradual disintegration of a wealthy provincial family, the Sakuradas. Starting at the end of the Second World War to the present day, the film is punctuated by the various ceremonies – weddings, anniversaries, funerals – at which the family is drawn together. As one family member points out, they only ever see each other at weddings and funerals, something that a lot of families can certainly relate to. These ceremonies, hugely important in Japanese culture, are an increasingly desperate attempt by the Sakuradas' patriarch to maintain an outward veneer of respectability, while inside all is rotten as dark secrets (suicide, murder, incest) are revealed.

The film begins as if it is going to be one of those long and formal Japanese sagas so beloved of classical directors like Ozu, but instead Ōshima subverts it totally; as he was to say, 'all families must be disinfected'. He seems especially interested in how the preservation of these traditions negatively affect the younger generation, as represented by his central character Masuo (Kenzô Kawarasaki), a young high-school baseball coach. This is best demonstrated in Masuo's wedding, which surely ranks among the most mortifying in film history. When Masuo's arranged marriage to a woman he's never met is cancelled, the stern and fearsome family patriarch, the grandfather, insists the ceremony continue as planned. Guests gather to watch as the humiliated Masuo stands at the altar alone, marrying a non-existent bride, just for the sake of the continuation of the ceremony and preservation of tradition.

In *The Ceremony*, it is the older, more authoritarian generation who show themselves to be both militaristic and feudal in their outlook, who hold sway over Masuo and his equally powerless and disillusioned contemporaries, making them unable to resist the status quo or discover new values to replace the old. The film suggests that modern Japan, like the Sakurada clan, is trapped between past and present.

The Ceremony employs a non-linear narrative, jumping back and forth between all the weddings and funerals Masuo has attended throughout his life, each ceremony coinciding with a year that reflects on the political upheavals and social transformations of post-war Japan. Stunningly beautiful to look at, with wonderful widescreen compositions, *The Ceremony* garnered great critical acclaim and reached Ōshima's largest international audience yet. And while *The Ceremony* is by no means as controversial as *In the Realm of the Senses*, or enjoyed the same exposure as *Merry Christmas, Mr Lawrence* (1983), due to the presence of David Bowie, it is arguably the director's most challenging and distinguished work.

(Japan: opening 5 June)

35 *THE ANDERSON TAPES*

After leaving the James Bond role following *You Only Live Twice* (1967), Sean Connery starred in a string of duds: *Shalako* (1968), a lacklustre cowboy picture; *The Red Tent* (1969), a drama of a doomed Arctic expedition; and *The Molly Maguires* (1970), a grim tale about deprived miners. Thanks to these failures Connery found that his reputation and status as a box office attraction was in doubt by the start of the 1970s. *The Anderson Tapes*, a slick caper movie, changed all that and returned him, albeit briefly, to America's list of top ten stars.

In his first film *sans* toupee, Connery plays Duke Anderson, a safe cracker fresh from a long jail term who plans to 'rob the guts' out of a luxury apartment block in New York over the Labor Day weekend. For this he requires the backing of the local Mafia and the help of some fellow cons, including Martin Balsam and, in his first major film role, Christopher Walken. The cast featured other familiar faces such as Dyan Cannon, Alan King, Garrett Morris, later part of the original line-up of TV's *Saturday Night Live*, and, in her final feature, Margaret Hamilton, immortalised as the wicked witch in *The Wizard of Oz* (1939).

The film works well within the conventions of the crime/thriller genre. It was also the first major film to focus on the pervasiveness of electronic surveillance in our daily lives, from security cameras in public places to hidden recording devices. While planning his caper, Duke is scrutinised by hidden cameras, wire taps and bugging equipment wherever he goes. The irony is that the various agencies doing the snooping, be it federal or state government, aren't interested in his activities, only the people he's associating with – like the Mafia or a suspected member of the Black Panthers – so the crime proceeds unchallenged. This is all pre-Watergate and a full three years before Francis Ford Coppola tackled the same subject in the critically lauded *The Conversation*.

This aspect of the story is almost certainly what interested Sidney Lumet and screenwriter Frank Pierson in adapting Lawrence Sanders's bestselling novel to the screen. Lumet once stated that he always gave a theme to every film he made, which influenced all the narrative decisions he made as a director. The theme that he gave *The Anderson Tapes* was 'the machines are winning'.

For his star, Lumet was happy to get Connery. The men had formed a strong bond working together on *The Hill* (1965), the first film that really disassociated Connery from the 007 image and saw him treated by critics as a serious actor. Following *The Anderson Tapes*, they would go on to make another three pictures together: *The Offence* (1972), *Murder on the Orient Express* (1974) and *Family Business* (1989).

Made on a tight budget in just six weeks, *The Anderson Tapes* was filmed on location in New York. In his memoirs Lumet told of one incident when the crew were shooting a mobster's funeral on the streets of Little Italy, outside St Patrick's old cathedral. During filming Lumet could sense tension developing in the crowd, with several criminal types getting agitated and vocally criticising why Italians were always portrayed in these types of movies as villains. The situation looked like getting serious when an assistant director informed Lumet that he'd overheard one of the mob guys saying they should grab the negative. 'So, after each shot,' said Lumet, 'we broke off the negative and gave it to a terrified production assistant, who quietly slipped away and brought the negative up to the Technicolor labs on the subway.'[156] St Patrick's old cathedral would be used the following year for the baptism scene in *The Godfather*.

Lumet brings an almost documentary feel to the film's climax, as the police are alerted to the crime and the gang try to escape from the building, which in effect has become their new prison. In the original ending the gang manage to escape. The film's distributor, Columbia, insisted that this be changed to one in which the villains are either killed or arrested, so that any future sale to television, where stricter moral codes are endorsed, would not be jeopardised.

The Anderson Tapes was a sizeable hit and received some favourable reviews. Interestingly, most critics argued the various merits and flaws of the film only as it related to the heist genre, ignoring its subtle sociopolitical commentary and prophetic take on electronic surveillance. Exactly one year after its premiere in New York, early in the morning of 17 June 1972, several burglars were arrested in the office of the Democratic National Committee, located in the Watergate complex of buildings in Washington, DC. The prowlers had been caught wiretapping phones. I wonder if any of them saw *The Anderson Tapes*.

(US: New York opening 17 June)

36 WILLARD

It was without doubt the strangest audition of Bruce Davison's life. He'd been asked by his agent to go to Paramount to read for this character called Willard in a new horror picture. He arrived, read a few pages and then was taken to an outbuilding containing an army of rats. The animal trainer grabbed what Davison thought to be the biggest of the lot and perched it on his shoulder, while asking how he fancied having a rat as a co-star. Just then the rodent started licking his ear. The next minute Davison was told he had the part. It was the rat that chose the actor, rather than the other way round.

Willard was based on the novel *Ratman's Notebooks* by Irish author Stephen Gilbert, and was directed by Daniel Mann. By the 1970s Mann was pretty much on his uppers, having been a top stage and film director in the 1950s and early 1960s – directing a pre-fame James Dean on Broadway and aiding Elizabeth Taylor to an Oscar-winning performance in *Butterfield 8* (1960). Maybe he got the job on *Willard* because not many others fancied working with a bunch of 'vermin'.

Working on the film was top animal trainer Moe Di Sesso, who purchased a dozen rats from a pet store, then spent a year training something like 500 of their offspring. The main rat protagonist, Ben, appeared only in close-ups, with fourteen stand-in rats of the same size and colour performing other tasks. Willard comes across these rats in the garden of the mansion he lives in with his ailing and demanding mother, and discovers he can communicate and control them. A socially awkward loner, the rats come to fill the gap in his life that should be occupied by human friends. They also become a tool of revenge against his boss, played by Ernest Borgnine, who treats him like dirt at work and who stole the business from Willard's father.

Davison enjoyed working with the veteran actor, although Borgnine himself had to overcome his own fear of rats. In the climactic attack scene, the crew smeared his body with peanut butter to attract the rodents to crawl all over him. Unfortunately, one ran up his trouser leg, while another bit him, resulting in the actor requiring a tetanus shot. For months after filming Borgnine suffered from nightmares about being attacked or smothered by rats. 'I actually woke up screaming more than once.'[157]

For someone who grew up a fan of the old Universal horror films, Davison was especially delighted when Elsa Lanchester was cast to play his mother. There he was, working with the original bride of Frankenstein. Sometimes Davison brought his Super 8 camera to work and Elsa would do her best 'bride' poses for him between takes. She gave him some good advice too, which he never forgot: 'If you ever have a director that's giving you a load of codswallop, just say – "oh, that's very good, let me try to incorporate that into what I'm doing" – then do whatever the fuck you want.'[158] Elsa had a sharp tongue and a great bawdy sense of humour.

Before *Willard* came out distributors Cinerama Releasing were unsure exactly how to market it. Should they emphasise the rat angle, or the more dramatic human elements of the story. In the end they came up with two ad campaigns, one featured the rats while the other did not.

Two test screenings were held in Pennsylvania, with the result that more people were encouraged to attend with the advertising that focused on the rats. On release, *Willard* appeared to perk the interest of the general filmgoer rather than just the usual horror crowd, turning what was a modestly budgeted film into a sizeable hit. *Cinefantastique* magazine called *Willard* the 'horror sleeper of 1971'. In truth, the actual horror content of the film is relatively mild and infrequent – the horrific exception being the final assault on Borgnine, where Davison instructs his rat army to 'tear him up'.

The surprise success of *Willard* at the box office was to inspire a whole subgenre of 'animal attack' horror films that flourished during the 1970s with everything from frogs, snakes, worms and spiders. It also gave rise to an inferior sequel, *Ben*, that arrived the following summer, a film best known today for its slushy title theme song by Michael Jackson. Another bonus was that Stephen Gilbert's hitherto obscure novel became a paperback bestseller. Horror historian Kim Newman argues that this success demonstrated to publishers the viability of horror as a mainstream literary genre and did much to bring about the boom of horror fiction in the 1970s, spearheaded by Stephen King and James Herbert. It's perhaps no coincidence that Herbert's very first novel, in 1974, was called *The Rats*.

Willard was remade in 2003 featuring Crispin Glover in the lead role.

(US: New York opening 18 June)

37 KLUTE

For a film that played such an important part in Jane Fonda's career, as well as earning her an Oscar for Best Actress, it's interesting to note that she only agreed to make *Klute* in the first place because she needed the money. Her political activism, such as her involvement in the movement to end the war in Vietnam, was such a drain on her personal finances that she was in danger of going broke. She also hadn't made a film for two years, and people in Hollywood were wondering whether her political causes would completely overtake her career as an actress.

When *Klute* came along, it helped that she liked the director Alan J. Pakula and felt that the story had something to say about how men exploited women in society. Along with her radicalism, Fonda was also experiencing the early stirrings of feminism. For her *Klute* was a cry in the dark for abused women.

When Pakula read the screenplay for *Klute* he saw only Fonda in the role of Bree Daniels, a cynical high-class call girl. Warner Brothers, however, saw anyone but Fonda and Pakula was told to cast someone else. He refused and was swiftly removed from the picture. Meanwhile several actresses turned the role down, including Barbra Streisand. With no takers, Warners had no choice but to bring back Pakula and his choice of Fonda was accepted.

Klute follows Bree as she assists a detective, played by Donald Sutherland, in solving a missing persons case. Some critics regard *Klute* as the first instalment of what has informally come to be known as Pakula's 'paranoia trilogy', a series of thrillers that continued with *The Parallax View* (1974) and *All the President's Men* (1976), two films that seized on a growing distrust of government in the wake of Vietnam and Watergate.

As part of his preparation for *Klute* Pakula read François Truffaut's book on Hitchcock, which discussed his career and techniques. 'He used it I guess as a primer to do *Klute*,' recalls production assistant Ralph Singleton, 'because the master of suspense is Hitchcock. And I think Pakula brilliantly captured the suspense of the story.'[159]

Klute was Singleton's big break in the movie business, and he went on to work on other seminal '70s movies like *The French Connection* and *Taxi Driver*. He started out working on low-budget movies until he was recommended for *Klute*. 'And that was a great experience. I loved working for Pakula. He was a very intelligent guy. And he was very much an actor's director.'[160]

For most of the shoot Singleton was stuck in the production office, but occasionally went out to find locations. *Klute* was a combination of studio sets and real locations. Bree's apartment was built at the Filmways Studio in Harlem. Before any of those scenes were shot Fonda asked Pakula if she could stay there for a few nights, just to get a feel of the place. Singleton says:

> She wanted to know where everything was in the kitchen, her living area, the bedroom and the rest of it. She really got into that place becoming her home, not just a movie set. It was terrific seeing Jane Fonda and being around her at that point in her career. She really got into that part.[161]

Fonda underwent her usual diligent preparation and research. She befriended call girls, visited them at home, watched how they worked in bars and clubs, and how they picked up their clients. On these recce evenings, not once was Fonda approached or solicited, which led to a devastating loss of confidence and a feeling she was totally wrong for the role. She approached Pakula with her concerns and the suggestion that her friend Faye Dunaway take over. 'Alan just laughed at me and told me I was nuts.'[162] Fonda later rationalised that maybe nobody recognised her. She didn't look like Barbarella anymore, having recently shorn off her long blonde locks for what was known as a 'hipster shag hairstyle'. Pakula liked it and thought it was perfect for her role. When the film came out it was a look that was quickly copied.

Pakula had hired a 23-year-old call girl to be technical adviser on the film, and she was on the set the whole time. Pakula also arranged for Fonda to go to the New York City morgue to look through case files and hundreds of photographs of women who had been beaten up and killed by their boyfriends, husbands, pimps or clients. It was a gruelling experience she never forgot. Afterwards she had to rush to the bathroom to throw up.

The partnership of Pakula and Fonda transformed *Klute* into something different to what was originally envisaged. Fonda was contributing ideas all the time, which Pakula gladly took on. There's one moment where Bree is having sex with a client, and she sneaks a look at her watch over his shoulder. That always got a big reaction from women in the audience. Pakula encouraged plenty of improvisation, especially in the scenes when Bree visits her psychiatrist. Pakula had a male actor in the role until Fonda said Bree would never open up to a man. Pakula had no choice but to replace him.

The character of Bree began taking over the film. In the original script the focus was a lot more on the detective, John Klute, but as Pakula began reducing what was a big screenplay down to a shootable length, it was at Klute's expense. Sutherland happily watched all this from the sidelines. He was in a relationship with Fonda at the time, deeply in love, and professional enough to realise that what was happening was for the good of the picture.

The only worry Pakula had was that Fonda's activism would disrupt filming. In a way it did. Roy Scheider, who played Bree's pimp, recalled that Black Panther members used to hang around the set and that between takes Fonda was invariably on the phone trying to raise money for some political cause or organising an anti-war appearance. Saying that, whenever she was required on the set for a take she'd drop what she was doing, take a moment or two to focus, and then bring her

A game. It wasn't without friction, though. Her anti-government views and radicalism did get the crew's back up, and one day they hung the American flag prominently near her dressing room. Fonda was devastated that her political views had been misrepresented as unpatriotic.

Klute is a masterpiece of American '70s cinema. A thriller and a whodunnit, it's also a fascinating character study and captures wonderfully the mood of early '70s New York. Pakula depicts the city as lawless, a moral vacuum, especially in its treatment of women. Bree lives in an apartment with five locks on the door. And Fonda has perhaps never given a better performance.

(US: Los Angeles opening 23 June)

38 | *WILD ROVERS*

Before *Brokeback Mountain* there was *Wild Rovers*. Well, sort of. While director Blake Edwards saw this western as 'a love story' between two men – an older, wiser man, played by William Holden, and a younger man, played by Ryan O'Neal – it was much more a mentor–apprentice situation, a search for a father. Edwards himself felt alienated and estranged from his own father growing up. In this way *Wild Rovers* was perhaps the most personal film he ever made, and the director always rated it as one of his best.

The film had a quirky quality about it, befitting the comedic talents of Edwards, best known for his *Pink Panther* movies, while at the same time being another of those 'Death of the West as We Knew it' type movies. What Edwards was keen to emphasise was the vast, open beauty of the western plains (it's stunningly photographed on location in Utah, Arizona and the famous Monument Valley), along with its barren, emptiness that can engender loneliness and boredom in those who lived and worked there. That's true of middle-aged Ross Bodine (Holden) and the young and cocky Frank Post (O'Neal). Both are employed by Walter Buckman (Karl Malden), a rancher who owns an impressive cattle empire. Bodine has become weary of a back-breaking life and Frank, fearful of following in his footsteps, impulsively decides that they should rob the local bank. Buckman gets his sons, played by Joe Don Baker and Tom Skerritt, to raise a posse and pursue the robbers. Rounding out an impressive cast is Welsh actress Rachel Roberts, who did the film because she'd always wanted to play a saloon bar madam.

During filming O'Neal and Holden struck up an interesting friendship – the grizzled old veteran and the young wannabe star. Both undertook a lot of impressive stunt work and horse wrangling. Edwards always took a helicopter to the next location, but Holden insisted on driving O'Neal and, during the long journeys, they talked and talked. O'Neal pumped Holden with questions about the industry and why he had become so disillusioned with it, and about his heavy drinking. Halfway through shooting, news arrived that O'Neal had been Oscar nominated for his performance in *Love Story* (1970). He pondered whether to turn up – it was obvious, he said, that George C. Scott was going to win for *Patton* (1970). And he did. Holden was adamant that O'Neal should go. O'Neal then asked where Holden's Best Actor Oscar was for *Stalag 17* (1953). 'The Bay of Naples,' Holden admitted, rather sheepishly. O'Neal couldn't believe it. 'Yeah,' said Holden, 'I threw it in when I was on Sam Spiegel's yacht with [French actress] Capucine.'[163]

Edwards not only directed *Wild Rovers* for MGM, he wrote it, too, and intended it to be a near two-and-a-half-hour epic. The recently installed James Aubrey, nicknamed 'The Smiling Cobra', brought in to sort out MGM's financial problems, had other ideas. Following disappointing previews, Aubrey cut twenty minutes from the running time. Edwards was incensed and pleaded with Aubrey not to do it; 'They still butchered it.' According to Edwards's wife, Julie Andrews, who was on location for the whole duration of the shoot, the failure of *Wild Rovers* left Edwards 'devastated', and that the whole experience 'challenged his reality. He took a nosedive into depression.'[164] For a time, Edwards even considered ditching Hollywood altogether. He later got his own back by satirising his battles with studios in his comedy *S.O.B* (1981), which also starred Holden.

It's doubtful whether Edwards's longer cut would have fared any better at the box office, though it might have garnered more critical fondness. One issue seemed to be the ad campaign and the original poster, which had a picture of Holden and O'Neal riding on the same horse, with O'Neal behind and his arms around Holden hugging him. An article in *Variety* magazine said that the ads had led to 'insider wisecracks' about a possible gay relationship between the characters. The studio ultimately withdrew that poster and replaced it with a more generic western image of the two of them wielding and firing pistols.

(US: New York opening 23 June)

39 | *LE MANS*

Steve McQueen was riding high as one of the biggest box office stars in the world. For years he'd dreamed of making the ultimate car racing film. That dream became reality when he got the finance for a drama set against the backdrop of the 24 Hours of Le Mans endurance race, which takes place every summer in France. Some of the best drivers in the world were hired, and McQueen took virtual creative control. That didn't last long as the production dissolved into chaos.

Peter Samuelson saw it happen first hand. He'd just finished high school and won a full scholarship to the University of Cambridge. While waiting for his studies to start, and because he spoke good French, Samuelson landed a job as interpreter to the production manager. 'When I left for France in my tiny little car, I was 18 years old and had no idea what awaited me.'[165]

His first exposure to McQueen was when he was told to hire bulldozers to turn the ornate gardens of the chateau the star had rented into a motocross track. 'I then flew to Sweden on a private jet to collect two Husqvarna motorbikes for his use.'[166] The presence of McQueen magnetically attracted women from all points of the compass, and Peter watched bemused 'as a steady stream of hot and cold running groupies rolled through the camp'.[167]

Inevitably with any sports film the trick is coming up with an adequate story on which to hang all the sporting footage; usually it's some romantic subplot. McQueen's determination to portray the reality of racing without the artifice of an imposed storyline led to script problems throughout the shoot. And it was never resolved. Writers came and went with alarming regularity. 'We never knew what we would be filming the next day because the script never coalesced,' confirms Peter, 'but we went through dozens of drafts, all mutually inconsistent.'[168]

McQueen brought in the experienced John Sturges to direct, with whom he'd worked on *The Magnificent Seven* (1960) and *The Great Escape* (1963). Sturges, too, wanted the racing scenes as real as possible, a view shared by the drivers. One of them was Derek Bell, who had experience in Formula 3 and Formula 2. Bell liked McQueen a lot and they ended up renting a house together for the last month of filming:

> The impression you got was that he wasn't bothered about acting. He wanted to be a racing driver. And he was very good. He loved being

with the drivers. Any chance he got he'd come over and hang out with us.[169]

Bell discovered McQueen liked to have fun. One Sunday, when there was no filming, McQueen, Bell and another driver took some Porsches and raced around the production village, a quadrangle of prefabricated huts that made up the offices, and in and out of the marquee that was normally used as the canteen. 'We made a right old mess of the place,' Bell recalls. 'But we had a blast. Of course, on the Monday all hell broke loose.'[170] Because it was McQueen, nothing was done about it. 'After all, it was his money,' says Bell.[171] However, that was starting to run out.

The level of embezzlement, pilfering and profligacy on the film was shocking. The production routinely ran out of cash. On one occasion they were unable to pay several hundred French extras. Samuelson recalls:

> These individuals then rioted in the production village. The producer hid in his prefabricated building, sitting on its concrete base. Fifty French extras pushed the entire building off its foundations with him inside it. The police were called. I had to lend the accountant the thousands of francs in unspent living allowance I had hidden under my bed.[172]

Money problems continued and it was obvious the film was going to run over its budget. 'About halfway through the shoot they stopped the movie and sent us all home,' recalls Bell. 'When we came back after two weeks there was a different hierarchy and John Sturges was gone.'[173] The backers, Cinema Centre, who were the theatrical film division of the CBS Television Network, considered shutting down the film completely, but eventually struck a new deal with McQueen, who agreed to forfeit his salary and creative control of the picture. Lee H. Katzin, primarily a television director, was brought in to finish the film, which still ended up over schedule and over budget.

It was a madhouse. People were being fired all the time. Samuelson watched as everyone above him in seniority left. When a driver was injured, Samuelson was seen as the best-placed person to replace the head of track safety. 'When my father came to visit, I remember him shouting at the producer, "Peter can't take care of himself, how the hell can he take care of track safety? He's a child!"'[174]

Accidents occurred throughout the shoot – none more bizarre than what befell Bell when he was on his way back in the Ferrari after racing along a stretch of the course for the cameras. Suddenly the cockpit of his car exploded into flames. Bringing the Ferrari to a halt, he leapt out and shouted to a passer-by to get the fire truck and an ambulance. As he waited, Bell watched his car burn to the ground. The ambulance arrived, along with Sister Brigitte, a nun who was looking after the medical side of things:

> She jammed this needle into my backside and put me on a stretcher in the back of the ambulance and banged on the door, 'Let's go.' The driver lets the clutch out in a very enthusiastic French way, and I go flying backwards and burst through the doors on my stretcher, out into the bloody road. I grabbed the rail to stop me going too far and the driver heard the noise, put his foot on the brakes in emergency fashion, and literally the bloody stretcher comes flying back inside.[175]

Bell escaped with just minor burns to his face.

He worked for six months on the film, and not just as a driver. Often he was asked for advice on things like how a driver prepares before a big race. At one point, McQueen wanted to know what to do if he was trying to get a fellow driver's attention, to rile him. Bell said in England you'd stick two fingers up, Churchill-style. McQueen used that and it became one of the film's most iconic images.

For Samuelson, when it all came to an end he drove back to England and found himself in academic robes at the University of Cambridge; 'but, touched by the sybaritic and puckish lunacy of Hollywood and the international racing community, I was never quite the same again'.[176] Samuelson later enjoyed a successful career as the producer of such films as *Wilde* (1997) and *Arlington Road* (1999).

As for Bell, his motor-racing career was to span over forty years. He returned to Le Mans many times as a competitor, winning it an extraordinary five times. However, when he first saw the McQueen film, he couldn't hide his disappointment. 'It wasn't as exciting or dramatic as it was when we were making it.'[177] Today, *Le Mans* is seen very differently. 'Now when you look at it, it's a bloody wonderful record of racing in one of the greatest eras of sports cars.'[178]

(US: New York opening 24 June)

40 | MCCABE AND MRS MILLER

Warren Beatty first met Julie Christie back in the swinging London days of the mid-1960s, but it was several years before their highly publicised on/off love affair that lasted well into the 1970s. It was David Foster, a former publicist trying to produce his first movie, who came up with a starring vehicle for the two of them. He had just bought the film rights to a book that he thought would make an interesting revisionist western, about a gambler who pitches up one day in a small mining town and goes into business with a prostitute to run a whorehouse. Foster knew it would be a huge coup getting Beatty and Christie together on screen – and so it proved. 'It was hot stuff. I mean, we had to beat the press away with a friggin' baseball bat.'[179]

Foster hired Robert Altman, a hot director after the success of *MASH* (1970). Beatty was in London when his agent told him about Altman. 'Who is Bob Altman?' said Beatty after a pause. *MASH* had yet to open in Europe. Beatty got on a plane to New York, saw *MASH*, loved it, and made a commitment to star in *McCabe and Mrs Miller*. But he wouldn't sign a contract. Foster reveals:

> Warren had a reputation for always being dragged kicking and screaming to commit to a movie. He kept putting it off until finally we called his agent and said, 'If he doesn't sign the contract by six o'clock Friday night, we're going to get another actor.' At quarter to six he signed the contract.[180]

On location in Vancouver, British Columbia, Altman and Beatty had a tetchy working relationship. Altman was meticulous in his preparation and assured in what he was doing. Beatty had his own ideas too. 'Warren was very intense,' says Foster. 'And he'd constantly question Bob on set-ups and dialogue, and Bob was like, "I'm the fucking director here!"'[181] There were frequent clashes. Beatty liked lots of takes, working his way into a performance. Altman preferred to shoot fast and loose. Take the scene where Beatty is drinking alone in his room. It was already take twenty, and Beatty wanted more. Pissed off, Altman announced to the crew, 'Print seven and eleven – I'll see you guys tomorrow,' and walked out. Altman referred to Beatty as a control freak and got his revenge by ordering him to do twenty-five takes of a scene in a biting cold snowdrift.

In contrast to Beatty, Christie put herself totally in Altman's hands, and the two became lifelong friends. Christie endeared herself to all of the crew, especially a young student called Don Carmody, who was in his second year at Loyola College in Montreal. The Professor of Film Theory at Loyola was Father Marc Gervais. Friends with a number of filmmakers, Gervais often loaned his students out as free labour on their productions. One day in class Gervais announced an opportunity for anyone interested in working on a Robert Altman film. 'The catch was you had to get yourself to Vancouver and put yourself up,' recalls Carmody. 'There was no pay but they would feed you. I was the only taker and ended up driving a Bell telephone repair vehicle across Canada to get to Vancouver.'[182]

Carmody showed up almost two weeks into filming and the production people didn't know what to do with him. 'I wasn't in the union and couldn't touch any equipment or help anywhere that I might displace a union member from working.'[183] The production manager, Jim Margellos, used Carmody mostly for photocopying and getting coffee:

> Then one morning he came in and tossed me the keys to his car and said go pick up Julie Christie at the hotel in Vancouver and bring her here. She had just arrived. I was also to help her if she needed any errands run or to pick anything up. Off I went and met the most beautiful woman I'd ever seen or dreamed of meeting.[184]

Carmody found Christie charming, and she seemed to like the fact that he was a nice, polite and well-spoken young man ('thank you years of Jesuit private schooling'). It also turned out that she knew Father Marc Gervais, so they hit it off:

> When we got to set, she asked me what my job was, and I told her I didn't really have one. She said, 'Okay come with me,' and we marched into Jim Margellos's office. She promptly informed him that she wanted me to be her driver and assistant during her stay. I'm sure Margellos was flummoxed but he knew better than to argue with one of the stars of the movie so he reluctantly agreed and even let me keep his car.[185]

Playing the brothel madame, Christie didn't work every day and, as the film was being shot pretty much in sequence, she had a lot of days off. 'That meant I was doing stuff for her or Warren,' says Carmody. 'He pretty much ignored me except to occasionally offer me tokes of his pot, which, since I was driving, I had to politely refuse (most of the time).'[186]

Carmody hardly ever got close to Altman except to say 'good morning', but from what he observed he seemed to always be in a pretty good mood. He liked to joke and tell stories:

> The set of the town of Presbyterian Church was being built around us during the shooting so didn't look like a typical western movie set. Everyday there seemed to be something new going up. And many of the crew were dressed as extras and wandered around the set doing their jobs with period tools and equipment.[187]

It was a real experience for an aspiring filmmaker, but sadly Carmody's time came to an end as his Christmas exams were coming up. 'Julie seemed genuinely sad to see me go and gave me a sweet gift with a photo of her she autographed to me. I also think she was aware I was smitten with her!'[188]

Carmody had worked on the film for a little over a month, enough time to at least appreciate the atmosphere of teamwork Altman brought to the film, which Carmody later tried to emulate as a producer on his own productions, such as *Porky's* (1981) and *Chicago* (2002). 'It always bothered me when I worked with a director who was autocratic or aloof or otherwise not building a team. I suppose that was my biggest takeaway from the Altman experience.'[189]

The modest critical and commercial success of *McCabe and Mrs Miller* was also the beginning of a distinguished career for David Foster, as he went on to produce the likes of *The Getaway* (1972) with Steve McQueen, and John Carpenter's *The Thing* (1982).

Over the years, *McCabe and Mrs Miller* rose substantially in critical esteem. At the time the nearest it got to winning any kind of award was Christie's Oscar nomination for Best Actress, but in recent years, the American Film Institute ranked it as the eighth greatest western ever made. It has another claim to fame too. During shooting, Christie and Beatty's rented home was the scene of numerous parties. It was supposedly at one of these parties that Beatty first met Jack Nicholson, then making *Carnal Knowledge* in Vancouver. Nicholson is said to have walked in, taken one look at Beatty and pronounced, 'Now that's what a movie star looks like.' It was the beginning of one of Hollywood's most enduring and renowned friendships.

(US: New York opening 24 June)

41 *SHAFT*

When James Aubrey, the no-nonsense head of MGM, gave Gordon Parks the chance to make his second-ever film, the Black director didn't hold out much hope for its success. The salary on offer was good and it was another notch on his CV, so he took the job. At least, he thought, this tale of a tough and suave Black detective might give young Black audiences their first cinematic hero to cheer on who was comparable to the likes of James Bond or Humphrey Bogart. It did more than that; *Shaft* became one of the pioneering blaxploitation films and saved MGM from bankruptcy.

Parks was the first African American to work as a staff photographer for *Life* magazine and broke more ground in Hollywood two decades later as the first Black artist to produce and direct a major Hollywood film: *The Learning Tree* (1969), a coming-of-age drama based on his own semi-autobiographical novel. Parks was a true Renaissance man; he was also a composer and poet.

Shaft began life as a novel by former *New York Times* reporter Ernest Tidyman, whose idea it was to create a Black detective hero in the Sam Spade/Philip Marlowe mould. Indeed, the plot could have come from any number of *films noirs*. Shaft is recruited to rescue the kidnapped daughter of a Harlem mob boss from Italian gangsters. A bestseller, it was quickly snapped up by MGM and Tidyman was asked to provide the screenplay, his first. 1971 was quite a year for Tidyman when film producer Philip D'Antoni, impressed by the grittiness and realistic New York setting of the *Shaft* novel, asked Tidyman to write the screenplay for *The French Connection*.

Parks knew the film would live or die with the casting of John Shaft. So, it surprised some when the actor he chose was a former male model with no film experience whatsoever. Richard Roundtree had done some stage work off-Broadway and a bit of television (driving a cab in New York to pay for acting lessons), but not much else. Roundtree himself was perhaps the most surprised to win the role, turning up at the audition to see familiar faces waiting with him and thinking he didn't stand a chance. MGM stood by Parks's decision to cast the unknown Roundtree, only to throw in a curve ball that threatened the entire production just twenty-four hours before filming was due to start. Aubrey wanted to cancel the New York shoot and for Parks to make the picture in LA instead. Parks was livid. Shaft belonged in the gritty streets of Harlem not downtown Beverly Hills. He caught the next flight to Hollywood to confront Aubrey, quite prepared to resign if necessary. With MGM haemorrhaging so much money, Aubrey's concern was the potential for budget overruns due to the extremely cold weather New York was then experiencing. Parks fought his corner and won, but with a warning shot from Aubrey that if he loused up, 'Your ass is mine.' In the end the film came in on time and on budget.

The picture was shot around Harlem, Greenwich Village and Times Square. Cleverly, the character of Shaft is seen to have roots in the neighbourhood of Harlem, something that resonated with Black urban audiences, but also presented him as upwardly mobile, with a bachelor pad in the predominantly white area of Greenwich Village. Other aspects of Shaft's character resonated too, not least his tough, streetwise savvy and conveyor belt of female lovers. However, much more than the novel, the film emphasised the political issues of the time. For example, Shaft relies upon a group of militant Black activists to help him complete his mission.

When it opened *Shaft* was an instant hit, proving that there was a Black audience out there for this kind of movie. A July 1971 *Variety* article noted that something like 80 per cent of the audience for *Shaft* during its first few weeks on release had been Black. Far from waning, the film's popularity crossed over to white audiences, and the large box office receipts helped a struggling MGM to pull itself out of financial difficulty.

Although not the first of its kind, *Shaft* is seen as the definitive blaxploitation movie. Some critics argued that it presented shallow, stereotyped characters, a criticism that was levelled at blaxploitation films in general. *Shaft* worked within the conventions of the detective movie, but what made it different was replacing what would have been a white protagonist with a Black protagonist and surrounding him with a largely Black supporting cast. It also established the first Black action super-hero. As the poster declared, Shaft was 'Hotter than Bond. Cooler than Bullitt.' In that respect the film is of huge cultural importance. Adding to the mix is the classic theme song by Isaac Hayes, who became the first African American to win the Academy Award for Best Song. Hayes was also nominated for his score.

With box office tills still ringing, MGM rushed a sequel into production, beginning the first film franchise to be headed by a Black actor. Made by the same team, *Shaft's Big Score* (1972) failed to match the impact of its predecessor. Nor did 1973's *Shaft in Africa*, despite the interesting concept of taking the character out of the New York ghetto and on to the trail of modern-day slave traders. This was followed by a television series in which Roundtree played Shaft in all but name. The restrictions of prime-time TV diluted everything that made him such a hit on film and, as a result, the show was short lived.

In 2000, Paramount remade *Shaft*, directed by John Singleton and starring Samuel L. Jackson as the police detective nephew of the original Shaft. Both Roundtree and Parks made cameo appearances.

(US: Los Angeles opening 25 June)

42 · WILLY WONKA AND THE CHOCOLATE FACTORY

Mel Stuart was relaxing at home when his 11-year-old daughter, Madeline, came running into his study. 'Daddy I've just read a book called *Charlie and the Chocolate Factory* and I want you to make a movie of it.' The title didn't mean anything to him. Stuart mainly specialised in documentary filmmaking, but he could tell that whatever it was, it had caught his daughter's imagination.

That night Stuart read the book and thought it was an interesting story. The following morning, he made a point of seeing his friend David L. Wolper, a film and television producer whose company he worked for. Stuart gave Wolper a quick outline of the story, about how this destitute young boy wins a golden ticket to tour the mysterious and magical chocolate factory of Willy Wonka. 'I left the book with him,' recalls Stuart. 'I don't think he ever read it.'[190]

Things might have been left like that, if not for a gigantic slice of luck. As Stuart reports:

> A few days later, David and myself were in the offices of Quaker Oats, we were doing documentaries for the corporation, and they asked if we had anything about chocolate. Quaker were thinking about making a chocolate bar. Suddenly Dave went into his pitch and told them about *Charlie and the Chocolate Factory* and that they should make their chocolate bar a Wonka bar. In the end the Quaker company gave us $2.8 million to make the movie.[191]

It was a remarkable turn of events; the food manufacturer having never financed anything like this before.

Once Quaker were on board, Stuart and Wolper had to get the rights to the book. Roald Dahl was happy to sell, provided he wrote the screenplay. He produced four drafts, none of which Stuart thought were quite right. 'So, I had a young writer called David Seltzer come in and do a rewrite job.'[192] Seltzer had only previously worked on documentaries for Wolper. A few years later Seltzer created the blockbusting horror film *The Omen*.

Perhaps the biggest decision of all was casting the right person to play Willy Wonka. Fred Astaire was one of the first names suggested, and he was interested in playing it. 'But I thought he was too old,' says Stuart. 'Then somebody suggested Joel Grey, who is a fabulous actor, but he wasn't much taller than the kids. And you needed someone with a presence for that role.'[193] At one meeting the name of Gene Wilder was brought up. He wasn't a big star yet, but had scored in the Mel Brooks's comedy *The Producers* (1967). He came in to see Stuart and Wolper. Stuart recalls:

> He sat down, and he just read a few lines from the book, and I knew he was Willy Wonka. He left the interview and walked out of the office, and I said to David, 'He's it. That's our Willy Wonka.' And David said, 'Don't tell him, it's going to hurt how much we'll have to pay.' I said, 'I don't care,' and I ran after him and he was at the elevator, and I said, 'Gene you've got the job.'[194]

Stuart found Wilder an absolute joy to work with. 'Great actors give you that extra something.'[195] Before filming they discussed the role together and Stuart stressed the point that they wanted Wonka to be this slightly off-beat character. 'We didn't want you to know exactly where he was coming from or what he was going to do next.'[196] Wilder certainly brings an edge to his performance and the role went on to be the actor's most famous. 'There are certain people that are just right for certain roles,' says Stuart. 'And Gene was unique. There was nobody in the world that could have done that role just the way Gene did it.'[197]

For the important role of Charlie, hundreds of boys were interviewed, before newcomer Peter Ostrum, who had previously appeared only in amateur theatre, was selected. Stuart also rewarded his daughter Madeline with a small role in the film as one of Charlie's schoolmates.

During pre-production Stuart was in his office when he was visited by a delegation of African American actors who raised concerns about how the Oompa-Loompas were going to be portrayed in the film. In the original novel, first published in 1964, the Oompa-Loompas were Black pygmies imported by Wonka from the African jungle to work in his factory. Given this was the time of the US Civil Rights Movement and the Black Panthers, Stuart could see their point. 'We sat there for about five minutes. They were waiting for me to say something. "Tell you what," I said. "I'll give them orange faces and green hair, how about that?"'[198]

Satisfied, the group stood up to leave. One of them lingered at the doorway, then turned to look at Stuart. 'You know who Mr Charlie is, don't you?' Stuart had no idea. It turned out that Mr Charlie was the name the Black workers used to call their white supervisors on the old plantations. Again, Stuart considered the implications and, the more he thought about it, the more he thought that Willy Wonka was by far a more interesting name than Charlie. So, despite Dahl's objection it became *Willy Wonka and the Chocolate Factory*.

A decision was also made not to shoot the film in Hollywood but in Munich. Harper Goff, who had worked on *20,000 Leagues under the Sea* (1954), was brought in to handle the production design. 'He did an outstanding job,' says Stuart. 'We only had two disagreements.'[199] The first was Goff's original design for the room where the Oompa-Loompas make the chocolate:

He had done the most beautifully designed room you've ever seen, with gorgeous silver tubes and everything, looking like a fantastic factory. 'No, that's not Wonka,' I said. 'Wonka is nuts. The room has to look the opposite of what you think it's going to be, this weird crazy looking place.'[200]

Goff had also designed a plush-looking office for Wonka:

Again, I said, 'No, that's not Wonka. We've got to do it all over again, cut every piece of furniture in half, tables, chairs, everything.' The only thing we couldn't cut was the light bulbs. Even the safe is cut in half. Because we had to keep the weirdness of Wonka all the way through.[201]

With no studio interference, Stuart had a lot of creative freedom. The only time the Quaker Oats company overruled him was their demand that this type of film would work better with a sprinkling of songs. Wolper first approached Richard Rodgers, then Henry Mancini to write the soundtrack, but both demurred. Wolper then hired the song-writing team of Anthony Newley and Leslie Bricusse, and they delivered a pleasing score with songs like 'Pure Imagination' and 'The Candy Man'.

When *Willy Wonka* opened, the reaction of the critics was a positive one. Roger Ebert called it 'probably the best film of its sort since *The Wizard of Oz*'. Oddly, the film did not light up the box office. Over the years, thanks to repeated TV showings and home media, the film attracted a huge new audience and today is regarded as a classic. Ironically, the Wonka chocolate bar, which was the whole reason Quaker invested in making the film in the first place, did not prove a success.

So, why has the film endured and why does it keep being discovered generation after generation? Stuart has his own theory:

> Parents want their children to see it because of the basic lesson of the film, treat children like adults and don't put up with bad behaviour. Most children understand that you should behave. And the parents want that lesson taught, and deep down the children want to know what the boundaries are too.[202]

Stuart's background in documentaries played a role as well. In spite of the story's obvious fantasy overtones, he wanted it to be as real as possible. 'I did not make this picture for children. I made it for adults.'[203] The film is littered with quotes from Shakespeare and from poems, and there's a dark humour running through the whole thing, although Dahl's books for children were not without their dark elements. This is probably why those who watched the film as a kid still enjoy it when they watch it again as an adult. And, in turn, they play it to their kids, and so it goes on.

(US: opening 30 June)

43 DRIVE, HE SAID

Key among the new Hollywood group of filmmakers that emerged out of the counterculture success of *Easy Rider* was director Bob Rafelson and producers Bert Schneider and Steve Blauner. Together they formed the groundbreaking BBS Production company and entered into an agreement with Columbia to make any picture they wanted, provided that the budgets did not exceed $1 million. The first film shot under this agreement was *Five Easy Pieces* (1970), directed by Rafelson, and starring Jack Nicholson. When Nicholson voiced a desire to direct his first movie, he went to BBS.

Drive, He Said is a feverishly shot and edited snapshot of what was happening in America during the early 1970s and, while the film itself is a flawed piece of work, today it's a remarkable historical document. 'The film is much better than anyone realised at the time,' says film-maker Henry Jaglom. 'It truly captured the insanity of the Vietnam War generation at home.'[204]

It tells the story of a disaffected college basketball player (William Tepper) and his increasingly radical roommate (Michael Margotta). It was shot at the University of Oregon, in the city of Eugene, then one of only two universities (the other was Colorado) that would allow film crews. With anti-war sentiment percolating around most university campuses tensions were high. Before Nicholson and his crew even arrived in Oregon, students had burnt down a campus building used as a recruiting office by the army. 'So, there were FBI all over that town before we even started,' says Margotta.[205] There was a real polarisation going on between the radical left and the hardcore right. Up in the Oregon mountains people were checking out by setting up communes to live an alternative lifestyle. Conversely, Margotta heard there was someone driving around Eugene in a pick-up truck shooting at anybody with long hair.

Directing his first film Nicholson surrounded himself with friends like Karen Black and Bruce Dern, playing the college's basketball coach; there's even a role for Robert Towne who later wrote *Chinatown* (1974). Henry Jaglom has a few scenes, too, and found Nicholson to be 'intense, spontaneously creative and willing to try anything'.[206] He allowed his actors space to experiment and follow their instincts. Nowhere is this better illustrated than in one moment with Margotta:

> I had the impulse to get up and walk out of the scene. And I kept talking off-camera. I didn't even know if I was going to go back again or if they were going to say cut. Then I walked right back in again, sat down and carried on. And nobody said cut. That kind of freedom was unique.[207]

Margotta had decided to stay in character throughout the entire shoot. On his last day, the leather jacket he'd been wearing the whole time literally began to fall apart. Margotta had been determined to integrate himself with some of the people in the radical underground groups and to understand what motivated them. One afternoon on campus he saw the camera truck and strolled over to sit and talk with some of the crew. Within a few minutes Blauner came running up shouting, 'Shit, all hell's breaking loose, get a camera.' One of the crew grabbed a camera and followed Margotta and Blauner to the administration building where a crowd had gathered. In front of them was a military transport vehicle and two rows of police in full riot gear. Some of the students had already been arrested and were being dragged off. Margotta got lost in the crowd when the police fired tear gas and he ended up injured with several other protestors. 'It was a pretty powerful experience. I forgot really who I was and that there was anything connected to a film.'[208]

After things calmed down the authorities put out on the media that no tear gas had been used. But the camera operator had captured the whole thing. 'Steve Blauner put that footage in his Porsche and headed immediately to California,' says Margotta. 'The Governor of Oregon sent down aides to the hotel and Jack had to deal with them, and with the police; they wanted that footage.'[209]

Prior to filming, Nicholson signed a contract that stipulated there would be no sex, no drugs, no nudity, nothing detrimental to the name of the university. After the hassle over the tear gas footage all bets were off. Nicholson really wanted to push the envelope and had included some full-frontal male nudity in the locker rooms and an explicit sex scene, although these were shot away from the university. Now, with a hidden camera, Margotta ran naked across the campus. He was spotted by security and the police were called. For his own protection against arrest, Margotta hid out in a beach house.

Amid all the pressure and police harassment, Nicholson arranged a river rafting trip with Robert Towne and his wife, along with Margotta. Margotta recalls:

We ended up going down this river and it was raging. After fifteen minutes we went over this drop and hit a rock and the floor of this raft ripped right open. I remember climbing up on the side trying to hold on like I was riding a horse. I looked and I saw Bob holding on,

Jack was gone, he popped up out of the hole about four seconds later flying straight up into the air.[210]

After about 10 miles, with a rip in the floor of this dinghy, Margotta declared he'd had enough and got out. The others carried on and finished the route:

> It was freezing water, and Bob Towne's glasses were broken, he was bleeding, and he was not your athletic kind of guy, he was more your intellectual kind of character, yet he stuck it out. Later we heard that four people died on that river that day.[211]

Margotta got to like Nicholson during the shoot and remembers that he had with him Stanley Kubrick's script for a film about Napoleon. 'Jack was talking all the time to Kubrick who wanted desperately Jack to play Napoleon.'[212] In the end, though, Margotta feels *Drive, He Said* was compromised in the editing. 'Jack took so much footage and I felt there were just too many cooks in the kitchen.'[213]

The film's showing at Cannes was a disaster. Perhaps following in the wake of *Easy Rider* and *Five Easy Pieces*, there was too much expectation surrounding *Drive, He Said*. Whatever the case it was not well received. 'After it finished the audience booed,' recalls Margotta, who was there. 'And that was tough on Jack.'[214]

(US: Los Angeles opening 30 June)

44 *CARNAL KNOWLEDGE*

Little Murders author Jules Feiffer first encountered Mike Nichols one night on the television, in his comedy double act with Elaine May. Thinking that this was someone he must meet, he quickly established a friendship with Nichols. When Feiffer wrote the play *Little Murders*, he sent it to Nichols to direct, only he never got an answer. So incensed at the rebuttal, Feiffer stopped speaking to Nichols for two years. After a screening of *The Graduate* (1967), Feiffer wrote to Nichols telling him how revolutionary a film it was. He got a hand-delivered letter back, wildly grateful, and the friendship was back on.

Feiffer had written another play depicting the sexually liberated 1960s in American society. Again, Nichols didn't want to do it, at least on

Broadway. This was a film, he told Feiffer, and asked him to adapt it into a screenplay. *Carnal Knowledge* traces the friendship between two former college roommates. Jonathan is a manipulative male chauvinist, unable to relate to women as anything other than sex objects; in one scene he presents a slide show of the significant women in his life, entitled 'Ballbusters on Parade'. Sandy is his shy, intellectual friend. It covers twenty-five years, from the late 1940s to the early 1970s, from their first sexual experiences with the same woman, Susan, through a series of dysfunctional relationships.

For these complex characters Nichols knew he didn't just need good actors, he needed the right people. Nichols's first choice for Jonathan was Jack Nicholson. That didn't sit too well with Feiffer, who'd written the part as a Jewish boy from the Bronx. He was asked to go see *Easy Rider*, which only made things worse: Feiffer hated the picture. Nichols convinced him that Nicholson was going to be America's most important actor since Brando. What's more, the character of Jonathan was one with which he was all too familiar. Nicholson's performance in *Carnal Knowledge* was to cement his devil-may-care image in the minds of the public, as well as make him *persona non grata* with the growing feminist movement in America.

Then best known as a folk superstar with partner Paul Simon, Art Garfunkel had already worked with Nichols, playing an innocent air force officer in *Catch-22* (1970). Confident in his acting abilities, Nichols cast him as Sandy and Garfunkel gives a highly affecting performance. As Sandy's college sweetheart Susan, Nichols wanted his friend Candice Bergen, who was delighted to join something that was already turning into a prestige project. 'There was some unspoken honour attached to being a part of this film, a feeling of privilege.'[215]

But the real surprise of the movie turned out to be Ann-Margret as Bobbie, a sensual but fragile woman who, because of the way she looks, always seems to attract the wrong kind of man, like Jonathan. Known primarily for her sex kitten roles and musicals, Ann-Margret hadn't really been taken seriously as an actress and Nichols took a gamble casting her. It paid off, despite the physical and emotional toil it took on her: 'It left me in a depressive stupor fuelled by pills and alcohol.'[216] Her performance was rewarded with an Academy Award nomination as Best Supporting Actress.

For a picture Nichols described as the darkest movie he ever made, he claimed to have had the best time working on it. Filmed in Vancouver, true to Nichols's theatre origins the cast rehearsed for three weeks before a foot of film was taken. The four leads, along with Nichols and Feiffer, sat round a table just going through the dialogue again and again, working things out, experimenting. It was a happy film; Bergen, Nicholson and Garfunkel shared a large house together and, after filming finished for the day, everyone usually met up socially.

In some of their intense moments together Ann-Margret found Nicholson to be a professional and unselfish partner. In one highly charged bedroom scene, Nichols wanted to capture Ann-Margret's reaction in close-up and, although he wasn't in the shot, Nicholson was jumping on the bed and screaming 'so violently and so loudly', recalled Ann-Margret, 'that he went home with laryngitis. All for the benefit of my close-up.'[217] Nicholson was also required to get naked, although these shots never made the final cut. The actor approached them in his usual 'don't-give-a-damn' style, getting undressed and pronouncing, 'Alright! Here comes Steve, get ready for him!' While the subject matter of the picture is sex, and there are occasional glimpses of nudity, Nichols's camera does not pruriently linger.

When it opened *Carnal Knowledge* was well reviewed, making *The New York Times* and *Chicago Sun-Times* 'Ten Best' lists for 1971. A substantial box office hit, the film stirred widespread debate about its raw, honest and unsettling depiction of how men treat women. Its frank language and depiction of sex was groundbreaking. The scene in which Sandy takes out a condom while in bed with Susan was the very first time a condom had been shown on-screen. It's also thought to be the first mainstream picture in which the word 'cunt' was spoken. Such was the film's notoriety that in 1972 a search warrant was issued in Albany, Georgia, leading to the arrest of the manager of the theatre in which it was showing, and the film was seized. The theatre manager was convicted, but the Supreme Court eventually overturned the decision. The film was briefly banned in most of Italy for alleged obscenity.

(US: New York opening 30 June)

45 *WALKABOUT*

The Donald G. Payne novella, about two children who are stranded in the Australian outback and rescued by an Aboriginal boy who leads them back to so-called 'civilisation', had long fascinated Nicolas Roeg. It's no surprise that he decided to tackle this subject when the chance came to make his first solo film as director after *Performance*. Made entirely on location in Australia, Roeg was also the cinematographer but insisted on bringing along another cameraman, Anthony B. Richmond. 'I had a good relationship with Nic [Roeg],' recalls Richmond. 'I'd been his clapper loader on two or three films. We were great friends and great drinking buddies.'[218]

Basically, Richmond acted as the second unit:

We started off in Sydney and we all had these jeeps; I had a trailer on mine and we were totally self-sufficient. We would do stuff without Nic and then we would meet up again and all camp together. We went to Alice Springs and hung out there for about three weeks and then we went to Darwin in the Northern Territory which is really fantastic. That's where all the buffalos are and the alligators. And we lived in tents. It was great. We had a grand old time.[219]

The main unit travelled all over the place too, starting off in the desert. While Roeg and the actors flew in to the location in a Cessna and out again at the end of the shooting day, the crew were given tents to sleep in. 'These tents were Mickey Mouse tents,' remembers Peter Hannan, who was the focus puller. 'They were literally Mickey Mouse tents with Huey, Dewey and Louie on the side and Donald Duck, they were kids' tents, our legs stuck out of the end. And the desert is freezing of a night.'[220] The unit eventually got better tents but there was still a lot of roughing it.

Some of the shots Richmond took are among the most breathtaking in the film – for example, the Aboriginal boy standing on one leg holding his spear as the sun sets behind him. And Richmond climbed up St Mary Peak in the Flinders Ranges, South Australia, still regarded as a sacred place for Aboriginal people, to capture the shot of the children staring out across a salt lake that looked like a sea. 'And I shot all the killings of the kangaroos. What would happen was the Aboriginals that were with us would eat them.'[221] The footage of animals being killed is distressing to watch and at the time caused controversy. However, it's made plain that this is how Aboriginal people lived, and there is no difference to an Aboriginal hunting and killing a kangaroo than the workings of an abattoir. At one point, Roeg intercuts an Aboriginal spearing and cutting up an animal for food with a city butcher preparing meat.

The role of the Aboriginal boy was pivotal. The lost children come across him while he is undertaking walkabout, which is a rite of passage in Australian Aboriginal society when they must live in the wilderness for several months to make the spiritual transition into manhood. Roeg scoured Australia for the right person and found David Gulpilil, a 16-year-old ceremonial dancer from the Northern Territory. 'He came along with a mate of his, with their digeridoos,' recalls Richmond. 'And he was fantastic. He picked up film work really quick.'[222] Hannan also has nothing but respect for Gulpilil, for the fact that he happily roughed it with everyone else. 'He stayed with the crew every night.'[223] Gulpilil went on to become a highly respected actor in the Australian film community.

For the children Roeg cast his 7-year-old son Luc and Jenny Agutter. 'She was a trouper, and part of the crew as well,' recalls Hannan. 'We would trek up mountains and she'd carry heavy equipment. She was a wonderful girl.'[224] Then just 17, Agutter found the whole experience making *Walkabout* extraordinary, but did feel uncomfortable with the scene where she was required to swim naked in a lake. Roeg explained to her how it was the most natural thing for her character to do. 'Nic could talk anybody into doing anything,' says Richmond who was on set for that day.[225] Most of the time, though, he and his team would be out shooting in the wilds of the outback:

> At the time I had long hair, and I wore these pink jeans and red cowboy boots, and I went into a bar with our art director Brian Eatwell, and they thought we were a pair of Pommie pussies. We went to the toilet and climbed out of the window because they would have beaten the shit out of us.[226]

To achieve the best possible footage, Richmond recalled the 1962 John Wayne safari film *Hatari!* where Wayne's character had a seat on the front of a truck so he could snare the animals. 'We had this guy who looked after the vehicles and I got him to weld this chair onto the front of my truck so I could sit in there and hand hold the camera while we were chasing the animals.'[227]

While *Walkabout* was not a success at the box office, it is now viewed as a revered work and one of the first important films in the Australian New Wave cinema movement. As for Richmond, he was asked to shoot Roeg's next film *Don't Look Now* (1973), and their relationship continued with *The Man Who Fell to Earth* (1976) and *Bad Timing* (1980). 'I had an extraordinary relationship with Nic. First of all, he was like a father figure to me. And then it was like we were brothers. And then we were just friends.'[228]

Looking back Richmond calls *Walkabout* 'an extraordinary film'.[229] It is a piece of unique visual art. There's nothing quite like it. It tells its story simply, while at the same time Roeg explores themes of spirituality and sexual awakening, as well as the collision of different worlds and cultures. Richmond recalls that, on one location recce, the art director Brian Eatwell found a small cave:

> He did some cave paintings on the wall, and we shot that. For some reason we had to go back a few months later to shoot something else there and some enterprising local chap was running tours and charging to see these 'old' cave paintings.[230]

(US/UK/Aus: New York opening 1 July)

46 *SUNDAY BLOODY SUNDAY*

Peter Finch had reached that point in his career where he wondered what was coming next. He'd languished in Rome for over a year making a picture no one would bother to go and see, *The Red Tent* (1969), and a proposed film with Fred Zinneman had just been cancelled. 'I've got that old showbusiness feeling that the phone is never going to ring again' he ruefully pondered.[231]

But ring it did. Over in London John Schlesinger was in deep trouble. His new film *Sunday Bloody Sunday* had only been in production a few weeks when it became obvious that he'd made a terrible error casting Ian Bannen as a gay Jewish doctor. Bannen was a good actor but was 'just not hacking it', in Schlesinger's words, 'and I knew the film would fail if we continued with him'.[232] Finch's agent allegedly called with an offer to take over. 'I'm not a queer,' said Finch. 'No dear,' said his agent. 'But I'd like to see you play one to prove you are an actor.'[233] If reported correctly this was a strange remark on Finch's part as, ten years earlier, he had brilliantly essayed Oscar Wilde.

Finch got on a plane and arrived in London. That evening he read the script and agreed to do it. He was on the set working within days. Such was the speed of things there hadn't been time to fit his wardrobe; most of the clothes Finch wore in the film were his own. Neither was there time for Schlesinger to talk over the role with him in any great detail, Finch simply plunged in, his acting instincts working overtime, and he proceeded to give one of his greatest screen performances, for which he received an Academy Award nomination.

Finch had been in Schlesinger's mind to play the doctor from the very start, only for Finch to rule himself out due to the Zinneman film. Alan Bates was considered; again, work commitments got in the way. Paul Schofield politely declined. The role certainly presented Finch with one of the most taxing of his career, not least because in essence the part he was playing was Schlesinger himself.

Schlesinger had been in love with a young actor, who at the same time was in a relationship with a woman. Both knew about the other and seemed to accept the situation. In 1966 Schlesinger began to turn this experience into a story of a middle-aged man and a divorced woman both in love with a free-spirited young bisexual artist. The focus was to be very much on the two older members of this love triangle and the emotional strain, inevitable frustrations and disappointments such an unconventional arrangement place on them. For this very reason *Sunday Bloody Sunday* is Schlesinger's most personal film and, out of all the pictures he made, his favourite.

Schlesinger also insisted that the character of the doctor be Jewish in order to make his personal conflict that much more important, as indeed it was in Schlesinger's own life as a gay Jewish man. There is an important scene of the doctor attending his nephew's bar mitzvah, which serves as a reminder of how alienated he feels from his family's Jewish heritage due to his homosexuality. This was another painful episode from Schlesinger's own life, having to field off the enquiries of cousins and aunts about when he was going to get married.

Thanks to the success of his previous film, *Midnight Cowboy* (1969), Schlesinger felt he'd never have a better opportunity to get this film made, writing in his diary, 'I can get away with anything now.'[234] UA agreed to back the film provided it could be made cheaply, for just £1.5 million.

For the divorced woman Schlesinger cast Glenda Jackson. Apprehensive about working with such a strong-minded actress, Schlesinger was pleasantly surprised by how playful their working relationship turned out to be. With Schlesinger having recently been made a CBE in the honour's list, before a take Jackson would sometimes play-fully ask him, 'Commander, am I standing in the right position?' For the artist, David Bowie was one of many to read for the part before actor and singer Murray Head, who'd been in the West End production of the musical *Hair*, was chosen.

The film was made at Bray Studios, the previous home of the Hammer horror movies; it was empty, so they had it all to themselves. Set in a London well past its 'swinging' era, there are location shots of Kensington, Wandsworth and Greenwich, and a seedy look at the junkies who congregated at midnight outside Boots, the chemist, in Piccadilly Circus for their prescribed drugs. Shooting in Greenwich Schlesinger required three youths to walk along scratching cars with broken glass. A few local kids were rounded up and Schlesinger chose the most mischievous-looking; one of them was 13-year-old Daniel Day Lewis.

Sunday Bloody Sunday opened in grand style with a royal West End premiere, with HM Princess Margaret and Lord Snowdon in attend-ance, alongside the Attenboroughs, the Oliviers and the Burtons. Afterwards, Princess Margaret was heard to say of the film, within ear-shot of Schlesinger, 'I thought it was horrific. Men in bed kissing!'[235] The critics were of a different opinion, heaping it with praise. It was a clean sweep at the BAFTAs too, where it picked up Best Film, Director, Actor and Actress.

While *Sunday Bloody Sunday* was groundbreaking in its depiction of a love triangle, the film's greatest achievement was the matter-of-fact way it dealt with a gay character. Schlesinger emphasised that the film was not about the sexuality of the people involved but their emotions. A case in point was a brief kiss shared between Finch and Head. It's something that wouldn't raise an eyebrow today, but back in 1971 this was a big deal. Screenwriter Penelope Gilliatt was against the idea of seeing the kiss and in the script wrote it as taking place in a long shot, almost out of the way. Schlesinger was adamant the kiss be in close-up, just like any other kiss in a film.

Gilliatt did not attend that day's shooting. Some of the crew had a similar reaction. One of them was seen to turn away muttering, 'What have we come to?!' UA wanted the kiss removed completely. Schlesinger recalled attending a private screening in Hollywood where some of UA's executives had brought their wives. One woman stood up after the 'kiss' scene and said to her husband, 'This isn't a film for nice people; come along, Harold.'[236] Schlesinger won the battle and the kiss remained.

(UK: London opening 1 July)

47 | *TWO-LANE BLACKTOP*

Less than four months after the release of *Vanishing Point* came a very different kind of road movie. *Two-Lane Blacktop* follows two long-haired car-freaks, played by singer-songwriter James Taylor and the Beach Boys' Dennis Wilson (in their only screen roles), as they ride across the country in a 1955 Chevy, challenging others along the way, among them an ageing driver (Warren Oates) in a bright orange Pontiac GTO.

Using two inexperienced actors, director Monte Hellman insisted on going across country for real, starting off in Los Angeles, knowing how this would affect Taylor and Wilson and also create a realism for audiences. 'It wasn't just a road movie,' says cameraman John Bailey. 'We truly lived on the road. We never stayed anywhere more than a week, maybe a week and a half. Sometimes only for a couple of days.'[237] Hellman wanted everyone to live the experience. Bailey says:

> Monte was very keen, as were so many of the young directors at that time, on what he considered lived experience rather than recreated or acted experience. That's why he cast the movie with non-actors really except for Warren. And that had both good and bad points, but that was very important to him.[238]

Bailey was just starting out in the business and got the job through his friendship with the cinematographer Gregory Sandor. It turned out to be a great adventure. 'And truly an interesting way to start a career because in the film business, especially at that time, almost all films were made on location. The studio set era and studio back lots were really out of favour.'[239]

Bailey had a lot of respect for Hellman. 'He was very intense and one of the most focused directors I ever worked with.'[240] Being young and inexperienced Bailey didn't really know much about how directors worked. He subsequently found out that some of them were almost craftsmen, bringing experience and sometimes obsessive preparation, using storyboards and things being done a certain way:

Monte wasn't like that at all. He was very much into a sense of improvisation. And really, he did not give that much direction. He would give indications of what he wanted. He would set the scene and use the dialogue as a reference. He felt very good about the script, but in terms of the interpretation of the scene and the interaction between one actor and the other, he tended to let it flow from take to take. So, he did a lot of takes.[241]

Hellman came from the theatre, starting his own small theatre company in Los Angeles where he staged one of the first US productions of Samuel Beckett's *Waiting for Godot*. And there's an interesting connection between *Two-Lane Blacktop* and Beckett's play; both take place in a kind of unspecified no man's land. Bailey states:

> The characters go right across the country but they are oddly untouched by anything visually, in terms of landscape or nature, around them. They're obsessed with the confined space of that car and getting there. I think Beckett had a tremendous influence.[242]

Coming from the rock world, there was a constant stream of music friends coming to visit Taylor and Wilson, like Joni Mitchell who was then dating Taylor. 'It was a cross-country caravan of musicians,' says Bailey. 'Especially on the weekends when they would sit around and jam.'[243] Bailey found himself gravitating much more easily towards Warren Oates:

> He was like an older brother figure to me. We had the same sense of humour. He had a very acerbic sense of humour which I think played through in his character. There's a tremendous sense of absurdity and irony in what he's doing. We have no idea why the hell he gets involved in this race.[244]

Oates's character, like the others, is nameless – he's just GTO, Taylor is the driver, Wilson the mechanic – and in his own way is caught in a no man's land. He picks up various hitchhikers, telling each of them a different story. In a way Oates's is the most unrevealing of all the characters. He doesn't really interact with anybody else. 'You get a sense of Taylor and Wilson, in the way they talk about their car,' says Bailey. 'But Warren you don't really do, you can project onto him almost whatever you want. He's got masks, he's got multiple personalities.'[245]

Travelling all the time, across country, it was difficult for the cast and crew to have their partners and families catch up with them. There was, however, one period when the unit stayed in Tucumcari, New Mexico, for about a week and a half. It was the perfect opportunity for a visit, so everyone came in on a bus. Bailey recalls:

> On this Sunday morning, I was getting up to go to breakfast at something like six in the morning and saw all these motel room doors open and women come pouring out of them, sort of road groupies, getting in their cars and driving off. And then half an hour later the bus pulls in with the wives.[246]

When it opened *Two-Lane Blacktop* was a box office disappointment, although it has since become a highly regarded cult film. Maybe audiences expected something even greater than *Easy Rider* and, of course, it had none of the zeitgeist of that movie. 'It was more a movie out of time,' says Bailey. 'They were expecting this road move to say something about where we were in terms of pop culture. Instead, what they got was an American road movie of *Waiting for Godot*.'[247]

As for Bailey, he went on to become a highly respected cinematographer on films like *American Gigolo*, *Silverado* and *Groundhog Day*. He also kept in touch with Hellman, they would meet every now and again at Academy screenings:

> He would usually be sitting by himself. He was a loner. He was not the kind of man that when you saw him you would go and say, 'Heh let's sit together and talk.' He was a man of few words and in many ways that film represents and reflects a lot of his temperament.[248]

(US: New York opening 7 July)

 48   *THE PANIC IN NEEDLE PARK*

'The intersection at Broadway and 72nd Street on New York's West Side is officially known as Sherman Square. To heroin addicts it's Needle Park.' So reads the title card at the start of this searing drama about a pair of drug addicts, Bobby and Helen, drifting through Manhattan's sleazy drug pits in a state of mutual self-destruction. It was also the first starring feature film role for Al Pacino.

Jerry Schatzberg had just completed his first directorial assignment, *Puzzle of a Downfall Child* (1970) with Faye Dunaway, and was pissed off. The lab had scratched the last six minutes of the negative and, although he managed to eventually sort it out, he was in no mood to contemplate taking on a new job. In his office was a recently arrived script. He gave it a quick cursory read and turned it down. A little while later Schatzberg was in his manager's office being told about this great screenplay that was out there called *Panic in Needle Park*. 'I think I've just turned that down,' said Schatzberg. Things changed when he was told Al Pacino was interested:

> I had seen Al before on stage and I was very impressed. I went backstage after, and the difference between him on stage and backstage was amazing. He was like a little pussy cat backstage but on stage he had such force. So, I always had him in mind for something.[249]

Schatzberg read the script again and was in.

Pacino was always first choice to play Bobby, but 20th Century Fox wasn't convinced. Pacino had a great reputation as a stage actor, but was untried in film, with just one small role to his name. So, Schatzberg and the writers, Joan Didion and John Gregory Dunne, went through the pretence of testing pretty much every young actor that was around, including Robert De Niro. Schatzberg recalls:

> The last person to come to see me was De Niro. And he was very good. But he wasn't Al. He was a wonderful actor playing the part, Al was a wonderful actor being the part. We told the studio, we still want Al. He's our guy.[250]

Previously the only film to touch the subject of hard drugs was Otto Preminger's *The Man with the Golden Arm* (1955) with Frank Sinatra. While controversial in its day, Preminger was still working in the confines of a '50s Hollywood industry. Schatzberg could go much further and brought to his film an almost documentary reality. He had read the original 1965 *Life* magazine article about two New York heroin addicts that formed the basis of Didion and Dunne's screenplay, and hung around the 'Needle Park' area talking to users:

We were lucky that Needle Park was still there. It had been cleaned up but most of the characters in my film had been druggies at one time. I depended a lot on these guys because they knew what it was like being on drugs. We'd have a discussion and go through things and they'd say, 'no it's not like that', or 'it is like that'. That's the way I am in all my work. I make my films as honest as I can get.[251]

That included Schatzberg's decision not to use music. 'As soon as I put a music cue in, it sounded like Hollywood. So, I'd take it out. The street had enough music in it for me, just the noise of the car horns and the people.'[252]

A lot of the supporting cast were recommended to Schatzberg by Pacino, who knew a lot of New York actors and had friends at the Actors Studio. Schatzberg states:

When we came to shoot, I said no drugs. I really laid the law down. I warned, If I catch any of you with drugs, I'll cut your part out of the film and do it over. They were pretty good except for this one actor who I didn't know until the very end when they told me that he'd been doing drugs. He's great in the film, actually.[253]

The role of Bobby's girlfriend, Helen, was played by another film newcomer, Kitty Winn. Schatzberg met her first over lunch. 'I adored her. She was just wonderful and so right for the part.'[254] Before leaving Schatzberg asked if she had any problem with nudity. Winn looked blankly at him, 'What nudity?' It was there in the script. It wasn't going to be exploitative, Schatzberg thought, what young couple cover themselves up in their own apartment? Winn was going on holiday and Schatzberg told her to take the script with her and let him know what she felt. When Winn got back, she said everything was fine. Schatzberg states:

Then every time we booked the scene or tried to book it into the schedule, she'd always have some excuse why she couldn't do it. We got to the very end of the shoot, and I said, 'Look, I'm going to clear the set, whatever makes you comfortable, we'll do. But we've got to shoot this.' It was only after we'd finished shooting, I found out her problem, that she was worried what her grandmother would say. And her grandfather was General George Marshall.[255]

The shoot went well, the only problem came when Fox president Richard Zanuck was sacked by his own father at a board meeting, and the old mogul took personal charge. Schatzberg recalls:

> One day Darryl Zanuck called me into his office, and told me he was taking over the film. He said, 'I've watched your dailies every day, they're terrific. I want you to keep on doing what you're doing.' He was very encouraging.[256]

During the shoot Schatzberg and Pacino grew close. They spent a lot of time hanging out, just walking round the city, talking about different things and the script. 'We had a great time.'[257] Well into production Schatzberg got a call from Francis Ford Coppola:

> Francis had seen Al on stage too, and wanted him for *The Godfather*. Paramount didn't want him. Francis called me and asked if he could see some footage of *Needle Park*. I said sure and gave it to him. He showed it to Paramount. And the rest is history.[258]

Schatzberg worked with Pacino again on 1973's *Scarecrow*, which ended in them falling out and not speaking to each other for something like two years. 'Then I was in a restaurant and Al walked in. We looked at each other. Hugged each other. And that was it. We've been friends ever since.'[259]

Unsurprisingly *Panic in Needle Park* caused controversy on release; it was banned in the UK for several years due to its graphic depiction of drug use. Before its release word had got round the industry about the film and Schatzberg's office received a phone call from Otto Preminger. He wanted to see it. Schatzberg recalls:

> So, we arranged a private screening. He showed up by himself. We were all sitting in the back, nodding at him when he came in. He didn't react to us. We were just workers as far as he was concerned. He took a seat in the middle, and we played the film. It finished. We put on the lights. He got up and walked out; never said thank you, never said anything. He just left.[260]

(US: New York opening 13 July)

49 | *BLOOD ON SATAN'S CLAW*

Coming as he did from the Royal Court Theatre and the BBC, Piers Haggard seemed an unlikely choice to make one of the archetypal British horror films of the decade. Haggard had managed to make a modest little film in Ireland called *Wedding Night* (1969), with Tessa Wyatt as a young girl who gets married but has a deep psychological fear of sex. 'Some people liked it and it got some good reviews,' says Haggard, 'but it was never released in the UK.'[261] Haggard organised an industry screening and just four people turned up, including Peter Andrews and Malcolm Heyworth, novice producers who had a deal over at Tigon to make a horror film in the mould of that company's *Witchfinder General* (1968).

Haggard was interested, although confessed to not being a fan of horror films. He ended up screening a whole bunch of them to familiarise himself with the genre. 'I watched *Witchfinder General* and thought, oh fuck, that's really good. I hope I can do as well as that.'[262] First something had to be done about the script. It didn't work. Andrews and Heyworth had brought in newcomer Robert Wynne-Simmons. 'He was very young,' says Haggard, 'barely out from Cambridge, shy and stuttering, and yet all these violent fantasies came out of this very quiet and retiring young man.'[263]

Tigon was run by the colourful Tony Tenser, a master of low-budget exploitation and he knew the market. He'd got Simmons to come up with three loosely connected stories about a rural community infiltrated by a demonic force. 'I thought the three-story idea was silly,' recalls Haggard. 'I said, let's make it one film. And we busted a gut to try and join them up. It blends pretty well considering, but there are a few holes.'[264]

Rather than the script itself, it was the seventeenth-century countryside setting that really interested Haggard. 'I grew up in the countryside and I had a feel for what the lives of the people should be like under that kind of a supernatural threat. So, I set about making a serious folk horror.'[265] What he definitely wanted to avoid was cliché Hammer horror melodramatics and to bring a more European cinema sensibility to the film.

Given Haggard's identification with the countryside it's no surprise that the land becomes a character in itself. Obviously, it was vital to get the right locations. 'We found a nature conservation area outside Henley,' recalls Haggard, 'with a farmhouse and a wonderful variety of woods and big rolling fields. It was perfect.'[266] This was Bix Bottom valley in Oxfordshire, where Haggard also came across an abandoned church and a nearby chalk pit.

When it came to casting, Haggard had no say in who played the crucial role of Angel Blake, a manipulative teenager and natural leader of the village children who ends up demonically possessed. Linda Hayden, 17 years old, was under contract to Tigon and came with the package. As it turned out Haggard worked well with her, and she gives an excellent performance. As the local voice of authority, the judge, Haggard chose Patrick Wymark, a highly respected actor:

> He was a pleasure to work with. His role wasn't terribly richly written, it was rather a symbolic and poetical character, but Patrick absolutely responded to that and had no problem in giving it the kind of severity and importance that it needed.[267]

Sadly, it was the last role he played. Wymark died within six months of finishing the film.

The production itself passed off relatively smoothly. There was one difficult scene, when one of the village girls is lured away to play a game and then held down by several teenagers and raped, before being murdered. In the script this sequence was far less explicit. Haggard wanted to emphasise, in a *Lord of the Flies* way, how children are just as capable of incredible violence and cruelty as adults. 'That scene is very strong. Perhaps too strong,' he admits.[268] It remains the film's most disturbing moment:

> But it was very important to me that it should also be cinematically beautiful. And on the day that we filmed it, I was driving up the valley and I'd seen all this May blossom and I suddenly had this idea of using it for a crown of thorns and flagellation.[269]

The scene begins with the children walking to the ruins of a church, chanting and indulging in a sort of mock pagan/religious ritual, whipping the victim with thorny branches.

Not surprisingly, this scene caused the most problems with the censor. Running the British Board of Film Censors was John Trevelyan, who had been in the post since 1958, but had never faced a year quite like 1971 with *The Devils*, *Straw Dogs* and *A Clockwork Orange*. Is it any wonder that by the end of the year he announced his retirement? Actually, Haggard got on well with Trevelyan. 'He was like an old public-school headmaster, straight up, honest, very old fashioned, but very liberal.'[270] For Trevelyan it was the combination of sex and violence that was the issue, and several cuts had to be made.

Originally called *The Devil's Touch*, then *Satan's Skin*, when Tigon sold the picture to America the distributors came up with *Blood on Satan's Claw*. 'And we all thought, yes, that's a much better title,' says Haggard.[271] It did reasonably well on the horror circuit but when it had its British release a couple of months later the reception was underwhelming. Maybe, thinks Haggard, it was too unusual for those expecting a typical horror. 'It's a bit arty perhaps, but it's not an art film. It's pretty horrific, but it wasn't really a horror film.'[272]

Vanishing from cinemas, *Blood on Satan's Claw* used to turn up occasionally on British television. 'Then in the '90s I started getting invited to these horror conventions,' says Haggard, 'and realised there was a whole network of fans and admirers.'[273] Haggard met Jonathan Demme once in New York, who admitted to being a huge admirer of the film. Today *Blood on Satan's Claw* stands alongside *Witchfinder General* and *The Wicker Man* (1973) as the foremost work of folk horror. Haggard says:

> I think the reason for the film having endured so long, is the blend of the story and the setting and the vulnerability of the children and the primitive nature of their rural life. And the film was made with complete sincerity. And I think that shows through. We were all passionate about the film.[274]

(UK: London opening 16 July)

50 GODZILLA VS. HEDORAH

Godzilla goes green! After ten instalments, Toho Studio's Godzilla franchise was fast becoming a tired formula. Just how many model skyscrapers and toy tanks can a man in a monster suit destroy without a sense of déjà vu taking over? Yoshimitsu Banno, given his first Godzilla directorial assignment, wanted to try something new and daring. The result is arguably the strangest entry in the entire Godzilla series.

Banno had previously worked as an assistant director to famed Japanese filmmaker Akira Kurosawa on such classics as *Throne of Blood* (1957) and *The Hidden Fortress* (1958). But it was his documentary feature

Birth of the Japanese Islands, which played at the 1970 Japan Expo in Osaka to record-breaking crowds, that encouraged Godzilla co-creator Tomoyuki Tanaka to sign him up to help revitalise the series after a two-year gap away from screens.

In Banno's view, the recent Godzilla pictures had become too childish. He wanted to bring the franchise into the 1970s and to embrace youth culture, hence the film's psychedelic imagery and animated interludes, criticised at the time but now part of the film's cult appeal. Neither did he want another silly monster to fight Godzilla, a giant cockroach or some such. He wanted the threat this time to be far more serious.

While travelling around Japan Banno had begun to notice the increasingly alarming problem of pollution, the flip side of the country's economic boom. He saw the black smog churned out by factories enveloping some of the cities and the sea filled with foam from all the detergent dumped into it. Recognising this as a real issue, Banno came up with the idea of a space virus affected by all this slimy pollution and growing into a hideous monster called Hedorah, or the smog monster in the film's American title. In the summer of 1970, Banno heard the story of some school children fainting in their exercise yard due to the heavily polluted air hanging over them. This incident is replicated in the film, where the creature flies over a school, spewing out vapour that sends the students reeling to the ground, clutching at their throats. With incidents like this making headlines across the nation, Godzilla's series producer Tanaka approved Banno's pollution idea. It also harked back to the environmental themes of the very first Godzilla picture, with its message about the dangers of the atomic age.

Due to the film's environmental theme, this Godzilla entry is much grimmer than others in the series. This time it isn't just property that is destroyed. We see the consequences of the creature's pollution and people die; we see an infant sink under polluted sludge and in another scene a child finds the acid-corroded bones of other victims.

Saddled with less than half the budget of prior Godzilla films, Banno was also given just thirty-five days to shoot the entire picture. Halfway through production Tanaka was hospitalised and when he came out and saw the finished film, he was not best pleased. There is a story that Tanaka told Banno that he had killed the Godzilla franchise. Certainly, he felt the film, with its surreal imagery (a vision of people with fish heads for example), had deviated too much from the formula and the character of Godzilla. Tanaka did approve Banno's suggestion that Godzilla should, for the first and only time in the series, demonstrate his ability to fly; this he does by firing his atomic breath towards the ground and propelling himself backwards. Banno later wrote a memoir appropriately titled, *The Man Who Made Godzilla Fly*. The outcome of all this was that Banno was never given another Godzilla film to direct and Tanaka ordered a return to more conventional Godzilla pictures. Banno, who had already made preparations for the next Hedorah movie, returned to scriptwriting and working in the documentary field, on projects mostly based around environmental issues.

Ironically, in 2004 Banno secured the rights from Toho to make a Godzilla IMAX 3D short film. When the funding for this project proved elusive, Banno instead approached Legendary Pictures, on behalf of Toho, to discuss the possibility of a new Godzilla feature film. It would take another ten years, but the 2014 Hollywood Godzilla reboot, with Banno acting as executive producer, was a worldwide smash and led to the creation of the MonsterVerse. Sadly, Banno passed away before he could work on another Godzilla film, but his drive and passion was recognised with posthumous credits on *Godzilla: King of the Monsters* (2019) and *Godzilla vs. Kong* (2021).

(Japan: opening 24 July)

51 | *THE DEVILS*

Aldous Huxley's book *The Devils of Loudun* was published in 1952 and described the true events of supposed demonic possession and sexual hysteria that took place in the small French town of Loudun in the 1600s; in other words, perfect material for the *enfant terrible* of British cinema, Ken Russell. And he had no hesitation in casting his favourite actor Oliver Reed as Father Grandier, the town's priest, whose knack for making political enemies ultimately led to his downfall; falsely accused of witchcraft he was tried and burnt at the stake.

As filming got underway at Pinewood in the winter of 1970 rumours quickly reached the outside world of diabolical happenings on Russell's closed set. However, no actress playing any of the supposedly 'possessed' nuns was made to perform any act against their will. Right from the off Russell informed them of what would be required, namely scenes of flagellation, masturbation and nudity. 'I mean, there were some of those nuns who couldn't wait to strip off,' says actor Murray Melvin. 'And there were some who were petrified.'[275]

The nun orgy was the talk of Pinewood. On a neighbouring stage *Carry On Henry* was being filmed and Barbara Windsor snuck in for a peek one afternoon. 'I came back all shock, horror and told Kenny Williams what I'd seen. "Oooh," he said, giving the nostrils a good airing, "it's a disgrace."'[276]

At one point, Russell ordered that Melvin's character, Father Mignon, should masturbate from a high vantage point at all this naked nunnery. 'Ken [Russell] explained that it was the highpoint of the scene, and I went, "Oh Ken, you know I'm not a flasher."'[277] Melvin was asked if he wanted a closed set and, out of bravado, told them not to make a fuss. On the day, Melvin walked on the set and there was a ladder at the side of the stage going right up to the top where they'd built a little platform. In his priestly robes Melvin began the climb, stopping often to gather up the material from under the rungs. 'You wouldn't be allowed to do it today because, had I fallen, I would be dead, but for Ken you did it.'[278] Melvin finally made his way up there:

> And there was no safety rail, it was just a piece of wood, and of course I crept forward and looked down and that's when I thought, oh Murray you fool, should have had a closed set, because I counted thirty-six people, all the stage boys, all the electricians, and the continuity girl. I was about to say, 'Ken I'm sorry, I really can't,' when Brian, the sound boy, said, 'Murray, what does it feel like to be doing it in front of a whole load of professionals.' That got me through because everybody fell about laughing, it broke the tension.[279]

Co-starring with Oliver Reed was Vanessa Redgrave as Sister Jeanne, a sexually repressed nun who incites the accusations of demonic possession out of her warped lust over Grandier. The likes of Georgina Hale, Brian Murphy, Michael Gothard and Dudley Sutton make up an impressive ensemble. In one scene Russell cast comedy icon Spike Milligan as a monk who visits Grandier in prison. It was quite a lengthy dialogue scene but, in the end, Russell took it out; it just didn't work. 'There was Grandier waiting to be taken out and burnt and in came Spike like a character from *The Goon Show*; people would howl.'[280]

It was a tough shoot, not least the terrifying torture climax scene where Grandier's legs are pulverised by a religious maniac with a hammer. Reed's legs were protected by huge oak planks, but even so poor Melvin found it hard to take:

> It just went on and on and on, and there was the screaming and the pounding, something went through you, your whole body was saying, 'We shouldn't be doing this, this is wrong.' Then Ken called the lunch break, and I went outside and threw up.[281]

Grandier's burning was shot outside on the studio lot. It was a dangerous stunt with Reed tied to a stake and the fire was for real. As a safety precaution he was given a device that he held behind his back that turned the gas off if he couldn't stand it anymore. Ever the professional, Reed often stayed the course, even when the heat scorched his face and burnt his eyelashes off.

When *The Devils* opened, people not unnaturally asked whether Russell had gone too far this time. In the judgement of the British censor he had, and numerous cuts were made, including shots of Redgrave's Sister Jeanne using a charred bone of Grandier as an improvised dildo. What was left after the hatchet job was still, without doubt, the most savage film ever made in Britain. The US version was even more heavily cut. Alexander Walker, film critic of the *Evening Standard*, who wonderfully denounced *The Devils* as 'The masturbation fantasies of a Roman Catholic boyhood', appeared with Russell on live TV and got thwacked over the head with a rolled-up newspaper for his trouble. 'When it was shown at the Venice Film Festival the Cardinal of Venice banned it,' recalls Russell. 'They made a dummy of Oliver Reed and hung it from a lamp-post and burnt it. The Cardinal withdrew his protest.'[282]

The media onslaught had its origins in an editorial in the *Daily Express*, which called *The Devils* 'The most shocking film of all', and claimed that at the press show two female journalists walked out in disgust. *The Sun* then labelled it 'filthy, perverted, degrading and vile', while in America reviewers at *New York* magazine couldn't recall, in all their broad experience wading through something like 400 movies a year, 'a fouler film'.

The Devils is an almost unique cinematic experience, by turns gross, comedic, tragic, dramatic and shocking – quite an achievement. What stands out today when you look at it are two things: firstly, the sheer beauty of it, the costumes, the make-up, and especially the production design by the then unknown Derek Jarman; and then there is Reed, giving perhaps his greatest performance.

(UK/US: London opening 25 July)

52 JOHNNY GOT HIS GUN

Dalton Trumbo's novel about the futility of war was first published in September 1939, just as Hitler's panzer tanks rolled into Poland. An immediate bestseller, today it is ranked as one of literature's great pacifist novels. The central figure is Joe Bonham, the survivor of an artillery shell attack during the First World War. In hospital, having lost his limbs, most of his face and the ability to speak, Bonham can only communicate by banging his head on his pillow in Morse code, letting the doctors know that he wants to end his life.

The novel had a convoluted path to the screen. In 1940 it was adapted for radio, with James Cagney starring as Joe. Later in the decade John Garfield showed interest in starring in a movie version. Things went quiet until Luis Buñuel announced in 1964 that he had purchased the film rights, but he ran out of funds. Finally, Trumbo decided to do it himself, sensing that the message of his novel was as relevant as ever with the unpopular war in Vietnam still being waged. Trumbo was 65 years old and had never directed a movie in his life.

Trumbo is an interesting figure in film history. One of the most accomplished screenwriters of his generation, with credits like *Roman Holiday* (1953) and *Spartacus* (1960), he was equally well known as one of the 'Hollywood Ten', a group who refused to testify in 1947 before the House Un-American Activities Committee. He was blacklisted and spent eleven months in prison.

Given the depressing nature of the subject, every studio in Hollywood turned *Johnny Got His Gun* down, saying it wouldn't earn a dime in profit. Trumbo and his producer Bruce Campbell had no choice but to raise the modest budget (under $1 million) from something like seventeen different sources.

Both Ryan O'Neal and Jon Voight were mentioned for the role of Joe. Trumbo even considered casting a young struggling stand-up comic by the name of Steve Martin, then dating his daughter Mitzi. The very last person he tested was Timothy Bottoms, who had only recently graduated from high school and had never made a film before; Bottoms didn't even know who Trumbo was. Someone else making his screen debut was David Soul, later best known for the television cop series *Starsky and Hutch*.

Also in the cast were Jason Robards as Joe's father and Donald Sutherland, who appears as Christ in a dream sequence. A big star, Trumbo wrote to Sutherland pleading with him to accept the role:

I am willing to rework the scenes to your taste and feel, to provide you with champagne baths, nubile dancing girls, little boys, pot, hash, dirty pictures: in short, I am prepared to endow you with anything and everything but money.[283]

Sutherland, a fan of the book, was on the film for just a few days before flying to New York to begin work on *Klute*. Most of the actors worked for scale or deferred payment.

Trumbo threw himself into the role of director with boundless energy, aided by his son Christopher, acting, as he saw it, as his dad's trouble-shooter. Trumbo micromanaged every production detail. He even appears briefly in the film: when the actor chosen to play an army doctor was disqualified by the Screen Actors Guild just four hours before the scene was to be shot, Trumbo had no choice but to get into make-up and play the part himself.

Despite winning both the Special Jury Prize and the International Critics Prize at Cannes, Trumbo found all the major American distributors lining up to turn the film down. Darryl Zanuck at Fox dismissed it as 'anti-American, anti-army and anti-patriotic'. Finally taken on by a small distribution company, its release in theatres was spotty. In New York servicemen were allowed in free of charge.

Reviews were mixed and the film never found any kind of audience. The fall-out was considerable. Trumbo, who had invested some of his own money, suffered serious financial losses, while Campbell never produced another picture and was forced to file for bankruptcy. Campbell, though, never lost faith in the project and took the picture around the country, showing it in churches and other venues. In a 1978 *Los Angeles Times* article, Campbell claimed that he had screened the film every week for the past seven years. 'It's been my entire life since I first saw the script in 1968.' It was a gallant effort to demonstrate that there was an audience out there for the picture – but there wasn't.

Johnny Got His Gun was destined to remain in obscurity until Lars Ulrich, drummer with the metal band Metallica, co-wrote the song 'One', about a First World War soldier who loses his limbs and begs God to take his life. Directly influenced by *Johnny Got His Gun*, the video also incorporated clips from the film. Rather than continue to pay the licensing fee for the clips, Metallica ended up buying the film rights outright.

While *Johnny Got His Gun* is flawed – its anti-war message is at times too heavy-handed – one must applaud its ambition and sincerity.

Interestingly, Trumbo chose to show Joe's horrific predicament in hospital in black and white, while his memories of growing up in a small town are in colour. At the end, the hospital staff decipher Joe's messages asking to die but refuse to help, and we are left with the awful final image of a desperate Joe weakly tapping out 'S.O.S. Help me' with his head.

(US: New York opening 4 August)

THE HIRED HAND

Hawk Koch was working on *Billy Jack* in New Mexico when he ran into Peter Fonda at a local hotel. They started talking and Fonda asked if he wanted to work as assistant director on a western that he was going to make. Koch liked Fonda; they connected real quick. Like Fonda, Koch had grown up in the industry, spending a lot of his childhood on movie sets: 'It was like a second home to me.'[284] Koch's father was the acclaimed producer Howard W. Koch, responsible for films like *The Manchurian Candidate* (1962) and *The Odd Couple* (1968). Hawk Koch had also worked with Fonda's sister Jane on *Barefoot in the Park* (1967), so that was another connection.

Even though this was going to be Fonda's first film as a director, Koch sensed that he had 'a real vision. He really knew what he wanted. And he was calm because he had all of this confidence from *Easy Rider*.'[285] The enormous success of *Easy Rider*, which Fonda produced, co-wrote and starred in, had given him a certain clout. So, when a former Clydeside shipyard worker called Alan Sharp submitted a script to him called *The Hired Hand* as a potential acting vehicle, Fonda decided to make it his directorial debut. What Fonda especially liked about Sharp's story was that it was a thoughtful western concerned with an independent woman in a man's world. As played by Verna Bloom, Hannah Collings has been living as a single mother, raising a daughter after her husband, Harry, played by Fonda, left to become a drifter and explore the wide-open plains. Then, after seven years, he suddenly returns.

Universal Pictures executive Ned Tanen greenlit the picture, part of his policy of letting young filmmakers make 'semi-independent' films for low budgets. 'And no one from the studio ever came on the set,' confirms Koch. 'They just let us make the movie.'[286] Shot in New Mexico, Fonda gave up his directing fee in order to have the funds to hire his first-choice actor, Warren Oates, to play Harry's drifter buddy. 'Peter really was committed to that movie,' says Koch. 'And he loved making it. He just had so much fun doing it. And he loved westerns. He'd grown up on his dad's westerns.' [287]

Someone else Fonda wanted was László Kovács, his cameraman on *Easy Rider*. Kovács was busy but recommended his fellow Hungarian Vilmos Zsigmond, who had primarily worked on exploitation pictures up to that point. Zsigmond went on to become one of the great cinematographers of American '70s cinema, lensing classics such as *Deliverance* (1972), *Close Encounters of the Third Kind* (1977) and *The Deer Hunter* (1978).

Fonda was a real outdoors kind of guy; he loved being out in nature and enjoyed scouting locations, often accompanied by Koch:

> This one time we were in a dry river bed, and I was walking along and all of a sudden, I said, 'Oh shit, rattlesnake!' And I jumped away. Peter snuck up behind it and he took out a buck knife and he cut the head off. And I thought, 'Wow, how cool is that guy.' [288]

At the end of the shoot, Fonda presented each member of the crew with a buck knife and on the side of the blade it said: 'Hired Hand'. Tragically, though, early in the production, one of the horse wranglers was killed while leaving a location site and attempting to board a helicopter; he was struck by the rotor blade.

When it came out *The Hired Hand* received generally mixed notices, with some critics dismissing the film as a 'hippie western'. Writer Alan Sharp was to criticise Fonda's leisurely direction and overuse of stylised visuals. 'Everyone compared it to *Easy Rider*,' says Koch. 'It was not received well. It was very disappointing for Peter.' [289] At one point, to flog the movie Universal planned to put up a billboard on Sunset Boulevard showing a shirtless Fonda with a cowboy hat and a pistol rammed down his pants with the tagline: 'That Easy Rider rides again'. Fonda was having none of it. 'I said you take that down or I will take it down. I was prepared to take it down with explosives. Needless to say, I was pissed off.' [290] As it was, the film was marketed as your standard western and was a commercial flop. Universal quickly sold it to television.

In Europe, *The Hired Hand* was better received; indeed the British magazine *Films and Filming* selected the picture as the Best Film of 1971. Certainly, in recent years, thanks to a 2001 restored director's cut that played at various film festivals, it has grown in critical estimation and is now viewed as among the best westerns the 1970s has to offer, beautifully evoking the rigours of frontier life and featuring well-crafted, naturalistic performances from the three leads.

(US: New York opening 11 August)

54 VILLAIN

Alan Ladd Jr, Elliott Kastner and Jay Kanter were young American producers operating in London. They came across a 1968 crime novel by James Barlow and brought in Dick Clement and Ian La Frenais, famous for their comedy sitcoms, to write a screenplay. Kastner was given the job of getting Richard Burton to play the lead, a sadistic East End gang leader called Vic Dakin, who has more than a hint of the Krays about him. Kastner had produced Burton's last big hit *Where Eagles Dare*, and they'd got on well. Burton liked the script, writing in his diary that it was 'the kind of "bang bang – calling all cars stuff" that I've always wanted to do.' He'd also long hankered to play a gangster, having admired the likes of Cagney and Bogart. He agreed to star for no fee upfront, settling for a share in the profits.

Elizabeth Taylor was around for most of the shoot; in the pub scenes filmed at the Assembly House in Kentish Town, she happily pulled pints for the cast and crew. Sadly, the Burtons' glory days of the 1960s, when they commanded million-dollar fees each, along with generous expenses, were pretty much over and, rather than taking up their usual suite at the Dorchester, they rented a modest house in north London.

One thing that did remain was Burton's drinking habit. He was knocking back at least two bottles of hard stuff a day. Co-star Ian McShane recalled being invited to Burton's dressing room at 8.30 in the morning to go over some lines and the star was already on the gin and tonics. Filming a robbery sequence in Bracknell, Burton only came out of his trailer to sit in the car and say his lines; the rest of the action he left to his double. 'At lunchtime Elizabeth Taylor would turn up with the Rolls Royce,' recalls Vic Armstrong, then a young stuntman. 'The boot would open and there'd be a Harrods hamper with champagne and old Richard would get hammered and be unable to work anymore.'[291]

You can tell that Burton is having a great time playing Dakin, chewing the scenery at every opportunity. Dakin is nothing short of a psychopath, good to his mum, bringing her a cup of tea in the morning, taking her out to Brighton Pier and buying her whelks, then slicing up hoodlums with a razor blade. Like the Krays he's got his own manor and a warped sense of morality, such as when he complains about today's youth: 'We should never have abolished National Service,' a line that predates the skewed patriotism of Bob Hoskins's Harold Shand a decade later in *The Long Good Friday*. It's only when his gang move up in the criminal world and try a wage snatch that they end up a cropper and Dakin's empire crumbles around him.

Quite risky for the time, Dakin is portrayed as gay and McShane plays his bisexual bit of rough, who deals drugs and pimps out his girlfriends to aristos. The rest of the cast is pretty solid – Nigel Davenport as the tough cop on Dakin's trail, Donald Sinden as a seedy MP, Fiona Lewis and Joss Ackland. In his memoirs Ackland recalled going to see director Michael Tuchner and Alan Ladd Jr, hoping to play a rival gang boss. Tuchner and Ladd didn't see him in that role at all. Deciding not to take no for an answer, he returned dressed up in hard man attire, a black shirt and white tie, with his hair slicked down:

> I swept past the secretary and burst in on Alan Ladd Jr, grabbed him by the lapels, thrust my face into his and said, 'If you don't give me this bleeding part, I'll break your bloody neck!' For a moment Ladd looked shaken, then he recognised me, grinned and said, 'The part is yours.' [292]

It was Ackland's big break.

There was another role for a young actor called Clive Francis. 'I played some aristocratic lord called Vivian, who enjoyed throwing orgiastic parties at his luxury pile in the country. I literally had two days on the picture.'[293] Time enough to get a rather special invite. 'One night Alan Ladd Jr invited myself, Fiona Lewis, Ian La Frenais and one or two others to dinner at his flat where the guest of honour was Marlon Brando, fresh from filming *The Godfather*.'[294]

Villain was not enthusiastically received by critics. 'Richard Burton being particularly savaged for his attempt at a Cockney accent,' says Francis. 'It did though coin the popular phrase: "Don't be a berk all your life, take a day off!"'[295] And it did not do well at the box office, having the misfortune of coming out not that long after *Get Carter*. However, it created a vivid and cynical portrait of the sleazy and violent aspects of London life and is regarded as one of the defining crime dramas of its era.

As for the Kastner, Kanter and Ladd partnership, it only lasted another year. Ladd went back to Hollywood and found himself head of 20th Century Fox, where one of his first acts was to green light a picture called *Star Wars*.

(UK/US: London opening 12 August)

 ## 55 ¦ *THE OMEGA MAN*

....

Richard Matheson's post-apocalyptic novel *I Am Legend*, published in 1954, must be one of the most influential of all modern horror stories. It tells of a scientist who believes he is the sole survivor of a worldwide pandemic that has turned the rest of the population into bloodthirsty ghouls, effectively vampires. George A. Romero has spoken about the inspiration he drew from the novel for his own *Night of the Living Dead* (1968).

Charlton Heston first read the book when he was making *Touch of Evil* in 1958 for Orson Welles. It was Welles who lent him a copy. What fascinated Heston the most about it was the intriguing premise of someone being the very last person left on the planet. Years later, when Heston resurrected the idea, he'd lost the book and told a producer friend Walter Seltzer to go buy it from a book store. Only he'd forgotten the title. 'It was something like My Name Is Legion,' said Heston. The producer bought the book but was surprised Heston wanted to make a film out of an academic study on population statistics.

Eventually the right book was found and Heston and Seltzer brought the project to Warner Brothers, who agreed to back it. Matheson's story had been filmed once before, cheaply, in black and white, but quite effectively as *The Last Man on Earth* (1964), starring Vincent Price. Matheson disowned the film, complaining that it strayed too far from his original story. He was to have even more cause to complain with *The Omega Man*.

It was decided to update Matheson's tale to incorporate early '70s themes like religious cults, hippies and Black power; also, to demythologise the story, to junk the supernatural element of vampires and go down the scientific route. The disease is the cause of bacteriological warfare, the victims become not bloodsuckers but mutants afflicted by albinism and photophobia – the reason they stay in the shadows during the day. Having come up with that idea, Heston later admitted he felt they botched it. The film was too rushed and the mutant make-ups weren't done well. Heston's right; they are a let-down. Wearing black cloaks and hoods, the mutants come across as a sort of hippie medieval religious sect, unlike the genuinely frightening creatures in the 2007 Will Smith remake.

To achieve the eerie effects of a deserted city, exteriors were shot in downtown Los Angeles early in the morning on weekends. It was a smooth shoot, although Heston complained that director Boris Sagal was an irritant on the set, given to outbursts of anger. Sagal was predominantly a television director. Matheson had heard that Heston had tried to interest Sam Peckinpah in the job, the pair having worked together on *Major Dundee* (1965). Following *The Omega Man*, Sagal went back into television, scoring a huge success with the 1976 mini-series *Rich Man, Poor Man*. It was while shooting a mini-series in 1981 that, getting out of a helicopter, he turned the wrong way and walked into the rotor blades. His injuries were so severe that he died later in hospital.

The Omega Man works best, and is at its most interesting, in the early scenes where Heston is all by himself, scouring the deserted city for food and supplies, searching out the creatures to destroy them. We watch how he passes his time alone, watching movies in a deserted picture house, talking to himself, playing chess with a marble head of Caesar Augustus, and dressing for dinner. He lives in a heavily fortified town house, where at night the creatures taunt him and try to break in. The town house set was on the Warners' lot in Burbank, and is today a historical landmark.

When Heston stumbles across a healthy survivor, played by Rosalind Cash, we find that he's not the last remaining human on Earth, that there are pockets of survivors. Following a small role in *Klute*, this was Rosalind's second movie, and it was the writer's decision for Heston to have an interracial relationship, something that was still considered quite a surprising thing to do in 1971. Cash herself was understandably nervous in her big love scene with Heston, telling him, 'It's a spooky feeling to screw Moses.'[296]

Heston's character Robert Neville was a scientist before the war; he's also immune to the virus and realises that his blood can help with a possible antidote. This essentially makes him the saviour of mankind and the Christ analogy that has been hinted at in the film becomes almost inescapable. For Neville's climactic death scene Heston decided to play around with the concept and, after being fatally hit with a spear, he adopts a crucifixion pose in a fountain turning red with his blood.

A sizeable hit at the time, *The Omega Man* is a decent watch and for the most part engaging and deserves its cult status. It also happens to be one of Tim Burton's favourite movies.

(US: New York opening 13 August)

56 THE DECAMERON

Pier Paolo Pasolini was one of the most controversial directors working in cinema, and yet he came into film late. He was already a published poet, did some teaching, tried to be an actor, was a journalist, a painter and a playwright. By the time he wrote his first screenplays he was in his 30s, and then almost 40 before making his directing debut with *Accattone* in 1961. Already he was one of the most dissenting public voices in Italian politics and culture.

In the early 1970s he embarked upon three bawdy adaptations of medieval works that offered religious themes (for a man who claimed to be an atheist he did seem to be overly obsessed by God and Christianity) and mysticism, along with ample scope for sex, nudity and broad humour. These were films, he said, intended for 'mass culture'. Branded collectively as 'The Trilogy of Life', *The Decameron* was followed by *The Canterbury Tales* (1972) and *Arabian Nights* (1974).

The Decameron is a series of 100 colourful stories, largely concerned with love and adventure, life and death, by fourteenth-century Italian writer Giovanni Boccaccio. Pasolini weaves a handful of these tales to create one of the most richly textured evocations of early Renaissance life ever put on film, populated by artists, peasants and priests. Pasolini himself appears as the great pre-Renaissance painter Giotto (after offering the role to two actors who turned him down), and acts as a guide for the viewer through this cinematic landscape. Pasolini becomes an artist operating inside his own work. He also changed the original location of the stories from Florence – too bourgeoisie he said – to the more earthy and proletarian Naples.

While Pasolini had been lionised by critics, *The Decameron* saw him make the move from relatively obscure European auteur to mainstream moviemaker, working with the biggest budget of his career and a major international distributor in UA. It was a deliberate rejection of his elitist following in order to broaden his appeal. Pasolini wanted *The Decameron* to be accepted as light-hearted fun, but some 152 legal complaints were lodged against the film from such diverse sources as a surgeon in Venice to two nuns in Milan. Pasolini was branded a pornographer. He hit back, saying, 'I wanted to show how eroticism was a warm, life-giving power for people, before it changed into a commerce for our time. My films are anti-pornographic.'[297] All of this controversy made for good publicity, although in some Italian districts, particularly in the south, the film was seized by police and there were calls for it to be banned. *Variety* reporting on it said: 'Pasolini has made the most sexplicit picture of the year and probably in the history of Italian cinema.'

Because of the controversy, the organisers of the Berlin International Film Festival refused to give it a screening. They eventually relented and the picture won the Silver Bear award. *The Decameron* was a huge success at the Italian box office, becoming one of the country's highest ever grossing films. In America it was the most popular foreign film of the year. Unfortunately, this enormous success resulted in numerous low-budget soft porn imitators and knock-offs, which of course did not carry the same political message or lyrical beauty. This greatly irked Pasolini and he would come to disown the film shortly before his tragic murder in 1975 at the age of 53.

(Italy/France/West Germany: opening 25 August)

57 *LET'S SCARE JESSICA TO DEATH*

It's strange to think that a film many critics have called one of the scariest ever made started life as a comedy about ditzy hippies being menaced on a camping trip by a creature that lives in a lake. Written by Lee Kalcheim and called *It Drinks Hippie Blood*, it was being financed by Charles B. Moss and his son, the owners of the Criterion Theatre at Broadway and 45th Street and sixteen other movie houses in the New York area. They wanted John D. Hancock to direct it on the strength of an acclaimed short film, but he didn't want to do it. 'The script wasn't that funny. It was a parody of a scary movie. It was bad.'[298] Instead of making a satire of a horror picture, Hancock wanted to do a movie that was legitimately terrifying. 'I took the genre seriously. There is actually something scary about the world and I wanted to capture that.'[299] It was agreed, and Hancock reworked Kalcheim's screenplay into something far more disturbing. 'And I cut out all the bad jokes.'[300]

Hancock wasn't a particular fan of the horror genre, coming as he did from the world of Broadway and theatre. 'So, I rented a 16mm projector and the Mosses helped me borrow a whole bunch of Hitchcock prints and I sat in my living room and watched them over and over.'[301] Hancock got on well with the Mosses. 'I had respect for their knowledge of audiences. They wanted a séance in the picture. I said, "There's really no place for a séance." But they said, "The people will like it." So, I put it in, and it worked.'[302]

Besides Hitchcock, Hancock pulled together other influences too, such as the Henry James novel *The Turn of the Screw*, Sheridan Le Fanu's novel *Carmilla* and the classic Robert Wise picture *The Haunting*, to create his creepy tale. Set in present-day New England, Jessica is a psychologically fragile young woman, recently released from a sanatorium. Along with her husband and his friend they decide to take a short break at a remote farmhouse in the country. Here they discover that a hippie girl Emily has been squatting in the farmhouse. Since she doesn't seem to have any place to go, the trio invite her to stay, but Jessica becomes disturbed by her likeness to a Victorian girl who drowned in a nearby lake.

As Jessica, Hancock cast Zohra Lampert, who was better known as a stage actress. She'd only made a few film appearances, notably alongside Natalie Wood and Warren Beatty in *Splendour in the Grass* (1961). Lampert later admitted to becoming totally lost in the role, as elements of the script resonated with her personally, and she spent much of the time between takes remaining in character. The rest of the cast were also filled by actors from the New York theatre community, most of whom Hancock had previously worked with. 'I had no idea really how to direct a feature film, so it was nice to work with people I knew. These were friends.'[303]

The film was shot in a brisk twenty-six days, on a budget of just $250,000, in and around various towns and villages in Connecticut. At one point the set was visited by the local Teamsters, a labour union. 'We were shooting without Teamsters,' admits Hancock. 'They said, "You really need to have union drivers on this because these cameras break soooo easy." We gave them some money and they went away. And then they came back a week or two later for more.'[304]

Hancock directs in such a way as to leave the viewer unsure whether everything is really happening or just mental delusions of Jessica's fervid mind. She is convinced the local townsfolk, who all bear strange marks on their faces, are zombies and out to get her. Jessica's psychological state and deterioration has been read by some as the fear and dread experienced during the death throes of the hippie and counterculture movement of the 1960s. Jessica and her friends drive around in a black hearse with the word 'love' scrawled on the car door. The hippie peace movement was something Hancock never got. 'I thought it was a form of sentimental insanity.'[305] And then there were the drugs:

> I was running a theatre in San Franciso in 1965 when our board members were starting to take acid, and then the actors started to take acid. I felt at one point that I was the most experienced director in the world of directing people on acid.[306]

Filmed without a distributor in place, *Jessica* was picked up by Paramount:

> They changed the title, which was a stroke of genius, and gave it a huge campaign, kind of old-fashioned ballyhoo. It opened at the Criterion, and they had horse-drawn hearses outside, and all across the country. Paramount did a great job, and it made a lot of money.[307]

Over the years the film began to attain a cult following and a critical reappraisal. In a 1992 interview Stephen King revealed it to be among his favourite horror films, alongside more familiar fare like *Dawn of the Dead*, *The Exorcist* and *Halloween*. 'I get invited to screenings where people come all dressed up in hoods and as witches,' says Hancock. 'There was a guy at one screening, he had his teeth filed so they looked like vampire teeth.'[308]

At a time when filmmakers were no longer constrained by the shackles of censorship and were pushing the limits of sex and gore, *Jessica* relies on suggestion and atmosphere to creep out its audience. None more so than when, during a daytime swim at a nearby lake, Emily disappears under the water, wearing a bathing suit, only to emerge in a nineteenth-century wedding dress. Hancock also handles Jessica's mental collapse, as she begins to question her own sanity, with sympathetic sensitivity and gets a terrific performance out of Lampert.

Hancock followed up *Jessica* with the Robert De Niro sports drama *Bang the Drum Slowly* (1973). But it was *Jessica* that landed him a huge job. 'Early in the picture there was a jump scare where the audience really jumped, and Richard Zanuck saw it and jumped too, and that's why he thought of me for *Jaws 2*.'[309] Sadly, Hancock's vision for the blockbuster sequel did not tally with the studio's and they parted company.

(US: New York opening 27 August)

58 *THE TOUCH*

This romantic drama marked the first English-language film made by the Swedish Ingmar Bergman, one of the true masters of cinema. And while *The Touch* is not among his best work – indeed the director himself later rather harshly dismissed the film – watching it remains a worthwhile experience, in spite of its flaws.

Bergman always felt that the film was compromised or 'bungled', as he wrote in his 1992 memoirs. At the time it was something he didn't want to make. On 5 July 1970 Bergman wrote in his workbook:

> I've finished the screenplay, although not without a fair amount of inner resistance. Now I'm going to take time off until August 3, when we begin the preparations in earnest. I feel depressed and ill at ease. I'd be happy to drop this film.[310]

He'd also wanted to release a version with both English and Swedish dialogue which, 'just possibly was slightly less unbearable' than the totally English-language version, which was made at the request of the American backers.

The backers in question were ABC and executive Martin Baum, who'd tied Bergman down to a contract after a meeting in London in 1970 when the director was working on a production of *Hedda Gabler* at the National Theatre. Among the most successful European directors of the 1950s and 1960s, Bergman had been courted by Hollywood for years, but had always rejected their advances. Perhaps he now wished he'd done the same with ABC, whose marketing campaign also irked him by focusing on the two leads, Elliott Gould and Bibi Andersson, when the story wasn't really about a couple, but much more about the woman. The eventual failure of the film was even more of a disappointment for Bergman since it was based very much on something deeply personal. He even declared it to be the first real love story he'd ever tackled.

There was much fanfare made about this being Bergman's first English-language film, and ABC threw a number of American star names at him: Paul Newman, Robert Redford and Dustin Hoffman, who said no because his wife was pregnant at the time. In the end Bergman settled on Gould, then a hot property thanks to the success of *MASH*. Bergman said he was drawn to Gould after watching him in the comedy drama *Getting Straight* (1970). The rest of the cast were filled with Bergman regulars Bibi Andersson and Max von Sydow, appearing in his eleventh and final film for the director.

Gould has said that he was stunned to be offered the part, and the chance to work with Bergman was too good an opportunity to decline. When the director first called him up, Gould recalled how the hairs on the back of his neck stood up. Gould plays David, an American archaeologist visiting Sweden, who meets by chance Karin (Andersson) a seemingly happily married mother of two. They begin a passionate and stormy affair, one that threatens the stability of Karin's marriage to a respected local surgeon (Sydow). Bergman had written the character of Karin with Liv Ullmann in mind, but Ullmann was unavailable.

The film isn't really a romantic triangle; Bergman's constant focus is on Karin. Her point of view and emotions are what interest Bergman throughout. Gould later revealed he had a feeling that Bergman wanted Bibi and him 'to share our intimacy off-camera, and that was not to be'.[311] In the script there was more than a hint of autobiography in the story, with Andersson's character having marked similarities to the woman Bergman was living with at the time and would soon marry, Ingrid von Rosen.

Interestingly, Bergman's screenplay was more akin to a novella, a written narrative, than a traditional screenplay. As was his method, Bergman worked from 9.30 a.m. until 3.30 p.m., writing on paper in long hand. If he made an error, rather than erase the mistake and correct it, he copied out the page in its entirety again. This meticulousness extended to his directing, the way he took care of all the details, from costumes to props, and the way he organised the shoot, with everyone starting and finishing and breaking for lunch at the same time every day on the dot. His sets were also private, with few visitors allowed, and he employed most of the same crew he'd worked with for years.

When it opened, *The Touch* received a mixed critical response and performed poorly at the box office. Bergman would make just one more English-language film in his career, *The Serpent's Egg* (1977). Four decades later, a restoration of the original bilingual version of *The Touch* was screened, leading to the widespread consensus that it was a great improvement.

(Sweden/US: Sweden opening 30 August)

59 BEWARE OF A HOLY WHORE (WARNUNG VOR EINER HEILIGEN NUTTE)

In the early 1970s Rainer Werner Fassbinder was the wonder boy of the new German cinema, or the *enfant terrible*, depending on your point of view. By the time of *Beware of a Holy Whore* he was just 25 years old, but already had an impressive career as a director on film and in the theatre.

Fassbinder was born in 1945 into a cultured bourgeois family and grew up in Munich. His parents divorced when he was 5 and Fassbinder found solace in a local cinema, where his mother stuck him when she was too busy working to look after him. The cinema was, he once said, the family life he never had at home. Fassbinder made his first short films at the age of 20, while also directing and acting in anti-establishment plays for a group of young actors that later formed part of his cinematic stock company. This group was known as the 'Anti-Theater', an ideological artistic commune that lived and performed together. It was largely Fassbinder's disillusionment with the ethos of the Anti-Theater that led to *Beware of a Holy Whore*.

His previous film, *Whity* (1971), a melodrama shot in Spain that took the form of a spaghetti western, had been a chaotic and dysfunctional production. *Holy Whore* was to be Fassbinder's own critique of the group, in a typical act of confession and self-analysis. When his cast read the script, a few recognised themselves, despite obvious name changes, and were not especially happy. There was a temptation to refuse to participate, but their dependence on Fassbinder had become too strong.

The story follows a film crew languishing in a Spanish hotel waiting for their director to show up. Lacking a purposeful way to spend their time, they drink, quarrel, have sex and engage in power trips. When the director and the lead actor finally show up, the director is enraged by the antics of his crew, and the production spirals into anarchy. In reality the cast and crew were waiting on location for Fassbinder to arrive, and when he did it was in his newly acquired Chevrolet Stingray.

This is a film about filmmaking, the 'holy whore' of the title. Fassbinder casts himself as a harassed and embattled production manager. But really the film offers a displaced portrait of Fassbinder as filmmaker in the character of the director Jeff, played by Lou Castel, who even wears Fassbinder's trademark beat-up black leather jacket. Jeff engages in all manner of abusive and self-abasing behaviour. He humiliates others and, in turn, is humiliated and brutalised by the cast and crew. Fassbinder was well aware that he was a challenging and difficult man to work with. At the start of every day on *Whity* he would demand ten Cuba libres, nine to drink and one to hurl at his cameraman Michael Ballhaus. He despised the fact Ballhaus came from television, but after several films together they built up a good, if complicated, working relationship. Ballhaus later went to Hollywood where he became Martin Scorsese's preferred cameraman on several pictures.

Fassbinder did everything in excess. He smoked in excess, drank in excess, took drugs in excess and took sleeping pills in excess. He also tormented his actors and was a cruel manipulator. Hanna Schygulla, who appeared in many of his film and television works, described herself as 'a survivor'.

Although set in Spain, *Holy Whore* was shot in Sorrento, a picturesque coastal town south of Naples. It was Fassbinder's most expensive film to date (1.1 million Deutschmarks) and his first international co-production. Playing the role of a faded movie star was the faded movie star Eddie Constantine, famous for his early gangster roles and Jean-Luc Godard's *Alphaville* (1965).

Holy Whore is a key work in the Fassbinder canon. It saw him moving away from his early esoteric films and maturing into an artist moving tentatively into some form of mainstream. He was a fan of American cinema, particularly the works of director Douglas Sirk. It also spelled the beginning of the end of the Anti-Theater experiment. It was partly Fassbinder's own realisation that this utopian ideal of an artistic collective living and working together was never going to work, even if the will was there to make it work. Given everyone's dependence on him, was it ever really a 'group' to begin with?

When Fassbinder died in 1982, aged just 37, following an overdose of cocaine and sleeping pills, he left a legacy of over forty films – quite a feat in a career that lasted only sixteen years. Such was his workaholic nature that when his body was found, a cigarette still between his lips, an unfinished script for his next film lay beside him.

(West Germany: opening 1 September)

60 THE BIG DOLL HOUSE

Shot for just $125,000 on location in the Philippines and ending up making millions for Roger Corman's freshly inaugurated New World Pictures, this grindhouse classic established the 'women in cages' flick that became a staple of exploitation cinema.

Looking for product for his new company, Corman was inspired by Jesús Franco's 1969 drive-in hit *99 Women*, set in a female prison colony off the coast of Panama. Sensing there was a market for films with scantily clad female inmates in a sweaty jungle setting (who'd have thought it?), Corman hired Don Spencer to come up with a script and Jack Hill as director.

Hill had worked with Corman before and had already made the cult classic *Spider Baby* (1967). When he read Spencer's script, Hill thought it was awful and took to rewriting chunks of it, introducing more campy humour. 'The only thing that was mandated was that I had to have girls fighting in the mud,' he revealed.[312]

In the Philippines, the scenery was stunning – and it was cheap. The locals worked hard too, and were eager, if lacking a certain professionalism. For Hill the experience shooting out there was 'a fun nightmare'. Stunt men would make the sign of the cross before doing falls. 'And if they want to have a man on fire, they just set a guy on fire who'll try and jump into the water as quick as he can.'[313]

The crew also had to contend with horrendous weather conditions, including a monsoon and a hurricane that blew off the roof of the soundstage. Economising was the name of the game. The cast returned to their hotel after one long day's work in the jungle only to discover the bill hadn't been paid and they were locked out.

The Big Doll House is pure sexploitation – wardens need little excuse to rip the clothes off female prisoners – and there are scenes of torture, bondage and sadism. In the end the inmates mutiny, machine-gunning their captors down like the Dirty Dozen in drag. Critics have argued that, despite the exploitative nudity, the fact that the female prisoners took on the kind of active, heroic roles traditionally performed by men marked the film out as a small step forward for women; perhaps even leading the way to kick-ass female characters like Ripley and Lara Croft.

Hill cast an interesting bunch of young American actresses to play the inmates, but the big breakout star was Pam Grier. Totally unknown at the time, Grier had come to Los Angeles hoping to get into movies and was working as a receptionist when Corman spotted her. Hill interviewed Grier and immediately sensed her strong personality and thought she was a natural. Hill and Grier would later team up for the blaxploitation classics *Coffy* (1973) and *Foxy Brown* (1974).

Hill took the young actress under his wing, told her to tap into her gut, not her mind, to find the real emotion. When the dailies came back it was obvious Grier was stealing the film. As a result, she was offered a starring role in a follow-up, *Women in Cages*, shot directly after *Doll House*, again in the Philippines, and released at the end of 1971. This time Grier is the one meting out punishment as sadistic prison warden Alabama. The plot centres on a naïve American woman staying in the Philippines who is set up by her drug dealer boyfriend and sent to a prison in the jungle.

Much of the cast and crew who worked on *Doll House* return for *Women in Cages*, except Jack Hill is absent. In his place is Gerardo de Leon, something of a revered figure in the Philippine film industry, whose career stretched back to the 1940s. There's also a prominent role for Philippine actress and singer Sofia Moran, one of the prisoners and plaything of warden Alabama. Moran fondly recalls working with Grier. 'The dynamics between Pam and myself was very good. We both got along really well and even when our scenes were intimate and sometimes violent, we were able to focus on our characters and our unique relationship in the movie.'[314]

Grier always came to their scenes together prepared. Moran remembers:

She was wonderful with ideas, as well as some coaching during our shoot. Outside of work, Pam and the rest of the main cast came to watch my Vegas-style show in Manila on more than one occasion. I loved being around Pam, she was very outgoing and funny at times.[315]

At first, Moran felt intimidated by the American actresses on the film. 'It was exciting and nerve-wracking at the same time.'[316] But they behaved graciously and made Moran feel part of the company. They needed to bond as a group, given the conditions everyone was under. Moran says:

Making that movie was tough and demanding. The location shoot was either in darkness or in the middle of nowhere, and also in unbearable summer, humid heat. There was a demand for many physical scenes that were challenging to shoot, but we all made it through.[317]

While not as big a hit as *Doll House*, *Women in Cages* still did well at the box office. 'To be honest,' says Moran, 'I did not realise the popularity of *Women in Cages* as a cult film until recently. Watching the movie with my close friends gives me such wonderful memories.'[318] Moran was also pleased when Quentin Tarantino included her fight scene with fellow inmate Roberta Collins in his movie *Planet Terror* (2007).

(US: Los Angeles opening 3 September)

61 A BAY OF BLOOD

By the time Mario Bava came to make *A Bay of Blood*, he already had a huge reputation in horror cinema as the man who defined the genre known as 'Giallo' – a name borrowed from murder mystery novels published in Italy with distinct yellow covers. His use of heavily stylised camera movement, operatic direction and imaginatively brutal murders was to have a profound and lasting impact on filmmaking, spawning talents such as Lucio Fulci and Dario Argento. *A Bay of Blood* is unquestionably his most violent film and is today considered the precursor to the 1980s *Friday the 13th* and the succession of slasher pictures that followed, making this a truly seminal work of horror cinema.

The story takes place in an isolated mansion, part of a large estate overlooking a beautiful lake. When the owner, a wheelchair-using countess, is murdered, all manner of characters, from estranged family members to illegitimate children and real estate agents, stake a claim to her valuable property. But the plot is of no real significance – this is an excuse for a conveyor belt of mayhem, as people are killed off in increasingly bizarre and gory ways – thirteen in total. What makes the film especially influential is the introduction of a group of young adults, with no relevance to the main plot, who suddenly arrive on the scene and break into a vacant cottage on the estate hoping for a bit of adolescent fun. One of the girls goes swimming in the lake and discovers a butchered body. Now a nuisance to the killer, the teens are mercilessly despatched. One is chased through the woods and has her throat slashed, another gets a machete full in the face, while a couple having sex in bed are simultaneously impaled by a spear; a death faithfully reproduced in *Friday the 13th Part 2* (1981).

It's this portion of the film that was to prove so significant and the forerunner of the slasher flick that was to dominate the horror genre in the 1980s and beyond. Of course, Bava had explored this kind of territory before, but here he introduces several 'slasher cinema' motifs, such as voyeurism and young people in cabins in wooded seclusion being horribly murdered one by one.

It's funny that such an influential film should owe its existence to the fact that Bava owed a large amount of back taxes and needed to make a film fast. As it was, he worked under severe budgetary restrictions. To save money the main location was the producer's own summer house and outlying property, and Bava undertook the role of cinematographer as well as director. Ironically, before shooting was completed the producer did a vanishing act, along with the money, but somehow Bava managed to complete the picture.

Handling the complicated and bloody effects was Carlo Rambaldi, whose innovative work here pathed the way for how gore effects would be done for decades after. Rambaldi later built a huge reputation in Hollywood, creating the aliens that emerge from the mother ship in *Close Encounters of the Third Kind*, bringing to life the designs of H.R. Giger in *Alien* (1979) and his most celebrated creation, Spielberg's ET.

Although *A Bay of Blood* gives its characters little time to develop any kind of presence, so swiftly are they all despatched, the cast is fairly competent, including ex-Bond girl Claudine Auger, Luigi Pistilli, veteran of several spaghetti westerns, and Laura Betti, an actress and cabaret performer who had appeared in Fellini's *La Dolce Vita* (1960).

On its initial release *A Bay of Blood* was criticised and vilified for its extreme violence, which some critics labelled pornographic. In Italy it did virtually no business at the box office and quickly disappeared. In America it went under the outrageous title of *Twitch of the Death Nerve* and was shown at drive-ins and grindhouses until the prints were so worn that they could hardly be played anymore. In Britain, the film was refused a certificate for eight years and, in 1984, was included on the infamous 'video nasties' list. It was finally released uncut in 2010.

Legend has it that Christophe Lee, who had previously worked with Bava, walked out of a festival screening of *A Bay of Blood* in disgust. He had seen the future of horror and didn't like it one little bit.

(Italy: opening 8 September)

62 | *OUT 1*

On the evenings of 9 and 10 September 1971 the Maison de la Culture in the port city of Le Havre in northern France was witness to an extraordinary event, the premiere of Jacques Rivette's bladder-crucifying thirteen-hour long film, still one of the longest in cinema history. Rivette didn't have enough money to make a projection copy, so the work print was screened. French director Claire Denis described the whole thing as 'like an acid experience where everyone was more or less stoned'.[319] This was the one-and-only public showing of *Out 1* until a print resurfaced again two decades later. Even then screenings were exceptionally rare, adding to the film's mystique. *The New York Times* called *Out 1* 'the cinephile's holy grail'.

Jacques Rivette's *L'Amour fou* (1969) had run over four hours and was a critical and public success. This time his intention was to subvert the traditional moviegoing experience altogether. Originally, though, *Out 1* was designed as a television serial (the finished film ended up divided into eight 90–100 minute episodes) but he was turned down by the national broadcaster. Remarkably, given its sheer length, Rivette shot the whole thing in just six weeks during the spring of 1970. He then faced the gruelling task of editing twenty-five to thirty-five hours of footage into some kind of shape.

Rivette devised his immense plot from Balzac's *Histoire des Treize*. A young man (Jean-Pierre Léaud) receives anonymous notes that put him on the trail of a mysterious group of thirteen individuals that operate a secret society in Paris following the failed revolution of 1968. The cast also includes Michael Lonsdale and Bernadette Lafont. Rivette left his actors pretty much to their own devices in how they developed their characters and then he found a way to integrate them into his scenario. Rivette kept the film's plot under wraps, not revealing it in any great detail until a week before shooting began. There was never a script as such anyway, more a multiple of storylines that weave in and out of each other, though it takes hours for these connections to be made. New characters appear and then disappear again for huge lengths of time.

The shooting style is largely *cinéma-vérité*, handheld grainy 16mm. There are long takes, sometimes lasting thirty minutes, and some that include actors fluffing their lines or continuity gaffes such as camera and boom microphone shadows, retained by Rivette. At one point a character, with no explanation, suddenly goes all *Twin Peaks* and starts speaking backwards on the soundtrack. And in one well-known scene Jean-Pierre Léaud walks down a street reciting a nonsense poem as real pedestrians look bemusedly at the camera crew, bystanders awkwardly get out of his way, and he is followed by gawping children.

Following its showing in Le Havre, Rivette spent almost a year reworking the film into a shorter, more commercially viable form, this one running four hours, presumably at the behest of distributors. Rivette always contested that this was not a digest of the long version but another film altogether, a ghost almost, which is perhaps why he called this version *Out 1: Spectre*. It was finally released in Paris in 1974.

The original long version would pop up at the odd festival or museum showing, rarely because that 16mm copy was said to be the only one in existence. Then finally, in 2015, the print was given an immaculate 2K digital restoration and brought out on home media for a wider audience to enjoy. If 'enjoy' is the right word. It depends how you view it. While this movie really is a one-of-a-kind experience, it's not advisable to view it in one sitting, probably practically impossible as well. Even Rivette suggested the best way to see his film was not all at once:

> One never reads a book in one sitting, one puts it down, stops for lunch, etc. The ideal thing was to see it in two days, which allowed one to get into it enough to follow it, with the possibility of stopping four or five times.[320]

Or maybe one should treat the film as if it were some mini-series or box set to dip into over its eight instalments. Those with a passion for the *Nouvelle Vague* may find it rewarding.

(France: opening 9/10 September)

 ## 63 *THE GO-BETWEEN*

At the Cannes Film Festival, the grand prize, the Palme d'Or, was awarded to *The Go-Between*, directed by Joseph Losey and written by Harold Pinter. It was to be their last collaboration, having worked together so fruitfully on *The Servant* (1963) and *Accident* (1967). L.P. Hartley's 1953 semi-autobiographical novel about a schoolboy who becomes a pawn in the forbidden romance of Marian, an aristocratic woman, and Ted Burgess, a tenant farmer, hurrying secret messages between the two lovers, was going to be their next film after *The Servant*. When it was discovered that someone else had the rights and Pinter's script wasn't working, they shelved it, returning to it six years later.

Originally Alexander Korda owned the rights, but he did nothing with it, buying the book purely as a piece of property. 'I was so annoyed when I learnt this,' said Hartley, 'that I put a curse upon him, and he died, almost the next morning.'[321] The project finally landed on the desk of the director, actor and writer Bryan Forbes, recently appointed chief of production and managing director of EMI Films. Forbes thought Pinter's script one of the best he'd ever read and, while he did not warm to Losey (the feeling was mutual), wanted to make a deal. Forbes negotiated a co-financing deal with MGM and its head James Aubrey.

Losey was keen on casting a young and unknown actress in the role of Marian, who was 18 or 19 in the book. He thought the role of Ted Burgess ought to be cast young too. MGM, however, demanded that Marian be played by a star – and that star had to be Julie Christie. Losey was told in no uncertain terms that it was Christie or there would be no film. Oddly, Losey had first considered Christie back in 1964, when the actress was in her early 20s, and she had agreed to do it. Now almost 30, Christie knew she was too old and refused to do the film. Losey used all his powers of persuasion to make her change her mind. Losey also added another marquee name, Alan Bates, in the role of the farmer Ted Burgess. The cast also featured Edward Fox, Margaret Leighton and Michael Redgrave.

Crucial to the film was the role of Leo, the 12-year-old schoolboy who stays at his friend's ancestral home during one long hot Norfolk summer in 1900, where he becomes the go-between. Losey looked at hundreds of candidates before choosing 14-year-old Dominic Guard, who hailed from an acting family and had done some television and stage work. For the role of Leo's school friend Marcus, Losey was after a genuine public schoolboy rather than someone from a stage school. Richard Gibson was attending Radley College in Oxfordshire and one day in the corridor the headmaster stopped him. 'I need to see you in my study after breakfast tomorrow.' 'Oh no,' thought Gibson, 'what have I done?' 'Is it good or bad sir?' he asked. 'As it happens it could be very, very good,' said the headmaster. 'Not being in a film with Julie Christie is it?' said Gibson, this being the best thing he could think of. 'How did you know?' said the surprised headmaster.[322]

The birth of a superstar. *The Big Boss* was Bruce Lee's first major film in a lead role. (Kobal/Shutterstock)

Gene Wilder as Willy Wonka, one of cinema's great fantasy characters. (Moviestore/Shutterstock)

Opposite: *Shaft* was one of the pioneering blaxploitation movies, starring Richard Roundtree as private detective John Shaft. (MGM/Kobal/Shutterstock)

Left: Clint Eastwood as Harry Callahan, his most iconic role, in *Dirty Harry*. (Warner Bros/Kobal/Shutterstock)

Below: One of the great police dramas, *The French Connection* won the Academy Award for Best Picture in 1971. (20th Century Fox/D'Antoni Productions/Schine-Moore Prods/Kobal/Shutterstock)

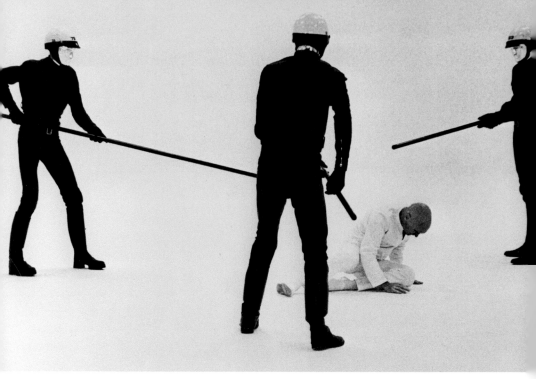

Before *Star Wars*, George Lucas began to dabble with sci-fi in his directorial debut *THX 1138*. (American Zoetrope/Warner Bros/Kobal/Shutterstock)

1971 was a golden year for horror. A highlight was Vincent Price in *The Abominable Dr. Phibes*. (Aip/Kobal/Shutterstock)

Michael Caine in *Get Carter*, arguably the best British gangster film ever made. (MGM/Kobal/Shutterstock)

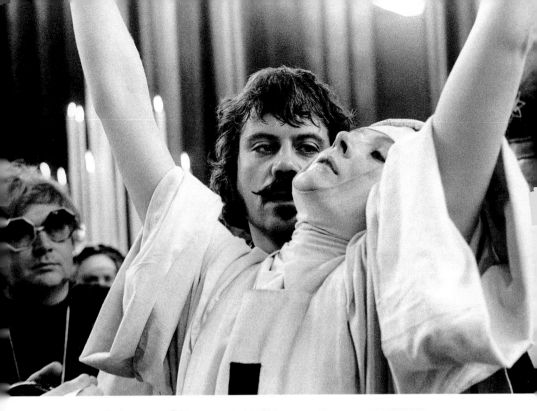

Above: Ken Russell, the *enfant terrible* of British cinema, pulled no punches in *The Devils*. (Warner Bros/Kobal/Shutterstock)

Right: One of the year's best comedies was Woody Allen's second directorial outing, *Bananas*. (Moviestore/Shutterstock)

Opposite: The lull before the storm. Dustin Hoffman and Susan George in the controversial *Straw Dogs*. (ABC Corp/Cinerama Releasing/Kobal/Shutterstock)

Luchino Visconti's *Death in Venice* was the art house hit of 1971. (Alfa/Kobal/Shutterstock)

Sean Connery's official reign as James Bond came to a close with *Diamonds Are Forever*. (Danjaq/Eon/Ua/Kobal/Shutterstock)

It was a happy shoot and the cast fell in love with the house Losey had found as the location, the grand-looking Melton Constable Hall, 20 miles outside Norwich. Gibson says:

It was almost like a character in the film. But before we arrived there had been a heat wave and all the grass had burnt and died. They got this green paint and sprayed all the grass as far as the eye could see. And they had to keep spraying it for about two weeks until we had a bit of rain and it grew back.[323]

Losey was keen on this arty shot of the two boys reclining on the ground, with the soles of their feet facing the camera. 'But they couldn't use it,' says Gibson, 'because the bottom of our shoes was covered in green paint.'[324]

Gibson and Guard fell naturally into a friendship, one that lasts to this day. Their dressing room was one of the bedrooms in the house where they'd muck about and blast out Steppenwolf and Led Zeppelin from their record player. As a director, Gibson found that Losey didn't so much direct Guard and himself as draw out their own naturalness, always picking up on their mannerisms and things they did. Gibson recalls one scene where everyone was having tea out on the lawn:

It was a blazing hot day. I was just about to chew on a French fancy when Losey sprang towards me, put his fingers in my mouth and snatched out this cake. And it had a wasp on it. You can die from a wasp sting.[325]

For the two boys Christie was a magical figure:

When you see somebody that's that famous you imagine them to be towering figures, but she was quite small and slight, but very charismatic. And she was a natural person. She was curious and she was friendly to people no matter what their status was. And Alan Bates was the same. There was nothing lofty about them.[326]

An occasional visitor to the set was Christie's boyfriend, Warren Beatty. The pair of them were renting a cottage on the Norfolk coast; Christie would cycle to the location every day. In their dressing room Gibson and Guard had a dart board and often played matches with Beatty, determined to beat him, despite his ignorance of the game. 'We also tried to teach him how to play cricket,' says Gibson. 'He had a good sense of humour.'[327]

After filming was complete problems arose in post-production, especially over Losey and Pinter's device of having flashforwards throughout the film. A late middle-aged Leo, played by Michael Redgrave, returns to the house, now derelict, to look back on the doomed love affair between Marian and Ted that was to shape his own life. There were arguments over whether these flashforwards made sense, but Losey and Pinter were adamant they stay. When Losey screened the picture for executives, James Aubrey was unimpressed, not disguising how bored he was by it, calling it 'the greatest still picture ever made'. With ironic bad timing, he withdrew MGM's support just days before the film won in Cannes. Columbia was only too delighted to take over.

On both sides of the Atlantic *The Go-Between* and Losey were praised. The film remains one of the directors most revered works. It is a beautiful examination of time and memory – the past is a strange place. Something like three decades later Gibson and Guard decided to pay a visit to Melton Constable Hall, just as Michael Redgrave does in the film as the older Leo:

> There was an open window and we climbed in and had a wander round. It was extraordinary because there were props left over from the film lying about. It was very atmospheric. And we went into the room that had been our dressing room and there were all these holes in the wall where we had been playing darts. And the further away these holes were the more likely they were to be Warren Beatty's.[328]

Both thought the place looked deserted but, as they left, a man appeared shouting, 'Heh, you.' Explaining how they had once made an award-winning film there cut no ice with him, 'Bugger off,' he yelled. And with a gaggle of geese reigning down on them, 'we scarpered'.[329]

(UK/US: London opening 23 September)

64 COMPANY LIMITED

(SEEMABADDHA)

Satyajit Ray is generally regarded as India's greatest director. More than any other filmmaker he articulated and interpreted the Indian way of life and, because of his gifts as a master storyteller, his work found acclaim and acceptance in the West.

Ray was an only child and came from an artistic family, both his grandfather and his father were writers and illustrators. He grew up in Calcutta (now Kolkata) and was raised by his mother after his father died when Ray was just 3. Following university, he became a commercial artist for a British company. But his great passion was the cinema and, together with some friends, Ray founded the first film club in India. By chance he heard that the great French director Jean Renoir was in Calcutta and staying in a hotel that was right next door to his advertising agency. Ray blagged his way into Renoir's suite, and they struck up a friendship. It was Renoir that encouraged Ray to follow his dream of becoming a director. Just as significant was a long business trip Ray undertook to London where most of his spare time was taken up going to the cinema; he saw over a hundred films. Upon his return to India he was determined to make his first picture.

Ray pawned his wife's jewellery and sold his precious book collection to buy film stock and hire a camera to make *Pather Panchali* (1955). Earning wide acclaim, it also formed the first part of the Apu Trilogy, along with *Aparajito* (1956) and *The World of Apu* (1959), which chronicled the life of a free-spirited child from his poverty-stricken early years in rural Bengal to his life as a young graduate in Calcutta. The films were lauded for their simplicity of narrative and are acknowledged masterworks of world cinema.

Company Limited also forms part of a trilogy, this time set in 1970s Calcutta during a time of great social and political unrest. It is no longer the city of the Apu films, a destination of learning and freedom; it is a place of violence and protest formed out of years of poverty, unemployment and social inequalities. The first film in what became known as the Calcutta Trilogy was *The Adversary* (1970), and was about a graduate looking for a job in a stagnant economy. Ray felt the next film should look at those who have the destiny of such people in their hands, the new middle and upper class that had grown up in India since independence. Ray never regarded himself as a political filmmaker, although he was always strongly critical of the executive class, and this informs much of *Company Limited*. It follows Shyamal (Barun Chanda), a young executive at a British-owned electronics firm in Calcutta, whose ambition overrides any doubts he may have about accepting the privileges remaining from colonial days and the rewards of Westernised industry. As Ray said at the time of the film's European release, 'In a sense the British have not really left. The whole intellectual middle class of India is a product of British rule.'[330]

When Shyamal's sister-in-law Tutul (Sharmila Tagore) arrives from the provinces to stay a few weeks, she is envious of the trappings her sister and Shyamal enjoy; cocktail parties, private clubs and a nice apartment, insulated from the stark realities of the city where bombings and shootings have become part of the fabric of daily life. Tutul has always admired Shyamal's idealism, and he in turn has repressed feelings for her. But everything changes when Shyamal engineers a strike at the factory to cover up a production flaw. As a result of his handling of the situation, Shyamal rises to a directorship, but loses Tutul's respect.

The film suggests that Shyamal is not inherently bad, that it is the system that makes him do the things he must if he wants to be part of affluent society. This is a theme further explored in *The Middleman* (1975), the final film in the Calcutta trilogy, and by far the bleakest in its tale of the corruption of a young man, from idealist to a businessman prepared to offer his best friend's sister to a client for a business favour. The film was made by Ray against the backdrop of national paralysis when the Congress government, led by Prime Minister Indira Gandhi, declared a state of emergency.

Taken together, this pair of trilogies amount to one of the richest imaginings of any city put onto the screen. It was a city Ray loved, it was the city of his birth and upbringing, and to which he always returned. And it was a city that came alive in his films, not merely as a backdrop but as a character in its own right.

(India: opening 24 September)

65 *MONTY PYTHON'S AND NOW FOR*

SOMETHING COMPLETELY DIFFERENT

When John Cleese bumped into Victor Lownes, the self-confessed rake and hedonist who ran the London Playboy club, he discovered the American was a big fan of Monty Python, then a current big success on the BBC. Cleese recalls:

> He'd never seen anything like it. He said to me, 'I don't think it will ever get onto American television' – in those days US TV was so conservative, so terrified of doing anything that might offend or puzzle anyone – 'but there are 2,000 college campus cinemas and, if we could get it into those, we might make a little bit of money.'[331]

Lownes's idea was to reshoot the best sketches from the first two series onto 35mm and release it as a film – a sort of 'greatest hits' package. The prospect of working in the cinema certainly appealed to the Pythons, as did the lucrative prospect of breaking America. Ian MacNaughton, who was in charge of the TV shows, was drafted in to direct.

With an extremely limited budget of around £80,000, the Pythons made do with a studio converted from a closed milk dairy in Totteridge, north London. 'It had these huge indoor areas and offices which we used as locations,' recalls Eric Idle. 'And we played five-a-side football all the time. It was great.'[332]

The limited funds affected all aspects of the production, as director of photography David Muir remembers:

> It meant we did not have the benefit of many paid extras, nor a big enough crew to control crowds in the street, so we just had to shoot in public as best we could. I was amazed how little notice passers-by took of the team's antics – such as with killer babies and murderous grannies.[333]

Filmed during the cold and bleak winter of 1970, the Pythons arrived at the dairy in the morning in pitch black and left in the evening in pitch black. 'By the end of four weeks I was more tired than I'd ever been,' complains Cleese.[334] It was enough to quash any thoughts he might have had of wanting to direct, since MacNaughton was always there an hour before everyone else and stayed at least an hour after everyone had left.

Having taken two months' unpaid leave from the BBC, this turned out to be MacNaughton's first and only cinema feature. 'He'd be fine in the mornings,' recalls Idle, 'and then he'd go to the pub and get shit-faced and go for a nap after lunch so we just carried on shooting.'[335] Things actually ran a little bit smoother without MacNaughton, since Terry Jones could do what he felt had to be done. 'Both Terry Jones and Terry Gilliam had always been itching to direct,' says Idle, 'especially Jonesy, who'd done a BBC directors' course and was always telling Ian where to put the camera. And so, there was a conflict.'[336]

Conflict came from Lownes too. The American wasn't around for the actual shoot very much; instead, he made his presence felt in post-production. For example, he hated one of the characters Michael Palin played, Ken Shabby, a smelly, unshaven individual dressed in a brown mackintosh, with a continuous hacking cough and sinister leer. Lownes found him repellent (that was the point) and the sketch he was featured in was removed.

Lownes also had a problem with the running time of 100 minutes. Reportedly Woody Allen had told him that comedy movies should never run for more than ninety minutes. Lownes organised an afternoon screening at an Odeon cinema in Hendon, advertised as: 'A sneak pre-view of a new British comedy.' 'So, the audience, mainly elderly people, were expecting something like the broad humour of the *Carry On* series,' recalls Muir, 'not the more sophisticated, rather undergraduate humour of the Monty Python team.'[337]

A sound recording was made of the audience reaction: 'Laughter being initially quite slow to catch on,' according to Muir, 'but greatly improved as the audience twigged this type of humour.'[338] Lownes then did something truly bizarre. He instructed the editor that, in order to shorten the running time, he should run the audience reaction soundtrack in parallel with the film and cut out all the bits where nobody laughed. Muir recalls:

There was a stunned silence in the editing room, until Thom Noble, the editor, had the courage to say, 'Well, that's an original idea! A film entirely of gag-lines, without any of the lead-ins! That should empty the cinemas.' In the end a couple of the weaker sketches were deleted to bring it down to ninety minutes.[339]

Thanks to the low budget, *And Now for Something Completely Different* recouped its costs in the UK market. However, Lownes's hope that it would score on the US college circuit and help break Python in America fell flat. It wasn't until 1974, when public service television began broadcasting the show, that the Pythons earned a cult appreciation, and the film was successfully reissued.

Ultimately the Pythons themselves were disappointed. 'I don't think the filmed versions were any better than the TV versions,' says Jones. 'I don't really put it in the canon of Python films.'[340] One lesson they learnt was a desire to retain creative control in the future. Idle reveals:

> Lownes never gave us the final cut. I think there were various arguments over the cuts, and we were pretty largely ignored. *And Now for Something Completely Different* was more a passage for us to get into movies. It showed us we could make films, but next time we'd have to direct it ourselves.[341]

Looking at the film today, it probably works better than it did back in 1971, as a standalone record of some of Python's best sketches from 'The Lumberjack Song' to the classic Parrot Sketch, Twit of the Year, Nudge, Nudge and many others. It really does play like a 'greatest hits' album.

(UK: London release 28 September)

66 THE LAST MOVIE

After the enormous success of *Easy Rider*, the world was waiting to see what its star and director Dennis Hopper was going to do next. *The Last Movie* is a parable about the impact of a visiting Hollywood film crew on a South American village. It was something Hooper personally experienced years before when he did a western with John Wayne in Durango, Mexico. Hopper plays a disillusioned stuntman who falls in love with a local woman and chooses to remain behind when the film unit leave. He is then disturbed to see that the villagers have succumbed to a kind of group hysteria and start making their own movie on the abandoned sets, unable to determine what is real and what is fantasy.

The film was shot down in Peru and, no sooner had the crew landed, they managed to score some cocaine. On location crew members were openly sniffing, smoking and dropping acid. 'That whole shoot was one of the most out-of-control situations I've ever seen,' recalls L.M. Kit Carson, who was there putting together a documentary about Hopper.[342]

In the middle of it all was Hopper himself, his talent blunted by drink and drugs, with an ego that threatened to destroy his career. Young singer Kris Kristofferson, hired by Hopper to appear in his first film role, recalled that at the time, 'Dennis was the most self-destructive guy I had ever seen!'[343] Hopper also gave a screen debut to Michelle Phillips, of The Mamas and the Papas. To give an indication of the kind of atmosphere going on, Hopper and Phillips fell in love and married. The union lasted all of eight days.

Physically drained after the shoot, Hopper faced the monumental task of editing the picture in the spring of 1970. He did this in a house he'd just bought in Taos, New Mexico, away from any Hollywood interference. His dream was to build a commune there, a hang-out for artists. There were a lot of dropouts and hangers-on there, too, ingesting industrial levels of drugs. Screenwriter Tom Mankiewicz, who knew and liked Hopper, was a visitor. 'Everybody was just blotto. You thought, everybody in this house is going to die.'[344]

It was a weird existence at Taos, then probably the last vestige of the 1960s left on the planet. 'Actually, Dennis was the perfect host for you to experience the '60s with,' claims L.M. Kit Carson. 'It was like the final scenes of *Withnail and I* where they're trying to count down the end of the '60s but they really can't.'[345]

The editing job Hopper faced was daunting, turning forty hours of raw footage into a coherent two-hour movie. It was taking months and months. The suits in Hollywood got nervous; whenever they called up asking for a progress report Hopper cursed and ranted down the phone at them. When they showed up in person, he'd ignore them. They even sent down a spy to infiltrate the commune and report back what was going on; Hopper turned him into a drug courier. Six months later Hopper was still cutting the movie; friends thought he'd never finish it, that he'd have a nervous breakdown first.

Finally, it was ready, but things didn't look good. This was not going to be another *Easy Rider*. What resulted, depending on your point of view, was either a massive ego trip or an audacious piece of experimental filmmaking. The Universal executives reacted to it with a mixture of bafflement, disillusionment and plain shock. One executive pondered whether the film reels had been shown in the correct order. Indeed, some sequences had been deliberately shown out of order without explanation. Hopper employs other filmmaking quirks, such as choppy editing, flashbacks and flashforwards, and at one point a blank screen with the words 'missing scene' scratched onto the film stock.

In no mood to recut the film into a more commercial and coherent form, Hopper stole a print and showed it at the Venice Film Festival, where it won the Critics Prize. That cut no ice at Universal. One executive merely assumed they'd paid for it to win. At the first test screening for the public, at the University of Iowa, Hopper was booed and jeered. Afterwards a female student, outraged by the film's explicit sex scenes, punched Hopper on the nose calling him a 'sexist fucking pig'.

The critics didn't much care for it either. Roger Ebert called it 'a wasteland of cinematic wreckage'. One even expressed a fear that, because Hopper had been given 'a virtual artistic blank cheque' and gone bat-shit crazy, future independent filmmakers would be limited in their opportunities from the big studios. Other critics, while disliking the film, did at least give a grudging acknowledgement of the sheer audacity of Hopper's filmmaking choices. That didn't do any good. After playing in New York briefly, then LA, and a few places in between, *The Last Movie* was pulled from distribution. Its failure put paid to any other directorial projects Hopper had on the go. It also proved a huge setback in personal terms. Hopper wouldn't direct another film for nine years.

The Last Movie pretty much faded from view for many years. Today it's seen as a counterculture classic.

(US: New York opening 29 September)

67 KOTCH

The partnership between Jack Lemmon and Walter Matthau is one of the most cherished in cinema. They appeared in ten films in all, starting with *The Fortune Cookie* in 1966, and were close friends off-screen too. Lemmon's son Chris said that in Matthau his father found the brother he'd always wanted.

Kotch is the odd one out in that series: Matthau stars but Lemmon doesn't, unless you count a brief cameo at the end, disguised with a moustache and glasses. Instead, Lemmon directs for the first and only time in his career. Like a lot of actors, Lemmon had for years held an ambition to direct. The chance came when his former press agent, Richard Carter, sent him a script that he hoped to produce called *Kotch*, about a 72-year-old widower determined not to act his age. Indignantly resisting his son's attempts to settle him in an old folks' home, he instead forms an unlikely friendship with a pregnant teenage runaway.

Carter saw Spencer Tracy in the role, but when the veteran actor died finance for the project dissipated. That's when he sent the script to Lemmon, to seek his professional advice. Lemmon loved it, especially the character of Kotch; here was a guy who felt young from the neck up. Recognising that it would be wrong to try and play an old man, Lemmon asked Carter about the possibility of directing the film.

With Tracy gone, thoughts turned to other veteran stars. Hopes of luring either James Cagney or Cary Grant out of retirement failed, before Lemmon approached Fredric March, who accepted, only to withdraw due to ill health when no one would insure him. Late one evening Lemmon got a call from Matthau asking if he'd cast the part of the old man yet and, if he hadn't, he'd like to do it. This despite the fact Matthau hadn't even read the script. His wife Carol had just come in from a night out with Lemmon and his wife Felicia and, after hearing them talk about the film, urged Matthau to make the call. Usually, Carol never gave an opinion on her husband's work, after telling him not to make *The Odd Couple* because it sounded rubbish. This time her judgement proved sound. Kotch ended up one of Matthau's most rewarding roles, and earned him a Best Actor Oscar nomination.

Even though Matthau was only in his early 50s, his craggy and lived-in face lent itself well to the ageing make-up process. But *Kotch* was always going to be a tough sell in a Hollywood that was chasing the counterculture dollar. Would they be interested in a story about a pensioner? The answer was no – every studio passed. In the end Carter and Lemmon made a deal with ABC Pictures, who provided the meagre $1.6 million budget. To keep costs low, friends and family were roped in both behind and in front of the camera. For instance, Lemmon's wife, Felicia Farr, played Kotch's daughter-in-law.

Cast as the teenage runaway, Erica, was a young actress called Deborah Winters. Still only 17, Winters had been acting since her early teens and making *Kotch* was 'two months of FUN! And I felt I understood the role of Erica very well. I enjoyed playing her.'[346] She used to call Matthau 'Waltz' and found him wonderful to work with:

> He had a terrific sense of humour, and was an expert on opera. He knew every opera ever written and all of the opera singers, as well.

He also taught me to always leave your trailer door open. He said that way, no one can ever lie about what you were doing inside your trailer.[347]

After years of friendship and working together, Lemmon and Matthau knew each other so well that they could almost anticipate how the other was going to react or behave. 'You're not going to tell me how to act, are you?' Matthau joked on the first day of filming, and Lemmon didn't really need to. Winters remembers:

Although Jack used to pull me aside and whisper to me that I should make a mistake in my dialogue if I ever felt Waltz was beginning to go overboard or ad-lib too much. I did, but didn't need to often. Jack was not a confrontive person, so kind of made me the bad guy once in a while.[348]

In the end Matthau's performance expertly avoids the mawkish sentimentality that usually pervades this kind of film. Lemmon's directorial debut was less well received by critics. Winters says:

Jack said it was the most work he ever had to do on a film. He said being an actor was much easier and lots more fun! But he was very easy to work with because he certainly understood an actor's insecurities and egos.[349]

Kotch did reasonably well at the box office, trading as it did on the Lemmon/Matthau partnership. They even appear as themselves in the film's amusing trailer.

(US: New York opening 30 September)

 ## 68 *THE LAST PICTURE SHOW*

Peter Bogdanovich was in a store glancing through a rack of paperbacks when one particular title caught his eye, *The Last Picture Show*. He turned it over to read the blurb on the back. It was about teenagers growing up in Texas; 'no thanks,' he thought, and put it back.

A couple of months later Bogdanovich's friend, the actor Sal Mineo, gave him the same book, saying how it would make a good movie. It lay around Bogdanovich's house for a while until he asked his wife, Polly Platt, a production designer, to give it a quick read. Her enthusiasm for the book made Bogdanovich finally give it a try.

At the time Bogdanovich was slated to direct a film for BBS on the strength of his impressive 1968 debut feature *Targets*. However, after a few meetings Bogdanovich was seen as too much of a square to fit in; offered some grass Bogdanovich had politely declined, saying he didn't do it. Then again, maybe that's what the company needed, a steady head rather than the crazy antics of a Dennis Hooper. Bogdanovich was in and suggested doing *The Last Picture Show*.

A bittersweet coming-of-age story, *The Last Picture Show* is set in a small Texan town during the early 1950s and follows a group of friends as they face the usual adolescent problems of parents, sex and the limitations of life in the sticks. After collaborating with the book's author Larry McMurtry on a screenplay, Bogdanovich began the process of looking for his cast. It was in another store that he happened to glance at the photograph of a stunning girl on the cover of a magazine. Buying the magazine, he gave it to his assistant with instructions to find out who she was. It was Cybill Shepherd. A model at the time, Shepherd had never acted before and was somewhat ambivalent about a career in movies. But she liked the script and wanted to play the role of Jacy Farrow, the glamorous daughter of a well-to-do family. During shooting Bogdanovich began an affair with the actress – a bit tricky since his wife Polly was the film's production designer. The two fell in love and began a highly publicised relationship that lasted for most of the 1970s.

For the two young male leads Bogdanovich cast Jeff Bridges, after being impressed with him at a general casting call, and Timothy Bottoms. For the pivotal role of Sam the Lion, who owns pretty much the only popular amenities in town – the diner, the pool hall and a run-down cinema set to close (hence the title) – Bogdanovich's first and only choice was the veteran western actor Ben Johnson. The problem was Johnson didn't want to do it – too many lines to learn he said, and too much coarse language. Even a phone call from director John Ford, who discovered the actor, failed to convince him. Exasperated, Bogdanovich told Johnson that if he played the role he'd get an Academy Award, or at least a nomination. This did the trick. Johnson did indeed go on to win an Oscar for Best Supporting Actor.

Something really noticeable about the film today is how many outstanding roles there are for women. Ellen Burstyn, Cloris Leachman and

Eileen Brennan all give beautifully judged performances. Leachman was to claim the Oscar for Best Supporting Actress, playing an embittered and lonely housewife.

Once assembled, the cast gathered for a week of rehearsals in Los Angeles before arriving on location in Archer City, Texas. Called Anarene in the film, Archer City was Larry McMurtry's hometown and where he based his semi-autobiographical novel. Some of the people McMurtry based his characters on still lived there and won small roles in the film or helped out. During filming the young cast became a tight-knit unit, spending a lot of time together, something encouraged by Bogdanovich to help with their performances.

Ultimately this is a bleak drama, one with a fine sense of period and place that evokes a lost era. Much of that is down to the excellent cinematography of Robert Surtees and the decision by Bogdanovich to shoot in black and white, on the recommendation of his friend Orson Welles. This was a brave and uncommercial choice, backed by BBS, something one doubts a major studio would have done. There's no traditional music score either; instead Bogdanovich uses songs from the period, which we hear, usually in the distance, on jukeboxes, record players and radios.

The Last Picture Show is widely regarded as one of the seminal American films of the 1970s. It garnered eight Oscar nominations and helped launch a new generation of stars, notably Bridges, Shepherd and Burstyn. It was also Bogdanovich's breakthrough film, and he was lauded as a major discovery. *Newsweek* acclaimed the picture to be 'The most impressive work by a young American director since *Citizen Kane*'.

In 1987, McMurtry published *Texasville*, his sequel to *The Last Picture Show*, which picked up the lives of his characters in 1984. Bogdanovich's film of the novel was released in 1990 and featured many of the same actors.

(US: New York opening 3 October)

69 *BLANCHE*

Walerian Borowczyk was a Polish director described by critics as a 'genius who also happened to be a pornographer'. His most infamous picture was 1975's *The Beast*, a corruption of the traditional *Beauty and the Beast* tale. Due to its erotic content and scenes of bestiality, the British censor refused it a general cinema release and one London cinema narrowly avoided prosecution for showing it.

The son of a railway worker, Borowczyk studied painting at the Academy of Fine Arts in Krakow and entered the movie business in 1955 designing posters. With another graphic artist, Jan Lenica, he began to make critically lauded and award-winning animation. After a series of short films Borowczyk moved into features in 1968. *Blanche* was only the third movie he directed, but it's perhaps his most lyrical, stunningly photographed and performed. Set in thirteenth-century France, Blanche is the young, beautiful wife to an ageing, almost senile, baron who keeps her heavily guarded in his secluded castle. They are visited by an amorous king, along with his page and the baron's son, and Blanche's unassuming and quiet life is turned upside down when these three new arrivals begin lusting after her.

Borowczyk prepared the film meticulously, using storyboards and designs, along with medieval paintings as references. His fine arts background shows in the beautiful compositions that lend the picture the look of a tapestry or medieval art. The film has been cited as a key inspiration in the work of directors like Terry Gilliam.

Borowczyk gave the celebrated Swiss actor Michel Simon one of his final roles, as the baron. Then in his mid-70s, Simon was best known for his performance in Jean Renoir's 1932 classic *Boudu Saved from Drowning*. As the king, veteran French actor Georges Wilson was cast. The real bone of contention came with who should play Blanche. Borowczyk insisted it be his wife, Polish actress Ligia Branice, but the backers would have preferred a marquee name and Jacques Perrin, who had been cast as the king's servant and put money into the film, wanted to approach Catherine Deneuve. Borowczyk would not budge. This led to some ill feeling and on the first day of filming: Perrin, still unhappy with the choice of Branice, halted production. Locks were put on the studio. This impasse lasted a whole two weeks. Work was allowed to continue, but there remained resentment towards Branice by some of her fellow actors who gossiped that she was only in the film because she was the director's wife. Despite creating tension and bad feeling on the set, Borowczyk was ultimately proved correct: Branice delivers a memorable and heart-rending performance.

Some of the actors were also thrown by Borowczyk's working methods, that he didn't give much instruction, basically left them to their own devices, only telling them what they'd done wrong if a take had to be redone. He didn't much care for delegation either, taking on numerous tasks himself. Assistant director Patrice Leconte came on the set one morning and noticed someone up a ladder repainting some of the scenery; it was Borowczyk. The director also created many of the strange props used in the film, such as a crucifix that turns into a dagger and a bible with a secret compartment for hiding a vial of poison. He clearly had his own way of doing things and, when it came to his vision for the film, he was stubborn. Michel Simon had a blazing row with him once on the set, but Borowczyk stood there like a brick wall, unmoveable.

On its initial release *Blanche* did not find an audience, but its critical reputation has grown over the years. Made on a tight budget, the film's beauty belies its humble origins. The musical score is memorable too, with its use of period instruments and musical arrangements drawn from the medieval *Carmina Burana* songbook; it was years ahead of its time.

Blanche began Borowczyk's series of erotic and decorative period pieces – films such as *Immoral Tales* (1973) and *Behind Convent Walls* (1978), which gained him a reputation as an art-porn auteur. While films like *Blanche* and his animated shorts had won him the admiration of critics, this interest in erotic cinema quickly alienated many of his former supporters, finally eroding any critical standing he may have had. Borowczyk reached the nadir of his career in 1987, when he agreed to helm *Emmanuelle 5*.

(Italy: Sanremo Film Festival opening 4 October)

70 | *THE FRENCH CONNECTION*

This is the film that put William Friedkin on the movie map and made Gene Hackman a star. One of the great police/crime movies of all time, shot with an almost documentary realism that influenced countless future movies and TV cop shows, *The French Connection* fully deserved to win the Best Picture Oscar; Friedkin also won, as did Hackman for Best Actor.

It's also one of the great New York movies. Today it's an extraordinary time capsule of a seedy and crumbling city that no longer exists. Production assistant Ralph Singleton states:

New York was a tough town. If you look at Wards Island, where we filmed the final shootout, all that was real. They weren't sets that were constructed and cosmetically done. A lot of that was the real look of New York. In the Bronx in the '70s, it was like Dresden. It was very bleak.[350]

The French Connection is based on a real case when New York detectives Eddie Egan and Sonny Grosso confiscated a massive horde of heroin smuggled in from France. The mastermind behind the drug ring, a French businessman, managed to escape. The remarkable story was told in a 1969 book by Robin Moore.

For something like six months before he shot a single frame of film, Friedkin rode around with Egan and Grosso, soaking up the mean streets of Brooklyn and Harlem, watching people shoot up on the pavement and sometimes hearing the crackle of nearby gunfire. To take on the roles of these two cops, whose names were changed in the film, Friedkin cast Gene Hackman and Roy Scheider. Friedkin and Hackman didn't have the greatest of relationships; there were regular conflicts and arguments on set, primarily due to Hackman's unease with the darker aspects of Egan's character – his racist views and tough, no-nonsense methods. At one point, Hackman quit, only to be talked into returning by his agent.

As for the villains, French actor Fernando Rey was cast as Alain Charnier, dubbed 'Frog One' by the detectives, and Tony Lo Bianco played a mobster and key component in bringing in the drug shipment. Friedkin had seen Lo Bianco in *The Honeymoon Killers* (1970) and the actor was also good friends with Grosso. Lo Bianco reveals:

> I used to travel with the police in New York and understood the grittiness of the streets, and the behaviour of the criminals. I had a great friendship with Sonny Grosso, and the rest of the cops on the film. We became one big family.[351]

Lo Bianco didn't know Hackman:

> But I found him to be absolutely wonderful and, of course, a great talent. Roy Scheider was an old buddy of mine. We had done five different projects together by the time we were cast for this movie and Roy, God rest his soul, was always wonderful.[352]

Smartly, Friedkin cast real cops in small roles to add an air of authenticity to the picture. 'You felt the reality of the characters because some of them were playing themselves,' says Singleton.[353] Both Eddie Egan and Grosso also make cameo appearances and were technical advisers.

The centrepiece of the film is, of course, the now legendary car chase. Friedkin makes it that much more exciting because it isn't your standard chase; Hackman is in a car, the baddie is in an elevated train. Singleton recalls they shot the sequence along something like twenty to thirty blocks in Brooklyn, with the unit having to block a section at a time. 'That first Pontiac that you see, by the time Hackman gets out of that car he's either in the fourth or the fifth Pontiac. We destroyed the rest in that scene.'[354]

Bill Hickman was the stunt co-ordinator on the film and drove for Hackman, although the actor was an excellent driver and did a lot of it himself. 'The daringness of Friedkin to shoot that with total abandonment,' says Lo Bianco, 'and the excellent driving of Hickman, made that for me the most exciting chase scene I'd ever seen.'[355]

Friedkin made the whole film on his own idiosyncratic terms. 'He was very sure of himself,' says Lo Bianco. 'He definitely ruled the film.'[356] The documentary-style cinematography was raw and ragged and a deliberate choice. Singleton doesn't recall one set being built for the film; it was all done on location. Take for example the auction house where the criminals buy a car to put the drugs in. 'That was a real auction house,' says Singleton. 'And the guy who was the auctioneer was I believe a real auctioneer.'[357]

With the film being shot in the winter of 1970/71, the weather was brutal, one of the coldest in recent memory. You can see the breath coming out of the actors' mouths and them stomping on the ground to keep warm. 'Gene Hackman deserved the Academy Award just for the weather,' jokes Singleton. 'He was a real pro.'[358]

Among the last bits of filming done was the famous scene where the cops rip apart a Lincoln car, convinced the heroin is hidden inside. This was shot at the actual police garage. 'And the older guy who says, "maybe it's in the rocker panels," was the guy who worked in the police garage,' says Singleton.[359]

Completed, the Lincoln was sent to the docks to be shipped out to France for some filming to be done on it. After a week, the car was still at the docks, so Singleton went down to find out what was happening. When he arrived, they all looked at him: 'Oh, so you're the guy with the Lincoln.' It turned out that the inspectors had found something alarming inside. Back when the unit finished filming, one of the detectives borrowed the car for the weekend. Singleton reveals:

The other cops decided to play a trick on him, and they threw a bunch of gun casings in the trunk and a couple of heroin bags. Obviously when the inspectors at the dock opened the trunk they went, holy god, and tore the car apart trying to find what else was in there. Then they put it back together again and waited for somebody to ask about the car. Then I show up.[360]

Ironically, what had happened to the car in the movie happened to it in real life. Singleton got the producer on the phone to convince the guys that it was a movie car. 'But they were still pissed off and said, "When this car comes back, we're going to tear it apart again."'[361] What they didn't know was the car had already been sold to someone in France and they never saw it again.

(US: New York opening 7 October)

71 WAKE IN FRIGHT

This savage and hard-hitting drama, which Australian singer Nick Cave once described as 'The best and most terrifying film about Australia in existence', was a hit at the Cannes Film Festival, only to fade into obscurity for the next thirty years. By the 1990s only bootleg versions existed, or faded and battered prints; the original negative was thought to be lost. Miraculously it was to be discovered in a warehouse in bins marked for destruction. An Australian film masterpiece had been saved from being lost forever.

Australian author Kenneth Cook's 1961 novel *Wake in Fright* told the story of John Grant, a young schoolteacher who has to make a short stopover in a tough mining town before heading on to Sydney. It didn't take long for people to work out that Cook had based his town on a real place, Broken Hill, a frontier mining town in the far west of New South Wales, in the Australian outback. Cook once had the misfortune to stay there and witnessed the heavily masculine culture of drinking, game shooting and gambling. It left such an impression that he was to later describe Broken Hill as an 'unmitigated boil of horror'.

The film rights to Cook's novel were bought in the early 1960s by Dirk Bogarde and Joseph Losey, who hoped to adapt it to the screen after their successful collaboration on *The Servant*. In the end they couldn't find suitable finance and the project died. The idea to bring the book to the screen was resurrected in 1969, and the unusual choice of director was Canadian Ted Kotcheff, who had primarily worked in television. He would make a big splash a little over a decade later when he made the first Rambo film, *First Blood* (1982). Many thought a Canadian, who knew very little about Australia and its culture before stepping off the plane at the airport, was not qualified to make a film out of what had become a seminal Australian novel. But after reading the script and the book Kotcheff felt Australia wasn't really any different to Canada, a massive country with a dispersed population and miles and miles of empty space.

The crew had decided to film all the exterior scenes at Broken Hill itself. 'That was an extraordinary place,' says Peter Hannan.[362] Hannan had just finished working on *Walkabout* when he was asked to stay on in Australia and work on the camera team for *Wake in Fright*. Hannan was himself Australian and had worked as a newsreel cameraman before moving to England. He found Broken Hill ultra-conservative: 'Books in bookshops were censored; you'd come across four or five blank pages. Indeed, Australia as a country was very conservative. When I arrived to work on *Walkabout* my wife's copy of *Lady Chatterley's Lover* was confiscated.'[363]

For the role of Grant, the schoolteacher, Kotcheff first tried to persuade Michael York, before casting another English actor, the much less well-known Gary Bond, who was largely a stage actor. As for the crucial part of Doc Tydon, the town's alcoholic doctor who attempts to acclimatise Grant to the ways, both good and bad, largely bad, of the local populace, Kotcheff brought in Donald Pleasence, who arrived in Sydney with a scraggly beard and a note-perfect accent. 'Working with Donald Pleasence was a real honour,' says Hannan. 'You knew you were in the presence of greatness. He was wonderful. And he became the unit cook.'[364] Towards the end of the shoot at Broken Hill there were personal issues at the motel the cast and crew stayed at, resulting in nobody being around to cook the food. And so Pleasence stepped into the breach. 'He did the evening meals,' says Hannan. 'His wife served at the table while Donald was cooking away. It was wonderful.'[365]

Interior work on the film was completed in Sydney. One large set was the recreation of a bar in Broken Hill. Kotcheff had cast the legendary Australian actor Chips Rafferty, then 61, as the local chief cop. It was to be his last film role. 'He was a total professional,' recalls Hannan. 'Except he wouldn't touch the non-alcoholic beer that the extras were all drinking. Donald was the same, he insisted on the real stuff.'[366]

The film's most controversial sequence is a kangaroo hunt, so vividly and grotesquely described in Cook's novel. Because Kotcheff did not want any animals destroyed especially for his film, the only solution was to shoot a real hunt that was going to be killing kangaroos anyway. Most of the crew were shocked and disturbed by what they saw. Hannan was taken off it, so sickened that he wanted nothing to do with it. 'I wasn't invited to the shoot that night, and I'm glad I wasn't.'[367]

Wake in Fright made its bow in Cannes, and Kotcheff never forgot the screening. For the entire duration of the film the man seated directly behind him was giving a sort of running commentary about how much he was enjoying it, pointing out its various merits, gasping at certain points too. He couldn't keep quiet. Afterwards Kotcheff pointed the man out to a colleague and asked who it was. It turned out to be a young American director by the name of Martin Scorsese.

When it opened in Sydney, *Wake in Fright* did not go down well with home audiences. 'The Australians didn't like it,' says Hannan. 'They said that it didn't represent them properly. They said they weren't that sort of people. They were out in Broken Hill, certainly.'[368]

Then the film seemed to vanish. And there was concern that the negative might have been lost. In the mid-1990s the film's editor, Anthony Buckley, began a personal mission to track it down, spending years following clue after clue. In 1998, he tracked the negative to a bonded warehouse in London, only to find on his arrival that the materials had been shipped to the USA just days earlier. Finally in 2002 he came across them in a Pittsburgh warehouse about to be destroyed. Over the course of the next two years the footage was digitally restored.

Along with *Walkabout*, *Wake in Fright* is a seminal picture in the revival of the Australian film industry that had lain mostly dormant since the end of the Second World War, and one that helped inspire a whole new wave of Australian filmmakers such as Fred Schepisi, Peter Weir and Bruce Beresford.

(Aus/UK/US: Sydney opening 8 October)

72 | *PUNISHMENT PARK*

The early 1970s was a traumatic time in the USA. The war in Vietnam was escalating, there was political polarisation and public unrest, especially on college campuses. The infamous Kent State University shootings, where four unarmed university students were shot dead by the National Guard, occurred in May 1970, just two months before President Nixon declared a state of emergency.

Into this maelstrom came British filmmaker Peter Watkins, best known for his unflinching BBC drama-documentary *The War Game*, depicting the aftermath of nuclear conflict. Watkins had come to America to produce a series of historical documentaries for television, but when that project fell through, he decided to stay in the country, shocked by the events at Kent State. His new aim was to put together an independent film that tried to make sense of what was happening. The result was a highly effective and deeply unsettling psychodrama that continues to shock to this day.

The idea of *Punishment Park* came about after Watkins's discovery of a piece of legislation called the McCarran Internal Security Act of 1950. This provided legislative powers to arrest and detain those accused of subversion by the government. Watkins speculated what might happen if Nixon enforced the McCarran Act against members of the anti-war or Black Power movements, or perhaps draft dodgers and other dissident groups. He envisaged the idea of government-run punishment parks set up to control the growing number of radical political activists, as well as the problems of overcrowded prisons. These parks could also act as field training facilities for law enforcement officers having to quell the rise in protests.

Once they arrive at these parks, following sentencing, dissidents are given an option – either confinement in a federal prison or the promise of liberty if they can evade pursuing police officers for three days to reach an American flag set up on a hill some 50 miles across the California desert. *Hunger Games* anyone? Watkins's film cuts between the desert and a large military tent on the edge of the park where the next group of dissidents are being judged and sentenced by an emergency civilian tribunal.

Watkins shot his film in the San Bernadino desert, about 60 miles from Los Angeles. The whole thing was captured by a handheld 16mm camera operated by Joan Churchill. As she recalls:

> Peter Watkins wanted the film to look like it was shot by a news crew, with Peter playing the reporter. His instructions to me were to 'crash zoom and find focus'. After viewing some of the rushes, Peter felt my shooting was too steady, so he would come up and jostle me in the middle of shooting.[369]

He also worked with the 'actors' before he brought them before Churchill's camera:

That way, I would have no idea what to expect; so the film really was shot as if it were vérité. If we did a second take, Peter would change something so that I would be caught off guard. He did not want the camera to anticipate the action. This added to the verisimilitude.[370]

The crew numbered no more than ten, and the whole thing was completed in under three weeks. With only a few exceptions, none of the cast had acted before, and for the most part they were playing themselves. 'Ex-cops and vets alongside peaceniks and hippies; Black Panthers mixing it up with white liberals and working-class people,' says Churchill. 'It made for really intense lunch breaks!'[371]

After its screening at the New York Film Festival, some American critics took umbrage with Watkins's perceived one-sided political views. *The New York Times* called his film 'The wish-fulfilling dream of a masochist'. Others just labelled it evil in the way it depicted America as a totally fascist state. A select few were more balanced, calling it a devastating indictment and a chilling prognosis of what might happen in America within the next five years. *Rolling Stone* voted *Punishment Park* one of the ten best films of the year.

Opening in a small cinema in the financial district of Manhattan, it was already clear to Watkins that the US distributor was not going to properly handle his film. 'It remains unclear whether the cinema owner (or the distributor) was affected by the hostile critics,' said Watkins, 'or whether the federal authorities issued threats.'[372] In any case, *Punishment Park* was withdrawn from the cinema after only four days. Since then, according to Watkins, the film has rarely been shown in the USA, and never on television. He was to recall a representative of a main Hollywood studio, when given the chance to release *Punishment Park*, saying he could never show the film because he would have the sheriff's office on their necks in five minutes.

Punishment Park was better received in countries like Britain and France when it opened early in 1972. Still, screenings of it were limited. In 2005 the film was shown at the ICA in London as part of a retrospective of Watkins's work, where it underwent a positive critical reappraisal and attained a new and horrible relevance in the post-9/11 world of Guantanamo Bay and the war on terror. What Watkins regarded as a metaphor for the social and political conditions of the USA at one of its most turbulent points in history had strayed into reality. Interestingly, on its initial release some people who saw the film came out believing that such things as punishment parks really did exist.

(UK/US: New York Film Festival screening 11 October)

73 | *TWINS OF EVIL*

In 1970 Hammer served up a heady brew of fangs and sex with *The Vampire Lovers*, based on the 1872 Sheridan Le Fanu novella *Carmilla* and starring Ingrid Pitt. With its somewhat daring exploration of lesbian themes, *The Vampire Lovers* was the first of Hammer's Karnstein Trilogy. *Lust for a Vampire* and *Twins of Evil* followed in 1971, and *Twins* is by far the more enjoyable slice of late gothic Hammer.

The novelty of the film is undeniably the casting of the Collinson twins, Madeleine and Mary, who gained notoriety as the first identical twins to pose for *Playboy* magazine. Born in Malta, they were both models and had made small film appearances before Hammer snapped them up. They play, unsurprisingly, twins – one innocent, one not so – terrorised by the vampiric Count Karnstein, played by RADA-trained Damien Thomas. Thomas recalls:

> In those days I was only just 6ft in shoes, and height was an important aspect of the casting. So, before my interview I went to the loo and stuffed folded up toilet paper in my heels and came back to be measured against a doorway and behold I was over 6ft and got the part.[373]

Having not made a film before, Thomas essentially had to learn on the job. He did that largely watching the vastly experienced Peter Cushing – 'Just watching what he did. Watching him in front of the camera.'[374] *Twins of Evil* was the first film Cushing made after the death of his beloved wife Helen, and it was obvious that here was a man totally broken by what had happened and was still grieving dreadfully. 'He was in a very bad state,' confirms Thomas. 'He was in deep mourning. He didn't say a word to me throughout filming, except good morning, that was about as much as I got out of him, he was pretty untalkative.'[375]

Judy Matheson recalls being told not to joke around Cushing too much. 'I met a different Peter Cushing to the one that he may have been before, or even much later. He was much more serious with me. And yet he was so lovely, very gentle and considerate.'[376] Cushing plays

Gustav Weil, a hard, cold man who is the leader of a clan of puritans ridding their village of supposed witches. His performance terrified Matheson, who plays an innocent girl confronted by Weil and his followers in the opening scene:

> When he burst through the door and rips the necklace off me and starts all that intoning business, holding his hands up, he was literally terrifying and that made it easy for a young actress to play the scene; I really believed the whole thing. I remember those moments very vividly. Peter was a fine actor. He had this evil look on his face, having just a few minutes before been this gentle, quiet man.[377]

Matheson's character is then burnt at the stake before the film even starts. 'They took tremendous care over that scene,' she recalls. 'A fire officer was on hand the whole time.' Coming as she did from theatre, Matheson enjoyed getting to play something a bit dramatic:

> And I did get caught up in the moment. And I had to scream for a long time because the director John Hough was going to put the credits over it. After they finished the shot, I got a round of applause from the crew.[378]

As usual with Hammer, the supporting cast is solid. David Warbeck is the dashing hero, and playing Weil's loyal wife was Kathleen Byron, so memorable as the nun that rebels in Powell and Pressburger's *Black Narcissus* (1947). For Thomas, a highlight of working on the film were the scenes he shared with Dennis Price. 'We had lunch together most days in the restaurant at Pinewood and people were constantly coming up to say words to him. Dennis was an absolute charmer but very subdued.'[379] At the time Price was seriously ill, the effects of years of alcohol abuse. 'He took me into his dressing room one day,' recalls Thomas, 'and opened a drawer, and there were rows and rows of bottles of Guinness. He didn't drink the hard stuff anymore because he'd been told it would kill him.'[380]

Filming went smoothly. Thomas recalls going to a dentist to have his fangs made to measure. They got through quite a bit of work and at one point broke when Thomas bit down on an actress's breast. 'They glued them back together.'[381] As for the grand climax, when Thomas's vampire is slain, it took a day to shoot his decomposition into dust. 'I kept having to go to make-up for the next stage and somebody bashed a nail into the set, and I rested my head against so I stayed in the same position.'[382]

As for the Collinson twins, quite a few of the crew tried to ask them out. Stunt legend Vic Armstrong worked on the film and recalls a mate of his going on a date with one of them. 'I couldn't believe it. I was so jealous.'[383] Still relatively new to the movie business, it was on *Twins of Evil* that Armstrong first saw the use of prosthetics. In one scene a man got his arm chopped off and the production used a real amputee, stuck a false arm on him, nailed it to a pole he was holding and hacked it off. Impressed, Armstrong later used the same technique when he was second unit director on Martin Scorsese's *Gangs of New York* (2002). 'It had stayed with me all those years. The old techniques are the best.'[384]

(UK: London opening 17 October)

 ## 74 HANDS OF THE RIPPER

Peter Sasdy arrived in Britain as a young penniless Hungarian refugee in the mid-1950s. He studied drama and journalism at Bristol University before getting into television. It was his work doing period dramas for the BBC that brought him to the attention of Hammer, and he was brought in to direct Christopher Lee's fourth outing as the count, *Taste the Blood of Dracula* (1970).

Following the atmospheric *Countess Dracula* (1971), Sasdy was offered his third Hammer outing, *Hands of the Ripper*. This was something very different, more of a psychological thriller than the usual monster mayhem. Eminent doctor John Pritchard takes in a young orphan, Anna, only to discover she is the daughter of Jack the Ripper. Not only that, she is possessed by her dead father's spirit and prone to acts of gruesome savagery over which she has no control.

When making his two previous Hammers, Sasdy was somewhat perplexed by the studio's policy that it was the casting department rather than the director that chose the actors. A list of candidates was drawn up for each of the main characters and, from that list, the director marked out who they wanted to interview. Coming from television, Sasdy never faced this system before. 'It was always the director's vision of who he wanted to play the part. How can a clerk in an office have the artistic imagination and give that idea to the creative person, the auteur. That's crazy!'[385] Sasdy insisted that he made all the casting choices on this film.

And that's what happened – Sasdy cast everyone in *Hands of the Ripper*, from the biggest to the smallest role.

In a part that would have suited Peter Cushing or Christopher Lee, Sasdy's first choice to play Dr Pritchard was Eric Porter:

> He was doing *The Forsyte Saga* at the same time I was working at the BBC and we would pass each other in the canteen and the corridor. I'd always liked him as an actor and thought he was perfect for this role.[386]

As Anna, Sasdy cast the young actress Angharad Rees after spotting her in a television drama and admiring her angelic look 'and the innocence in her eyes'.[387] Rees found fame a few years later in the BBC period drama *Poldark* and was particularly drawn to the innocence of the Anna character 'because she wasn't aware of what she was doing'.[388]

Rees's first day on set was a bitter experience when she was pressurised into doing a topless bath scene, despite insisting beforehand that her contract obliged her not to have to do any such thing. On working with Porter, Rees said:

> He was a charming man with a great sense of humour, very wry. I learnt a lot from Eric Porter. I could ask him anything. We talked about my character quite a lot and worked out our relationship, which was obviously a father/daughter relationship, although there were hints of something else.[389]

A noted actor, with a Shakespearean pedigree, Rees detected no sense that Porter felt he was slumming it in a Hammer horror. 'He took it all very seriously and put everything he could into the film and the part.'[390]

It's Pritchard's relationship with Anna that drives the plot and gives the film its emotional heart. As a psychiatrist Pritchard employs Freudian techniques in an attempt to cure Anna's psychopathic tendencies. The killings are particularly gruesome, some of the most savage in the entire Hammer canon – poor Dora Bryan gets pinned to a door by a poker, Lynda Baron's motherly prostitute has a bunch of hat pins pushed through her eyeball, and an innocent maid's throat is slashed by a broken hand mirror. Rees recalls:

> I never knew exactly what I'd done until I went to the film's opening. They would shoot my reaction and then say, you can go now, see you

tomorrow, and then they would do the shot of my victim, so I was quite horrified when I saw it all put together.[391]

The climax in St Paul's famous Whispering Gallery is one of Hammer's most grandiose. When permission to film at the real cathedral was rejected, the sequence was achieved by the use of front projection and a partial set. 'I also went into St Pauls with a few dressed extras, their costumes hidden under raincoats,' confesses Sasdy, 'along with a photographer and pinched some stills from various angles that were then used for backdrops.'[392] The film also made use of the large Baker Street set at Pinewood, left over from Billy Wilder's *The Private Life of Sherlock Holmes*, made the previous year.

Of the three films he made for Hammer Sasdy ranks *Hands of the Ripper* as his favourite, precisely because it didn't follow the pattern of their usual gothic fare, dealing as it does with Freudian themes and psychoanalysis within the drama. It's not without some supernatural elements; when Anna feels the urge to kill, her hands become those of her father, powerful and with syphilitic scarring. It is above all a tragic story. An element of melancholy runs all the way through it because you know that, however hard Pritchard tries to cure her, Anna is doomed.

(UK: London opening 17 October)

75 *PLAY MISTY FOR ME*

Early in his career Clint Eastwood was determined to be a director. This desire went back to his TV days on *Rawhide*, when he'd watch a procession of directors being nursemaided through episodes, thinking to himself, 'I could do a better job myself.' But how was he ever going to get the opportunity?

A property had come his way from a young aspiring screenwriter called Jo Heims. It was about a radio disc jockey being stalked by a female fan and was based on a woman Heims knew, who followed her victim around and tried to kill him. The idea appealed to Eastwood, not least because something similar, though less drastic, had happened to him.

With Eastwood's own production company, Malpaso, putting up the funds it ended up being no big deal landing the director's chair. 'All you need to get into the Director's Guild is for someone to give you a job. So, I gave myself a job. I said, kid, you got the job.'[393] It was also a given that Eastwood would take the lead role of DJ Dave Garver, who has a one-night fling with an obsessed fan, Evelyn, that turns into a nightmare. Eastwood's choice to play Evelyn was a masterstroke; Jessica Walter turned in a truly terrifying performance, one moment seductive, the next unhinged.

The second female lead, Garver's steady girlfriend Tobie, proved more difficult to cast. Eastwood had seen a number of women but not liked any of them. One night he bumped into his friend Burt Reynolds in a bar and told him his problem. Reynolds was then making a TV detective series called *Dan August* and had just worked on an episode with an actress he was sure Eastwood would like. He showed him the dailies and she was hired on the spot. Her name was Donna Mills.

Mills was back in New York and working on a daytime soap opera when she heard the news. 'I finished the soap opera on the Friday, got my wardrobe on the Saturday, flew to the location on the Sunday and met Clint in the bar of the hotel that night, and started shooting on the Monday morning.'[394] Mills had never met Eastwood before.' He had a tremendous amount of charisma. Even though he was a very laid-back, gentle guy, he had this aura around him. I was totally intimidated. But he put me at ease right away.'[395]

The fact Eastwood was starring, as well as directing, a picture for the first time didn't seem to faze him at all. 'He knew exactly what he wanted and how to get it,' says Mills. 'He had it all in his head. Every day he came on that set totally prepared. And he brought that movie in under budget and under time.'[396]

Eastwood had given director Don Siegel a small role in the film and, according to Mills, he was around the set quite a bit. 'He and Clint were very good friends. I don't think Siegel helped Clint with his direction, but I think he was there for Clint if Clint wanted him.'[397] Like Siegel, Eastwood liked to work fast. 'If you wanted another take, he would do it,' says Mills. 'But he'd usually go, "But why? It was fine."'[398] In that respect Eastwood wasn't what Mills would call an actor's director. He hired the person he thought was best for the role and then pretty much left the performance to them. That was especially true of Jessica Walter, with whom Mills grew friendly during the shoot. 'She was brilliant in that film. And she crafted that whole performance herself. She had a vision of who that character was and just went for it.'[399]

The story was originally set in San Francisco but changed to Carmel at Eastwood's request. Eastwood lived in this small beach community on California's Monterey Peninsula and the film was entirely shot there. 'It's a beautiful place,' says Mills. 'The town is so charming, and I've been back many times.'[400] Eastwood still owns property in the area and in the late 1980s was famously Carmel's mayor.

Music, of course, played a huge role in the film, notably Erroll Garner's song 'Misty', which Evelyn asks Garver to play every night on his show. Eastwood also insisted on the inclusion of the song 'The First Time Ever I Saw Your Face', sung by Roberta Flack. One morning Eastwood played the song to Mills, explaining that it was going to be used over a montage of Garver and Tobie spending a romantic day together that ends with them making love. Mills says:

> And that scene was not in the script. And Clint said, 'There's a part in it where we're going to be naked.' I went, 'Oh my God. My parents aren't going to like this.' But he was so nice; he said, 'I'll tell you what, we'll film it and I'll show it to you and if you don't like it, and you think it's salacious in any way, I won't put it in the film.' And that was so generous of him because he knew it made me a little nervous. Then he played me the song and I fell in love with it.[401]

'The First Time Ever I Saw Your Face' was originally released in 1969 to little fanfare, but the success of *Play Misty* turned it into a hit.

Play Misty for Me is a smartly directed and superior thriller that stands up well even today. It clearly inspired the 1987 monster hit *Fatal Attraction*. 'When I first saw *Play Misty*, I knew what was going to happen, but I was scared anyway,' says Mills.[402] It amply demonstrated Eastwood's directorial skills and he went on to have an outstanding career behind the camera. For Mills, too, it was a breakthrough: 'That film was really good for my career.'[403] In 1980, she landed her most prominent role, that of the scheming Abby on *Knots Landing*. Mills was in the prime time soap for almost ten years.

(US: Los Angeles opening 20 October)

76 | THE BIG BOSS (TÁNG SHĀN DÀ XIŌNG)

A year before the film that launched Bruce Lee as a cultural phenomenon, the actor was speaking frankly about his conviction that he was going to become an international star. A producer friend tried to make

Lee see sense, that western audiences would never accept an Asian actor as a star. 'We shall see,' he said.

Lee grew up around the Hong Kong movie business. As a child actor he appeared in something like twenty films. Leaving Hong Kong at the age of 18, he travelled to America, where he attended university and taught martial arts in his spare time. While appearing at tournaments, he came to the attention of Hollywood, and won the role of Kato in the TV crime series *The Green Hornet*. When the show was cancelled in 1967 after just twenty-six episodes, work was thin on the ground; certainly, the top jobs he felt he deserved weren't coming along. Lee started to get restless. He was also running out of money.

When a personal project he was developing called *The Silent Flute*, a kung fu western that focused on the philosophical and zen aspect of martial arts, collapsed, Lee turned in frustration to his old hunting ground of Hong Kong cinema. He had never lost touch with his Hong Kong roots and during a radio interview revealed he might return to do a movie there if the price was right. Within days he started to get offers. One of them came from Raymond Chow, head of the production company Golden Harvest. Chow offered Lee a contract for two films with a combined fee of $15,000. Lee accepted.

The first film in that deal, *The Big Boss*, sees Lee play Cheng Chao-an, a country hick who travels from Hong Kong to Thailand to live and work with his cousin, Hsiu Chien (James Tien), at an ice factory. Unbeknown to Cheng the boss is operating the factory as a front for a drug-smuggling operation, with heroin encased in each ice block. *The Big Boss* pretty much set the mould for every character Lee subsequently played: the lone outsider who arrives in a new place and things start to happen. In that respect he's a variation on Clint Eastwood's 'man with no name' character, a sort of avenging angel. The films usually end the same way, too, with Lee coming face to face with the big villain for a final showdown – think the fight on the lawn in *The Big Boss* or the fight in the room of mirrors in *Enter the Dragon* (1973). This again harks back to the western genre and the final shootout.

The genius of *The Big Boss* is that for nearly half of the running time Lee doesn't throw a single punch. He has promised his family back home not to fight again, after years of trouble-making. After each loss of face it's not only Lee that's seething but the audience as well, so by the time he finally lets loose, expectation is at fever pitch.

Arriving in Thailand for his first major picture as a leading player, Lee was not happy with the way things had been organised. The equipment the crew were using was antiquated and in poor repair, and there was barely any script to speak of. The budget was less than $100,000. Worst of all, the director Wu Chia-Hsiang had a violent temper that he took out on the cast and crew at every opportunity. He and Lee also clashed over the style of the film. Wu Chia-Hsiang wanted to adhere to the traditional stylised martial arts that came out of Cantonese opera, while Lee was pushing his own philosophy of a more realistic, almost street-fighting kung fu. Things got so bad Chow had no option but to get another director, Lo Wei. While Lo didn't rant and rave, he was a chronic gambler and would sometimes listen to the commentary of a horse race while the actors were trying to play a scene.

Lee and Lo also clashed, again over the tone of the film. In the now famous ice house fight a villain is kicked through a wall and Lo wanted his departing body to leave a man-shaped hole. Lee thought this was veering too much into parody, but Lo won the argument. Lee did insist on choreographing his own fight routines, bringing with him the film experience he had gained in Hollywood.

Lee had persuaded Raymond Chow not to place too much emphasis on weaponry. Chinese martial art films tended to replicate the Japanese samurai film with their use of sword play. Lee wanted the action to concentrate on the fighting man alone. In this way *The Big Boss* differed greatly from previous martial arts films, and Lee's fluid, lightning-fast martial arts style was a complete revelation.

During filming Lee suffered numerous injuries and did not enjoy the location. Pak Chong was a remote village 90 miles from Bangkok. The month's filming happened to coincide with the hot season, the accommodation had no air conditioning, the food was inadequate and the tap water in the hotel came out yellow. Lee lost something like 10lb and got by eating canned meat and taking vitamin tablets.

Confident *The Big Boss* was going be a success, not even Lee anticipated what was to follow. Along with his wife Linda and Raymond Chow, Lee attended the midnight premiere in Hong Kong, where local audiences were notorious for not holding back their feelings if they disliked a picture. After it finished there was complete silence in the auditorium. Then the cheers started. Lee had been able to arrive at the theatre without too much hassle; on his way out he was mobbed. *The*

Big Boss went on to become the most successful film of all time at the Hong Kong box office. All over Asia the pattern was repeated. In the Philippines it ran for six months, packing out theatres. In Singapore, some showings were cancelled due to traffic jams.

As *The Big Boss* cleaned up around Asia, Lee had already started work on his second film for Golden Harvest, *Fist of Fury* (1972). The legend of Bruce Lee had begun.

(Hong Kong: opening 23 October)

 ## 77 *A FISTFUL OF DYNAMITE*

(DUCK, YOU SUCKER!)

The undisputed master of the spaghetti western was Sergio Leone. After all, he single-handedly created the genre with the enormous success of the Dollar trilogy starring Clint Eastwood. These films demythologised and deromanticised many of the conventions of traditional Hollywood westerns. And it was while he was making his epic *Once Upon a Time in the West* (1968) that Leone was presented with an early draft of a film that provided him with the opportunity to do much the same with the Mexican Revolution. The climate was right for such a film. The Paris riots of 1968 had led to a glut of political filmmaking and in Leone's estimation a naïve romanticising of revolution on the part of the left. As a result, *A Fistful of Dynamite* stands as Leone's most political film.

While set during the Mexican Revolution the real theme of the film is friendship. And betrayal. Juan Miranda is an amoral peasant-turned-bandit, robbing stagecoaches with his gang. John Mallory arrives, an Irish revolutionary on the run. Together, they set out to rob a bank but get caught up in the fervour of revolution.

Leone had begun to tire of the grind of directing movies and the original plan was for Peter Bogdanovich to direct and Leone produce. When that didn't work out, Sam Peckinpah's name was mentioned. Finally, Leone promoted his assistant director Giancarlo Santi.

There was trouble, too, casting his Mexican bandit. As the role of Juan took shape it was obvious that it was merely an extension of Tuco from *The Good, the Bad and the Ugly*. So, it made sense to cast the same actor, Eli Wallach. According to Wallach's memoirs, he had already agreed to make a film in France; Leone begged him to turn it down, which he did. Then Leone's backers, UA, said Wallach wasn't a big enough name, and to use Rod Steiger instead. Wallach wasn't best pleased when Leone phoned him up with the news. Having essentially lost two jobs, Wallach asked for some form of compensation. When Leone said he couldn't do that, Wallach threatened to sue him. 'Get in line,' said Leone, then slammed the phone down. It was the end of their friendship. The two men never spoke to each other again.

James Coburn had passed on the chance to work with Leone on two separate occasions, turning down *A Fistful of Dollars* and the Charles Bronson role in *Once Upon a Time in the West*. Now Leone wanted him for Mallory. Coburn asked Henry Fonda, who had worked with Leone, what he was like and was surprised by the answer – that he was the best director Fonda had ever worked with. This from a man who had been directed by John Ford and Alfred Hitchcock. Coburn accepted the role.

Arriving for his first day on set, Steiger was perplexed, to say the least, that Santi, and not Leone, was the man behind the camera. Leone assured Steiger that Santi was more than capable. He was like his brother and worked just like him – he was not to worry. Fine, countered Steiger, tomorrow he would send his cousin to the set. He was just like him, and Leone was going to love him. The next day Leone took over as director. Reluctantly no doubt. Leone wouldn't direct another picture until 1984's *Once Upon a Time in America*. *A Fistful of Dynamite* also turned out to be his final western.

This wasn't the only clash between the director and his star. Steiger's method acting led to some notable friction on the set. His habit was to psychoanalyse everything and work himself up into an Actors Studio lather to deliver the simplest of lines. Leone, known for his frequent volcanic outbursts, was unusually tolerant, until one day he could take it no longer, telling Steiger that he didn't care if he'd won an Oscar, he could fuck off back to Hollywood. Steiger did indeed walk, but not back to Hollywood, only getting as far as the local hotel in Almeria. Reportedly there was an impasse of several days where actor and director communicated through messages relayed to each other by assistants. Steiger did ultimately apologise, and everything seemed to pass smoothly after that.

As well as Spain, the film's pivotal flashback scenes were shot in Dublin, Ireland, in locations scouted for Leone by Irish filmmaker John Boorman. These scenes, played mostly in slow motion and bathed in Ennio Morricone's heart-rending music, reveal Mallory's past and how he was betrayed by a fellow revolutionary.

A *Fistful of Dynamite* was only marginally successful in Italy, falling behind the box office takings of Leone's previous westerns. In America the film was called *Duck, You Sucker!*, and when it failed to find an audience the distributors gave it the more exploitative British title of *A Fistful of Dynamite*. In both countries the film was shorn of something like twenty minutes. In Mexico it was effectively banned until 1979 because it was considered offensive to the Mexican people and the revolution.

For many years, the film was seen as a minor work in the Leone canon, not spoken of in the same hushed reverential tones as the Dollar films or *Once Upon a Time in the West*. Yes, it's too long in its director's cut, and a bit messy and sprawling, but the epic quality of the film is impressive, as is Leone's trademark operatic style. It's also arguably his bleakest and most melancholic work. As his final western, the genre in which he made his name, *A Fistful of Dynamite* is a fitting finale.

(Italy/US: Italian opening 29 October)

78 | FIDDLER ON THE ROOF

Based on the short stories by Sholem Aleichem, the most beloved classical Yiddish writer, about Jewish life in a village in pre-revolution Russia, *Fiddler on the Roof* was one of the most successful Broadway musicals of all time. Opening in 1964, and starring Zero Mostel as Tevye, a dairyman faced with the challenge of marrying off three of his five daughters, it ran for over 3,000 performances and went on to spawn a number of international productions. This confounded investors and commentators worried that the show might be considered 'too Jewish' to attract mainstream audiences. Far from it: the themes of family were universally relatable.

When the time came to produce the film version the same worries existed. UA had taken the plunge by buying the rights, for something close to $3 million, and brought in hot director Norman Jewison, just coming off the back of huge successes with *In the Heat of the Night* (1967) and *The Thomas Crown Affair* (1968). Adapting a play to the big screen always means moving it from a largely artificial environment to a much more realistic setting, and that is doubly difficult when it's a musical. To succeed Jewison knew there could be no tinge of Broadway or even America for that matter; it's the reason why he decided to shoot on location in Yugoslavia. He also fought against the studio's insistence on casting Mostel; Jewison just felt the actor seemed too New York, not Old World enough. Despite people like Danny Kaye and Walter Matthau voicing an interest, Jewison ended up choosing the Israeli actor Topol, who had starred in the London production; his father was a Russian Jewish immigrant, and that made him closer to the root of the character.

The offer to direct *Fiddler on the Roof* also came at an opportune moment for Jewison, who, in the aftermath of Robert Kennedy's assassination in June 1968, was worried where America was headed. He took this chance to move his entire family to London, where interiors were to be shot at Pinewood Studios. Jewison ended up living in England for seven years.

The whole project was a huge undertaking and, from start to finish, took two and a half years out of Jewison's life. He described it as one of the most difficult pictures he ever made. Prior to shooting Jewison immersed himself in the works of Sholem Aleichem and Jewish traditions. For him, that's what the story was about: a mixture of history and Jewish folklore. Tevye is a man of tradition in a world of rapid change, whose daughters want to marry their own men rather than have them picked by a matchmaker. While all this is going on Tevye battles to maintain his Jewish tradition under a tsar and a country where anti-Jewish sentiment is growing.

To play opposite Topol as Tevye's wife Golde, Jewison cast Norma Crane, after Anne Bancroft turned down the part. Jewish herself, Crane saw the role not only as the most important of her career, but deeply personal as there were echoes of the story in her own family history. However, during location filming Crane revealed she had breast cancer. In London for studio work Crane would work in the mornings, have radiation treatment in the afternoon and then take the next day off. This meant the schedule had to be altered and a lot of things worked around her, but the producers and Jewison were as accommodating as they could be as the actress bravely battled through and worked as hard as she could to finish the role. Two years later, she sadly passed away.

Gorgeously photographed by Oswald Morris, who won an Oscar for his work, and performed by a talented group of actors and singers, including the young Paul Michael Glaser, *Fiddler on the Roof* was a runaway success, ending up the third highest-grossing movie musical of the decade according to *Variety*. There are a host of great musical set pieces; some of the show's most famous and recognisable songs are 'Tradition', 'Matchmaker, Matchmaker', 'Sunrise, Sunset' and, of course, 'If I Were a Rich Man'. Jewison brought in John Williams to conduct and adapt the original score by Jerry Bock, as well as compose some additional music. This included an original cadenza for the film's opening titles, to be performed by Isaac Stern, one of the greatest violinists of the twentieth century. Williams won his very first Academy Award for his work on the film. In all, *Fiddler on the Roof* was nominated for eight Academy Awards including Best Picture, Best Actor and Best Director.

(US: New York opening 3 November)

 ## 79 *DR. JEKYLL AND SISTER HYDE*

Brian Clemens and his producing partner Albert Fennell were having lunch in the Elstree Studio restaurant one afternoon. Both had made a name for themselves on the hugely popular television series *The Avengers*, for which Clemens wrote numerous episodes. Sat with them was the director Roy Ward Baker and at a nearby table was James Carreras, head of Hammer films. Clemens recalls:

> Because of that, our table started discussing Hammer's product, the fact that it was getting a bit stale. Then suddenly I said, 'I've got it, Jekyll and Hyde, but he turns into a woman', and Roy fell about laughing. Then when I got up to go, Jimmy Carreras stopped me. 'I like the sound of that idea,' he said. 'Can you come to the office on Wednesday.' This was Monday.[404]

Clemens walked into Hammer House on Wardour Street and got into the lift. The Hammer offices were on the second floor:

> It was one of those old lifts where you can see out and, as it came up to the offices, there facing me on the wall was this huge poster of *Dr. Jekyll and Sister Hyde*. And I hadn't written a word yet.[405]

For Clemens, the script came together quickly once he arrived at the plot device of Jekyll trying to create an 'elixir of life', by using female hormones stolen from the glands of fresh corpses. 'Hyde could use his female alter ego to go out and murder women,' says Clemens. 'It was the perfect alibi.'[406] The plot also used elements of Jack the Ripper and Burke and Hare. And there's a nice line in dark humour: 'Most of my scripts had a touch of humour in them. I learnt from Hitchcock, who was my idol. He never made a film that didn't have some element of humour in it.'[407]

The job of director went to Clemens and Fennell's companion at that fateful lunch, Roy Ward Baker, already a veteran of several Hammer horrors, who had also worked on *The Avengers*. Installed alongside Fennell as producer, Clemens found himself on the set for much of the shoot. 'And near the end of that picture Albert said to me, "I think you could have directed this film. I think you're ready to direct." So, I did the next one we made for Hammer, *Captain Kronos: Vampire Hunter*.'[408]

As producer Clemens had a hand in the casting. Installed as Jekyll was Ralph Bates, then under contract to Hammer and being groomed as their next big horror star. 'And I had no objection to that,' says Clemens, 'because Ralph was a fine actor and a nice person to get on with.'[409] The real challenge was matching Bates up with the right actress:

> That took some time. We went through an awful lot of young actresses without success. And it was Michael Carreras [son of James] who said we ought to see Martine Beswick. We did and she was perfect. And as the picture went on, Martine seemed to become more and more like Ralph.[410]

There is a startling resemblance between the two actors – they could almost be twins – and this was a key element in helping make the story believable. Clemens was on the set when they filmed the first transformation scene and, together with Baker, worked out a way to show it in one complete shot, without cuts. The finished result is skilfully done and highly effective.

Clemens's first experience working for Hammer ended up being an enjoyable one. 'The good thing about Hammer was they left you alone. They only interfered if you went over budget. James Carreras never showed up on the set. He was only interested in making deals.'[411] As Clemens recalls, his script was shot pretty much as he wrote it. 'When you've got just a six-week schedule and a low budget it's not a good idea to start changing the script. You're just grateful to have a script that works.'[412] Clemens always prided himself in tailoring a script to a specific set of circumstances, especially on *Sister Hyde* where he was also a producer. 'And I wrote like a producer in a funny sort of way. I used to say, "if we can't do the *Titanic*, I'd rather do the best row boat disaster ever filmed."'[413]

There was also Hammer's house style to consider, and the audience's expectation of lots of blood. Like Hitchcock, Clemens always preferred not to show extreme violence on the screen, keeping it where he believed it worked best, in the mind of the audience. As a consequence, the Ripper-style murders in *Sister Hyde* are not overly gruesome, and Clemens faced no pressure to up the ante in the gore department.

Dr. Jekyll and Sister Hyde was quite well received by some critics, grudgingly one suspects. Like that other film series, the *Carry Ons*, critics dismissed the Hammer horrors as so much factory fodder, little realising that they would become part of British film heritage. Box office-wise, *Sister Hyde* was a sorry failure, evidence that Hammer's style of horror was going out of fashion. Even so, *Sister Hyde* ranks as one of the best of the later Hammers and a favourite for many fans.

(UK: London opening 7 November)

80 BLOOD FROM THE MUMMY'S TOMB

Facing a new decade, Hammer realised that the gothic horrors of its past weren't going to cut the mustard anymore. To attract new audiences, they were going to have to offer something different, or at the very least present old themes in a new way. In its search for fresh ideas and 'new blood' Hammer welcomed pitches from a score of independent producers. One of these was Howard Brandy, who thought of adapting Bram Stoker's little-known 1903 mystery *Jewel of the Seven Stars*. This was going to be a mummy film with a difference – there was no mummy in it. Instead, the supernatural force is a long-dead Egyptian queen whose spirit possesses Margaret, the daughter of the professor responsible for breaking into her tomb.

Screenwriter Christopher Wicking hoped that Hammer might keep Stoker's original title; instead, the studio took all the words associated with mummy movies, jumbled them around and *Blood from the Mummy's Tomb* was the result. Wicking's next suggestion was looked upon more favourably: that Seth Holt should direct. Holt had worked with Hammer before, notably on *The Nanny* (1965), expertly handling the temperamental Bette Davis. However, he hadn't directed a picture since 1967 due to ill health and alcohol problems.

Cast in the role of Margaret was Valerie Leon, who had made brief film appearances in *Carry On* comedies and on television; *Blood from the*

Mummy's Tomb was her first starring role. 'And I was incredibly shy.'[414] As a result, she largely kept to herself during the production and didn't mix very much with the other actors. To counterbalance Leon's relative inexperience, Holt assembled a supporting cast of veteran British actors: James Villiers, Rosalie Crutchley and Aubrey Morris. But by far the film's greatest casting coup was Peter Cushing as Margaret's father Professor Fuchs. Leon fondly remembers their first day on the set together, filming the pivotal scene where he gives her Queen Tera's ring. Then, late that afternoon, Cushing received a call that his beloved wife Helen, who had been ill for some time, had been taken to hospital. Cushing rushed to her side, only to be told by doctors that there was little hope and to take her home and make her comfortable. She passed away just a few days later.

Inevitably, Cushing's agent cancelled his appearance in the film. 'Everyone was devastated,' Leon recalls.[415] Quickly Andrew Keir, an actor already familiar with the house of Hammer, having made *Dracula Prince of Darkness* (1966) and *Quatermass and the Pit* (1967), was brought in. Living in Wales, Keir travelled overnight, picked up the script and, within a few days, had learnt the role and was on the set. 'I liked Andrew very much,' says Leon, 'but it would have been wonderful to have done the movie with Peter. It was just that one day and I had no real chance to get to know him.'[416]

The production was facing other problems too. Producer Howard Brandy had fallen out with Wicking and barred him from the set. In defiance, Wicking met with Holt in secret to see how things were progressing. Like everyone working on the film, Wicking got on well with Holt. Leon loved him dearly. 'Seth was a lovely man. He had a great sense of humour and was very artistic.'[417] This being Leon's first starring role, Holt worked extremely closely with her.

And so it came as an awful shock, with just a week left of the schedule, when Holt died suddenly. 'Seth had given a dinner party the previous night and, just as the guests left, he turned to his wife and said, "I'm going," and died of a heart attack,' Leon remembers.[418] In the week leading up to his death he'd suffered terribly from hiccups, now seen as a possible symptom of a potential heart attack. 'We used to think that was quite funny,' recalls Leon. 'We would watch rushes and you'd hear these hiccups in the background.'[419]

What was particularly distressing for Leon was not being allowed to go to his funeral as work on the picture had to continue. 'It was just awful. We were filming the scene in the asylum, and I remember crying and them having to patch me up between takes. I was really upset. It did affect me.'[420]

With no director, Michael Carreras, son of James and a producer and director in his own right, took the reins. Michael faced what could have been an insurmountable problem. Holt's way of working was to plan everything in his head rather than take notes, and that left Michael with a lot of material but very little idea of how Holt wanted to put it all together in post-production. There were also several incomplete scenes to finish shooting. Watching the film today, one can't really tell it had such a troubled history. Indeed, it's since achieved huge cult status. Leon confirms that she gets more fan mail about it now than she ever did at the time.

Blood from the Mummy's Tomb held its premiere at the National Film Theatre in London, as part of a Hammer retrospective. James Carreras noted that his company had finally been acknowledged by his industry peers. Sadly, Hammer's days were already numbered, and by the mid-1970s they were to be no more.

(UK: London opening 7 November)

81 *200 MOTELS*

In November 1968 Tony Palmer's landmark documentary on the rock music scene, *All My Loving*, was broadcast on BBC1, featuring interviews and concert footage from the likes of Paul McCartney, Jimi Hendrix and Pink Floyd. Also appearing was Frank Zappa, who two years later contacted Palmer again asking if they could work together on a new project.

Zappa had approached UA to finance a feature film to be called *200 Motels*, a surreal evocation of life on the road with his band The Mothers of Invention. UA were not that enthused, and so Zappa offered to use his next record advance to finance the film if UA would agree to distribute. This sounded like a fair deal, but the studio insisted on a safe pair of hands to oversee the whole thing. Enter Tony Palmer.

When they met Zappa gave Palmer the script, which the director recalls comprised:

300 pages, some handwritten, some paste-ups, some incomprehensible, a few lyrics, and a frequent use of the word 'penis'. The opening line on page 1 of 'the script' read: 'If you were forced by a crazy

person to insert a mysterious imported lamp into the reproductive orifice of a lady harpist, would you do it?'[421]

The plan was to co-direct the movie. The credit would read 'Tony Palmer (visuals) Frank Zappa (characterisations)'.

Pinewood Studios had been booked for ten days, a little short for a full-length feature, Palmer thought. But Zappa appeared confident, and Palmer was under no illusion as to his supreme musicianship. The score relied extensively on orchestral music, and it was obvious they needed a full orchestra to realise it. 'Your job,' said Zappa. Palmer had worked before with the Royal Philharmonic and brought them on board, 'although somehow, I failed to mention to them that they would be seen throughout the film in a prison camp with the percussionists dressed as Nazi guards.'[422]

It was Palmer's job to hire the cast too. 'I called up every crazy rock 'n' roller I could think of who owed me a favour; enter Ringo Starr (disguised in the film as Frank Zappa) and Keith Moon, the drummer with The Who.'[423] Moon, making his film debut, plays an asexual nun who is trying to become a groupie. One of the main roles was originally intended for Zappa's bassist Jeff Simmons, but when he quit the group just before filming, Palmer brought in Wilfrid Brambell, famous for the BBC sitcom *Steptoe and Son*, who was to be billed as the oldest bass player in the world. Brambell gamely took on rehearsals but was never comfortable in the role. 'I think he felt it just didn't suit him,' says Palmer.[424] Somewhat baffled by the story, on the last day of rehearsal he finally had enough and retreated down a corridor yelling, 'This is crazy!' and never came back. Stumped at what to do, Zappa announced that the next person to walk into the rehearsal room would play the part. The door opened and in came Starr's chauffeur, Martin Lickert, who'd been sent out to get a pack of cigarettes. Everyone said, 'You.' Lickert had just one week to learn the part.

The real challenge was how to realise Zappa's concept of portraying the wacky life of a band on the road, 'and with a budget that today wouldn't even pay for the wigs,' says Palmer.[425] 35mm film was out, both economically and because of the time constraint. Palmer told Zappa that the only hope was to shoot it on colour video and then transfer it to film. UA were not to be told. 'I was sure they would cancel the whole thing at the very mention of the word "video" and blame … me,' says Palmer.[426] Video was relatively quick and cheap. Most important for Palmer, it gave them the chance to experiment with a technology still in its infancy. *200 Motels* became the first feature to use the video-to-film process.

The actual shoot, understandably, was hectic. 'Partly because Frank kept interfering,' says Palmer, 'wanting to conduct the orchestra, direct the cameras, lecture the actors etc. I think I even at some point threatened to kill him! Heat of the moment stuff.'[427]

Zappa did enjoy filming at Pinewood, frequently telling Palmer how humble he felt sitting in the dining room surrounded by the photographs and memories of the many great films that had been made in those studios down the years.

To publicise the film Zappa wanted to perform the score at the Royal Albert Hall. Unfortunately, the performance was cancelled at short notice due to the obscene nature of the content. Zappa sued the Hall's management for breach of contract and the matter finished up in the High Court. Palmer recalls:

> I was called as a so-called expert witness. Did I really think that a piece which included 'homosexual material' was suitable for performance in the home of the Proms, the judge asked me? It so happened that Britten's great opera *Death in Venice* had been performed the previous year in the Proms. When I mentioned this, the judge said, 'And who wrote that?' 'Benjamin Britten,' I replied. 'And how do you spell that?' the judge said.[428]

Surely *200 Motels* must qualify as one of the most unhinged films of the year; Zappa's road manager, for example, plays the role of a vacuum cleaner. It mixes various avant-garde visual techniques, including superimpositions, dissolves, matte shots, special effects, animation and fast- and slow-motion sequences to create a surreal and psychedelic experience. Several years after its release Palmer met an unexpected fan of the film in the personage of David Lean:

> Whereas I wanted to ask him about *Lawrence of Arabia* and the rest, all he wanted to talk about was *200 Motels* and how it had been done. Astonishing to me that he had seen it at all; that was a truly humbling experience.[429]

(US: New York opening 10 November)

82 *BEDKNOBS AND BROOMSTICKS*

Walt Disney was on a personal mission to persuade author P.L. Travers to allow him to bring her novel *Mary Poppins* to the screen. The negotiations, held in person between Walt and the mercurial Miss Travers, were tough and challenging. Worried that at any moment the whole thing could fall apart, Walt devised a back-up plan. He purchased another similarly themed book, this one called *The Magic Bed Knob* by Mary Norton, along with its sequel *Bonfires and Broomsticks*. It was about three young children and a witch. In the end Travers gave permission, and the rest is history. *Mary Poppins* was released in 1964 and *The Magic Bed Knob* was put on the shelf.

What originally drew Walt Disney to Norton's tale, aside from its magical elements, was the chance to salute the heroism and bravery of the British people when they stood alone against invasion by the Nazis. Published in 1943 and, in its small way, a bid to help keep wartime spirits up after the country had gone through the Blitz, it tells the story of three young children evacuated from London to the countryside where they end up living in the house of Eglantine Price who, thanks to a correspondence course, has learnt the ways of witchcraft.

Due to its similarity to *Mary Poppins*, *Bedknobs and Broomsticks* was put on hold until early 1970 and was filmed entirely at the Disney Studio in Burbank. For one extended sequence, three blocks of Portobello Market, circa 1940, were faithfully reproduced on the soundstages.

It was hoped that the role of Eglantine would lure Julie Andrews back into the Disney fold after her iconic performance as Mary Poppins, but it was not to be. Other choices included Lynn Redgrave, Judy Carne and Leslie Caron, before Angela Lansbury was cast. Still riding high from his portrayal of Fagin in *Oliver!* Ron Moody was cast as Emelius Browne, a bogus professor of witchcraft. However, when Moody learnt that he would be second-billed to Angela Lansbury he left and was replaced by fellow Brit David Tomlinson. Of course, Tomlinson had starred in *Mary Poppins*, and the similarities didn't stop there: the films share the same songwriters, Richard M. Sherman and Robert B. Sherman; director, Robert Stevenson; and producer, Bill Walsh. Like Mary Poppins, Lansbury's Eglantine is another stern yet sweet guardian figure. And she's able to fly, not with the use of a magic umbrella but a broomstick, befitting her trainee-witch status.

Both films also combined live action and animation. Without doubt the highlight of *Bedknobs and Broomsticks* is a twenty-minute sequence when everyone lands in the sea, courtesy of a bewitched bed knob that transforms a bed into something akin to a flying carpet. Here they join an underwater dance, only to resurface on the legendary Isle of Naboombu, where Emelius Browne is coerced into refereeing a bizarre game of football between two teams of wild animals, featuring everything from cheetahs to rhinos. This sequence was directed by Disney stalwart Ward Kimball, who was the animation director on *Dumbo*, *Cinderella* and *Peter Pan*. It took a year to complete at a cost of $1 million. This, along with the film's climax, where a Nazi raiding party are defeated by suits of armour from a museum that Eglantine has brought to life, deservedly won *Bedknobs* an Oscar for Best Visual Effects.

The three child actors, cast from hundreds of candidates, add a bit of cockney savvy to proceedings, as opposed to the rather sugary pair from *Mary Poppins*. And there's an appearance from Roddy McDowall as a village pastor with designs on Eglantine. One unusual casting choice was British entertainer Bruce Forsyth playing an East End spiv. The story David Tomlinson heard was that when Forsyth arrived in Hollywood, the Disney people asked that he do his trick with the hat in one of his scenes. Brucie was stumped – what trick? What hat? 'You know,' they said, 'whaddya call it – the fez.' It then dawned on Forsyth that they thought he was Tommy Cooper. Despite the casting error, he stayed on the film.[430]

Bedknobs and Broomsticks was chosen as the Christmas attraction at the prestigious Radio City Music Hall in New York. And that's when the problems started. Radio City issued a decree that the film had to be under two hours because it was to be packaged with the theatre's elaborate festive stage show. Disney went in with the scissors and took out almost half an hour of footage, removing pretty much the entirety of Roddy McDowall's performance and, to the consternation of the Sherman Brothers, three of their songs. These songs, they contested, added much to the character development of both Eglantine and Browne, and their removal did nothing less than rip the heart out of the film. This cut footage remained missing for twenty-five years, until most of it was discovered in the Disney archives, restored and reinstated into the movie for home video release.

Bedknobs and Broomsticks was not the big success at the box office that Disney hoped for, but over the years it has become a real family favourite and a Disney classic.

(US: New York opening 11 November)

83 *MON ONCLE ANTOINE (MY UNCLE ANTOINE)*

This evocative and bittersweet portrait of a boy's coming of age during one 1940s Christmas in rural Quebec was consistently cited by critics and scholars as the greatest Canadian film of all time. However, in recent years it has been overshadowed by a controversy that saw its director scrubbed out of existence.

Claude Jutra was at the forefront of establishing Quebec as a national cinema distinct from the rest of Canada. He had been making films since the early 1960s, had worked in France as an apprentice to François Truffaut, and was acknowledged as part of the New Wave of Canadian filmmaking. *Mon oncle Antoine* was to bring him international recognition.

The story was a personal one and belonged to Clément Perron, a Quebec filmmaker and screenwriter, who had grown up in a small town in an asbestos mining region, working at his uncle's general store. These deeply felt childhood recollections had shaped his script and the lead protagonist of Benoît, a 15-year-old orphan who goes to live with his uncle, the local store owner and undertaker. After approaching Jutra with his script, Perron reacted badly when it was dismissed out of hand and considered to be of little merit. Sensing his disappointment, Jutra took Perron out for a drink to cheer him up. They talked, and Perron began to describe his childhood and some of the little vignettes that had informed his script – how the wealthy mine owner used to dress up as Santa every Christmas and ride through the streets on a sleigh distributing presents like some benign ruler; and the Christmas night when he accompanied a boozy relative to pick up the body of a teenage farm boy and how it fell off the back of the sleigh. Suddenly the story and its events came to vivid life in Jutra's head. He reversed his original decision and the two men worked together to revise the script. Backing came from the National Film Board of Canada.

Filming was carried out on location in the Abitibi region of western Quebec, whose barren and beautiful landscapes are startlingly captured by cameraman Michel Brault. For the pivotal role of Benoît, Jutra cast the unknown Jacques Gagnon, a young actor he had discovered after picking him up hitchhiking. The veteran actor Jean Duceppe played the uncle, Antoine.

Inexplicably, the film sat on the shelf of the National Film Board of Canada unreleased for over a year. When it finally opened, *Mon oncle Antoine* swept the Canadian film awards and was critically lauded wherever it was shown. No other Canadian film had reached such popularity. What made the film such a success and an enduring classic is its universal theme of someone having to deal with that difficult transition from childhood to adulthood, learning about friendship, sex, work, death and the hypocritical world of adults. Setting the film in rural 1940s Quebec also gives the story an intriguing political backdrop. The asbestos miners strikes of 1949 and 1952 are viewed as the first stirrings of the political agitation and labour unrest that led to the Quiet Revolution, a series of drastic political, societal and cultural changes that transformed Quebec in the 1960s. Jutra had gone there as a student in a show of solidarity.

Mon oncle Antoine established Jutra's international reputation, though its success was to overshadow his other work. Following the commercial failure of his expensive historical epic *Kamouraska* (1973), Jutra's career suffered a disheartening decline, though he continued to make films. At the start of the 1980s he began to recognise the early stages of Alzheimer's. In the winter of 1986, he disappeared. At his home were several notes that referred to a 'decision' and a 'departure'. In the following spring, after months of mystery and public speculation, his body was found in the St Lawrence River, Cap-Santé, near Québec City. It was presumed to be a suicide. He had made an earlier film in which a character leaps into the same river.

The death of Jutra came as a huge shock to the film world and his local community. To commemorate a famous son, several locations in Quebec and Canada, as well as prizes and scholarships, were named in his honour.

In 2016 allegations were brought to light that Jutra had sexual relationships with boys in their early teens, a fact that was known within the industry, but nothing had been done about it. The news made national headlines and raised numerous questions relating to the filmmaker's legacy. Within twenty-four hours of this becoming public, the Canadian film industry and government started scrubbing the name Claude Jutra from every film prize, park and street sign. In a Montreal park, a sculpture dedicated to Jutra was defaced. Few public figures have fallen so utterly, so swiftly.

(Canada: opening 12 November)

84 *DUEL*

When writer Richard Matheson heard the news of the assassination of President John F. Kennedy in Dallas on 22 November 1963, he abandoned his game of golf and drove home. On the way he was continually tailgated by a huge truck. Every time he stepped on the gas, the truck sped up. In the end he pulled off the road and the truck hurtled past. Shaken, it didn't take long for the writer inside him to realise here was something that would make for an interesting story.

After television rejected the idea; Matheson published it as a short story. In an era before the term 'road rage' had been coined, Matheson's protagonist is David Mann, a travelling salesman (an everyman figure), pitted against a viciously aggressive truck driver who is stalking him on a stretch of desolate road in the California desert.

Meanwhile, over at Universal Studios a young director was making waves. Steven Spielberg's first contact with Universal was when, as a kid, he took the famous studio tour and went AWOL to spend the day hanging out around the sound stages and the lot. Years later, his award-winning short film *Amblin'* secured him a seven-year contract after studio executive Sid Sheinberg recognised the young filmmaker's talent. His first job was directing Joan Crawford in the pilot episode of Rod Serling's new anthology show *Night Gallery* in 1969. More TV assignments came his way, and he gained a reputation as someone who was imaginative and took risks. All the time, Spielberg was looking for his chance to break into features.

That opportunity came when someone told him about this script that Matheson had written based on his short story, which Universal had purchased and were going to produce as an ABC television Movie of the Week. Spielberg was already an admirer of Matheson, especially his episodes on *The Twilight Zone*, and when he read *Duel* he started a campaign to persuade his bosses that no one else at Universal was better qualified to direct it. Spielberg felt an emotional resonance to the material and Mann's predicament, this feeling of being victimised, having been bullied as a kid at school for being Jewish. Spielberg has said that *Duel* was his life in the schoolyard. The truck was the bully, and he was the car.

To play Mann, Spielberg remembered Dennis Weaver's nerve-twitching performance as a motel night manager from Orson Welles's *Touch of Evil*. At the time Weaver was the star of the popular police drama series *McCloud*. Weaver knew the offer was something special when his agent said he was sending over a script, and he ought to say yes to it before even reading it.

With a budget of $300,000 Spielberg was given a shooting schedule of just ten days. The film was entirely shot on location in California, on the edge of the Mojave Desert. Spielberg, just 24 years old, brought creativity and tenacity to the shoot. Rather than the traditional storyboard he meticulously pre-planned every shot using a gigantic overhead map of the locations, which identified where to position cameras, blocking for the stunt drivers and the continuity of the film. Spielberg stressed that the car driven by Mann, a Plymouth Valiant, had to be red in order to stand out from the desert landscape in the wide shots.

Matheson visited the set for one day, during the scene in the coffee shop, and mistakenly thought the place was open as normal and the people were actual customers, not actors – it all looked so real. He was also surprised when numerous members of the crew approached him to say they had experienced very similar incidents on the road involving truck drivers. In his script Matheson stressed that the driver should never be seen, aside from shots of his arms and boots. It was a clever trick; the fear of the unknown is far greater than something you can see. Spielberg used this again in *Jaws* (1975), keeping the shark largely hidden until the climax in order to build up the suspense – although much of this was beyond his control since the prop shark didn't work.

The driver's motives are also never revealed and, because we can't see or understand him, the truck itself becomes the villain, the monster. As the story unfolds the vehicle takes on something of a supernatural presence. When it crashes over the cliff at the end and mangles in a cloud of dirt there is an almost primordial roar. Looking for the right sound Spielberg went through several alternatives, including mixing truck noises with the sound of a screaming woman. In the end a sound editor came up with the idea of distorting the noise of the Gill-Man from *Creature from the Black Lagoon* (1954).

Excited by the rushes, Universal executives allowed Spielberg to film an extra three days. This was followed by a fast edit, and *Duel* debuted on television less than five weeks later. It won a healthy audience and positive reviews, but its reputation was forged in Europe where Universal decided to release a theatrical version. This entailed Spielberg, Weaver and a crew returning to the same locations and shooting an additional fifteen minutes of footage. The film was a big success, bringing Spielberg to the attention of international critics for the very first time. The praise the theatrical version of *Duel* received proved to be a pivotal stepping-stone in Spielberg's ambition to be a film director. And, as it developed its reputation, becoming a cult film, admirers began reading into it all manner of meanings and symbolism. For Spielberg it was always 'an exercise in paranoia'. Amusingly, when Sid Sheinberg was trying to persuade Spielberg to make *Jaws*, he told him, 'Why don't we simply make it *Duel* with a shark.'

Duel was also responsible for bringing Spielberg and George Lucas together. The pair had crossed paths a few times but never really connected. On the night *Duel* was shown on US television Lucas was at a party at the house of Francis Ford Coppola. He was curious to catch the movie and went upstairs, thinking he'd watch maybe ten minutes of it. He ended up watching the whole thing; he couldn't tear himself away. Afterwards he thought to himself, 'I've got to get to know this guy better.'

(US: TV airdate 13 November)

 ## 85　TWO ENGLISH GIRLS (LES DEUX ANGLAISES ET LE CONTINENT)

François Truffaut's love affair with France's great beauty Catherine Deneuve was at an end. Depressed, he entered a clinic for a sleep cure, and took one book with him: Henri-Pierre Roché's *Les Deux Anglaises et le continent*. Truffaut was not unfamiliar with Roché's work, having already had success with the author's *Jules et Jim* (1962). He set about bringing this new novel to the screen, perhaps in a bid to wipe away his depression. It's perhaps no surprise that the end result is a dark picture that almost wallows in its own misery.

Truffaut chose Jean Gruault, who had skilfully adapted *Jules et Jim* a decade previously, to write the screenplay. The director's identification with the source material was so strong that the narrative voice-over was read by Truffaut himself, and taken directly from the novel. Roché's story takes place in the years before the First World War and concerns Claude Roc, played in the film by Jean-Pierre Léaud, a young middle-class Frenchman who befriends Ann Brown, a young Englishwoman. While spending time in Wales with Ann's family, Claude falls in love with her sister Muriel. This being an intricate study of siblings, Truffaut hoped to cast actresses who were sisters, an idea that may have lingered from his romantic involvement with both Françoise Dorléac (whom he directed in 1964's *The Soft Skin*) and her sister Catherine Deneuve. Truffaut was to say that one of these sisters had deserted him in death (Françoise died as the result of a car accident in 1967), while the other deserted him in life.

Instead, Truffaut cast two unrelated British actresses; Stacey Tendeter played Muriel, while Kika Markham was Ann. Markham had done a lot of stage work and television, particularly in period drama, but this was her first major film role. Markham remembers that her first meeting with Truffaut was very formal:

> It was not like an audition at all because he really couldn't speak English. The thing about Truffaut was, he was quite childlike. His background was very unhappy with his parents. He didn't get on with his father. He didn't even know whether they cared for him or not. That's why he made films like *The 400 Blows* and worked a lot with children. He felt a lot of passion towards children. He identified with anybody that had been lost or left. He was very kindly like that.[431]

In one sequence, where Ann, played by Markham, confesses to her sister that she has slept with Claude, a very intense and emotional scene, it was a little disconcerting for both actresses when Truffaut insisted on bringing in a young boy that had been hanging around the location and having him stand there on the set and call 'action'.

Filming began in the spring of 1971 on the coast of Normandy, a location chosen to substitute for the Welsh coastline and moorland where most of the action takes place. Markham enjoyed the shoot enormously. 'Truffaut hardly directed you. You sort of knew what to do because the writing was good. It was all there. So, there was never any confusion between us. The path was fairly straight forward. He required simplicity, really.'[432] Usually, the actors knew if Truffaut was satisfied with a take or instinctively could understand what he wanted. If not, his assistant Suzanne Schiffman was always there to interpret. Schiffman was a screenwriter and director in her own right and had previously worked closely with Jean-Luc Godard.

Outside work, Markham and Truffaut often discussed politics, with the actress keen to interest him in her passion for left-wing causes. But

Truffaut liked his luxuries too much and living well. 'Once we went to a terribly expensive hotel and he said I had to have a new bag or I couldn't go. I think he was rather conservative, not in his politics, but in his life.'[433]

Markham enjoyed making the film: 'It was an incredible experience.'[434] And there was the added charm of working with her father, the actor David Markham, whom Truffaut cast in the role of a palmist in a brief scene where he reads the two sisters' fortunes. The two men got on extremely well. Markham recalls that Schiffman told her, 'Truffaut loves fathers. His own family was a mess. He thinks everyone else's is wonderful.'[435] Truffaut later cast David Markham in his *Day for Night* (1973).

Truffaut was extremely pleased with *Two English Girls*. It remains one of the director's most visually beautiful films; Nestor Almendros's camera seems to evoke the work of the great impressionist painters. However, when it opened the reviews were mixed. There was much comment about the scene in which Claude and Muriel make love and we see the bed sheets steeped in blood. It was unusual for Truffaut to be so explicit in his imagery. 'People said that was too much and they tried to make him change it,' says Markham, 'but he absolutely refused.'[436]

The film's commercial failure, and complaints that it was too slow, forced Truffaut to remove twenty minutes; but this didn't make a difference and he sank into another depression. This film, indeed all his films, were so personal. 'Cinema was everything to him,' says Markham, 'actually his whole being.'[437] The missing minutes would later be restored.

Truffaut had a reputation for falling in love and having affairs with his leading ladies and indeed he did fall in love with Markham, who was warned that it wouldn't last very long:

> When the film finished, I was full of grieving and thought, 'well, that's that.' Then he sent a telegram asking me to come to the south of France where he was staying, and it was all quite awkward. And he drove me back to the airport. And that was the end of it.[438]

They did sort of stay in touch and met up again years later. 'By then I was married and had a baby. He was such a sweet and lovely man.'[439]

(France: opening 18 November)

86 A TOUCH OF ZEN (XIA NU)

Blending art house aesthetics with the more commercially minded martial arts genre, *A Touch of Zen* is regarded as a masterpiece of Chinese cinema and martial arts moviemaking. It was directed by King Hu, whose films of the 1960s and 1970s reshaped martial arts cinema and influenced subsequent Hong Kong action directors like Ang Lee, John Woo and Jackie Chan, who was a stuntman on *A Touch of Zen* and also played a small role.

Although Hu worked in Hong Kong cinema he was actually born in Peking (now Beijing) and in his youth was captivated by Peking opera, especially the stylised martial arts movements and depiction of ancient legends. Arriving in Hong Kong in 1949 he worked as a set decorator and an actor, before making his directorial debut with the war drama *Sons of the Good Earth* (1965) for the famous Shaw Brothers Studio. Next, Hu made a big impact with *Come Drink with Me* (1966), his first wuxia martial arts film, a genre that featured stories of chivalry and fantasy set in ancient China. Hu introduced a heightened sense of realism and highly stylised choreography that ushered in a whole new boom of modern wuxia pictures.

The downside was Hu's growing reputation for a slow and meticulous way of working. This led to him leaving the Shaw Studio and going to Taiwan to make his next two films. It was the success of the first of these, *Dragon Inn* (1967), that gave him the clout to make a martial arts epic. For years Hu had been a fan of the ghost and fantasy tales of the Ming dynasty scholar Pu Songling. His initial inspiration came from a very brief story in Pu's *Strange Stories from a Chinese Studio*, written around 1679. To expand on the idea, Hu thought of introducing the theme of zen Buddhism – full of grandeur and mystery, and leisurely paced, the first combat scene doesn't happen until an hour in. *A Touch of Zen* follows a provincial painter (Chun Shih) who becomes involved in imperial machinations when he tries to protect a fugitive noblewoman, Yang (Feng Hsu) from an army of warriors.

The production was a mammoth undertaking. The main set of a ruined town took almost a year to construct. After that it was left for months to become suitably weathered. The set didn't come cheap and was built to last. Over the next several years, according to Hu himself, some 200 pictures were shot there. Equal effort was expanded in finding other locations; these were sometimes in isolated places, most notably a fight that takes place in a bamboo forest. Hu took twenty-five days to shoot this now legendary sequence, largely because the location site was in a valley and sunlight hit it only four hours a day. Later reworked by Ang Lee in *Crouching Tiger, Hidden Dragon* (2000), this set piece, like others in *A Touch of Zen*, was influenced by the balletic movements of Peking opera that Hu loved as a child. The film's fight choreographer was Han Ying-Chieh, who originally trained in Peking opera acrobatics and stagecraft. He said that he designed all his fight scenes like ballets. In the bamboo forest fight warriors leap 20ft into the sky, somersaulting and fighting in mid-air. One of the female warriors leaps onto the trunk of a tree, clasping against it like a forest creature, before dive-bombing her foe. These impressive leaps were enhanced by trampolines hidden in the set.

Taking almost two years to complete, *A Touch of Zen* was so long, over three hours, that the original Taiwanese release came in two parts, first in 1970 and then 1971. It was not a success. In November 1971, a condensed version, running two and a half hours, debuted in Hong Kong. Again, it was not a success. Eclipsed by the extraordinary popularity of Bruce Lee's *The Big Boss*, it played for only one week on two screens.

It wasn't until the full three-hour version was revived for a screening at the 1975 Cannes Film Festival that *A Touch of Zen* gained international attention. Shown in competition, it won a prize for technical achievement, becoming only the second Chinese-language film to win an award at Cannes. Despite its festival success, no distributor was willing to take it on, as the kung fu craze was beginning to wane, following the death of Lee in July 1973. As a result, the film was only seen sporadically in America and Europe, usually in art houses. Only in recent years has the true mastery of *A Touch of Zen* been appreciated by a wider audience.

(Hong Kong: opening 18 November)

87 | *STRAW DOGS*

Katy Haber was at home in London when she got a call from producer James Swann. Sam Peckinpah was looking for an assistant on his new movie, to be shot in the UK – was she interested? Not really. Haber was taking a short break from the business and just off to watch a tennis match at Wimbledon. Weeks later, Haber was rejuvenated and looking for a new job. Exhibiting perfect timing, Swann called again, saying that

Peckinpah had hired and fired three assistants and desperately needed someone. When Haber walked into Peckinpah's office in Piccadilly he hardly appeared to notice her. Instead he thrust a script into her hand, with an almost illegible scrawl all over it, and asked her to type it out. It was the rape scene from *Straw Dogs*. 'Somehow, I could read his writing, or at least read his mind, because at 11 that night I had finished his changes. And at 11 that night I was hired.'[440] Haber's life was never to be the same again.

Straw Dogs was based on the novel *The Siege of Trencher's Farm* by Scottish author Gordon Williams. As the script took shape, Peckinpah asked Harold Pinter to take a look and offer some comments. Pinter was appalled by what he read, and didn't hold back in a letter to the director: 'I detest it with unqualified detestation,' adding, 'How you can associate yourself with it is beyond me. I can only say I consider it an abomination.' Peckinpah replied with: 'Of course! But that's the point, isn't it?'[441]

The story centres on the relationship between American academic David Sumner, played by Dustin Hoffman, and his young wife Amy (Susan George), who retreat to the village where Amy grew up in a bid to save their marriage. Here the couple are menaced in their home by a local gang of vigilantes pursuing a suspected child-killer David is protecting.

Shot on location in Cornwall, Haber found out fast what it took to work with Peckinpah, and that meant not just working as his secretary/assistant. 'They were just titles. On all the films I worked on with Sam, we were tied at the hip. I fulfilled many and sundry roles including continuity, second unit director and dialogue director.'[442] For a middle-class girl like Haber, learning to work with the unpredictable Sam Peckinpah was like suddenly being thrown into the Wild West. And it was tough acclimatising 'because Sam was already at loggerheads with the producers. Dan Melnick wanted Sam fired early on during pre-production and we had to fight to stay on the picture.'[443] Added to that the weather was miserably cold and Peckinpah was constantly sick.

After Cornwall, interiors were done at Twickenham Studios in London. 'Every rock that was thrown through the window in Cornwall had to land correctly on the set at Twickenham weeks later,' says Haber. 'Matching the rocks was another of my many jobs. It was also my job to do continuity during the rape scene because the continuity lady refused to be on the set.'[444]

Straw Dogs's enduring notoriety rests on the rape of Amy. Peckinpah wanted the scene, which did not feature in the book, to be realistic, visceral and horrifying. It caused consternation for George, then just 21 years old, as the sequence was only loosely described in the script, and Peckinpah refused to discuss what he wanted from her. At one point she threatened to quit if the scene was shot too explicitly.

According to Haber, Peckinpah would resort to any means necessary to get what he wanted from an actor. After the rape, Amy attends an event at the local village hall, the trauma still clearly evident on her face. Just before the scene, Peckinpah took George aside and said to her, 'Your father is not as young as he used to be and not too well, he might not even live to see the release of this film.' As Susan absorbed this information she started to cry and Peckinpah rolled the camera and called 'action'.

As for Peckinpah and Hoffman, 'They were both perfectionists,' says Haber.[445] Hoffman explained to Peckinpah how suppressing laughter and keeping a straight face helped him portray intense emotion, such as anger. Often, he'd ask Peckinpah to try and make him laugh in some of his character's most intense moments. Hoffman also took to using this technique with his fellow actors. 'On one of his off-camera entrances into the village pub,' recalls Haber, 'when Del Henney and Ken Hutchison were in the bar, Dustin came in without his pants on. Henney, an intense actor to say the least, was definitely not amused.'[446]

In America *Straw Dogs* was trimmed of several minutes, mostly from the rape scene, in order to receive an R-rating instead of an X-rating, which was the kiss of death commercially. Even with the cuts the picture caused huge controversy; many reviewers, while admiring Peckinpah's skill as a filmmaker, lambasted the gratuitous depiction of violence. Some felt he had taken his obsession with toxic masculinity to extremes. Famously the *New Yorker* critic Pauline Kael called *Straw Dogs* 'the first American film that is a fascist work of art'. And *Life* reviewer Richard Schickel labelled the film 'unredeemed, unrelenting evil'. Peckinpah was personally stung by those two critiques. In a *New York Times* piece in October 1971, he defended his film, stating: 'We're violent by nature. We're going to survive by being violent. If we don't recognize that we're violent people, we're dead.'

The irony of all this was that *Straw Dogs* became Peckinpah's most successful picture at the box office up to that point; certainly, it remained the most controversial of his career. It was especially successful in the UK, despite similar critical condemnation. The British censor was forced to defend passing the film uncut, stating their belief that the film was a serious attempt to do something about societal violence. Things were a little different on home video when *Straw Dogs* was caught up in the video nasties controversy of the mid-1980s and ended up banned. It didn't return again to the home market in the UK until 2002.

For Haber *Straw Dogs* was the beginning of a seven-year relationship with Peckinpah, both professionally and on a personal level. 'I learnt more about movie making than I could have done in a lifetime of film school.'[447] It was a rough ride; besides working on the films she was Peckinpah's enabler, nurse, his other half, and the one who understood him like few others. She was also the buffer between him and the studios. 'I was there to fight the powers that be, to cover for problems, to make excuses and be there through thick and thin.'[448]

Towards the end of production on *Convoy* in 1977, Katy quit. She and Peckinpah had parted ways before, on no less than five separate occasions, only this time it was final. Haber never spoke to or saw Peckinpah again. When he died in 1984 her first emotion was anger. 'He never gave me a chance to tell him thank you.'[449]

(UK/US: London opening 20 November)

88 | MAN IN THE WILDERNESS

By the dawn of the 1970s, one of the great hellraisers of the 1960s, Richard Harris, was in something of a career nosedive. His 1970 western *A Man Called Horse* had done well, but that was sandwiched between two very expensive flops that same year, *The Molly Maguires*, a coal mining drama that paired him with his acting pal Sean Connery, and the historical epic *Cromwell*. Adding to his woes his latest film *Bloomfield* (1971) was booed off the screen at the Berlin Film Festival and never really seen again. His next picture had to be chosen well.

Sandy Howard was the producer behind *A Man Called Horse* and believed he'd found exactly the right project for Harris, a revisionist western with a difference. While scouting locations in the wilds of Dakota for another movie, Howard came across the true account of Hugh Glass, a fur trapper and frontiersman who survived a vicious bear attack in 1823. Left for dead by his companions, Glass managed to crawl 200 miles to Fort Kiowa on the Missouri River, despite a broken leg and shredded torso, where he threatened to take revenge on the men who abandoned him. It was the kind of story that had been told over frontier campfires year after year.

Too many campfires as it turned out. Howard discovered that the Glass story had been the subject of a 1954 novel by Frederick Manfred, who had also hoped to turn it into a Hollywood movie. Faced with these facts, Howard either had to buy the film rights from Manfred or alter some of the names and events. Howard chose the cheap option, and thus Harris became Zachary Bass. Manfred was cheesed off to say the least when the film came out and threatened to sue the producers. The case ended up being settled out of court.

If the story of Hugo Glass sounds familiar, that's because Leonardo DiCaprio portrayed him in the 2015 movie *The Revenant*, winning an Academy Award for Best Actor. The film was also nominated for Best Picture. The productions are similar, of course, although *Man in the Wilderness* is less contrived and more faithful in its telling. And while Harris never received any kind of acting nod or award, he gives an excellent performance. Harris had clashed several times with director Elliot Silverstein on *A Man Called Horse*, so Howard brought in Richard C. Sarafian to helm this picture. Wisely, Howard also made the actor a partner in the movie and found him to be a willing and enthusiastic collaborator. Asked for his reasoning in making Harris a partner, Howard simply declared, 'Well, it made certain that he showed up each day! And he was first on set in the mornings, and last to go home.'[450]

Harris had got pally with a gentleman by the name of John Bindon, who had a reputation among the criminal elements of west London, and took him over to Spain to play one of the fur trappers in his picture. It wasn't long before they were drinking and brawling. Sarafian wasn't having any of it and insisted Bindon be removed and his character hastily killed off with a convenient spear in the back. His remaining lines of dialogue were shared out between the other actors.

Other cast members included Dennis Waterman and James Doohan, *Star Trek*'s Scotty. John Huston, who plays the leader of a gang of fur trappers, was cast in the role because he just happened to be in Spain, having just days before quit as the director of a film called *The Last Run* following fierce disagreements with its star George C. Scott. We first see him commanding a group of men dragging a boat over some rocky terrain Fitzcarraldo-style. Harris got on well with Huston, and in their free time the famous director introduced him to the books of Georges Simenon and his famous detective hero Maigret. Harris was instantly hooked and read something like sixty of them. It became an obsession to one day play the character, which he finally did in a TV movie made in 1988.

Man in the Wilderness is an uncompromising film. Sarafian doesn't hold back in his depiction of life in the wild as a constant battle for survival. In one scene Bass comes across a bison being devoured by wolves. Starving and unable to walk, he crawls on his hands and knees and beats the wolves off with a club, before ripping off a chunk of bloody raw meat for himself and eating it. There is also a heavy religious aspect to the film. In flashbacks we learn that Bass is at odds with his Christian upbringing. During his journey through the wilderness, as he recovers and gains his strength, the film changes into a story about a man finding true redemption and forgiveness.

(US: Los Angeles opening 24 November)

89 NICHOLAS AND ALEXANDRA

Sam Spiegel was the last of the great independent movie producers who sprang from the golden age of Hollywood. By the early 1970s his power was diminishing but his passion for epic moviemaking remained. And there was no bigger canvas than the fall of Imperial Russia and the 1917 revolution.

For a man who had worked with some of the biggest stars in movies, from Marlon Brando to Elizabeth Taylor, Spiegel took a gamble by casting two unknowns as the fated Tsar Nicholas II and Alexandra. Michael Jayston was a theatre and television actor with a good reputation. 'I remember going for the first test with Liv Ullmann,' says Jayston, 'who was supposed to be playing Alexandra. She was charming and very good. Afterwards she wished me all the best.'[451] At Jayston's second test there was no sign of Ullmann. Instead, he found himself performing opposite Janet Suzman, who had come from the Royal Shakespeare Company. 'Apparently Spiegel didn't like Liv Ullmann's accent,' says Jayston.[452]

Spiegel surrounded his two young leads with the cream of British acting royalty: Laurence Olivier, Michael Redgrave, Jack Hawkins, Eric Porter and Harry Andrews. They would fly in for a few days, work and then fly out again. Curd Jürgens, Jayston recalls, was on the set for one, maybe two days. 'Spiegel paid him with a brand-new Mercedes.'[453] Olivier, cast as the tsar's adviser, was there a bit longer, around ten days. 'He was marvellous,' says Jayston. 'He also offered me a job at the National Theatre, which he ran at the time, and I happily accepted.'[454]

Olivier also solved the thorny question of who ought to play the legendary character of Rasputin. Various names were bandied around.

'Spiegel turned down Max von Sydow,' recalls Jayston. 'He didn't even test him. He wanted O'Toole to play it and I was in Spiegel's office when O'Toole, who didn't like Spiegel at all, refused to play the part and Spiegel went barmy.'[455] Jayston was sat in make-up one day when Olivier mentioned they ought to get Tom Baker to play Rasputin. 'He's a bit eccentric, but we've got him at the National playing small parts.' Spiegel took Olivier's advice and Baker was cast. 'He hardly got any money for it, a pittance really,' says Jayston. 'But I remained great friends with Tom.'[456]

Spiegel had an equally awkward time finding the right director: Ken Russell, Lindsay Anderson, John Boorman were all considered. Finally, Franklin J. Schaffner, who had two big recent hits with *Planet of the Apes* and *Patton* (1970), signed on. During the shoot Spiegel and Schaffner clashed. It got so bad that a top executive of Columbia, the backers, had to be called in to hold peace talks. Jayston recalls that while Spiegel wasn't always around the set, he still made his presence felt:

Sam always had to put his oar in, and he was nearly always wrong about a lot of things. His influence was not very conducive for Schaffner to do good work and Schaffner was trying to keep his temper in most of the time.[457]

For example, Spiegel would see rushes and order Schaffner to reshoot various things, most of which weren't used because Schaffner's original work was deemed better. This constant interference was draining. 'It annoyed Schaffner,' says Jayston. 'It impinged on his authority, and he couldn't do anything about it.'[458] One day Schaffner said to Jayston, 'I'd like to strangle that son of a bitch.' Jayston replied, 'I'd buy tickets.'[459]

Jayston, too, was not fond of Spiegel, finding him something of a vulgarian:

I remember going to his place in New York and there were ten Toulouse-Lautrec paintings in one of the downstairs lavatories. It was like, this is my money. At one party we had Persian caviar and Sam was putting his cigar out in some of the caviar jars.[460]

Shot in Spain, the picture cost a whopping $9 million. Spiegel had been refused permission to shoot in the Soviet Union, 'And the film wasn't shown in Russia for a long time,' says Jayston.[461] Despite the tensions, Jayston enjoyed the shoot; a lot of his acting friends and colleagues, like

Julian Glover, Ian Holm and Brian Cox, making his film debut, had been cast in small roles. Steven Berkoff had a small role and asked Spiegel if he could play Rasputin. 'Sam admired his hutzpah,' says Jayston, 'and the fact they were both Jewish, but he said, "I've never heard of you."'[462]

Before playing Nicholas II, Jayston did plenty of research. 'I don't think he liked being tsar. He was really like a country gentleman. He admired the English a lot. Of course, his cousin was King George V.'[463] There is a general view that Nicholas was a weak man, particularly in his decision-making, and Jayston reveals that he played to the strengths of Janet Suzman because Alexandra was that much stronger a person. 'I know he was ruthless, but I felt sorry for him because events took over. The revolution was on its way and that took everybody by surprise.'[464]

The final scene of the family's massacre at the hands of the Bolsheviks is utterly harrowing and by far the most effective moment in the entire film. Nicholas and Alexandra, along with their children, are led into a sparse, colourless room to await their fate. Finally, a group of men enter with guns and open fire. It took all day to recreate this infamous moment of history and for the actors it was very unsettling. Jayston says:

> I'm not a method actor, and neither is Janet, but when we were doing that scene there was something about it. Janet got quite upset about it and the girls did as well. I spent about an hour in a bar afterwards having a few drinks trying to get it out of my mind.[465]

Despite being nominated for an Academy Award for Best Picture and for Janet's performance, *Nicholas and Alexandra* was on the whole poorly received by the critics and flopped at the box office. 'I thought at three hours it was too long,' says Jayston.[466] Spiegel took the film's failure badly, and it effectively ended his career. He was already 70 years old. Spiegel produced just two more films before he died in 1985.

(UK/US: London opening 29 November)

 ## 90 BLEAK MOMENTS

This painful, tragic tale of Sylvia, a young woman tied to her elder, mentally disabled sister, began life as a stage play directed by Mike Leigh and performed in 1970 at a London fringe theatre. Anne Raitt had done some theatre work with Leigh and was invited to join the cast, playing

Sylvia. While the structure of the play had been mapped out before-hand and the actors knew where they were going, the piece lent heavily on improvisation. 'There were moments when we didn't know what the other person was going to say,' recalls Raitt, 'which meant that the piece was very much alive.'[467] It was this kind of experimentation that enthused Albert Finney when he came to see it.

Along with his business partner Michael Medwin, Finney had his own production company, Memorial Enterprises, and was keen to promote original work and new talent. Mike Leigh certainly fitted into that category, despite being totally untried. He had never directed a film or anything on television. Even so, Finney agreed to help finance a film version of the play; the fact that he and Leigh were both Salford Grammar School boys may have sealed the deal. Even with further backing from the BFI, the budget was only £18,000, with the cast and crew working for £20 a week.

To some extent Finney and Medwin took on *Bleak Moments* sight unseen. There was no script. The film was to be an expansion of the play and the script was constructed during rehearsals, which is how Leigh preferred to work. 'We spent ages rehearsing in a wretched hall,' recalls Raitt.[468] At first Leigh split up his actors and made them work on their own. He wanted them to imagine where their characters lived, what their homes were like, their individual situations, what their mental state was. Raitt reveals:

> You were living with yourself before you met any of the other actors. It was very extreme. And then you were put in with another actor and Mike would give you a situation to act and try out. In that way Mike gradually got an idea of who to put with whom and in what situation.[469]

It's an interesting way of working. 'A lot of the dialogue comes from the actors and the characterisation comes from the actors totally,' Raitt confirms.[470]

During rehearsals Raitt and Sarah Stephenson, the actress playing her mentally disabled sister, were encouraged to go outside in character, to places like shops and post offices. 'I felt so guilty,' recalls Raitt, 'because the people in the shops were trying to help out and going, "Oh what a shame, we're so sorry."'[471]

As a backer Finney was often at rehearsals and, when filming started, was an occasional visitor to the main location, a house in south London.

In post-production, too, he was around and always gently encouraging. He even donated some cans of film stock from the picture he was then working on, *Gumshoe*, to help with costs. The lack of money does show in the finished film; it's a bit rough round the edges. The crew really did have to improvise due to shortages. In one long tracking shot between two characters walking along a pavement talking, the entire crew and some of the actors hid behind a hedge, passing a hand microphone to each other in order to capture the dialogue as the actors passed.

The budget heavily restricted a lot of outdoor location filming. So the bulk of the picture takes place indoors, lending the film even more of a gloomy atmosphere. This filtered through to Raitt who, having also done the play, had lived with Sylvia for almost a year. 'It took me quite a long time to get over that film because I got so into the character. I became that person.'[472] If they were working late on the film, instead of going home, which necessitated a long journey across half of London, Raitt would sometimes sleep in the house, in her character's room. 'At the very end of the shoot when the crew started to dismantle my room I was really upset. Mike thought it was funny. I could have punched him.'[473]

This was clearly a symptom of the way Leigh worked. 'He deals with the actor's psyches almost completely,' says Raitt.[474] To find Sylvia and understand her, this woman, who, like all of the characters in the story, is unable to understand or express herself and is therefore isolated from everyone, Raitt drew from a time in her life when she was ill for a very long time, which cut her off from almost everything. 'And so, what I did was to feed on that part of my life which I had spent years climbing out of and so *Bleak Moments* rather flung me back into that psychological area.'[475]

Bleak Moments was highly acclaimed critically, but its dour subject matter restricted any kind of mainstream audience, and beyond the art house circuit it had no commercial impact. 'If you're watching that film, you kind of need a bottle of scotch beside you,' admits Raitt. 'It's so gloomy.'[476] *Bleak Moments* did, however, announce Leigh's artistic credentials, although it was television that took advantage. That was where the work was, with the film industry in Britain for the rest of the decade in near collapse. Leigh was to make nine feature-length plays, mostly for the BBC, the best known of which was *Abigail's Party*, based on one of Leigh's most successful stage works. It would be another seventeen years before he embarked on another cinema release, 1988's *High Hopes*.

(UK: London Film Festival opening 30 November)

91 FAMILY LIFE

By the time Ken Loach came around to making *Family Life*, his third feature, his modus operandi, which he considered to be central to the kind of films he wanted to make, was one that he has strictly adhered to for the entirety of his career. That is to make films for the class he considered to be the only politically important class – the working class. 'And therefore, not to make elitist films, or cineaste films, but to make films which can be understood by ordinary people.'[477]

You couldn't get more working class than playwright David Mercer – his father was an engine driver, his mother a maid and both of his grandfathers were coal miners. Early in his career, after the collapse of his first marriage, Mercer suffered a nervous breakdown and spent a lengthy time in psychoanalysis. Much of his personal experience of mental illness and psychiatric hospitals was to inform his 1967 BBC television play *In Two Minds*, which was directed by Loach. It was based on the ideas of the controversial Scottish psychiatrist R.D. Laing, who railed against the barbaric way he felt the mentally ill were treated, and believed that such patients should be looked after outside an institutional environment. Laing also challenged the traditional view that people with schizophrenia were born with the condition, theorising that social pressures were to blame – more often than not the fault of the family structure, in other words, parents. As Philip Larkin so famously observed in probably the darkest poem ever written: 'They fuck you up, your mum and dad. They may not mean to, but they do.'

Following the success of Loach's previous film *Kes* (1969) it was comparatively easy to get another of the director's films off the ground. The finance came from the National Film Finance Corporation and EMI, which each put up half the £190,000 budget. The idea to make a film version of *In Two Minds* came from Tony Garnett, a producer responsible for some of the most politically radical dramas ever seen on British television, usually in collaboration with Loach, such as *Up the Junction* (1965), which included a backstreet abortion sequence, and *Cathy Come Home* (1966). Garnett read psychology at university and was in tune with Laing's theories. Loach was less enthused about making a film of the play; his working relationship with Mercer hadn't been great and they were to clash once again. Keen to approach the film, as he'd done on the television version, in a quasi-documentary style, Loach encouraged his actors to improvise. Conversely, Mercer was one of those writers for whom every word and syllable were sacrosanct. Inevitably there were tensions, and Garnett was usually the one stuck in the middle. In the end Loach did press the actors to improvise in some of their scenes.

The story concerns the plight of Janice, a 19-year-old suicidal schizophrenic girl, whose own dysfunctional family is the real cause of her disturbance, especially a domineering mother who has made her unable to establish her own identity. Janice's parents respond to her depression by taking their daughter to see a psychiatrist, a follower of the theories of Laing. When he is asked to leave by the hospital board Janice is instead transferred to a harsh regime of drugs and electro-convulsive therapy.

For the role of Janice, Loach found a young actress called Sandy Ratcliff. Like a lot of the actors Loach likes to work with, Ratcliff had very little acting experience, save doing a few dramas for school television programmes. To prepare for the film, she spoke with psychiatrists, and Loach accompanied her on visits to mental homes, where she watched first hand women enduring electroshock treatment. Ratcliff was able to draw upon her own troubled and rebellious upbringing: she was expelled from her local grammar school and sent to the Tavistock clinic, a specialist mental health trust based in north London.

During filming she and Loach battled over the character. Loach didn't want the actress to wear make-up and also forbade her to wash her hair for the whole seven-week shoot. He used to examine her scalp to see if she was cheating. After the film Ratcliff was tipped by Lord Snowdon to be one of five 'Faces for the Seventies' in a *Sunday Times* magazine article of 1972. However, it wasn't until the mid-1980s that she found fame as Sue Osman in the original cast of the BBC soap *EastEnders* – ironically a character who finished her run on the show by being sectioned and admitted to a psychiatric hospital.

Unsurprisingly, *Family Life* did not connect with audiences in the same way that *Kes* did. The film, like the play, did court some controversy. Interestingly the letters the makers received were split down the middle. Some said, 'Oh, the poor parents, with a girl like that, what a terrible time they had,' while the other half said, 'The poor girl, with parents like that, no wonder she went mad.'[478] In France the film was initially banned due to concerns it might encourage people to commit suicide. By the time it was allowed to be shown in cinemas, the theories of Laing had become well known in the country and, as a consequence, *Family Life* did well and made Loach's reputation there. However, its failure in Britain made it almost impossible for Loach to find finance for more films and he went back into television, not directing a feature again until 1979.

(UK: London opening 2 December)

92 GUMSHOE

Eddie Ginley works as a bingo caller and compere at a local working men's club in Liverpool. He's a wannabe comedian, too, and, as an avid reader of Raymond Chandler, also rather fancies himself as a Humphrey Bogart type. As a laugh, Eddie places an ad in the local paper posing as a private detective. But the joke backfires when someone takes him up on the offer and he becomes embroiled in a real-life case involving drugs, blackmail and murder.

This is the intriguing premise of Stephen Frears's first film as a director. Coming from the Royal Court Theatre, Frears started in films when Karel Reisz employed him as an assistant director on *Morgan – A Suitable Case for Treatment* (1966). Frears worked in the same capacity on Lindsay Anderson's *If* (1968) and *Charlie Bubbles* (1968), both of which were made for Albert Finney's production company, Memorial Enterprises. As well as working on television, Frears had directed an admired short film, *The Burning*, about apartheid in South Africa, when he told his friend, the writer Neville Smith, that he should write a thriller, a genre they were both fans of. *Gumshoe* was the result and Frears had a feeling that Finney might like to do it. He did, responding to the piece in much the same way he did with the fantasies of Billy Liar, a character he played on stage. Finney was something of a daydreamer as an adolescent, and it was going to the movies and getting lost in their fantasy world that allowed him to think and dream of life beyond the grimy environs of where he lived in Salford.

Smith was much the same. He had in large part written the script in homage to those *film noir* classics of the 1940s that he saw as a young working-class kid growing up in Liverpool. In order to enable Smith to concentrate and finish the script, Frears carted him off to a vicarage, so he was able to write in isolation. Smith also makes a brief appearance in the film as a gun expert.

When Memorial Enterprises came on board, they offered the distribution rights to ten companies. With Finney starring, Columbia took less than eight hours to snap them up. On his first day on the set Frears recalled feeling only one emotion – terror. Doing a feature was a big step up from television. He also found the movie industry to be quite a conservative world. Here was Frears, along with Smith and cameraman Chris Menges, again from television, these young Turks, and there was a degree of conflict between them and the traditional filmmaking that went on in Britain at the time.

Supporting Finney is an excellent cast including Billie Whitelaw, Frank Finlay and the American actress Janice Rule. In a small role was Carolyn Seymour, just starting her career:

> When I heard Finney was in the film I said, 'I'll do it, whatever it is.' And I just sat there and watched all these extraordinary actors. I could have watched Billie Whitelaw all day. And Frank Finlay was an absolute dream. Albie was lovely to work with too.[479]

At the time Finney was married to French actress Anouk Aimée, who was around all the time. 'Albie had just fallen in love with her, and she was so French and difficult. And he was constantly exhausted,' says Seymour.[480]

Frears was also looking to cast someone as a modern version of the 1940s Sidney Greenstreet 'Fat Man' character from films like *The Maltese Falcon* and *Casablanca*. When he was on a location recce to Liverpool with Menges, driving in the centre of the city and stopping at some traffic lights, a corpulent gentleman began walking across the road. He was perfect. Menges urged Frears to get out of the car and go see who he was. His name was George Silver, and he was in the catering business; in fact, he owned a fifth of the Wimpy restaurants in the country. In his 50s, Silver agreed to play the role, and from then on made something of a career for himself appearing as 'heavies' on film and television.

Gumshoe was well received critically but didn't really find its audience. The film doesn't seem to be able to make up its mind whether it's a spoof of the detective genre or wants to take itself seriously. It has a social realist setting, but Finney talks this absolutely fantasy-based private-eye speak reminiscent of characters like Sam Spade. *Gumshoe* is an odd amalgamation of Walter Mitty and *The Maltese Falcon*. Perhaps the fault lay in the conditions in which the film was made, with Frears and Smith aiming for pastiche, while the backers, Columbia, wanted more of a straightforward detective story. The result was a film that fell between the two stools. Despite all that, it's an entertaining watch and Finney is outstanding.

Listen out, also, for the first film soundtrack by Andrew Lloyd Webber. He would do just one more, *The Odessa File* (1974), before concentrating on theatre musicals. His score for *Gumshoe* is highly reminiscent of those classic gangster dramas, and portions of it would later be incorporated into his musicals *Evita* and especially *Sunset Boulevard*.

As for Frears, he went back to television and didn't direct another feature until *The Hit* in 1984 and then *My Beautiful Laundrette* in 1985, which launched his career as one of Britain's most important directors.

(UK/US: London opening 9 December)

93 *THE HOSPITAL*

Writer Paddy Chayefsky had just come out of a decade-long slump in his career when he won the Oscar for this blistering screenplay, a 'gothic horror story' he called it, set in a metropolitan hospital. The project began life as a series of hard-hitting dramas meant for television: the idea was to use a large city hospital as a metaphor for everything that was wrong with contemporary American society. Instead, Chayefsky approached UA with it.

Before writing the script Chayefsky immersed himself in research, reading medical books and journals 'by the truckload' and visiting hospitals in the New York area. One emergency room in the Bronx was so full of the sick and wounded that 'it looked like something out of a World War II movie'.[481] Interviews he conducted with doctors, nurses, surgeons and administrators brought up a cavalcade of horror stories about their day-to-day life. Chayefsky was proud that some of the best reviews of the movie came from medical journals, pointing out that this was what really happens in a hospital. Chayefsky insisted that everything in the movie had happened in a hospital somewhere at some time.

He spares the audience nothing, depicting doctors as more interested in making money than the welfare of their patients, a staff that can barely cope, bureaucratic inefficiency, and an institution that hasn't the time or inclination to worry about the human being behind the number and harasses critically ill patients to produce proof of their medical insurance. The film begins with a young man coming into hospital complaining of chest pains and, thanks to a misdiagnosis, is given the wrong drugs and dies in less than twelve hours. Chayefsky doesn't sugar-coat his pill; he rams it down the throat of the audience.

His protagonist is Dr Herbert Bock, who is going through something of a mid-life crisis. His suffocation at the hands of bureaucracy parallels the impotency of his own life; his wife has left him, he's thrown his son out and he's contemplating suicide, when he isn't drinking himself into oblivion. Faced with a monstrous administrative system that is out of control, Bock gamely soldiers on. But when a string of mysterious murders take place at the hospital, he finds himself in the role of detective. This is an interesting aspect of the film – with sudden death so commonplace in emergency rooms, somebody clever could do horrible damage before being caught. It's easy to kill in a place where people die all the time.

It was a great role for any actor, with wonderful monologues containing some of Chayefsky's best writing. UA wanted Burt Lancaster or Walter Matthau, while Chayefsky's first choice was George C. Scott. When Scott demanded a $300,000 salary, the studio baulked and offered Rod Steiger the part. When he asked for even more money, Scott was back in.

For director, UA brought in the up-and-coming Michael Ritchie, who had just the one picture to his credit, *Downhill Racer* (1969) with Robert Redford. Chayefsky and Ritchie scouted New York for the right hospital to shoot in, selecting the Metropolitan Hospital on the Upper East Side of Manhattan. As pre-production continued, however, Chayefsky realised he couldn't work with Ritchie; they simply didn't see the film the same way. He was replaced by Arthur Hiller, who intended to give the film a semi-documentary feel.

For the role of Barbara Drummond, a free-spirited young woman who Bock has an intense fling with, UA were keen on Jane Fonda. Scott refused to sanction the actress, considering her to be 'still too much of a hippie, and in need of a bath'.[482] Chayefsky went with the British actress Diana Rigg, admiring her theatrical credentials and that she was ballsy enough to handle Scott. The character of Barbara was a strong one, but in other areas women were underrepresented. The production was picketed by a group of actresses protesting the fact that not one doctor in the film was female. The leader of the protest was a young actress by the name of Trish Van Devere, who just happened to be Scott's girlfriend and later wife. The actor was incensed, and Trish agreed to pull out of the picket line. Roles for two women doctors were written into the script.

The start of filming coincided with a tumultuous period in Scott's life. At the best of times he was a troubled soul and notorious drinker, but his marriage to the actress Colleen Dewhurst had recently collapsed. On the first day of shooting Scott was a no-show. Hiller knew of his alcoholism, but recalled him only once turning up on the set the worse for wear. The actor approached him asking, 'Arthur, how do you play drunk when you're drunk?' Then there would be days when Scott didn't show up at all because he was at home in a stupor. This presented Hiller with the problem of always having to make alternate plans in case Scott didn't show up. If he did go missing, Scott was always contrite the following morning on set. Hiller recalled:

> He never said anything, but I could feel his determination to make it up to me, that he felt so badly that he had given me a problem, but he couldn't help it. It's an illness, and he had it. But he would just hold himself together all day to give me what he could.[483]

In the end Scott missed so many days that a warning was sent to his agent that, if this persisted, he would be replaced.

Scott ended up giving a towering performance and was again Oscar nominated, despite refusing to accept his award for *Patton* the previous year. Favourably reviewed, *The Hospital* did well commercially too, and was one of UA's biggest hits of the year.

(US: New York opening 14 December)

94 *MACBETH*

Roman Polanski's *Macbeth* was in trouble. Awful weather on location in Wales, combined with Polanski's infamous attention to detail, saw the production two days behind schedule after the first week. People started to get nervous, especially the completion bond company, Film Finances. They had been nervous about taking on the project in the first place, and warned Timothy Burrill, the producer on the ground, to get Polanski to keep on schedule. But the director was adamant: 'I'm going to make the film my way.'

Sure enough, after another week they were again falling well behind. 'Film Finances said they were going to have to pull the plug,' recalls Burrill. 'And under the conditions of the guarantee of completion they had the right to sack Roman and bring in another director.'[484] That director was going to be Peter Collinson. This did not go down very well with Victor Lownes, a business colleague of Polanski who, along with Columbia, was financing the film. Lownes ran the London Playboy Club and was in regular touch with Hugh Hefner. 'Together they acknowledged that Peter Collinson's *Macbeth* was not going to be as commercial as a Roman Polanski *Macbeth*,' says Burrill. 'So, Hugh Hefner flew over in his bunny jet, with his backgammon board and ladies, for talks.'[485]

There followed a lengthy discussion, the outcome of which was that Film Finances withdrew and Playboy agreed to pick up any financial overage; Columbia were not interested in putting any more money in. Essentially the film became a Playboy production. 'As filming continued, we were pushed for money,' says Burrill. 'Happily, at that time the Playboy Club in London was doing tremendous business and we almost had sacks of money coming down every week to pay the salaries of the crew.'[486]

Ever since his film student days in Poland, Polanski had been interested in doing a screen version of a Shakespeare play. It's interesting to note that he chose to film *Macbeth*, by far the Bard's bloodiest drama, so soon after the tragic murder of his wife Sharon Tate at the hands of the deranged followers of Charles Manson. And the screen is full of violence and gore. 'Roman made his own blood,' says Burrill. 'He had this wonderful mixture that included Nescafé coffee, there were gallons of it spread around the set.'[487]

Ditching tradition, Polanski wanted his Macbeth and Lady Macbeth to be young. Burrill remembers Polanski telling him, 'These are kids who would be on a motorcycle.' After numerous auditions, it was down to two upcoming actors: Martin Shaw and Jon Finch. 'We tested both of them,' recalls Burrill. 'And it was debated amongst the crew and Roman. It was a tough decision because Martin longed to play it.'[488] In the end Shaw was deemed to be perhaps too earthy to play a king, and so Finch got the part. Shaw had to make do with playing Banquo. Acclaimed stage actress Francesca Annis, just 25, played Lady Macbeth.

Burrill admits it was his idea to start shooting in Snowdonia in North Wales. This might have worked had the film begun as planned in late summer. Instead, the schedule was pushed back to November when the conditions were far from ideal. 'We all went through a tough time, working long hours in the wind and rain. You'd end the day soaking wet and have to go back to your hotel to find somewhere to dry off.'[489]

On the very first day of shooting Lownes turned up, along with Kenneth Tynan, the noted drama critic Polanski hired to help with the adaptation. Both men asked to be in the film. Polanski happily obliged, hanging them from a gibbet.

Other locations included Bamburgh Castle in Northumberland and Lindisfarne Castle on Holy Island, all beautifully captured by cameraman Gilbert Taylor. The rest of the picture was shot at Shepperton Studios, where Polanski demonstrated his remarkable working method, which though very slow and detailed, brought remarkable results on the screen. Few directors can match the way Polanski composes a shot so beautifully and so carefully. 'Each frame that Roman set up he would spend time making sure everything was correct,' says Burrill. 'That the mug on the table was in the right position and so on. He was meticulous.'[490]

While filming the scene in which Macbeth enters the witch's coven, coming face to face with something like twenty elderly ladies of various shapes and sizes, all completely naked, Polanski realised that it was Hugh Hefner's birthday, Burrill recalls:

> He got Jon Finch with a clapperboard to stand in front of the naked ladies and say to camera, 'Scene 69. Take 69.' And they all sang 'Happy Birthday' to Hugh Hefner. We took it to the lab and got a print and sent it to him.[491]

Polanski's version of *Macbeth* is rightly regarded as one of the best screen adaptations of a Shakespeare play. As for Burrill, he worked again with Polanski a number of times, notably on *Tess* (1979) and *The Pianist* (2002).

(UK/US: Los Angeles opening 15 December)

 ## 95 *FOUR FLIES ON GREY VELVET*

Michael Brandon was renting a room in a former monastery and was a bit puzzled when an Italian gentleman arrived out of the blue one day holding a script and asking him to telephone his son Dario. Not sure what to make of it, Brandon's agent quickly filled him in saying, 'Dario Argento is the biggest cult director in the world. You should read the script and take it seriously.'

The role on offer was that of a young jazz drummer Roberto Tobias, framed for a murder he didn't commit and pursued by a psychopathic killer. Brandon flew from the USA to Rome on Air Italia. It turned out to be a memorable flight. Brandon found himself in the same row as a bunch of American marines:

> All shaved to the skull, and I'm there with hair down around my shoulders, about to play this rock n roll hippie, and they're going, 'is that a girl or a boy?' I thought, 'I can't take this for ten hours.'[492]

He walked to the back of the plane and saw a very attractive woman stretched out. He sat down. Then Brandon recognised her; it was the German actress Romy Schneider:

> Later on, we hit a storm and, boy, were we being thrown about, and she was terrified and held on to me. It was glorious; when I wasn't feeling absolute fear, like being on a rollercoaster. That's how I flew into Rome.[493]

Brandon was given virtually the entire top floor of a hotel, and a set of drums was delivered so he could learn how to play. 'The lifestyle was great.'[494] Argento didn't speak a word of English and Brandon didn't speak any Italian at the time, so it was usually the task of the script girl to act as interpreter. But Brandon began to grasp and understand. 'I knew when I could tell a joke in Italian I was getting there.'[495]

Argento had complete autonomy on set. It helped that his father, Salvatore, was the producer. This way he could take the time to make things right or the way he wanted them. Brandon reveals:

> Dario would have a vision of how he wanted to see something. He articulated this vision while the crew stood there, arms folded staring; and then they would create it. He took his time, if say he wanted a certain angle or he wanted to create and build a shadow. The lighting was a very important thing to him in creating the suspense. He was exciting to work with.[496]

At one point, instead of using a camera dolly, the cameraman was on a kind of pulley system, like something out of medieval times, and the crew lifted him into the air by hand and rolled him along.

Surrounding Brandon was a good supporting cast. Mimsy Farmer was an American actress who had spent a lot of time in Rome. Francine Racette was a French–Canadian actress who later married Donald

Sutherland. And there was Bud Spencer, a big star in European movies, who took the job as a favour for his friend Argento. Brandon recalls:

> Bud was great. He had his own trailer that had an amazing kitchen, and he had a cook that took all morning to make the lunch. He said to me, 'Today you have lunch with me.' It was five courses. And then the food was removed and the beds come out and then you sleep. Everything shut down for two hours; that's the way it is in Italy. You get used to that style of life.[497]

Four Flies on Grey Velvet is an excellent example of early Argento, when he was just getting into his stride. Of course, one can criticise his films for being all style over content and having convoluted plotlines, but they are pure cinema, and few directors brought such artistry to the horror film. *Four Flies* is full of typically flamboyant Argento touches, such as the camera following the slow-motion trajectory of a bullet fired from a gun, an effect that predates *The Matrix* (1999) and many Hong Kong action films. The climax, when the killer is decapitated in a car crash, is again staged in slow motion and accompanied by the haunting strains of an Ennio Morricone score.

Argento originally approached rock band Deep Purple to handle the music, but work commitments ruled them out and he returned to Morricone, who'd scored his previous two pictures. However, the two men fell out during production and would not work together again until the 1990s. It's interesting that Argento was thinking about using rock music to accompany his flashy imagery this early in his career and, indeed, would later work extensively with the Italian progressive rock group Goblin, notably on *Deep Red* (1975) and *Suspiria* (1977).

Looking back on working with Argento, Brandon has nothing but fond memories. 'He treated me as an artist.'[498] When filming closed, Argento had one last surprise for his star. 'He organised for me to go and have tea with Fellini. That was amazing. It was a special surprise. He was shooting *Roma* at the time. It was quite something.'[499]

Argento had another *giallo* open earlier in 1971, *The Cat O' Nine Tails*, which was his second feature. While not quite vintage Argento, *giallo* fans will find much to enjoy.

(Italy: Rome opening 17 December)

96 A CLOCKWORK ORANGE

Michael Tarn was just 16 when Stanley Kubrick cast him in the role of Pete, one of the Droogs, in his infamous screen adaptation of the Anthony Burgess novel, *A Clockwork Orange*. Word had gone around the London stage schools that young people were required for a new film; no details were given. Tarn had been at the Italia Conti stage school since the age of 12. He was asked to go to a house in Notting Hill Gate. Inside were Malcolm McDowell and Stanley Kubrick – quite a shock as Tarn's favourite film was *2001*. They had been holding auditions for weeks, 'improvising scenes from the film with potential Droogs,' says Tarn.[500] Now it was his turn.

It was something like six months before Tarn heard he'd got the job. As the only actor in the Droog gang who was a real teenager (McDowell, Warren Clarke and James Marcus were all in their mid- to late 20s), Tarn was often used as a sounding board regarding a teenager's view of things. Before filming began, the four actors spent a couple of weeks at Kubrick's house to get to know each other, do improvisations, chip in their ideas about their roles and costumes, and develop a chemistry. 'But because they were all so much older than me,' says Tarn, 'I didn't feel I had the necessary experience to get fully involved in their conversations about the film.'[501] These were men with vastly more experience. 'I realised after a couple of days that the only thing I could do was listen, maybe contribute, but generally make the tea and the coffee.'[502] During shooting Tarn spent a lot of time playing board games with Vivian, Kubrick's daughter, who was allowed to abscond from school and come down to the set. Neither did he develop any kind of relationship with McDowell. 'It was very much Stanley and him all the time.'[503]

For the most part it was a closed set. Early on Tarn was approached by a reporter and offered money to take photographs of the filming. He refused. 'You didn't say anything. You didn't talk about it. And that was understood.'[504]

The Burgess novel, first published in 1962, was set in a dystopian near-future Britain plagued by a subculture of extreme youth violence. Kubrick said the picture's focus was the dangerous extremes to which society will go to fight crime, and this is explored when the Droogs' anarchist leader Alex is sent to prison and volunteers for an experimental rehabilitation programme. Essentially the film is in two parts – the

Droogs' violent rampages and then the consequences for which Alex ends up having to pay. For Tarn, the group were at their strongest in the early part of filming:

> As actors we all knew we could trust each other, thanks to the improvisation process. Then, as Stanley started to look at all the other parts of the film, there wasn't really an opportunity to build on what we had established early on.[505]

In those early days, Tarn got on well with Kubrick. Kubrick never stopped him from entering his van to look at the rushes when he was going through them. 'Now and again, he would ask me what I thought, which I thought was super.'[506] Once he told Kubrick that he should make a film out of the book he was reading. 'What's that Mr Tarn?' Tarn said, 'It's called *Lord of the Rings*.' Kubrick replied, 'Mr Tarn, I'm not going to do another *Spartacus*.'[507]

Curiously, it was during the filming of the movie's most controversial sequence, where the Droogs invade a house and rape and kill a woman, that Tarn thinks they were all at their closest. 'That's where we became the foursome, and Stanley the fivesome, because we were in that house for a long time.'[508] This was in early December. 'And it was bloody cold. We had to get on our knees almost to beg Stanley to get a heater for the tent that we were all huddled up in as we waited to do the scenes.'[509] These were rare but very special moments, when Tarn felt the group were as one. 'Even though that was a very difficult scene because we were looking at nudity, rape, and suddenly introducing the song "Singing in the Rain."'[510] That purely came out of an improvisation. 'My annoying habit,' says Tarn, 'was me tapping away between scenes trying to remember the routine I was supposed to do at my stage school's Christmas show. And it developed from that.'[511]

After Christmas, as filming began to overrun, the mood changed. The unit was hit with various illnesses and delays, although Kubrick was the main instigator. 'Several times Stanley just threw a whole week's filming in the bin, and we had to start again,' says Tarn. 'He also went through about three or four first assistants. Simply because he was so demanding.'[512] And often no one knew what he was demanding. Sometimes he didn't know himself and would sit alone and think and ponder and wasn't to be disturbed. 'Once Stanley had an idea, he'd follow it through to the end, and you had to let him work through the process,' says

Tarn.[513] The crew started to dub the film *A Clockwork Odyssey*, which didn't go down too well.

For Tarn some of the impetus was lost, too, as filming entered the last couple of months. There weren't so many Droog scenes required, and his fellow actors were already talking about other jobs they had lined up, while all Tarn had to look forward to was his upcoming exams. The work changed too. 'It went from being very flexible and very, "let's try this, let's try that," to "no, this is what you do," just because Stanley was feeling the pressure from Warner Brothers to finish the film.'[514]

Ironically, when *A Clockwork Orange* opened Tarn was unable to attend any of the premieres because he wasn't 18 yet. He also had no clue that the film would become a classic. 'I thought people would recognise it as a unique little one-off film, and then forget about it.'[515] Others felt the same way, like Clive Francis, who played the lodger who takes over Alex's bedroom:

> In all honesty I don't think I really appreciated how lucky I was at the time to be working with someone as iconic and as brilliant as Stanley Kubrick or, indeed, how remarkable a film *Clockwork* would turn out to be.[516]

Francis's scene took three days to film. 'I had to eat a piece of toast and, as Kubrick wanted to cover it from every possible angle, it meant consuming something like one and a half loaves of bread, leaving me feeling bloated and sick.'[517] As they sat quietly together, Francis felt compelled to ask Kubrick something about his work:

> I haltingly asked, 'Stanley, tell me about *2001: A Space Odyssey*. I bet that wasn't such an easy picture to make.' Considering it took over four years to complete, and is noted for its pioneering special effects and ambiguous imagery, such a question hardly warranted much of a reply. He looked at me for the briefest of seconds. Opened his mouth as if to say something. Thought better of it and moved away![518]

A Clockwork Orange caused huge controversy, especially in the UK. In 1973 a number of newspapers attributed the murder of a homeless person to a teenager said to have been influenced by the film. A year later, after other copycat crimes, and upset about how the movie was being used as inspiration for gangs to enact violence, Kubrick banned any further screenings in British cinemas, any sale to television and later video. Before his death in 1999, Kubrick removed the ban. Francis says:

> What my 85-year-old grandmother (who insisted on seeing it one afternoon at the Picturedrome, Eastbourne) made of Adrienne Corri being attacked by a 6ft plaster penis is hard to imagine. I would like to think it went gently over her head.[519]

(UK/US: New York opening 19 December)

97 | HAROLD AND MAUDE

At first glance it's a miracle any studio gave this movie the green light. After all it's a story of a troubled teenager who falls in love with an 80-year-old woman. *Variety* famously called it 'as much fun as a burning orphanage'. And yet this droll and subversive film has resonated down the years with people who feel at odds with society, or who are not sure they fit in. Today it still feels fresh and funny.

Colin Higgins was a UCLA film student who wrote the screenplay for *Harold and Maude* for his graduate thesis. His hope was to make it as a short film. Struggling financially, Higgins got a job at the home of producer Edward Lewis, cleaning the swimming pool and sweeping the tennis court. Lewis got to hear about the *Harold and Maude* script and sent it to his friend Robert Evans, head of production at Paramount. Evans loved its quirky nature and bought it.

Higgins hoped to direct the film himself, but Paramount brought in Hal Ashby, who had impressed with his first film, the racial satire *The Landlord* (1970). Ashby's first task was selecting the right actors to play Harold, a wealthy, death-obsessed teenager, and Maude, a vivacious senior citizen. Richard Dreyfuss and Bob Balaban were high on the list to play Harold, but from the start of auditions a young actor called Bud Cort just felt right. Cort, who was headed for the priesthood before getting into acting, had played the lead in Robert Altman's whimsical comedy *Brewster McCloud* (1970).

For Maude, Hal talked to or considered just about every actress of a certain vintage still breathing. Flying to London he met Dame Edith Evans who, after being told about the role, said to Ashby, 'That doesn't sound like me, ducky. Why don't you get Ruth Gordon.'[520] Which is exactly what he did. Gordon was an actress predominantly known for her work on Broadway, but had come to international prominence with her creepy role in *Rosemary's Baby* (1968).

As one of Harold's prospective girlfriends, Sunshine Doré, Ashby cast Ellen Geer, daughter of *The Waltons* star Will Geer. Told to go to an audition at a house up in the Hollywood Hills that had been turned into a production office, Geer felt uneasy. 'The idea of going alone late in the evening made me nervous. So, my Pop said he would wait in the car and barge in if it took too long. He didn't have to barge in.'[521]

Geer immediately took to the way Ashby worked with his actors: 'I loved him. He gave you the space to work. His calm presence released the actor to contribute in every way. He also let us go to dailies. Rare for actors.'[522] According to Geer, three quite separate camps naturally evolved at these screenings:

> 1: On the floor in the front there were scattered mattresses and cushions and always the smell of burnt vegetables. Hal was there. 2: The middle group on chairs (not too many of us) with sodas or milk. Squares, I guess. 3: At the rear, filmmakers on high stools with a bit of booze to end the day.[523]

While Higgins set his story in LA, Ashby shot far away from the studio suits in and around the town of San Mateo, near San Francisco, and in an old mansion they managed to find. Geer has never forgotten her very first scene. It was a long entrance, and she was wearing knee-high white plastic boots. Of course, she slipped. 'I heard a snicker behind the camera, but being a theatre actress, I kept going, blessing my balance that I didn't hit the floor!! They used that shot.'[524]

Harold's mother is determined, against her son's wishes, to find him a wife. One by one, Harold frightens them off by appearing to commit gruesome acts of suicide. With Geer, he chooses to commit hara-kiri. Before committing the deed, the samurai kneels on a bamboo mat – only there wasn't one and Bud Cort required it for the scene. 'We waited until someone went into town for a mat,' recalls Geer. 'That's the kind of respect Ashby had for an actor. Many wouldn't do that, nor understand the young actor's need. Hal gave the world to the actor.'[525]

Ashby had taken a lot of footage, and it was going to be a chore in the editing rooms to get it all to come out right. But Paramount had a bigger problem on their hands. Their big release for Christmas 1971 was going to be *The Godfather*, only it was way behind schedule. So, what did Paramount decide to rush out in its place? Yes, *Harold and Maude*, hardly suitable festive fare! Then again, nor was a film in which a horse's head ends up in someone's bed. Predictably, the subject matter of *Harold and Maude* turned off audiences. An avalanche of hostile reviews didn't help either: *Time* magazine even called up Paramount, saying they were doing them a favour by not reviewing it. After bombing at the box office *Harold and Maude* was quickly yanked from distribution.

Out of its failure came some good things. Ashby became one of the most important American directors of the 1970s while Higgins went on to direct hits like *Foul Play* (1978), giving Chevy Chase his film debut, and *9 to 5* (1980).

As for Cort, the actor came to see *Harold and Maude* as both a blessing and a curse, so intense did his identification with the role become. The legacy of the film for Geer is much more positive. In 2000 Geer appeared in a stage production at her local theatre:

> My daughter, Willow, played Sunshine, and I endeavoured to play Maude. A great opportunity. One young man came up to me afterwards and whispered in my ear, crying after a performance: 'You helped me ... thank you ...'. That has been one of my best compliments on any of my work.'[526]

(US: New York opening 20 December)

 ## 98 *MARY, QUEEN OF SCOTS*

In early 1969 Alexander Mackendrick, who had made several Ealing classics, including *The Ladykillers* (1955), was deep into pre-production on his long-cherished film of Mary Stuart, perhaps the best-known figure in Scotland's royal history, who rivalled her cousin Elizabeth I for the English throne. He had scouted locations in Scotland, met with actors and took budget meetings. Mia Farrow was reported to be playing Mary. Then, bad news. His backer, Universal, pulled out.

Mackendrick had worked on the script for years. It was to be a character study of Mary rather than your typical Hollywood historical epic. When news reached him of the project's cancellation it was a body blow. And while he hadn't lost his desire for filmmaking, he had grown tired of the business end of the industry and took a teaching job at California Institute of the Arts (CalArts). He never directed again.

Following the success of his historical dramas *Becket* (1964) and *Anne of the Thousand Days* (1969), veteran American producer Hal B. Wallis began looking for another interesting slice of British history with cinematic possibilities. He found the story of Mary Stuart, whose life provided tragedy and romance, irresistible and wrote in his memoirs that here was a figure of 'great mystery and appeal', whose image he wanted to change 'from victim to active protagonist'. Essentially Wallis took over the abandoned Mackendrick production, rekindled the interest of Universal, and reunited the director, Charles Jarrott, and writer, John Hale, of *Anne of the Thousand Days*. Jarrott and Wallis clashed over the religious aspect of the story: the Catholic Mary pitted against a Protestant Elizabeth. Mindful of how the film might play in middle America, Wallis wanted a more straightforward telling of the story. He and Jarrott worked extensively on the script together, chopping and changing, and, in the end, they never really got it to work.

Several big names were mentioned to play Mary, including Vanessa Redgrave. Jarrott had lunch in London with the actress, who responded immediately to the material and the role. Mary, she said, was one of her historical heroines. She accepted at once.

For Wallis there was only one choice to play Elizabeth, and that was Glenda Jackson. Unfortunately, the actress had just played the role to great acclaim in a BBC drama and didn't want to revisit it again so soon. A top executive from Universal flew to London in a personal bid to make her change her mind. Suitably impressed by him and the meeting, Jackson accepted the job. Another inducement was the opportunity to work with Vanessa Redgrave; the pair had met a few times but never worked together. Wallis now had his leads. To play two of history's most famous monarchs, he had brought together two of the most formidable acting talents of the age.

Jackson's price to play Elizabeth was for all her scenes to be done first, and in three and a half weeks, 'before boredom affected her performance,' said Wallis.[527] This required changes to the script and the schedule, but for Wallis it was a price worth paying. Although in real life Mary and Elizabeth never met, Wallis decided for dramatic purposes there needed to be a showdown between these two titans. The dialogue was to be based on letters the two monarchs exchanged. There was much excitement and anticipation in the days leading up to the scene, and

Redgrave and Jackson approached it, said Wallis, 'like thoroughbreds'. Shot in a wood on the outskirts of London, filming was repeatedly interrupted by aircraft passing overhead. Frantic calls were put through to Heathrow, where it was discovered management had been forced to change its flight paths. For what was the most important scene in the movie the sound was rendered completely useless. The whole scene had to be redubbed.

As she had done for the BBC drama, Jackson refused to wear a skull cap, claiming it looked fake, and shaved her hairline daily. As it turned out, she regretted making the film, calling her own performance a bit of a rehash. As with Jane Fonda on *Klute*, Redgrave brought her political activism to the film. At Pinewood she went round the canteen collecting money in the lunch hour for the Upper Clyde shipbuilders, who had just been made redundant. On her days off she was marching for some left-wing cause or addressing rallies in Hyde Park. Wallis recalled that, shooting on location in France, she refused to eat in restaurants with the rest of the cast and instead sat on the roadside with the crew, the workers. 'I regarded her as a harmless case of English eccentricity,' said Wallis.[528] Her performance earned Redgrave an Oscar nomination.

In these types of historical dramas, the frame is stuffed with British acting royalty, and *Mary, Queen of Scots* is no exception: there's Patrick McGoohan, Timothy Dalton, Trevor Howard, Nigel Davenport and Ian Holm. During filming Redgrave began a relationship with Dalton that lasted until 1986. It must be said that the acting raises the film above the inadequacies of the script, making this well-mounted production worth watching. And it's topped off by a suitably sumptuous John Barry score, his fifth that year.

Curiously, Alexander Mackendrick's version of the Mary story was finally given an airing in 2018 as a BBC radio play. Providing the narration was Glenda Jackson.

(UK/US: Los Angeles opening 22 December)

99 *DIRTY HARRY*

The year 1971 marked a turning point in the career of Clint Eastwood. *Play Misty for Me* and *The Beguiled* had already opened. However, it was the release of this classic cop thriller that established him as a genuine superstar. Another bonus was the actor's positive dealings with Warner

Brothers on the film, which influenced his decision a couple of years later to move his production company, Malpaso, from the Universal lot to Warners, where he was to stay for the remainder of his career.

It almost didn't happen. Warners wanted Frank Sinatra to play the role of police inspector Harry Callahan, after John Wayne rejected it on moral grounds. The script, by husband-and-wife writing team Harry Julian Fink and Rita M. Fink, had been polished by a couple of other writers, including John Milius. It was Warners' production chief, John Calley, who was responsible for bringing him in. 'We've got this treatment,' Calley told Milius. 'We want you to make it into a screenplay and we've got to meet with Frank Sinatra, who's going to star in it, in four weeks. Can you write this in twenty-one days?' 'Sure,' said Milius. 'I don't recommend it, but it can be done.'[529]

Writing the script, Milius poured himself into the character of Harry Callahan:

> I always considered myself to be a loner, so I suppose there's some degree of that in there. And I'm a bit of a fanatic, and Harry is too. Originally, Harry was just a regular tough cop; it was my idea that he was God's lonely man. He was the other side of the bad guys, the other side of the coin.[530]

With Irvin Kershner installed as director, cameras were ready to roll when Sinatra went into hospital for urgent surgery on his right hand. Warners scrambled around for a replacement. Reportedly, when Paul Newman declined the offer he made the suggestion they try Eastwood. It was a stroke of genius. The role of Harry Callahan fitted Eastwood just as perfectly as did 'the man with no name' in the Dollar westerns, and today it's the role for which he remains most fondly remembered.

San Francisco is Callahan's turf and in *Dirty Harry* we see him track down a psychotic killer who calls himself Scorpio. 'He was fun to write,' says Milius. 'Although he was a lot worse in the script – when he gets on that bus with the kids at the end, he has a flame-thrower.'[531]

Played unforgettably by Andrew Robinson, Scorpio was based on a real-life serial killer who murdered five people in the San Francisco Bay Area in the late 1960s. Dubbed the 'Zodiac Killer', like Scorpio he taunted police with messages and threats. Much earlier in 1971 a low-budget film entitled *The Zodiac Killer* was released. During its run in San Francisco director Tom Hanson hoped it might tempt the killer to attend a screening. Moviegoers were asked to answer a questionnaire, with the written answers later examined by experts for any similarities to the distinct handwriting of the murderer. The identity of the Zodiac Killer remains a mystery to this day. Interestingly, in David Fincher's 2007 film about these crimes, called *Zodiac*, a police inspector pays a visit to a San Francisco theatre during a screening of *Dirty Harry*.

Brought onto the project, Eastwood immediately enlisted Don Siegel as director and the film was shot almost entirely on location in San Francisco. The famous bank robbery sequence that takes place early on, when Callahan's hot dog lunch is interrupted by gunfire, was filmed on a Hollywood studio back lot. As Callahan strides across to the scene of the crime, a movie theatre marquee is clearly visible in the background, showing *Play Misty for Me*. Callahan blows away most of the robbers until just one is left – and here we get the first taste of the unorthodox Callahan, when he plays a form of chicken with the suspect. And what he delivers has become one of cinema's most quotable lines. It was Milius who came up with it, not least because of his own personal liking for guns:

> I love .44 Magnums, the most powerful handgun. It will blow your head clean off. You've just got to ask yourself – do you feel lucky punk? And what makes the speech is, 'well, do you?' I always wanted to do that.[532]

It was scenes like this that personified Callahan's ruthless methods, along with the film's general violent tone, that led many contemporary critics to take against it. Famously, the prominent *New Yorker* critic Pauline Kael called the film a 'right-wing fantasy' and labelled it 'fascist medievalism'. Audiences didn't agree; they went to see *Dirty Harry* in droves and made it a huge hit.

Very quickly *Dirty Harry* turned into an icon of popular culture. During a spate of murders and attacks perpetrated by a group of serial killers in San Francisco during 1973 and 1974, someone daubed a piece of graffiti on a wall in the area that read: 'Dirty Harry, where are you when we need you.' I wonder what Kael thought about that. Callahan would indeed return in four sequels of slowly diminishing quality: *Magnum Force* (1973), *The Enforcer* (1976), *Sudden Impact* (1983) and *The Dead Pool* (1988).

(US: New York opening 22 December)

100 DIAMONDS ARE FOREVER

James Bond was the cinematic sensation of the 1960s, but as the series moved into the 1970s it faced something of an existential crisis. *On Her Majesty's Secret Service* (1969) was a more serious entry, truer to its literary antecedent, but had not fared that well at the box office. George Lazenby had also proven to be an inadequate replacement for Sean Connery and, in any case, no longer wanted to be Bond. So, the producers faced the twin dilemmas of breaking in a new actor and where to take the series next.

The man they chose as the new James Bond was 40-year-old John Gavin, a former naval intelligence officer with the dark handsome looks of a Rock Hudson. Since working with Alfred Hitchcock on *Psycho* (1960) and Stanley Kubrick in *Spartacus* (1960), in which he had played the young Julius Caesar, Gavin had languished mostly in television. UA were still nervous about introducing another new Bond in the wake of the previous film's perceived failure. There was only one solution – bring back Connery. David Picker, studio president, called the producers to see if there was any chance of making a deal, only to learn that, after years of tension, their relationship with the actor had broken down completely.

Picker took personal charge and flew to London to negotiate a deal. The offer was unprecedented: a fee of £1.2 million, a healthy share of the profits and a promise by UA to finance, to the tune of $1 million, any two films of Connery's choosing. Ultimately only one film was made under this agreement, *The Offence* in 1972. Connery agreed to return one more time and Gavin was paid off.

For *Diamonds Are Forever* it was back to the fantastical world of James Bond, and the producers brought in a young writer called Tom Mankiewicz. Just 27, Mankiewicz was elated; here he was writing a James Bond movie at a time when 007 was the only real movie event in town. 'There was no *Indiana Jones* yet, no *Superman*, no *Star Wars*, no anything. The world waited for the Bond movie to come out every eighteen months or so. Harry and Cubby really did have the world by the tail.'[533]

Mankiewicz produced one of the series's wittiest scripts, even if the story was a little cheesy, with Bond investigating a diamond-smuggling racket that turns out to be a SPECTRE-led mission to use large quantities of gems for a laser satellite to hold the world to ransom.

Mankiewicz soon learnt just how bad things had got between Connery and the producers. The actor had tried to get a clause in his contract that he didn't want to see Harry Saltzman anywhere near the

Las Vegas location. 'I don't know why, but Sean had a particular dislike for Harry. In those days Sean and Cubby got along pretty well.'[534]

Mankiewicz also had a hand in a key casting decision, that of Bond girl Plenty O'Toole. Lana Wood, younger sister of Natalie, had just done a heavily publicised *Playboy* pictorial, and was a friend of the writer, so Mankiewicz put her name forward to Cubby. Other roles went to Charles Gray as Blofeld and Jill St John as diamond smuggler Tiffany Case. Making a strong impact was Bruce Glover and Putter Smith as a pair of homicidal killers Wint and Kidd. It was only after reading the script that Glover discovered his character was gay, something he had no problem with. His first day working with Connery was out in the desert, the scene where Wint and Kidd bury Bond in an underground pipe. It was the first time Glover had met Connery, and he decided to make a joke. Looking down at the star he said, in his Wint affectation, 'I think I'm getting emotionally involved.' Glover was expecting Connery to laugh. 'But he didn't. I thought, "should I tell him it was a joke. I'm not gay." Then I thought, "to hell with it."'[535] This deception lasted for the whole of the US shoot. Moving to Frankfurt Airport, there was a group of three very attractive stewardesses. Glover went over and started chatting to them:

I was flirting my ass off and, all of a sudden, I could feel the energy behind me, and I heard this voice say, 'You son of a bitch.' It was Sean, and he was waving his finger at me scoldingly and laughing.[536]

There was also a role for an old pal of Cubby's, Bruce Cabot, who had played the lead in the original *King Kong* (1933). Already suffering from cancer, this would be Cabot's last film. Another old friend of Broccoli's proved particularly useful to the production. By 1971, Howard Hughes had become an eccentric recluse, living with his entourage of personal aides in the top-floor penthouses of various Vegas hotels. Publicly he was never seen, but he was a huge Bond fan. As the owner of several top casinos in Vegas, Hughes allowed the Bond team unrestricted access to shoot anywhere they wanted.

The cast and crew certainly made good use of the Vegas location. It especially amused Glover to see how willing people were to lose their livelihoods. 'And there were hookers all over the place. I remember I watched Broccoli lose something like $30,000 playing one of those big games; he laughed about it. He was so friendly and fun to work with.'[537]

Opening in time for the Christmas holidays, *Diamonds Are Forever* was a worldwide smash and successfully navigated Bond into the 1970s, especially in its more comedic approach, which signalled the way the series was headed. It had been Connery who wanted more wit in the film and Broccoli encouraged it. On occasion, when Mankiewicz would say that maybe it was going too far, Cubby would say, 'Don't worry about it, keep writing.'[538]

Saltzman and Broccoli were determined that Connery make the next Bond, *Live and Let Die* and arranged for Mankiewicz to persuade him:

So, we had this lunch and I told him, 'Look Sean, we've got crocodiles, we've got a boat chase, we've got a lot of great stuff going on in case you want to do one more.' And Sean said a really interesting thing, he said. 'I read in the papers sometimes that it's my fucking obligation to play Bond. Well, I've done six of them, when does the obligation run out, at ten, twelve, fourteen?' And Sean, being very much an actor by then, and he wasn't when he started, I think he just couldn't wait to go out and act and play other parts.'[539]

(UK/US: London opening 30 December)

THE GOOD, THE BAD AND THE WEIRD: THE BEST OF THE REST

1971 was such a rich year that even picking 100 films doesn't quite do it justice. And so here is an A–Z rundown of some of the films that almost made the top 100, along with some hidden gems, some interesting oddities and cult items, some worthwhile entries, and some downright wacko films. And, for a bit of fun, a few of the very worst too.

THE BAREFOOT EXECUTIVE

Kurt Russell made his first Disney picture when he was just 15 years old and was the studio's teen star of the 1960s and early 1970s. He'd make twelve pictures for Disney over time and call his adolescent years there 'my education in the film business'.

Here Russell plays an ambitious mailroom clerk at a TV network who discovers his girlfriend's lovable pet chimp has a knack of picking out hit television shows. There were a number of chimps Russell had to work with; one in particular was smart and tough. If he got a little rough and disobedient, the trainer said it was alright for Russell to give the monkey a little whack, just to show him who was boss. On this one occasion, the chimp was going off the rails and Russell gave him a big wallop, just as five guests were being shown around the studio. 'Oh my God,' they said. 'This is what they do at Disney!'

BELIEVE IN ME

When producer Irwin Winkler read author Gail Sheehy's heartfelt *New York* magazine article about her sister's descent into drug addiction, he bought it. Michael Sarrazin and Jacqueline Bisset, then romantically involved in real life, play a young couple, Pamela and Remy. Indulging in speed and barbiturates, the pleasures are soon forgotten as they begin to lose control. Pamela quits her job and Remy is thrown out of medical school. When Remy gets hooked on heroin Pamela is forced to leave him in a bid to go clean.

You can sense that director Stuart Hagmann's instinct was to bring a documentary realism to the social crisis of drugs, in much the same vein, excuse the pun, as other 1971 anti-drug films, like *Panic in Needle Park*. They didn't reckon on James Aubrey, head of MGM. Aubrey didn't like the film; maybe he thought he was getting a stoned version of *Love Story*, and demanded extensive cuts along with three weeks of reshoots done by another director, John G. Avildsen.

The tinkering showed. *The New York Times* noted the film was 'not so much edited as maimed'. As a positive, when Winkler was later looking for a director to helm *Rocky*, he remembered Avildsen and hired him.

BLACK BEAUTY

Anna Sewell's timeless novel *Black Beauty*, first published in 1877, is brought to the screen here by director James Hill of *Born Free* fame, and told from the perspective of the horse as it changes owners during its tumultuous lifetime. Born on a farm, Beauty is looked after by a little boy, played by Mark Lester, until it's taken away by a drunken squire. When the squire is killed in a riding accident the horse comes into the possession of a travelling circus, before seeing service with the British army in India. Returning to England, it's put to work hauling a coal wagon. Here its plight is noticed, and rescued by Anna Sewell herself, an early champion of animal rights.

This is a pleasant if lightweight film, shot in Ireland and Spain. Although Lester only appears in the opening scenes and worked on it for just ten days, he received top billing. 'I had a good agent in those days,' he says.[1]

BLESS THE BEASTS & CHILDREN

During his career Stanley Kramer earned the nickname 'Hollywood's conscience' through his willingness to tackle controversial topics, with films like *The Defiant Ones* (1958) and *Guess Who's Coming to Dinner* (1967), which aimed to inform as much as entertain. *Bless the Beasts & Children* is no different, with its statement about gun culture in America.

Based on Glendon Swarthout's book, the story revolves around a group of misfit teenage boys, dumped at summer camp by their wealthy parents, who decide to free a herd of buffalo from slaughter by hunters. Attacked by some critics for being too preachy and heavy-handed, the film ended up less than Kramer had hoped for. 'And when you fail in a good cause, the frustration is difficult to bear.'[2] The title theme, sung by The Carpenters, received an Academy Award nomination.

BLINDMAN

This spaghetti western, featuring Ringo Starr as a Mexican bandit, was co-produced by Allen Klein, the tough-talking American lawyer whose controversial tenure as manager of The Beatles led directly to McCartney's exit from the band and its eventual dissolution. Klein also makes a cameo appearance; the irony of him playing a double-crossing bandit was not lost on Beatles' fans.

Blindman owed much to the Zatoichi character, a blind swordsman who featured in a long-running series of Japanese films. Tony Anthony plays a blind gunslinger hired to escort fifty mail-order brides to mine workers in Texas. When he is double-crossed by his partner, who kidnaps the women to sell them to the Mexican Army, Blindman is determined to get them back.

Filmed on location in Spain, production was briefly interrupted when Starr left to perform at the Concert for Bangladesh, a benefit gig organised by George Harrison. Released in Italy in 1971, *Blindman* wasn't seen in the US or Britain until 1972 in a butchered version.

BORN TO WIN

George Segal gives a career-best performance as a former trendy hair-dresser reduced to hustling and petty crime on the streets of New York to maintain his heroin addiction. Alternating tragedy with farce, UA were appalled when they saw it. It was too depressing, they said, and ordered a recut to play up the comedy. Even then they barely gave it much of a release.

Born To Win was the first American feature for Ivan Passer, a leading filmmaker of the Czech New Wave, who fled the country with Miloš Forman. Passer interviewed ex-addicts during his research and actual junkies appear in the film. Passer also clashed with Robert De Niro, playing a small role as a plainclothes cop hassling Segal. More than once Passer and Segal thought of replacing De Niro when his method acting practices went too far. The impressive supporting cast features Karen Black, Paula Prentiss and Hector Elizondo.

THE BOY FRIEND

Ken Russell was at some glitzy showbiz function chatting with Twiggy, the famous model and face of the 1960s. They were sipping champagne and getting quietly merry, but being pestered by a journalist. To get rid of him Russell announced that he was going to make a movie of the famous Sandy Wilson 1920s set musical *The Boy Friend*, starring Twiggy. 'There's your exclusive,' said Russell, 'now sod off.'

The next morning the news was splashed all over the front pages and Russell received a phone call from an irate lawyer representing MGM who wanted to know why he'd made that statement, and if he was aware that MGM owned the screen rights. Instead of being threatened with litigation, Russell was asked if he actually fancied having a go at adapting the musical, which premiered on the London stage in 1953. Nobody had yet found a way of doing it properly on film. The 1920s aesthetic that worked so well on stage just didn't seem to translate to the screen; it came over all mannered and stilted. Russell's idea was to change the original setting from the French Riviera to a struggling theatrical troupe putting on a production of *The Boy Friend*. Twiggy plays Polly Browne, a mousy assistant stage manager who has to replace the leading lady

(Glenda Jackson in an unbilled cameo) after she twists her ankle before the curtain goes up.

Reportedly Sandy Wilson disliked the film version. His show was a 1920s jazz-inspired spoof, whereas Russell's joke is that this is a mediocre production transformed into something better than it is through the eyes of the players fantasising about making the big time. Russell even throws in a few extravagant dance numbers, executed in the style of famed film musical director Busby Berkeley.

BROTHER JOHN

This was something of a personal project for Sidney Poitier. Not only did he come up with the idea, but he also produced this story of a mysterious figure visiting his Alabama hometown for his sister's funeral. Playing opposite Poitier was Beverly Todd as a schoolteacher who falls in love with him. Beverly had previously worked with the star on Broadway:

> We stayed in touch and developed a wonderful friendship. At lunch one day Sidney talked about a series of films he was making and asked me to be in them. I wanted to jump up and scream YES!!! But we were in the very refined Russian Tea Room, so I responded with a dignified yes.[3]

Todd subsequently featured in *The Lost Man* (1969), *They Call Me Mr Tibbs* (1970) and finally a co-starring role in *Brother John*. 'I was in heaven! And Sidney taught me the difference of working on a film set and on the stage.'[4] On the first day of filming, Todd had a face full of make-up. 'Sidney had me take it all off. He, of course, was right. I was playing a shy schoolteacher and he wanted her innocence to show.'[5]

When Poitier's character first arrives, racial tensions rise in the town and local law enforcement label him as an agitator. Others suspect him of a more spiritual purpose. Is he a messenger from God, an angel of judgement? 'I think he was trying to save humanity,' says Todd of Poitier's intention for the film, 'wake people up, warn them about the dying Earth. But no one would listen.'[6]

THE BURGLARS

French star Jean-Paul Belmondo had something of a reputation for performing his own daredevil stunts. Famously on *That Man from Rio* (1964) he crawled along the ledge of a building high above Copacabana beach. Later, for fun, he went up there naked and waved at the people below in the street.

The Burglars was the fifth of eight collaborations with Belmondo for director Henri Verneuil, who knew all about his star's reckless behaviour, but was tested beyond endurance here. Belmondo plays an ace safecracker and leader of a bunch of thieves who break into a villa on the outskirts of Athens to steal $1 million in emeralds. Unfortunately, the gang have already drawn the attention of crooked police detective Omar Sharif, who proves less keen on cracking the case than grabbing a slice of the takings himself.

In the film's impressive car chase sequences, Belmondo was behind the wheel most of the time, gunning though the streets of Athens. At one point he jumps across a number of car roofs before hurling himself at a speeding bus, grasping the barred window at the last minute. His *pièce de résistance*, however, was being dumped from the back of a construction truck down a steep rocky hillside. This stunt was one too far for the director, who tried to persuade Belmondo not to do it. When this failed Belmondo's agent flew in from Paris to dissuade him – without success. Belmondo ended up doing the stunt not once but twice!

The Burglars, enhanced by a great Ennio Morricone score, was the French response to the new breed of Hollywood action thrillers that came in the wake of *Bullitt*, with its emphasis on car chases and stunts, and it cleaned up at the home box office.

BUSINESS IS BUSINESS (WAT ZIEN IK)

This ribald comedy about the customers and personal lives of two female prostitutes in Amsterdam's red-light district was the first feature film directed by Paul Verhoeven. It was written by Gerard Soeteman, who first collaborated with Verhoeven on a 1969 Dutch TV series Verhoeven directed called *Floris*, which starred a young Rutger Hauer as a medieval knight. To prepare for the film Verhoeven spoke with street walkers, while Soeteman studied scientific papers on prostitution.

At first conflicted about making the film, fearing he may only be offered sex romps afterwards, Verhoeven was pleasantly surprised when the film became a monster hit, pulling in almost two and a half million punters – making it the fourth most popular Dutch film ever made. Its success allowed Verhoeven and Soeteman the freedom and clout to make the critically acclaimed *Turkish Delight* (1973).

THE CASE OF THE SCORPION'S TAIL (LA CODADELLO SCORPIONE)

Sergio Martino was nothing if not prolific. His work encompassed spaghetti westerns, sex comedies, cop dramas, horror and sci-fi. Quentin Tarantino, a big fan, once playfully knelt in front of Martino at the Venice Film Festival. From 1971 to 1973, Martino created an impressive series of Giallo thrillers, of which *Scorpion's Tail* is a standout.

After her husband dies in a freak plane accident, Lisa (Ida Galli) is summoned to Athens to collect his generous life insurance policy, only to discover others are willing to kill to get their hands on it. There is the usual complex, multifaceted narrative typical of the genre. And while not as bloody or body-strewn as the usual Giallo, there is one highly graphic scene when the killer takes a broken bottle to the eye of the victim. And, in a nod to *Psycho*, the female lead is killed off a quarter of the way into the film. Highly atmospheric and creepy, *The Case of the Scorpion's Tail* is a must for any fans of Giallo or the works of Dario Argento and Mario Bava.

CATLOW

Louis L'Amour was the most popular and prolific exponent of western novels. British producer Euan Lloyd had already brought one of his literary works to the screen with *Shalako* (1968), pairing Sean Connery and Brigitte Bardot. Its box-office success encouraged him to try his luck again.

Yul Brynner plays Catlow, a lovable outlaw riding with an entourage of vagabond cowboys and a wild, sex-crazed lover played by Daliah Lavi in her last film before deserting the silver screen to pursue a singing career. On Catlow's tail is Marshal Ben Cowan, played by Richard Crenna, an old army buddy.

Directed by Sam Wanamaker, *Catlow* is fairly mediocre, but a pleasant enough watch for western fans, with broad comedic overtones in addition to outbursts of violence. A highlight is Leonard Nimoy's turn as a vicious bounty hunter, a million light years away from Mr Spock.

LE CHAT

Few films in the history of cinema have given as bleak a commentary on married life as *Le Chat*, adapted from a novel by Georges Simenon, the creator of Maigret. It recounts the story of an elderly couple, Julien Bouin and his wife Clémence, whose love has worn away over the years, replaced by indifference and loathing. They live in a rundown house, stranded in a landscape of urban redevelopment, waiting for the wrecking ball to move in – a perfect analogy for their lives together. One day Julien brings home an alley cat that becomes the source of bitter battles when Clémence complains he shows the animal more affection than her.

Director Pierre Granier-Deferre cast two icons of French cinema, both nearing the end of their careers, Jean Gabin and Simone Signoret; surprisingly the two had never worked together before. And it nearly didn't happen this time. The producer rejected Signoret because her previous film had flopped. Gabin called up the producer and threatened to quit if Signoret was not cast. Just six hours later the director was told he could have Signoret.

The French public flocked to see the couple on screen together, and they weren't disappointed. They are brilliantly matched, and their interplay is a joy to watch.

THE CHRISTIAN LICORICE STORE

In its story of a young tennis champ seduced by outside commercial interests this picture makes fun of the superficial showbiz side of California. The original choice to direct was Steven Spielberg. Producer Michael Laughlin liked and admired Spielberg, an occasional dinner guest at the house Laughlin shared with his wife, actress Leslie Caron. Instead, financiers Cinema Center Films went with James Frawley, who cast two attractive young actors in the leads, Beau Bridges and Sweden's Maude Adams, who was making her film debut.

The unusual title was taken from the lyrics of the song 'Pleasant Street' by Tim Buckley. The cult singer/songwriter also makes an appearance in the film performing the song. There's a cameo appearance, too, by famed French director Jean Renoir. Laughlin and Caron knew Renoir, and asked if he would like to appear. The scene, shot in Renoir's home in Beverly Hills, was mostly improvised. Cast in small roles were Penny Marshall and Cindy Williams, soon to achieve TV fame in the US sitcom *Laverne & Shirley*, but both ended up on the cutting room floor.

The film never found an audience and was shelved by Cinema Center Films after just a few screenings.

CHROME AND HOT LEATHER

The success of Roger Corman's *The Wild Angels* (1966) ushered in a craze for motorcycle gang films. *Chrome and Hot Leather* is a biker film with a twist in that the heroes are Vietnam veterans out to avenge the death of their friend's fiancée, killed when her car is forced off the road by a bike gang. The film poses the question of whether it is acceptable for lethal skills learnt in war to be used in society. Ultimately military might triumphs and the bikers are marched off to face justice. In the original script the vets kill the gang, wrapping them up in barbed wire and dragging them behind their bikes.

Exploitation maestro Lee Frost directed the picture, despite thinking it was 'the worst piece of shit I've ever read'.[7] He gave an unlikely feature debut to Motown legend Marvin Gaye, who had been taking acting lessons in between recording his seminal album *What's Going On*. Frost liked Gaye a lot. 'He was a sweetheart of a guy, always smiling.'[8] They did have to teach him how to ride a motorbike. The failure of *Chrome and Hot Leather* put paid to Gaye's interest in acting, and he went back to singing. Future *Charlie's Angels* star Cheryl Ladd also makes her film debut.

COLD TURKEY

Dick Van Dyke had been trying to quit smoking for years. He knew he wasn't alone, that millions of his fellow Americans were struggling too. He thought that maybe a story about someone going to great lengths to quit might make a good film. He wrote a treatment and gave it to a colleague, Norman Lear, the king of television satire in the 1970s. Lear liked it, but told Van Dyke that, instead of one guy, how about a whole town trying to quit. The idea was forged about a tobacco company staging a publicity stunt by offering $25 million to any American town that can stop smoking for thirty days.

Van Dyke plays the Reverend Clayton Brooks, a minister who urges the economically depressed midwestern community of Eagle Rock to go for the prize. The excellent supporting cast included Bob Newhart, Jean Stapleton and Vincent Gardenia. Singer/songwriter Randy Newman provides the score, his first, launching his career as a soundtrack composer. Newman went on to write dozens of film scores, most famously *Toy Story* (1995).

While the tobacco industry is a prime target of satire, *Cold Turkey* also rips into big business, religious hypocrisy, right-wing fringe groups, political corruption, gun violence and small-town America, making it one of the darkest, most despairing social satires of the Nixon era. Perhaps too dark, UA held up the release of the film, shot in 1969, nervous about how it would play to audiences.

CONFESSIONS OF A POLICE CAPTAIN

This could be one of the most brutal and cynical political thrillers to come out of the 1970s. Giacomo Bonavia is a disillusioned police captain nearing retirement, determined to bring down a local Mafia boss. Both Anthony Quinn and then Ben Gazzara were originally cast in the role, but demanded so many script changes that director Damiano Damiani fired them. Martin Balsam took over.

As Bonavia wades through the morass of official corruption, he clashes with a young district attorney, played by Franco Nero, who does everything by the book. The story takes place in Palermo, the capital of the Italian island of Sicily, where historically the Mafia began. It's made chillingly obvious that anyone crossing the syndicate is swiftly despatched. One female character is murdered, her body put in cement and buried in the foundation of a building under construction; one of many such victims entombed in the newly erected Palermo skyline.

A big hit in Italy, *Confessions of a Police Captain* won the Golden Prize at the Moscow International Film Festival.

COUNTESS DRACULA

Elizabeth Bathory was a sixteenth-century Hungarian noblewoman, reported to have tortured and killed hundreds of young women and bathed in their blood to retain her youth. When director Peter Sasdy read an article about her in a Sunday newspaper, he quickly put together a one-page story treatment, called it *Countess Dracula* and went to see Hammer's James Carreras at his office. Carreras quickly read it and seemed interested. He then said he had a business lunch meeting to go to and, when he returned a few hours later, saw Sasdy to ask, 'Can you start shooting in six weeks' time at Pinewood. I've just arranged a release over lunch.'[9]

With such a quick schedule to meet, Sasdy brought in Jeremy Paul, a writer he knew from television drama who could work fast, and put together his regular crew. His aim was to go for atmosphere over the usual Hammer gore. One thing Sasdy had no real control over was the casting of scream queen Ingrid Pitt; from the beginning he was under no illusion that she was who the Hammer bigwigs wanted in the title role. Despite having Pitt thrust upon him, Sasdy found her easy to work with and a total professional. Alongside Pitt is a nice supporting cast, headed by Nigel Green and a very young Lesley-Anne Down. Sandor Elès plays a young army officer who the countess has the hots for. During the shooting of their tryst in a stable, Sasdy heard everyone laughing. 'I thought, "why are they laughing?" I got a bit angry and yelled "cut." Then I saw that half of Sandor's moustache had remained on Ingrid's breast.'[10]

The film's most iconic scene is when the countess is disturbed bathing in the blood of her latest victim. 'Ingrid asked me to let her know half an hour before I was ready for her,' recalls Sasdy, 'because she wanted to drink a small bottle of vodka first.'[11]

CREATURES THE WORLD FORGOT

The success of Hammer's 1966 *One Million Years BC* launched a short-lived series of similarly themed prehistoric/cave girl movies, of which this is the last. It starred Hammer's latest screen glamour queen, Norwegian ex-model Julie Ege.

Due to budgetary restraints, there isn't a single dinosaur in the entire picture. Instead, what we have are various stone age tribes either fighting each other or struggling to survive in an arid desert landscape. Originally the film was conceived on a much grander scale, featuring all manner of perils including giant bats, spiders, crocodiles and ants. The best we get is the appearance of a cave bear, which is so laughably obviously a man in a cheap costume.

Back in the director's chair was *One Million Years BC's* Don Chaffey, and he shot it on location in the Namib Desert in southern Africa. The scenic vistas give the film a nice, broad visual scope. Given the less censorious times, there is increased brutality and sexuality than in previous Hammer prehistoric films. In summary, this pulp adventure film is not as bad as its reputation suggests, but *Quest for Fire* it ain't.

CRUCIBLE OF TERROR

Mike Raven was a former Radio 1 DJ who was said to have had a genuine interest in the occult. Not dissimilar in appearance to Christopher Lee, with this film he sought to make himself the new star of British horror. The problem was he lacked any kind of screen charisma, spoke in a somewhat weedy voice and, frankly, couldn't act. He was overly serious too, and did not endear himself to the crew. In one scene Raven had to perform a series of kisses all the way up a woman's leg. 'The crew put chili pepper on her skin, and it got up his nose,' recalls co-star Judy Matheson. 'He was absolutely furious. He didn't really have a sense of humour.'[12]

In this low-key shocker Raven plays a reclusive artist who makes bronze nudes out of living women encased in molten metal. Directed by Ted Hooker on a shoestring budget of £100,000, it was filmed on location in Cornwall, the barren landscape lending the film a moody atmosphere. Matheson recalls everyone going down by coach and staying in basic accommodation. 'The film's base was at this local farm and the lady there would cook us all these wonderful farmhouse breakfasts. We had a great time in Cornwall.'[13]

Alongside Raven, Hook cast ex-Likely Lad James Bolam and Ronald Lacey, ten years away from his turn as the arch-villain of *Raiders of the Lost Ark*. *Crucible of Terror* failed to make any impact, and Raven soon gave up on films and retired to Cornwall to become a sheep farmer and a sculptor.

THE DEADLY TRAP

This suspense drama was made by René Clément, one of the most respected post-war directors in France. By the early 1970s his powers had somewhat diminished – he was nearing his 60s – although star Faye Dunaway agreed to do the film largely for the chance to work with him. Dunaway and Frank Langella, then best known as a Broadway actor, play a married couple with two children, living in Paris. In the past Langella worked for an espionage organisation and, when the children go missing, it looks like they are being used as pawns to get him to return to the spy game.

Langella was to recall that Dunaway would sometimes cause shooting delays 'for any number of reasons' – on one occasion it was her inability to decide on what style of shoes to wear. 'So, shooting shut down for a few days as assistants went scurrying in search thereof.' Fed up, Langella caught a flight to London and went to the Ascot races.[14]

THE DEVIL'S NIGHTMARE

What could have been just another trashy European sexploitation horror flick manages to raise itself above the average thanks to its creepy atmosphere and the extraordinary presence of Italian actress Erika Blanc. And not least in her startling wardrobe – especially one item.

It was a dress that I used for a theatrical piece and that was given to me, and I modified it for the movie. It was a black dress, and I created a sort of opening where the belly is. And I have to say that it was very sexy. I was so proud of it![15]

Blanc had fun in the role of a succubus seducing and killing her way through a bunch of tourists in an old castle. For Blanc what added immeasurably to the atmosphere of the film was the fact it was shot in a real castle:

> The atmosphere on the set was a bit strange. We were influenced by the story and had the feeling that around us there were some strange energies, almost like ghosts. Many of us were quite scared or uncomfortable. There was an actor that asked me if he could sleep in my room!![16]

Beside the magical and scary atmosphere, there were some fun moments. In a scene one of the actors had to have blood pouring from his mouth. Blanc recalls:

> They used condoms, with the fake blood inside that he had to put in his mouth and break in order for the blood to come out. Well, we laughed so much that he wasn't able to break the condoms and he swallowed a few of them. Can you imagine my face while shooting? I was the devil and I was killing a man, but couldn't stop laughing![17]

DIE SCREAMING MARIANNE

After a successful stint in the sexploitation game, Pete Walker made his first foray into the suspense/horror genre in which he specialised for the rest of the decade. Shot mostly in the Algarve, where Walker owned a villa, Susan George stars as Marianne, a nightclub dancer who stands to inherit a family fortune, along with several documents that could incriminate her corrupt judge of a father, all of which puts her life in danger.

Playing a shady character was Christopher Sandford, who'd appeared in Walker's previous film *Cool It, Carol!* (1970):

> I think Pete was a little bit insecure about being in the film business. He was always watching the clock, watching the budget. I think he had to settle a lot of the time for not exactly what he wanted.[18]

Poor old Leo Genn, who played the judge, came from the Old Vic and had appeared in distinguished Hollywood pictures like *Quo Vadis* (1951) and *Moby Dick* (1956). 'I think he suddenly found he was in a cheap movie, and he didn't want to be there,' says Sandford.[19] Also in the cast were Barry Evans and Judy Huxtable, then dating Peter Cook, who turned up at the location and stayed for the whole shoot. 'We used to play golf together,' says Sandford. 'He was great fun.'[20]

Sandford also recalls a scene involving a car crash:

> Pete Walker took two cars out to Portugal, one was a wreck, he had to tow it out there, and he just pushed that over a cliff, and he kept the good one. But he got the shot, that's the thing. I did admire him.[21]

DOC

In old westerns, figures like Wyatt Earp and Doc Holliday had been turned into almost mythic figures. Director Frank Perry and journalist Pete Hamill figured the time was right to re-examine these legends and to tell their story in a more realistic way. A huge replica of the town of Tombstone, scene of the famous gunfight at the O.K. Corral, was built out in Spain. Stacy Keach played Doc and Harris Yulin Wyatt Earp. Faye Dunaway was top billed as Kate Elder, a true pioneer woman who, history tells, drank and fought as good as any man.

While *Doc* aims to tell a more revisionist tale, it's not nearly as entertaining as the likes of *My Darling Clementine* (1946) or *Gunfight at the O.K. Corral* (1957), which tell the same story. A solid western in its own way, the film just didn't catch the interest of the moviegoer. On location, both Keach and Yulin took against Hamill's script that dismantled these old western heroes, especially the idea of a gay liaison, and set about rewriting scenes, much to Hamill's anger. This tension lasted for the whole shoot. Notwithstanding the film's reception, the three leads give excellent performances.

$ (DOLLARS)

Warren Beatty and Goldie Hawn make a fun team in this modest heist thriller shot in Europe under the direction of the experienced Richard Brooks. Beatty plays a security expert out to rob safe-deposit boxes in Hamburg; Hawn is a hooker and former Las Vegas showgirl. After the seriousness of *McCabe and Mrs Miller*, critics questioned what Beatty was doing wasting his energy making a lightweight caper, but he'd enjoyed himself and out of it came a lifelong friendship with Hawn.

There are a couple of standout sequences – one in a bank vault and another where Beatty plays cat and mouse with a chasing car on a frozen lake. While shooting on some train tracks, Beatty almost died when he stumbled and fell, and only just managed to drag himself from the path of an oncoming locomotive.

DRACULA VS. FRANKENSTEIN

This was originally shot under the title *Satan's Blood Freaks*, and starred horror veterans J. Carrol Naish, as a mad scientist living in an old amusement park, and Lon Chaney Jr, as his manservant sent out to grab girls for blood experiments. Both stars were making their last film appearances. Naish couldn't remember his lines and resorted to huge cue cards that he could barely read with his coke-bottle lenses and one glass eye. Chaney was ravaged by lung cancer and could hardly talk, so it was decided to make his character mute. Co-star Regina Carrol recalled that between scenes Chaney would walk off set to be violently sick, then come back and work: 'He was fighting just to stay alive. Just fighting it with all he had.'[22]

Completed, the backers didn't like the film. So director Al Adamson decided to beef it up by making Naish's scientist the last of the Frankensteins trying to revive the monster and, hey, why not throw in Dracula as well?! Adamson brought in his stockbroker Raphael Engel, who'd originally trained as an actor, to play the role. Engel wasn't deemed enough of a horror name, so he was credited as Zandor Vorkov. New footage was shot, including a climactic battle between the two titans of terror.

This is fun despite its amateurish awfulness. There's even a cameo from legendary horror buff Forest Ackerman. Horror devotees will recognise some of the electrical lab equipment props originally used in *Frankenstein* (1931). Thanks to the intervention of Ackerman, Ken Strickfaden, who designed all the electrical gadgetry in the Karloff classic, agreed to supply the equipment.

EVEL KNIEVEL

George Hamilton was looking for someone to do a bit of stunt work on a TV series he was making. A producer mentioned the name Evel Knievel. When Knievel showed up for the interview he could scarcely walk and was so busted up he was about to have an operation to put 11lb of metal in his leg. Hamilton was impressed; here was the most outrageous character he'd ever met. Forget the stunt work, Hamilton wanted to film his life story.

Armed with the script, Hamilton went to see Knievel, who was holed up in a motel room nursing an injury and sipping whisky from a bottle. Knievel wanted the script read out loud. Hamilton said he didn't read scripts, he acted them. 'Read,' demanded Knievel, 'and literally put a gun to my head. And cocked it. And so, I read. For more than two hours. I gave the performance of a lifetime, as if it might be my last.'[23]

While Hamilton cast himself as Knievel, the daredevil did most of the stunt work, including jumping over nineteen cars, even though his right hand was broken from an earlier practice jump and taped to the handlebar. This world record stood for twenty-seven years.

Director Marvin J. Chomsky also found Knievel a bit of a 'character'. Filming in Butte, Montana, Evel's hometown where as a kid he got in trouble with the law stealing and causing mayhem, Chomsky welcomed the odd bit of advice. One day, Knievel told Chomsky he wanted to blow up city hall for a robbery sequence, and knew where he could lay his hands on some dynamite. 'We can't blow up city hall!' Chomsky explained.[24]

This biopic found little favour with critics, but the public liked it enough to make it a modest hit.

FLIGHT OF THE DOVES

Director Ralph Nelson performs a complete about-face from the savage brutality of *Soldier Blue* (1970), his previous picture, to this gentle piece of family entertainment about two Liverpool orphans who run away to Ireland to escape their wicked uncle.

Boasting excellent location photography and a fine score by Roy Budd, *Flight of the Doves* reunited two of the stars of *Oliver!* in Jack Wild and Ron Moody; it was Fagin and the Artful Dodger back together again. Playing the dastardly uncle allowed Moody to show off his versatility as he adopts a range of disguises, from a vaudevillian magician to an old maid, in his desperate efforts to catch the children. The film also marked the return to the screen of actress Dorothy McGuire, after a six-year hiatus, and a role for Irish singer Dana.

FOOLS' PARADE

This drama set in the Great Depression presented James Stewart with what turned out to be his very last starring role. Based on a novel by Davis Grubb, best known as the author of *The Night of the Hunter*, Stewart plays an eccentric, one-eyed reformed murderer released from jail after serving forty years. With two other convicts, Strother Martin's ex-bank robber and a young Kurt Russell, they plan to open a store, but are menaced by an obsessive prison official played by George Kennedy.

Shot on location in Moundsville, West Virginia, assistant director Hawk Koch recalls shooting one afternoon outside a penitentiary with the four leads:

> I'm standing with them about to shoot something and all of a sudden, a school let out down the street. And these kids come running up the road. As the assistant director the first thing I did was say, 'Quick, Jimmy, over here.' And I got Jimmy Stewart off into a corner. Then I looked back and all the kids attacked Kurt Russell, because he was a big Disney star. And to this day when we meet Kurt says to me, 'You left me. You arsehole.'[25]

FORTUNE AND MEN'S EYES

John Herbert was one of Canada's most important playwrights. This is his best-known work and was the first play to dramatise the inhumane conditions faced by gay men in prison. Banned from public performance in Canada, the play was taken up by the Actors Studio in New York and done as a workshop in 1966, with Dustin Hoffman and Jon Voight in the leads, four years before their partnership in *Midnight Cowboy*. A year later the play was produced off-Broadway and its evocative content spurred audience discussion around criminal justice, eventually leading to the founding of the Fortune Society, which performs outreach services for ex-prisoners and publicises the shortcomings of the prison system.

Writer/director Jules Schwerin was equally inspired by the play and bought the film rights, intending to use the piece as a general plea for prison reform, rather than focusing on the sexual politics. Managing to interest MGM in backing the low-budget feature, Schwerin presided over thirty-one days of shooting, before he was dismissed by the film's producers. Early on there had been artistic differences; Schwerin later stated that the producers were more interested in emphasising nudity and exploitative sexual material over the social content implicit in the play. Schwerin was replaced by Harvey Hart. As a result, the finished film, while remaining hard-hitting for its time with its scenes of male rape, was heavily compromised.

FOUR NIGHTS OF A DREAMER

(QUATRE NUITS D'UN REVEUR)

'Robert Bresson is French cinema, as Dostoevsky is the Russian novel and Mozart is the German music.' So said Jean-Luc Godard, one of the director's greatest admirers. Interestingly, Bresson's first films in colour, *Une Femme douce* (1969) and *Quatre Nuits d'un reveur* (1971), were both taken from Fyodor Dostoevsky stories.

Bresson was writing an original screenplay when he was given some money by a production company to make a film quickly. He recalled the Dostoevsky novella *White Nights* (1847), and was struck by how this story of love and youth still seemed very contemporary. Dostoevsky's protagonist is a dreamer and a lonely man who wanders the city of St Petersburg at night. He meets a young woman and, although her heart belongs to another man, they spend four nights getting to know each other, before she returns to her lover.

The story had already been filmed in 1957 by Luchino Visconti, who moved the action to Italy. Bresson relocates the story to Paris and had his young couple meet on the Pont Neuf. The director lived by the Seine and was familiar with the sights on the left bank, lovers walking hand in hand by the water, and the illuminated boats that pass along in the summer months. Jacques, our romantic dreamer, is played by Guillaume des Forêts, and Bresson made him a painter, a choice inspired by the director's own early aspirations to paint, something he abandoned when he committed to the cinema. At one point, Bresson was going to use some of his own canvasses in scenes set in Jacques's studio. Oddly, the people in Jacques's paintings have no faces, just large splotches of colour.

Jacques encounters Marthe (Isabelle Weingarten) as she's contemplating suicide on the Pont Neuf. They talk and agree to see each other again the next night. Gradually, he discovers that her lover had promised to meet her on the bridge that night, and had failed to turn up. Over the next couple of nights, Jacques falls in love with Marthe, but on the fourth night she encounters her lost lover and goes off with him. Jacques returns to his paintings and his illusions.

FRIENDS

This teen romance was very much a personal project for director Lewis Gilbert. His original idea was to make a film that featured three individual love stories – one about two young teens, another concerning a middle-aged couple and, lastly, one featuring an elderly couple. It was going to be called *Morning, Noon and Night*. Paramount boss Robert Evans liked the idea and asked Gilbert to write a treatment. Gilbert set about working on the teen story first and, when Evans read it, he told Gilbert to forget about the rest and just concentrate on that one.

Friends tells the sentimental tale of Paul and Michelle, a British boy and a French girl who meet, fall in love and run away from their families to live an idyllic life together in a remote cottage. For the young leads Gilbert tested hundreds of candidates, before choosing 16-year-old Sean Bury, who had appeared as a school kid in Lindsay Anderson's *If*, and Anicée Alvina, who went on to have a strong career in French cinema. Gilbert had been keen to cast 15-year-old Isabelle Adjani, but things didn't work out.

Featuring a soundtrack that included songs by Elton John, *Friends* was an international hit, despite receiving generally poor critical notices. In 1974 Gilbert picked up their story again in *Paul and Michelle*, again starring Bury and Alvina. It was not a success.

THE GANG THAT COULDN'T SHOOT STRAIGHT

Just about the only merit of this misconceived gangster spoof is that it presented Robert De Niro with one of his earliest starring roles, and he is by far the best thing in it. Originally the role was going to be played by Al Pacino, until the actor won the part of Michael Corleone in *The Godfather* and was freed from his contract. Ironically, De Niro, who had a small part in *The Godfather*, was allowed to leave that film to replace Pacino.

Based on a novel by journalist Jimmy Breslin, the film was shot entirely in New York. Director James Goldstone gave his actors a rehearsal period prior to shooting. For De Niro and Leigh Taylor-Young, who played lovers in the film, Goldstone told them to spend the day sightseeing in character. De Niro, playing a kleptomaniac, took these instructions literally and, during a visit to Macy's, was arrested by the store detective for stealing shirts. Protesting they were actors preparing for a role, both were only released when a cop recognised Leigh from TV's *Peyton Place*.[26] De Niro also flew out to Sicily with a tape recorder to capture the local dialect. This marked the first occasion the actor had done heavy research for one of his film roles, something that later became a trademark of his acting method.

The film also marked the feature film debut of Hervé Villechaize, the diminutive actor who later played a Bond villain and starred in TV's *Fantasy Island*.

GIRL STROKE BOY

The 1970s is generally regarded as an era of rampant political incorrectness. So, imagine a film in 1971 that features a positive portrayal of a trans woman of colour and her romance with her cisgender, white boyfriend. Yes, such a thing exists.

George and Lettice are two middle-class parents looking forward to meeting their son Laurie's new girlfriend Jo. However, when Jo arrives both are uncertain of their gender identity. While George seems more willing to accept Jo on face value, it is Lettice, who considers herself a liberal woman, who is not happy with the situation.

Girl Stroke Boy was based on David Percival's acclaimed play and adapted for the screen by Ned Sherrin and Caryl Brahms. At the helm was Bob Kellett, whose direction is serviceable – but he cast the film with a brilliant eye. Playing George and Lettice were two estimable British character actors, Michael Hordern and Joan Greenwood. For the part of Laurie, he cast Clive Francis, while Jo was played by Jamaican-born actor and singer Peter Straker. Straker recalled that Kellet encouraged him to play the role in a straightforward way and avoid the more cliched mannerisms that infected portrayals of gay characters in the media back then. 'Infuriatingly, though, they dubbed Peter with a more feminine-sounding voice to make his transgender appearance all the more plausible,' recalls Francis. 'Instead, it had the opposite effect.'[27]

Filmed on a shoestring budget across a breathless two weeks on location at a house in Hertfordshire,[28] one must admire the film for its positive and progressive portrayal of a trans character at a time when most people hadn't even heard of the term, let alone knew what it meant. 'For a time, *Girl Stroke Boy* was shown annually at various gay film festivals, together with *Entertaining Mr Sloane* which I'd made two years earlier,' recalls Francis. 'It even turned me into a bit of a gay icon!'[29]

GOING HOME

This tough drama about a man who kills his wife in front of their 6-year-old son during a drunken rage stars the uncompromising Robert Mitchum. Out of prison after fifteen years, he starts a new life when his traumatised son, played by Jan-Michael Vincent in his breakthrough role, turns up desperate to understand what drove his father to such an act.

Every morning on location in New Jersey, director Herbert Leonard visited Mitchum's motel room to go over the scenes for that day and invariably found Mitchum smashed, having already drunk half a bottle of vodka; it wouldn't be long before Mitchum reached for a big pipe of hash.[30] And yet on set he knew his lines and was always prepared and ready. One night assistant director Hawk Koch was with Mitchum in his motel room along with Vincent and actress Brenda Vaccaro:

> Mitchum had just got this huge bag of grass. There was a young cop called Jerry who was assigned to us to keep people away while we were shooting. We're smoking and all of a sudden there's a knock on the door. It was this cop. Shit. Mitchum flushes this giant bag of grass down the toilet. 'We'll be with you in a minute.' We open the

windows and start waving the smoke away. Finally, we open the door and Jerry says, 'Can I come in? Have you guys got any grass?'[31]

Koch liked Mitchum, but was less keen on the director. A lot of the crew didn't think he knew what he was doing. After a clash Koch was fired – the only time ever in his career. When Koch left, 'eighteen members of the crew left with me'.[32]

GOODBYE UNCLE TOM

In a year of controversial films this Italian Mondo docudrama really takes the biscuit. Indeed, it is without doubt one of the most infamous movies ever made. Written and directed by ex-journalist Gualtiero Jacopetti and Franco Prosperi, creators of the Mondo film genre with 1962's *Mondo Cane*, *Goodbye Uncle Tom* is the most shocking depiction of slavery ever committed to celluloid, showing the racist ideology and degrading conditions of African slaves.

Relying on historical documents, the film was shot primarily in Haiti, where Jacopetti and Prosperi were welcomed by dictator Papa Doc Duvalier and allowed to film anywhere on the island and the use of as many locals to act as enslaved people. Further scenes were shot in the US.

The filmmakers positioned themselves almost as historical documentarists. However, as is sometimes the case with such films, depicting controversial themes can stray into outright exploitation. This was certainly the case here. In America it received a barrage of criticism, despite fifteen minutes of footage depicting modern-day American Black militants killing white people being excised before any distributor would even touch the film. Esteemed critic Roger Ebert did not mince his words when he called *Goodbye Uncle Tom* a 'vomit-bag of racism and perversion-mongering'. Pauline Kael called the film 'the most specific and rabid incitement to race war'. The film truly has to be seen to be believed, if you have the stomach for it.

THE GRISSOM GANG

Director Robert Aldrich earned so much money off the back of his film *The Dirty Dozen* (1967) that he was able to buy his own studio, the old Mary Pickford Studio in East Hollywood. It was the realisation of a long-held dream, one that he hoped would lend him the clout and freedom to make movies his own way without big studio interference. Unfortunately, his first three movies, *The Killing of Sister George* (1968), *The Legend of Lylah Clare* (1968), and *Too Late the Hero* (1970) were all box-office flops. When *The Grissom Gang* went the same way Aldrich was forced to sell his studio and go back to being a director for hire.

The failure of *The Grissom Gang* both irked and surprised Aldrich. The film tapped into the nostalgia boom for the 1930s begun by *Bonnie and Clyde* (1967) and exploited by other early '70s pictures such as *The Great Gatsby* and *The Sting*. Unlike *Bonnie and Clyde*, Aldrich's gangster film does not romanticise the criminals; there are no redeeming characters here and Aldrich was heavily criticised for his use of explicit violence and cruelty.

Based on the sensational novel *No Orchids for Miss Blandish* by famed British writer James Hadley Chase, the story concerns Barbara Blandish, a wealthy socialite kidnapped by a violent, sexually twisted family of criminals. Following on the heels of her 1969 breakout hit, *True Grit*, Kim Darby plays the petulant and spoilt heiress and Scott Wilson is Slim Grissom, a feeble-minded psychopath who takes a fancy to her. Initially revulsed by his advances, Barbara realises that the only thing keeping her alive is his desire for her. The film originally ended with Barbara committing suicide after the gang are slaughtered but, following test screenings, this was changed as it was felt unnecessary since 'her life was lost and useless anyway', according to Aldrich.

A GUNFIGHT

This Kirk Douglas western was made by his own production company and financed by the Jicarilla Apache tribe, who wanted to invest in movies using earnings from oil wells on their reservation lands in New Mexico.

Douglas had come across this script and liked its story of two old-time gunslingers running into each other and the local townsfolk laying bets about who would win in a gunfight. In the end both men agree to a public showdown. As the other gunslinger Douglas cast country and western superstar Johnny Cash in his first screen appearance in a decade. It was a role that suited his persona well and a short clip from this film, of him saying – 'You stay the hell away from me, ya hear' – featured in Cash's final music video before his death, the widely acclaimed 'Hurt'.

Unusually for a western, seen as a macho genre, there are two strong female performances from Jane Alexander as Douglas's wife, desperate to stop the shoot out, and Karen Black. The film also saw film debuts for Eric Douglas, Kirk Douglas's son, and Keith Carradine, son of actor John Carradine.

HANNIE CAULDER

This revenge western features an impressive cast led by Raquel Welch as a frontier wife who is raped and her husband murdered by a trio of outlaw brothers, played by Ernest Borgnine, Strother Martin and Jack Elam. She recruits Robert Culp's bounty hunter to train her how to use a gun before hunting down her attackers. Christopher Lee and Stephen Boyd play small roles, and Diana Dors turns up as a brothel madame.

Director Burt Kennedy and Welch didn't have the best of relationships, according to assistant director Julio Sempere. Welch was a tough cookie. Sempere had a huge argument with her one day when she was late on set:

> When she arrived, I reproached her, and she tried to hit me. We were so close that the brims of our hats were touching each other. We cut for lunch. When she returned, perhaps persuaded by her husband Pat Curtis, who was the film's producer, she assembled the crew and apologised to me in Spanish. From then on, we had minimal dialogue.[33]

On the last day of shooting, which took place in Spain, Welch threw a small party on the set. Sempere refused to go. Welch sent her secretary to ask him to attend. 'I agreed, she gave me a kiss and a picture of her, almost without clothes, just the blanket she wore in her role, and wrote: "keep the guard up till next time."'[34]

THE HORSEMEN

John Frankenheimer spent two and a half years on this film, based around *buzkashi*, the ancient and brutally violent Afghan sport requiring an individual on horseback to transport a dead calf over a goal line. Starring Omar Sharif and Jack Palance, the logistics of shooting on location in Afghanistan were extreme. And there were other problems too. Frankenheimer required a crowd of around 5,000 for one of the buzkashi games, but there simply wasn't the money for that many extras. Someone came up with the bright idea of a car raffle. What nobody realised was the national wage was so small that owning a car was a luxury beyond most of the population. On the day of the game, rather than 5,000 people showing up at the stadium there were 300,000 people clogging the streets for miles. The army had to be called in and it took them two days to get things under control.

Frankenheimer planned *The Horsemen* as a three-and-a-half-hour epic, but Columbia took charge and severely edited and restructured the picture. It did not do well at the box office.

THE HUNTING PARTY

British actors usually make a pig's ear out of playing cowboys; they just look false, out of place. Not Oliver Reed. He appeared to be perfectly at home in a western setting and thoroughly enjoyed the experience, practising his draw sixty times a day and borrowing his cowboy's accent from a New York hamburger seller he'd overheard. Reed's dark menacing looks also suited the character of outlaw Frank Calder, leader of a band of rustlers and thieves. They kidnap a school teacher, played by Candice Bergen, unaware she is the wife of a ruthless cattle baron, played to the hilt by Gene Hackman, who mercilessly hunts down the group and systematically kills them off as if he's on some perverse safari.

It sounds nasty and that's exactly what *The Hunting Party* is, without doubt one of the most savage westerns ever made. The film is loaded with brutal slayings, mostly in Peckinpah-style slow motion, and Bergen is thrown about like a piece of left luggage at Paddington Station. She did not enjoy the experience, and in her autobiography revealed that Reed stayed in his outlaw character off-set too, 'brawling drunkenly and flinging plates of food after fleeing waiters'.

I, MONSTER

This version of *Dr. Jekyll and Mr Hyde* was saddled with a rather dodgy 3-D process that was the creation of Amicus co-founder Milton Subotsky. Two directors had already turned the job down due to his insistence on employing it. In the end it was Christopher Lee who suggested a young filmmaker called Stephen Weeks.

Weeks's youth – he was just 22 – and perceived inexperience presented problems. 'The camera operator, when he found out that I was at least two years younger than his son, could hardly bring himself to do what I asked him – and we had to communicate through my first assistant.'[35] Then there was Subotsky. Weeks soon realised why he'd wanted a young director – to push around. 'He would find out that I wasn't quite so malleable as he hoped.'[36] For starters Weeks found Subotsky's 3-D process 'a nonsense', and a fortnight into a six-week schedule pulled the plug on it. 'Milton never said a word. He knew it was a crazy idea.'[37]

Then there was Subotsky's ponderous script, which was far too reverential to the source material, to the point of lifting entire chunks of dialogue from the book. Weeks did his best to pare this down but could do nothing about Subotsky's insistence on keeping reams of Freudian psychobabble about the dual nature of man, most of which came, courtesy of Subotsky's psychologist wife, straight from a textbook!

Weeks got on much better with his two stars, Lee and Peter Cushing. Weeks found Cushing 'gentle and always helpful', while Lee had issues 'as well as a big but sensitive ego'.[38] One afternoon Lee didn't appear on set. 'Eventually he was found in his dressing room,' Weeks recalls, 'the door locked, listening to himself on an LP – singing operatic favourites!'[39]

Despite a flawed script, *I, Monster* has commendable production values. And Lee's performance as the doomed scientist almost certainly ranks among the best he ever gave.

THE INCREDIBLE 2-HEADED TRANSPLANT

Mad scientist Bruce Dern decides to transplant the head of an escaped homicidal maniac onto the body of his burly mentally defective handyman, with predictable results; the creature breaks loose and terrorises the neighbourhood.

This is drive-in, exploitation fodder at its crudest, shot in just six days. Dern himself was the film's most articulate critic, calling it 'a real dog-shit movie'.[40] It didn't help that his $1,700 cheque for playing the role bounced. When he went back to the studio the day after filming was completed to confront the makers, he found the place boarded up. He never got his money and he never managed to track them down.

JENNIFER ON MY MIND

When Michael Brandon signed on to make this drug drama it was clearly inspired by the true 1966 case of Robert Friede, a 25-year-old publishing heir and his girlfriend, Celeste Crenshaw, a drug-addicted 19-year-old socialite who died of an overdose. Brandon reveals:

> The boyfriend didn't know what to do. He put her body into the bath tub with ice, and then eventually snuck it into his car. The police stopped him and found one of those little packets of heroin. That led to his car being searched and the body was in the boot. I was loving the script. It was a love-gone-wrong story.[41]

Pretty soon the film went wrong. The writer Roger L. Simon called Brandon, revealing he'd been fired and replaced. After that things started to change for Brandon:

> I remember sitting with Robert De Niro, who played a New York cabbie in the film. I said, 'Bobby, I don't know what I'm doing. And nobody else knows what they're doing. One day it's a comedy, another day it's a tragedy.' It was really strange.[42]

In the movie, flashbacks show how the two lovers, called Marcus and Jennifer, first meet in Venice. Brandon says:

> For one shot I swam the Grand Canal. It wasn't a healthy thing to do. I swam across and the cameraman, Andrew Laszlo, saved my life because, when I got to the other side, I couldn't get up because of all the algae on the stone, it was so slippery. Andy grabbed my hand and pulled me up.[43]

In the end Brandon wasn't thrilled with the experience. 'It was not the movie that I signed to do. And it wasn't the movie our director set out to make. The powers that be make these creative decisions and you've gotta go with the flow.'[44]

LADY FRANKENSTEIN

This Italian production has the distinction of starring veteran Joseph Cotton as Baron Frankenstein, who at least has the acting chops to make the lamentable dialogue sound halfway decent. Only he's quickly bumped off and his daughter Tania takes over in the monster-making stakes. The reason for Cotton's brevity in the role was purely economic; his asking price was too steep and so his part was truncated and he only worked for two weeks.

Believe it or not there's a feminist message among all the creature mayhem, as Tania laments the resistance she faced as a woman in the halls of academia. Tania is played by Italian exploitation actress supreme Rosalba Neri, who appeared in sword and sandal pictures as well as Bond rip-offs and spaghetti westerns.

The film was directed by Mel Welles, a former actor best remembered as the flower shop owner in *The Little Shop of Horrors* (1960). Welles left the US to make a career in Europe, acting in and directing B pictures. It was his ex-employer Roger Corman who provided most of the funding for this one. A sequel was planned, but wise heads terminated it at birth.

THE LAST RUN

Coming off the success of *Patton*, George C. Scott could do no wrong and had enormous creative power. He wanted to make *The Last Run*, playing a former getaway driver coming out of retirement to prove to himself he hasn't lost his touch, because it reminded him of the kind of part Bogart might have played. The perfect director then was John Huston, the man who made six films with 'Bogie', including *The Maltese Falcon* (1941). From the start there were problems on location in Spain. Huston liked the premise, but not the script and started extensive rewrites. This led to heated disagreements with Scott and finally shouting matches that threatened to sink the picture. Three weeks into the schedule Huston walked and was replaced by Richard Fleischer.

Scott had taken to drinking – lots – and his wife, actress Colleen Dewhurst flew out to the location to calm things down, ending up playing a small role. A young actress called Trish Van Devere had been cast as the love interest. When Dewhurst returned to America, Scott and Van Devere began an affair that wrecked Scott's marriage. Dewhurst divorced Scott in 1972, and he married Van Devere that same year. They remained married until Scott's death in 1999.

THE LIGHT AT THE EDGE OF THE WORLD

Producer Ilya Salkind was having trouble casting his movie. He had made a list of top stars, but they'd all turned him down. There was only one name left, Kirk Douglas. In a magazine, he read that Douglas was vacationing in the south of France – and so put a call through to his hotel. Salkind let his dad Alexander do the talking. He'd been producing movies since the mid-1940s and knew his way around the business. Douglas wanted a $1 million fee. 'And if you put $80,000 in my bank in the next four weeks then I'm interested,' he said. Salkind says:

> My father was an absolute genius at finding money, and he got the $80,000 and sent it to Kirk and Kirk called back and said, 'Alright, now you have a month to get me the million dollars, but you can use my name.' At that point Kirk was still a very big star and with his name attached to the movie everything started to move and we raised the financing.[45]

Based on a little-known Jules Verne novel, it told the story of a ruthless gang of pirates who capture and imprison the keeper of an isolated lighthouse so they can loot the ships that crash on the rocks. Salkind managed to bag Yul Brynner as the pirate leader and his scenes with Douglas's lighthouse keeper bristle with intensity. Brynner had a reputation for being demanding and difficult, 'But we had no problems with him,' Salkind recalls; Douglas too was 'very professional'.[46]

Salkind recalls the shooting went smoothly on several locations around Spain, including Cadaqués, in the heart of the Costa Brava, home of the artist Salvador Dali, who paid the set a visit. On release the film did not do well at the box office and was criticised for its excessive violence, but this was a conscious decision by Salkind 'to make a more adult adventure film'.[47]

The Light at the Edge of the World was Salkind's first producing credit and a valuable lesson in putting together an international co-production. It was an experience that came in handy later in the decade when he made *The Three Musketeers* (1973) and *Superman* (1978).

A LIZARD IN A WOMAN'S SKIN

This is surely contender for the most grotesque Giallo of all, and no surprise that it's courtesy of the master of gore himself, Lucio Fulci. An Italian–Spanish–French co-production, shot on location in London, Florinda Bolkan plays Carol, the wife of a successful lawyer, plagued by bizarre dreams about her decadent neighbour Julia presiding over noisy parties and orgies. When Carol dreams about viciously stabbing Julia, she is disturbed to find out the following day that her neighbour has indeed been murdered in the exact same manner, and Carol finds herself the subject of scrutiny from a police inspector, played by Stanley Baker.

By far the film's most sensational scene is when Carol is chased through a clinic by a mysterious figure and finds herself in a room where six dogs are being horribly experimented on. Strung up and howling, the dogs' chests are exposed revealing their pulsating hearts, while their heads move and their eyes twitch. The effects here are gruesome if understandably dated. However, at the time they proved to be all too realistic when the Italian authorities took the producers to court for animal cruelty, convinced they had tortured and killed six dogs for the movie. Fulci faced a two-year prison sentence. Carlo Rambaldi, the effects supervisor, had no choice but to bring the animatronic dogs into the courtroom to prove that they were not the real thing. All the charges were dropped. This was the first time that an effects artist had to testify in court that their work was fake.

LUST FOR A VAMPIRE

The success of Hammer's lesbian vampire film *The Vampire Lovers* necessitated a sequel, and *Lust for a Vampire* was hurried into production. Ingrid

Pitt refused to reprise her role and was replaced by Danish actress, Yutte Stensgaard. This was the first of numerous setbacks that were to mar the film. Hammer's grandmaster Terence Fisher was the original director, but broke his leg and was replaced at the last minute by Jimmy Sangster. Then Peter Cushing withdrew in order to look after his wife, who was terminally ill, and he was replaced by Ralph Bates.

Lust for a Vampire significantly ratchets up the sex quota, as Stensgaard's sensual vampire enrols in a girl's school, conveniently located near her ancestral castle, and unsurprisingly runs amok among the girls and staff. 'Ralph and Jimmy loved all the girls running around them, and there was a lot of teasing and flirting going on,' recalls Judy Matheson. 'But they all behaved quite gentlemanly. It was really a happy time.'[48] This was Matheson's second Hammer horror of the year, and she loved working for the company. 'The production values were all fantastic, the hair and the make-up, the costumes, the cameramen, they were all talented people.'[49]

THE MAGNIFICENT SEVEN DEADLY SINS

The comedy actor Graham Stark had just directed a short film called *Simon Simon*, which had been selected for the Sans Sebastian Film Festival. Back in London he got a call from a producer: did he have any ideas for a low-budget comedy 'with lots of saucy girls'? That phrase was actually used.

Stark came up with a comedy made up of seven separate stories, each illustrating one of the Seven Deadly Sins. In a smart move he brought in separate writers for each segment, including Galton and Simpson, Graham Chapman and Marty Feldman. He then filled the screen with a cavalcade of familiar comedy faces: Bruce Forsyth, Harry Secombe, Spike Milligan, Leslie Phillips, Bernard Bresslaw, June Whitfield, Harry H. Corbett, Ronnie Barker and Ian Carmichael.

The format worked in much the same way as those horror anthologies in that each segment isn't long enough to really wear out its welcome, although some are better than others. For one episode a naked lady was required to be photographed in a studio. Like his friend Peter Sellers, Stark was a keen photographer and wrote a column about cameras for *Penthouse* magazine. Stark got in touch with *Penthouse* founder Bob Guccione and suggested he play the photographer, even though he'd never acted in his life. Guccione was game and arrived at Pinewood in a limo with one of his magazine's top models. Stark even gave him a line of dialogue – 'Beautiful baby!'

THE MEPHISTO WALTZ

Spurred by the phenomenal success of *Rosemary's Baby* (1968), famed television producer Quinn Martin paid over $250,000 for the rights to Fred Mustard Stewart's novel about satanic possession. What he ended up with was a pale imitation of the Polanski shocker. Still, it's better than a lot of satanic rip-offs that arrived in the wake of *Rosemary's Baby*, and for a mainstream Hollywood film this is fairly subversive stuff, dealing as it does with themes of witchcraft and incest. It also features a strong cast. Alan Alda, here just seventeen months away from his eleven-year run on TV's *MASH*, and Jacqueline Bisset play a young and beautiful couple living in LA. Myles is a former pianist while Paula runs an antique shop. They meet Duncan Ely, a renowned classical pianist (played by Curt Jürgens), and his daughter Roxanne (Barbara Parkins). Paula soon becomes suspicious of their new friends, and with good reason – they are Satanists and intend to place the dying Duncan's soul into Myles's young body!

It all sounds better than it actually is. The plot gets too complicated for its own good, but there are some nice visuals and creepy dream sequences, and director Paul Wendkos lends the film a degree of style.

MINNIE AND MOSKOWITZ

John Cassavetes was the definition of an independent filmmaker. For many he was the progenitor of American independent cinema. All his previous projects had been funded from friends or his own resources, sometimes mortgaging his home to make a picture. This time he went to Universal and wished he hadn't when they failed to back the film with an adequate advertising campaign. Cassavetes resorted to organising his own press screenings.

Minnie and Moskowitz is Cassavetes's most accessible, straightforward and light-hearted film. It's a revisionist take on the screwball comedy; Cassavetes was an admirer of Frank Capra, and this is a veiled self-portrait of his often stormy relationship with his wife Gena Rowlands.

It tells the unlikely love story between Minnie (Rowlands), a lonely museum curator who is hooked on romantic movies even though she knows they fill her with unattainable ideals about love, and Moskowitz, an eccentric, uncouth parking lot attendant played by Seymour Cassel.

Cassavetes cast many of the supporting roles with family and friends – the Cassavetes' three children feature, as does his mother; Rowlands's mother and brother; and Cassel's wife, mother-in-law and two children. Behind the camera, too, the crew were filled by associates and family. Cassavetes also used his own home and the homes of friends as sets. For Cassavetes, making a film was not a business, the point was to be comfortable and relaxed and surrounded by trusted colleagues. The shoot wasn't without friction, however, with Cassavetes going through three cinematographers.

MR FORBUSH AND THE PENGUINS

This was produced by Bryan Forbes and features the first screenplay by Anthony Shaffer, who later wrote *Sleuth* and *The Wicker Man*. John Hurt stars as Richard Forbush, a brilliant biology student gallivanting round London boozing and womanising. In a bid to impress a new girl, Forbush accepts a six-month research post in the frozen isolation of Antarctica to study a penguin colony.

Hurt and the crew spent months in the Arctic wastes, pretty much cut off from the outside world. Acclaimed Swedish documentary filmmaker Arne Sucksdorff had been hired to shoot the penguin footage, while award-winning commercials director Alfred Viola was making his feature debut. When everyone returned and the film was put together it was obvious that the location footage did not sit right with the more conventional scenes shot in London. The backers, British Lion, fired Viola and replaced him with Roy Boulting to carry out drastic reshoots. The original leading actress, playing Forbush's girlfriend, was also replaced by Boulting's wife Hayley Mills. Hurt was furious, and it took all of Forbes's persuasive skills to stop the actor walking off the picture.

As it stands, the film still has two very distinct halves, and the filmmakers never quite fixed the join. The scenes of Forbush with the penguins, almost 2,000 of them, are the most impressive, as he becomes increasingly obsessed with trying to stop predators attacking the colony

– especially gulls that feast on the eggs and later the helpless chicks. But whatever he does he cannot stop nature taking its course.

NECROMANIA

Even though it's hard to believe that the director of *Plan 9 From Outer Space* (1957) could stoop even lower, by the early 1970s Ed Wood was reduced to making hardcore sex horror films as his career came to a close.

Back in those pre-*Deep Throat* days, *Necromania* numbered among the first US-made 'hardcore' features, and so can be seen as something of a trend-setter. In classic Ed Wood style, it was shot literally over one weekend, with Wood sometimes directing behind the camera in a pink baby doll outfit. With a budget of just $7,000, there was both a soft and hardcore version.

The plot revolves around a young couple with sex problems visiting an occult sex clinic. The cast are mostly adult film performers, although Wood tried to lure Vampira herself, aka Maila Nurmi, then 50 years old, to appear naked in a coffin while getting banged by a young stud. She politely declined.

A NEW LEAF

Henry Graham is a wealthy self-absorbed New York bachelor whose expensive lifestyle is in jeopardy due to his profligate spending. Almost flat broke, the solution is to marry into money and then bump off his new bride and keep her loot. The ideal candidate turns out to be introverted and socially graceless Henrietta Lowell, a millionaire botanist.

That's the premise of this pitch-black comedy written, directed and starring Elaine May, and which was very much an extension of the comedy style she developed with Mike Nichols at the improvisational group The Second City, in Chicago. *A New Leaf* marked the first time a woman simultaneously performed the three functions of writing, directing and starring in a major feature film. May's co-star, Walter Matthau, though admiring of her talents, felt May was taking on too much. And so it proved when the film went over budget and over schedule. A perfectionist, May gave no consideration to how long it took her to get things done the way she wanted. The rumour was that May then took ten months to edit the picture and submitted a three-hour cut to Paramount. The studio took the film over and pruned it to 102 minutes. May took unsuccessful legal action to have her name removed, complaining that the studio had reduced her work to a 'cliché-ridden banal story'.[50] Matthau actually preferred the studio cut and the film has since become a cult comedy. Both May and Matthau deliver strong comic performances, with Matthau skilfully balancing Henry inspiring revulsion and affection. One wonders if his growing affection for Henrietta will cancel out his psychotic tendencies as he packs *A Beginner's Guide to Toxicology* as his honeymoon reading.

THE NIGHTCOMERS

By the start of the 1970s Marlon Brando was box-office poison, with a trail of flops to his name. Even so, Michael Winner thought that, with Brando's name attached to his new project, he'd find a backer. 'Quite the contrary, they ran away even faster.'[51]

The film was a sort of imaginary prequel to the classic Henry James novel *The Turn of the Screw*. Brando liked the script and agreed to appear for just a percentage. Winner found Brando a consummate professional; 'Very restrained, didn't need an atmosphere of reverence.'[52] During one scene a crew member dropped a heavy object with a very loud clang. 'Oh shit,' thought Winner. 'Marlon's bound to have heard that.' After saying cut, Winner went over to apologise:

'Terribly sorry, sir, somebody dropped something.'
'What?' said Brando.
'Well, they dropped something, dear, there was a big bang. I thought you did very well, you didn't react.'
'What?'
'MARLON, THEY DROPPED SOMETHING!'[53]

Just then Brando took out a pair of earplugs. 'He acted with earplugs so he could only hear the people next to him,' confirms Winner. 'Rather clever.'

Then there were the explicit sex scenes with Stephanie Beacham. The trouble was Brando insisted on wearing not only his underpants but a pair of wellington boots. 'I was crying with laughter,' recalls Winner. 'I said, "cut," and I'm crying on the floor. Marlon went, "What's so funny Michael?" I said, "I don't know what it's like from where you are, but from here it's absolutely fucking hysterical."[54]

During the shoot a large, bearded man arrived on the location in Cambridgeshire. For days he hovered about in the distance, always on the periphery of the set. It was Francis Ford Coppola.

'Isn't that Francis standing behind the barrier, Marlon?' Winner asked one morning.
Marlon looked across. 'Yes.'
'Shall we let him through?' asked Winner.
'No.'[55]

Coppola had flown over from America with the express intention of asking Brando to play in *The Godfather*.

NIGHT OF DARK SHADOWS

Dan Curtis's groundbreaking daytime serial *Dark Shadows* ran from 1966 to 1971 on ABC-TV. Essentially it was a horror soap opera and featured all manner of monsters, notably the debonair vampire Barnabas Collins, played by Jonathan Frid. As it gained in popularity, inevitably a movie spin-off arrived, *House of Dark Shadows* in 1970, with many of the regular TV cast. The film did rather good business, so MGM asked Curtis for a follow-up.

The idea was to do a direct sequel, only Frid refused to play his vampire character anymore, for fear of being typecast. Instead of recasting the role Curtis worked with writer Sam Hall to concoct an all-new storyline featuring a pair of newlyweds, Quentin and Tracy Collins, played by David Selby and a pre-*Charlie's Angels* Kate Jackson, moving into Quentin's ancestral manor. Unfortunately, the spirit of a witch hanged 200 years previously returns to exact revenge.

The film was not a success, and reviewers complained about its slapdash plot construction and poor character development. The fact that MGM forced Curtis to remove thirty-five minutes from the completed film, and gave him just twenty-four hours to do so, might have had something to do with it. Much of the excised footage was recovered in 1999, but minus sound.

THE NIGHT VISITOR

Max von Sydow and Liv Ullmann were scheduled to appear in Fred Zinneman's long-cherished project to film André Malraux's epic novel *Man's Fate*, about the failed communist insurrection in Shanghai in 1927. When that production was cancelled, literally just days before shooting was due to start, both actors found themselves suddenly available, and signed up to this interesting if flawed psychological thriller that was shot on location in Denmark and Sweden. Sydow plays Salem, wrongly convicted for an axe murder, who escapes from an asylum for the criminally insane. He burns with one obsessive desire, to seek revenge on the people who framed him. Trevor Howard appears as a dour police inspector. It's interesting to watch Sydow and Ullmann here, more accustomed to the complex work of Ingmar Bergman, running around in what is essentially a snowbound Giallo.

Hungarian director László Benedek had studied to be a psychiatrist in Vienna before switching to the cinema, and so knew much about the subject matter. His most notable Hollywood work was the Marlon Brando biker movie *The Wild One* (1953). Benedek's camera wonderfully captures the wintry atmosphere, and there's a strong sense of claustrophobia with much of the picture taking place in the lunatic asylum and a family farmhouse. The atmosphere is enlivened by an interesting score from Henry Mancini.

THE ORGANIZATION

This was the third and final film to feature police detective Virgil Tibbs, the character Sidney Poitier so successfully portrayed in the classic *In the Heat of the Night* (1967). The follow-up to that film, *They Call Me Mister Tibbs!* (1970), in which Tibbs is assigned to the case of a murdered high-priced call girl, was something of a disappointment. *The Organization* is an improvement, thanks to a more engrossing plotline. Shot on location in San Francisco, Tibbs joins up with a group of idealistic vigilantes (including a young Raul Julia in an early film role) in order to bust an international drug ring controlled by powerful businessmen.

Directed by Don Medford, *The Organization* was a modest hit and there was talk of a fourth instalment for Tibbs. But Poitier had grown bored of the character and it never materialised.

PERCY

This infamous British comedy concerns itself with the world's first penis transplant. Despite the exploitative subject matter, the film managed to draw an impressive cast including Denholm Elliott, Elke Sommer, Britt Ekland and Hywel Bennett as Percy, the beneficiary of said organ. There's even a cameo from football legend George Best and a theme song from The Kinks.

Directed by Ralph Thomas, of the *Doctor* film series, subtlety was never an option. At times the film doesn't quite know whether to go all out for knob jokes, or tread a more contemplative path about the consequences of Percy's predicament post-op. Just a few weeks prior to shooting Thomas brought in Monty Python pair Michael Palin and Terry Jones to rewrite the script. How much of their stuff got in remains unknown. It didn't earn them a screen credit.

In an era when British comedies were able to push the boundaries of permissiveness, *Percy* ended up as the eighth most popular film at the British box office in 1971. Bennett did not reprise his role in the inevitable sequel; instead, Leigh Lawson took over for the less successful *Percy's Progress* (1974).

PINK NARCISSUS

This landmark of gay cinema is the erotic daydreams of a male prostitute (Bobby Kendall), a series of interlinked fantasies populated by matadors, dancing boys, slaves and leather-clad bikers. The mix of kitsch and beautiful imagery is a paean to the male form. Shrouded in mystery following its release, with its director credited only as 'Anonymous', *Pink Narcissus* was falsely attributed to a number of filmmakers (including Kenneth Anger and Andy Warhol) until it was rediscovered in the 1980s and revealed as the work of artist and photographer James Bidgood. Incredibly, the whole thing was shot on 8mm over the course of seven years, between 1964 and 1970, on sets Bidgood designed and made in his own cramped New York apartment.

Bidgood arrived in New York in the early 1950s and worked as a drag queen, set designer and then photographer for male physique magazines. His aim was to photograph male models in the same lush and erotic way that magazines like *Playboy* presented women. Bidgood created his own distinct style, which later inspired the careers of Pierre et Gilles, and David LaChappelle.

A lot of the 'models' in the film were picked up in the street. Many of them were straight and hadn't done anything like this before – they were druggies or hippies, some were hustlers. One night, Bidgood was shooting on a guy and a gun fell out of his trousers on the floor.

Influenced by MGM musicals and Powell and Pressburger's *The Red Shoes*, with its exaggerated use of colours the film has lost none of its highly charged hallucinogenic quality.

PLAZA SUITE

Before it even opened in February 1968 the film rights to Neil Simon's new Broadway play were snapped up by Paramount. Directed by Mike Nichols, it comprised three acts featuring George C. Scott as a trio of guests staying in the same suite at the famous New York Plaza hotel – first a jaded husband whose marriage is failing, then a Hollywood producer and, lastly, a father whose daughter is getting married.

In the film version Walter Matthau replaces Scott. Curiously, Maureen Stapleton, who appeared opposite Scott on Broadway in all three acts, was only used in the film's opening story; Barbara Harris and Lee Grant were cast in the others.

Directed by Arthur Hiller, *Plaza Suite*'s stage origins are all too obvious. Simon later blamed himself for some of its failings, namely not making enough changes from the stage version and opening it out much more for the screen. Still, there's much to enjoy in Simon's sharp dialogue and to watch Matthau is always to watch a comedy master at work.

PRETTY MAIDS ALL IN A ROW

This marked Gene Roddenberry's first and only theatrical film that wasn't based on his creation *Star Trek*. And it's a very strange film indeed, one that certainly could never be made today.

Directed by Roger Vadim, it's set at a California high school where a teacher is bedding his female students and a serial killer is on the loose. A sizeable hit at the time, it features a strong cast: Rock Hudson, Telly

Savalas, Angie Dickinson and Roddy McDowall, along with a roster of young actresses including Diane Sherry Case. Sherry Case was home for the summer from college and auditioning for a television show on the MGM lot when she passed Vadim and Roddenberry. 'They tried to get me to stop but it felt like they were trying to pick me up, so I kept walking.'[56] They managed to track her down and asked her to test. There was going to be a lot of nudity, including a *Playboy* spread as part of the film's publicity. Sherry Case refused:

> I kept turning down the role and they kept offering me more money and finally I took it. I was hoping that they wouldn't insist on the nudity, and I think they actually found it sport to see if I would go nude.[57]

In the end Sherry Case was cast in a smaller role because she refused to bare all. Then came the *Playboy* shoot;

> I went in wearing a turtle neck but, after the photographer gave me some wine, I posed topless. Afterward, I wasn't happy about it and didn't want them published and they destroyed the negatives, I believe. Now I wish I had those pics, they were lovely.[58]

Sherry Case got to like Vadim. 'He was funny. Los Angeles was grey with thick smog in those days and Vadim smoked; he said that cigarettes protected his lungs from the smog!'[59] Also she remembers:

> We shot in a church, and they gave the church a fake script because, if they read the real one, they wouldn't have let us shoot there. Probably true about the school also. And for one of John David Carson's close-ups [he played a nerdy student], Angie flashed her breasts to get him to salivate.[60]

PRIVATE ROAD

When Barney Platts-Mills's *Bronco Bullfrog* opened in 1969 it was viewed as one of the freshest films of post-war British cinema. It was made in black and white on a meagre £18,000 budget in east London, using teenagers with no previous acting experience. Mills secured a £26,000 budget for his next project, *Private Road*, along with a larger crew and professional actors – Bruce Robinson (later the writer and director of *Withnail and I*) and Susan Penhaligon – who play a young couple experimenting with sex and drugs and a new way of living.

Private Road covers much of the same ground as *Bronco Bullfrog*: a youthful struggle for social and personal freedom. It was a conscious effort by Mills to move into the commercial film world, but he came away from the experience exhausted by having to concern himself with things outside the actual creative process, such as distribution deals, financial returns and how much ice cream a cinema sells. While the film did well and was awarded a Golden Lion at the Locarno International Film Festival, Mills was to distance himself from the commercial end of the movie industry, preferring to remain on its periphery.

RAID ON ROMMEL

This was an odd picture, using action footage from the 1967 Rock Hudson war film *Tobruk*; audiences with a reasonable memory must have felt cheated sitting in the stalls. For Richard Burton, this was one of the reasons, apart from the large cheque, why he made it, intrigued by how they could make a brand-new film out of a lot of footage from another film. The answer was not very well. Burton himself was under no illusion as to the merits of the piece, confessing to his diary: 'The writing is to be dialogue sufficiently credible to get us from one explosion to another.'

Shot in three weeks in Mexico under the direction of the veteran Henry Hathaway, the result was dreadful – easily one of the worst pictures Burton ever made, and there's stiff opposition. When Universal's publicity department asked Burton to lend his dulcet tones to radio and TV ads for the film he replied, 'Good God, do you think I'm a double fool? It's bad enough that I made the picture. Why would I want people to see it?'

THE RAGING MOON

If you have a project that you want greenlit it helps if you're the boss at the studio. This was the case with Bryan Forbes, head of production for

EMI Films at the time he directed this romantic drama about two young people in wheelchairs, who meet and fall in love. He kept up with studio matters during rushed lunch breaks and at the end of the shooting day, resulting in sixteen-hour work days.

Based on a 1964 semi-autobiographical novel by British author Peter Marshall, Forbes cast his wife Nanette Newman and Malcolm McDowell as the young lovers. McDowell demonstrated his wicked sense of humour during location shooting in Canterbury. Forbes had a hidden camera across the street for a scene where Newman and McDowell visit a jeweller to buy an engagement ring. While Forbes was setting up the shot, the Archbishop of Canterbury came strolling down the road. McDowell spotted him and, as he passed, flung off the blanket covering his legs and staggered out of the chair, declaring, 'It's a miracle. I can walk!' Visibly shocked, the archbishop sped off down the road.

A 15-year-old Gary Oldman watched a TV showing of this film and was so captivated by McDowell's performance he decided to become an actor.

RED SUN

This Franco-Italian co-production spaghetti western is worth watching for the cast alone: Charles Bronson, Toshiro Mifune, Alain Delon, Ursula Andress and Capucine. Add to that Terence Young, director of the early Bond films, and an intriguing storyline. Mifune is an ageing samurai warrior accompanying a Japanese diplomat to Washington to present a golden samurai sword to the US president as a symbol of friendship. Travelling through the west their train is ambushed by a pair of outlaws, Delon and Bronson. When Bronson is double-crossed, he joins forces with Mifune's samurai to track Delon down and recover the sword.

Shot in Spain, *Red Sun* flopped in America, but did excellent business in Europe and especially Japan. In an interview John Huston ranked *Red Sun* alongside *Stagecoach* (1939) and *Red River* (1948) as his three favourite westerns.

For cinema buffs, it's interesting to see Bronson and Mifune sharing the screen together. Mifune of course appeared in the 1954 classic *Seven Samurai*, while Bronson starred in the western remake *The Magnificent Seven*.

THE RESURRECTION OF ZACHARY WHEELER

This science fiction drama was arguably the first film to depict the medical exploitation of cloning. The interesting premise concerns a shadowy organisation that makes zombie-like cloned people in order for their body parts to be farmed out to politicians and important dignitaries who need them.

The idea came about after Tom Rolf, who was better known as an editor, read an *Esquire* article about organ transplants. Together with his friend Jay Simms, they put together a script in three weeks. This was Rolf's one-and-only writing credit. He continued as an editor on such films as *Taxi Driver*, *Heaven's Gate*, *The Right Stuff* and *Heat*.

Shot on videotape and transferred to film for theatrical release, Angie Dickinson and Leslie Nielsen star.

RETURN OF COUNT YORGA

Originally intended as a bargain basement sexploitation flick, *Count Yorga, Vampire* (1970), one of the first vampire movies located in a recognisable contemporary setting, in this case Los Angeles, was a huge hit for AIP. It also made a horror star out of Robert Quarry as the debonair count. A sequel was rushed into production, again with Quarry, this time terrorising a rural town and its orphanage, aided by a harem of female bloodsuckers. In one scene Yorga is seen relaxing at home watching Hammer's *The Vampire Lovers* on television.

Made with a larger budget and heavier quota of blood and shocks, *The Return of Count Yorga* did not repeat the success of the original. AIP considered a third outing for Yorga, but instead put Quarry in their *Dr. Phibes* sequel and the count was laid to rest.

REVENGE

This was pretty gritty for its time: James Booth and Joan Collins play a married couple running a pub, who turn vigilante when a reclusive local man, suspected of raping and murdering their young daughter, is released due to insufficient evidence.

Playing Booth's teenage son and Collins's stepchild was Tom Marshall, who got on well with both Booth and Collins, although he found the actress rather stuck in her ways:

I was a young actor then and quite keen on trade unionism. I went into Joan's dressing room at one point and said, 'You know there's a meeting of Equity?' and she went, 'What?' I said, 'Equity, our trade union.' She said, 'Are you a communist?'[61]

In one scene Marshall throws bottles at the suspected paedophile that they've tied up in the cellar. Collins tries to stop him, only she and Marshall got their timing wrong, and she caught an elbow in her eye. 'She had a big shiner. Steaks were sent for in those days and she couldn't shoot for the rest of the day. I was in the dog house.'[62] In the same scene Marshall was required to roughly rip off her nightie. 'She had all the gantry and the stage cleared. I heard one of the sparks say, "I'm not worried about Joan Collins. I've seen Ursula Andress."'[63] She came on wearing a sort of corsage, with camera tape wound round and her nightie on top so nothing could be revealed.

Playing Marshall's girlfriend was Sinéad Cusack, then friendly with footballer George Best. Marshall was a Chelsea fan and asked Cusack if Best could get him tickets for Manchester United's upcoming match at Stamford Bridge. Then, just days before the match, Best went AWOL from training and the press learnt he'd spent the night at Cusack's London flat and were camped outside. 'We were supposed to shoot our love scene that morning,' recalls Marshall, 'and of course she didn't turn up. And I didn't get my tickets.'[64]

A SAFE PLACE

The friendship of idiosyncratic filmmaker Henry Jaglom and Jack Nicholson went back to the mid-1960s when they used to hang out together in all-night restaurants on Sunset Strip, spending hours 'dreaming our movie dreams'.[65] Jaglom began his career working with Nicholson on the editing of *Easy Rider*, and got the opportunity to direct his first film thanks to the patronage of BBS.

The men made a pact to appear in each other's first film as director. Jaglom appeared in *Drive, He Said* and Nicholson was now happy to return the favour, even though by this time he had become a big star, and no one thought Jaglom could get him:

> And yet, fulfilling our agreement, Jack made it possible for me to have him act in my first effort as a director by waiving the large fee he was entitled to and doing the part for a new colour TV set of his choice.[66]

Orson Welles, after being introduced to Jaglom by Peter Bogdanovich, also agreed to play a brief role.

A non-narrative story of the emotional vulnerabilities of a young girl, played by Tuesday Weld, *A Safe Place* received a heated reception at the New York Film Festival. This surprised Jaglom, as several European filmmakers were working along similar lines and their films were greeted warmly. Nicholson suggested a genius notion. 'He said we should pull the film, dub it in French, put English subtitles on it and change my name to Henri Jaglom. He insisted that it would be a huge hit if we did that.'[67] Ultimately *A Safe Place* was left to its fate. 'It was a commercial disaster of unbelievable proportions,' admits Jaglom.[68]

SAY HELLO TO YESTERDAY

This revolves around a brief liaison between a younger man and an older woman. Director Alvin Rakoff's choice for the woman was Jean Simmons, then in her early 40s. 'She was the loveliest actress to work with, a real straightforward, no-nonsense lady.'[69] For the young man Rakoff cast Leonard Whiting. 'And he was devoted to Jean. They got on very well.'[70]

Playing Jean's mother was the veteran stage and film actress Evelyn Laye. In one scene Leonard dances wildly with her and they fall on a sofa. Unfortunately, he got a bit carried away and crushed her arm and broke it. 'But Evelyn, being of the old school, went off to hospital, had the arm put in a cast and came back to finish the day's filming,' reveals Rakoff. 'She was a remarkable lady.'[71]

Rakoff did a lot of location shooting around London. 'I was trying to capture the London of that time. It was a sparkling city back then.'[72] One day Rod Steiger, a friend of Rakoff, turned up when they were shooting a street scene, and asked if he could casually walk through a shot.

Rakoff was pleased with how the film turned out, except for the music. He wanted to use the Joni Mitchell song 'Both Sides Now' as a theme for the couple that runs throughout the film, but the producer refused to pay for permission to use it. 'I pleaded with him, but he didn't back down. It was a great pity. The whole feel of the film could have been different with that song.'[73]

SEE NO EVIL

This effective thriller from the pen of Brian Clemens stars Mia Farrow as a young woman recently blinded in a riding accident, who returns to her uncle's English country home, unaware that a psychopathic killer is on the loose.

For the role of Farrow's boyfriend director Richard Fleischer spotted a young actor called Norman Eshley in a West End play:

> Fleischer was great, and very much an actor's director. He was one of those directors, and they're the best sort, who says, 'What do you think?' He knows what he wants, but he allows you to guide yourself to where he wants you to be.[74]

Farrow, too, far from being the big Hollywood star, was fun. 'She made me feel very welcome. She had no side to her at all.'[75] In a horse-riding scene, Eshley was required to kiss Farrow:

> But I'd never kissed a big star before. I was trying to say how professional I was going to be, but I was mumbling around like an idiot, and it came out as, 'Don't worry Mia, it's alright, I don't fancy you.' I thought, 'Oh God, what have I just said?!' She looked at me, and burst out laughing.[76]

When Eshley signed on, Columbia put him on a three-picture deal. However, the contract all depended on the American reviews. 'When the film was released one of the best notices that we got was, the most attractive thing in the film, apart from Mia Farrow, are the horses. And that was the end of my Hollywood contract.'[77] Instead, Eshley won TV fame in the hugely popular sitcom *George and Mildred*.

SHOOT OUT

This western was produced by the same team behind *True Grit*, director Henry Hathaway, screenwriter Marguerite Roberts and producer Hal B. Wallis. It had much the same plot too, a tough ageing loner saddled with a feisty youngster in pursuit of some bad guys. Instead of John Wayne we have Gregory Peck as a bank robber just out of jail looking for the partner who double-crossed him, and lumbered with a 7-year-old girl who may or may not be his daughter. No longer the star he once was, Peck agreed to defer his usual salary for a percentage of the profits, the first time he'd done this in his career.

During filming in New Mexico, Peck grew irritable at Hathaway's attempts to mould his performance into that of Wayne's. Hathaway had a reputation for being cantankerous and one of the most difficult directors in the business to work with. On the set Peck often had to stop Hathaway's abusive nature towards some of the crew. In contrast, Hathaway was deferential to Peck, who said of the veteran filmmaker, 'He was fine, except from nine to six when he became paranoiac.'[78]

SOMETIMES A GREAT NOTION

This was Ken Kesey's second novel, following in the wake of *One Flew Over the Cuckoo's Nest*, and was a sprawling epic set in Oregon about a tough family of loggers who continue working for a local mill in opposition to unionised workers who go on strike. Paul Newman bought the rights for his production company and went down to Newport, Oregon, to familiarise himself with the life of loggers, even learning to climb trees 80ft high with a chainsaw, despite a fear of heights.

Henry Fonda co-starred as the family's proud old patriarch and the largely inexperienced Richard A. Colla was hired to direct. After a few weeks things weren't working. First Newman was thrown off a motorcycle rehearsing a racing sequence and broke his ankle, necessitating a month's shutdown. Then Fonda complained that Colla was too preoccupied with camera set-ups than the actors. Things didn't improve and, reluctantly, Newman had to fire Colla and take over. Newman did not take to the experience of both starring and directing, and took to drinking whisky too much and taking out a motorbike for dangerous joyrides with his foot still in a cast.

Sometimes A Great Notion was not a success, but did make a little piece of history as the first programme telecast on HBO when it premiered in November 1972 when the station had just 365 cable subscriber households.

SUPPORT YOUR LOCAL GUNFIGHTER

This was a sequel of sorts to the 1969 comedy hit *Support Your Local Sheriff* and used many of the same cast and crew, including star James Garner and director Burt Kennedy. Both films poked fun at western conventions, in particular Garner's own TV characterisation of Maverick. He plays a con man arriving in a small western town who quickly takes advantage of a local rivalry between gold-mining factions – a plot with more than a hint of *A Fistful of Dollars* about it.

The film was shot almost entirely on the western street set of the Studio City lot, CBS Studio Center in LA. Although a draft script was written for a third film, entitled *Support Your Local Coward*, it was never made.

TALES OF BEATRIX POTTER

These classic children's stories are brought to life through a series of impressive dance sequences performed by members of the Royal Ballet. This was a passion project for producer Richard Goodwin. Managing to secure the film rights from the Potter estate, where the Walt Disney company had tried and failed, Goodwin developed the film for two years.

He was backed by EMI, despite some reluctance from board members. Nat Cohen had never heard of Beatrix Potter, while another opined 'ballet films are shit'. Nicely timed for the Easter holidays, it was one of the most popular movies of the year in Britain.

Choreographed by Frederick Ashton, one of the most influential ballet figures of the twentieth century, and with the dancers in beautifully rendered costumes of Beatrix Potter's most famous creations, from Mrs Tiggy-Winkle to Jeremy Fisher, this is a quite unique film.

THERE'S ALWAYS VANILLA

If you're George A. Romero, how do you follow the groundbreaking *Night of the Living Dead*? Why, with a romantic comedy, of course! At the time Romero didn't want to do another horror picture, reluctant to typecast himself as a horror director. The idea was to do another small independent movie, but in another genre. The plot concerns a young drifter, Chris (Raymond Laine), who literally bumps into a beautiful model Lynn, played by Judith Ridley from *Night of the Living Dead*, and the pair start an affair.

Romero shot the film on 16mm, directed and edited it on a shoestring $100,000 budget. At the time Romero's company was involved in shooting commercials, so it was only when he could spare the time that they'd get the cameras and cast together and shoot a few scenes. The film's schedule dragged on for almost a year.

Although at the time Romero felt it was a worthwhile exercise, later he came to see the film as a compete mess, and rarely talked or cared much about it. He certainly never attempted another romantic comedy.

THEY MIGHT BE GIANTS

George C. Scott is Sherlock Holmes – or is he? Scott in fact plays Justin Playfair, a successful New York criminal lawyer who, psychologically disturbed by his wife's death, believes himself to be the great detective, to the point of dressing up like him, smoking a pipe, playing the violin and making deductions. Playfair's brother is intent on having him committed so he can get his hands on his money. Justin meets a psychiatrist called, obviously, Doctor Watson, played by Joanne Woodward. A lost soul herself, she latches onto Playfair and follows him around the city as he endeavours to solve a mystery that may lead him to Professor Moriarty.

Based on James Goldman's play and directed by Anthony Harvey, this offbeat romantic comedy is a must for Holmes fans. The film is distinguished by excellent performances by Scott, showing a flair for comedy, and Woodward, whose husband, Paul Newman, was producer. According to Harvey, Newman briefly considered playing the lead himself. Future Academy Award-winning actor F. Murray Abraham makes his feature debut here in a small role.

TOGETHER

This relatively inauspicious film brought together the two men that came to dominate '80s horror cinema: Sean S. Cunningham (*Friday the 13th*) and Wes Craven (*Nightmare on Elm Street*). A pseudo-documentary about sex in America, this was Cunningham's directorial debut, and he brought in the struggling Wes Craven, who was keen to get into movies, to help out with editing duties.

A big hit, the distributors of the film, Hallmark, asked Cunningham to come up with a horror film next. This time Cunningham took on the role of producer, leaving the writing and directing job to Craven. The result was the groundbreaking *The Last House on the Left* (1972).

A TOWN CALLED BASTARD

Another in a conveyor belt of tough, violent spaghetti westerns, this one is blessed with a superior cast to many: Robert Shaw is a priest with a shady past, living in a town ruled by bandit Telly Savalas. Widow Stella Stevens arrives on the scene, promising to pay $20,000 in gold to anyone who can deliver the man who killed her husband. There are also roles for Martin Landau and Fernando Rey.

Playing the widow's faithful servant was Dudley Sutton, fresh from *The Devils*. Assistant director Julio Sempere remembers make-up man Fernando Florido telling him that, while working on Stella and Dudley Sutton, he always felt dizzy. 'Later he told me that he discovered what was wrong. The two actors, while relaxing, smoked cigars of certain herbs.'[79]

The film was directed by Robert Parrish. He was having difficulties with a mysterious character in the story called Águila (Spanish for 'eagle'), who did not appear physically, only in a photograph. In the end Parrish chose his production supervisor Gregorio Sacristán as the face in the photo. 'At the end of the editing,' recalls Sempere, 'Parrish decided that it was necessary to shoot a scene with "the eagle" so that the film could be better understood. So, the production supervisor became a key player in the film.'[80]

TRINITY IS STILL MY NAME

This sequel to the enormously popular *They Call Me Trinity* (1970) was rushed into production only for its release to be postponed because the first movie was still playing to packed theatres in Italy.

The original film made stars out of Terence Hill and Bud Spencer, and the pair return as wannabe outlaw brothers Trinity and Bambino, who this time defend a Mormon settlement from Mexican bandits. The emphasis now is more on the comedy elements that worked so well in the first film and less on the savage violence typical of spaghetti westerns from this period. It's clear that the producers wanted to make the sequel more 'family friendly', and it certainly worked: the film went on to become the top-grossing Italian film of all time, beating the previous record holder, *They Call Me Trinity*. Hill and Spencer went on to make eleven more films together.

THE TROJAN WOMEN

At the core of this screen adaptation of one the most powerful works of classic Greek theatre is the bringing together of a staggering quartet of actresses: Katharine Hepburn as Hecuba, the aged Queen of Troy; Vanessa Redgrave as Andromache, the wife of Hector; Geneviève Bujold as the Trojan priestess Cassandra; and Irene Papas as Helen of Troy, all of whom face enslavement after the fall of their city.

Director Michael Cacoyannis had staged the play in Italy, New York and Paris in the mid-1960s, and believed the writing of Euripides still had much to say about the folly of war and the human disease of slaughtering other people. Shot in the Spanish village of Atienza, 80 miles north-east of Madrid, with the destruction of Troy replicated by mounds of burning rubber tyres, the cast suffered heat exhaustion, diarrhoea and sundry ailments, all save for Hepburn who battled through unscathed like an unsinkable battleship. She had agreed to make the film because she had never played Greek tragedy before, and wanted to work with Redgrave, who she considered the most accomplished actress of her generation. In turn, Redgrave always rated *The Trojan Women* as a career 'high point' for the simple reason it afforded her the chance to work with Hepburn who, during filming, took the younger actress under her wing.

UNIVERSAL SOLDIER

On paper this project looked promising. Its star, George Lazenby, had just finished playing James Bond, and the director was Cy Endfield of *Zulu* fame. The premise was interesting too, with Lazenby playing a mercenary hired to train an army for an exiled African leader who suddenly gets a conscience. 'The script seemed alright,' reveals assistant director Mike Higgins, 'but instead of becoming a thriller it turned into this flower power, give peace a chance rubbish, and the main players were all on drugs.'[81]

The film trades on Lazenby's masculinity. In one scene he comes up against a gang of skinheads. The casting director hired a group of totally inappropriate actors. In the end Higgins was asked if he could perhaps find some 'real ones'. At the time Higgins had some contacts in the East End, including an ex-boxer with former links to the Kray twins. 'I called him up and he got a group of half a dozen real hard men together. They shaved their heads and came into the office. When Lazenby saw them, he almost shat himself.'[82] Higgins was told by the production manager that the scene was no longer going ahead, and they weren't going to pay the heavies, either. 'You want to actually leave the building tonight?' asked Higgins, 'Or would you rather go straight to the hospital? Because they will beat the shit out of you.'[83] They got paid.

Whatever audience the film was made for, it didn't reach it. Halfway through shooting Higgins realised he'd made a mistake. 'At the time you think, "What am I doing here? Why did I agree to do this?" It was not an enjoyable experience.'[84]

UNMAN, WITTERING AND ZIGO

This is an odd title (it refers to the last three names on a school register) for what is actually quite a decent thriller. David Hemmings plays a teacher at a boys' school who fears his class was involved in his predecessor's tragic demise.

Hemmings had been a big star in the 1960s, but his career was starting to falter. 'He was so beautiful and just a mess, poor darling,' recalls Carolyn Seymour, who played his wife. 'He was a storyteller, a drunk and a delightful louche guy.'[85] In only her second film, Seymour recalls on her first day Hemmings walking into her dressing room and plonking a bottle of champagne on the table at 7 a.m. 'This is how we make movies,' he said.[86]

The pair shared a complicated love scene that was tough to shoot, 'and fuelled by a certain amount of vodka to loosen us up,' adds Seymour.[87] Shot in an isolated cottage, after the crew packed up a knackered Hemmings and Seymour fell asleep. The crew had turned off the generator so, when they woke a couple of hours later, it was in pitch blackness. 'We dressed in darkness and got into David's Roller and drove across these bumpy roads to the hotel. Everybody assumed we'd been at it like rabbits.'[88] Hemmings's wife, Gayle Hunnicutt, was there waiting. 'She took one look at us, turned around, and then came back with a couple of pint glasses full of beer and tipped them over our heads.'[89] They were wearing each other's tops.

In another unsettling scene Seymour's character is threatened by the schoolboys and is almost gang-raped:

> It was terrifying. One of the boys kept coming up to me and apologising; but the rest of them were just having a blast. I knew that I was safe because it was a movie, but I also found it quite intimidating.[90]

Luckily, Seymour had supreme confidence in her director John Mackenzie: 'He was so supportive. I adored him.'[91] Mackenzie was to finish the decade strong, directing *The Long Good Friday*.

VAMPYROS LESBOS

This erotic tale hails from the arch exponent of Eurotrash cinema, Jesús Franco, and is one of the most explicit examples of the lesbian vampire movie for its time. Set in modern times, it features Soledad Miranda as a vixen vampire, a descendant of Dracula, who lures women to a Mediterranean island to satisfy her insatiable lust for female flesh and blood. As with most of Franco's oeuvre, the story is a mere excuse for scenes of softcore sex and sadomasochism. A definite highlight is the experimental jazz score, segments of which were used by Quentin Tarantino in *Jackie Brown* (1997).

However jumbled the narrative, the Mediterranean locations are beautiful to look at, along with the spellbinding presence of Miranda, who tragically died in a car accident not long after finishing the film.

VON RICHTHOFEN AND BROWN

Roger Corman has a reputation for cheap schlock, but this was an ambitious First World War flying drama he directed for UA. But the rebel filmmaker found it almost impossible to tolerate the outside pressure from the big studio and, when they redubbed the film, against his wishes, with actors doing cheesy German accents, that was the last straw. Corman didn't direct another film for twenty years. Instead, he formed his own production company. Better to be his own boss.

Interestingly, the film remained an important one for him. He saw the two protagonists – the daring, aristocratic German ace, the Red Baron, and Roy Brown, the Canadian garage mechanic who shot him down – as reflecting the 'warring' aspects of his own personality, 'the elitist artist and the hustler maverick destined to defeat him'.[92]

The film was shot at Ireland's Ardmore Studios, where Corman made good use of all the planes left over from the 1966 big-budget war movie *The Blue Max*. The aerial sequences took three weeks to complete. When UA overruled his plan to cast Bruce Dern as Von Richthofen, John Philip Law was cast. Don Stroud played Brown. Shooting was marred by several aerial accidents and the tragic death of one of the stunt pilots.

WELCOME HOME SOLDIER BOYS

Directed by Richard Compton, this is a brutal, if at times outlandish, drama about four shell-shocked soldiers returning from Vietnam who go on a cross-country trip that leads to murder and mayhem. Something of a thematic predecessor to Sylvester Stallone's *First Blood* (1982), Joe Don Baker stars as the leader of the group, travelling down to California with his comrades-in-arms to start a new life as a farmer. But all of their personalities are so fundamentally changed by their harrowing experiences that each of them has found it difficult readjusting back into normal society. It's the final realisation that they don't fit anywhere that sends them over the edge. Out of money, they rob a gas station in a small town; but when the locals start fighting back at them, they don their Green Beret uniforms and take revenge. Finally, coming face to face with the National Guard, they all meet their inevitable slow-motion demise.

WHAT'S THE MATTER WITH HELEN?

Following the success of *Whatever Happened to Baby Jane?* (1962) it seemed that every ageing actress in Hollywood was making horror films. The genre even spawned its own name: Grande Dame Guignol. This one, directed by Curtis Harrington, paired Debbie Reynolds and Shelley Winters as two mothers who, after their sons commit a horrible murder in their Iowa hometown, decide to leave for LA to start a new life.

The actresses had known each other since the 1950s but never worked together. Reynolds labelled Winters as bananas, though much of Winters's behaviour was done for shock value. Before starting work, Winters told Reynolds that her psychiatrist had told her not to make the picture, 'Because it will probably flip me over the edge.'[93] This did little for Reynolds's nerves, knowing that in the final scene Winters kills her with a kitchen knife.

A method actress, Winters became the character in the film and drove everyone nuts. After agreeing to the design for her costumes, on the first day of shooting she threw them all away and stormed out of her dressing room virtually naked. Complaining that Reynolds was thinner than she was, Winters ransacked her trailer and kicked the door off its hinges. Then there was her habit of bringing a portable gramophone onto the set to play selections of Puccini operas before a scene. When Reynolds complained, Winters said, 'This is the only way I can work. I've won two Academy Awards you know.'[94] Finally, Reynolds flipped, halted the scene they were playing, ripped a fire hose off the wall and let Winters have it full blast.

WHO IS HARRY KELLERMAN AND WHY IS HE

SAYING THOSE TERRIBLE THINGS ABOUT ME?

This surreal social satire stars Dustin Hoffman as Georgie Soloway, a Bob Dylan-type singer unable to cope with the problems of life despite his celebrity status. Plagued by insomnia and suicidal fantasies, he is also on the hunt for one 'Harry Kellerman', an invisible foe spreading lies and rumours about him, but who is in fact not real, just a figment of Soloway's troubled mind.

Hoffman and director Ulu Grosbard had been friends in New York since 1957, and worked together in local theatre. Indeed, this whole movie has an off-Broadway quirky feel about it. Enlivened by a minor tour-de-force from the ever-dependable Hoffman, the film met with mixed reviews and failed at the box office. For almost thirty years it was thought to be lost, until the film's writer Herb Gardner tracked down the negative and it was finally released on home video.

Made on location in New York, the concert sequence was shot in front of a live audience before a Grateful Dead appearance at Fillmore East, the famous rock venue on Second Avenue. Barbara Harris plays Soloway's girlfriend, a failed actress, and ironically received an Oscar nomination for Best Supporting Actress. Dom DeLuise is also a standout in his brief scene as Soloway's accountant.

WOMEN IN REVOLT

Produced by Andy Warhol and directed by Paul Morrissey, this satire on the women's liberation movement stars Candy Darling, Jackie Curtis and Holly Woodlawn, drag queen superstars of Warhol's famed New York studio, the Factory.

With no budget or script (the dialogue was improvised) shooting took place erratically over a year and, on completion, no distributor would touch it – largely due to the full-frontal nudity and depiction of numerous sex acts. In the end Warhol hired a cinema and put it on himself.

Women in Revolt is seen as Warhol's mocking revenge on the radical feminist and visual artist Valerie Solanas, who in 1968 walked into Warhol's studio and shot him. He was critically injured and spent several months recovering in hospital. Solanas was the founder and sole member of an organisation called the Society for Cutting Up Men (SCUM). In *Women in Revolt*, Darling, Curtis and Woodlawn play the roles of women's libbers and members of PIG (Politically Involved Girls). In one scene Jackie pays a former Mr America for sex so she can 'find out what we're fighting against'.

The music soundtrack comes courtesy of the Velvet Underground's John Cale.

ZEPPELIN

This *Boy's Own* war picture stars Michael York as a First World War British officer asked to infiltrate a German airship factory. There he finds himself aboard the maiden voyage of a powerful new prototype Zeppelin, tasked with stealing the Magna Carta from its hiding place in a Scottish castle. It all sounds a bit barmy, but it's a well-mounted production with some impressive model work.

Tragically, during the shoot a replica First World War biplane collided in mid-air with the camera helicopter, resulting in the death of four crew members, including top helicopter pilot Gilbert Chomat and acclaimed cameraman Skeets Kelly.

NOTES

Introduction
1. Michael Margotta, author interview.

100 Films

1. Peter Hannan, author interview.
2. Ibid.
3. Ibid.
4. Ibid.
5. Ibid.
6. Ibid.
7. Ibid.
8. Michael Deeley, author interview 2014.
9. Ibid.
10. Ibid.
11. Ibid.
12. Ibid.
13. Ibid.
14. Ken Russell, author interview 2005.
15. Ibid.
16. Ibid.
17. Ibid.
18. *Daily Mail*, September 1981.
19. Rex Reed, *People Are Crazy Here* (Delacorte Press, 1974).
20. Christian Roberts, author interview.
21. Ibid.
22. Ibid.
23. Ibid.
24. Michael Caine, *What's It All About?* (Century, 1992).
25. Michael Attenborough, author interview.
26. Ibid.
27. Ibid.
28. Ibid.
29. Ibid.
30. Ibid.
31. Ibid.
32. Ibid.
33. Ibid.
34. Mike Higgins, author interview.
35. Ibid.
36. Ibid.
37. Ibid.
38. Ibid.
39. Ibid.
40. Mike Hodges, author interview.
41. Ibid.
42. Tony Klinger, author interview.
43. Ibid.
44. Ibid.
45. Mike Hodges, author interview.
46. Ibid.
47. Ibid.
48. Ibid.
49. Tony Klinger, author interview.
50. Ibid.
51. Mike Hodges, author interview.
52. Tony Klinger, author interview.
53. Mike Hodges, author interview.
54. Ibid.
55. Ibid.
56. Ibid.
57. Ibid.
58. Tony Klinger, author interview.
59. Ibid.
60. Mike Hodges, author interview.
61. Stephen Lighthill, author interview.
62. Ibid.
63. Ibid.
64. Ibid.
65. Ibid.
66. Ibid.
67. Ibid.
68. Ibid.

69. Ibid.
70. Ibid.
71. Ibid.
72. Ibid.
73. Kate Buford, *Burt Lancaster. An American Life* (Knopf, 2000).
74. Michael Winner, *Winner Takes All* (Robson, 2004).
75. Jimmy Perry, *A Stupid Boy* (Arrow, 2003).
76. Graham McCann, *Dad's Army. The Story of a Classic Television Show* (Fourth Estate, 2001).
77. Bill Pertwee, *Dad's Army. The Making of a Television Legend* (Pavilion, 1998).
78. Jo Ann Harris, author interview.
79. Ibid.
80. Ibid.
81. Ibid.
82. Ibid.
83. Ibid.
84. Ibid.
85. Ibid.
86. Ibid.
87. Christopher Beach (ed.), *Claude Chabrol Interviews* (University Press of Mississippi, 2020).
88. *Guardian*, June 2001.
89. Mark Lester, author interview.
90. Ibid.
91. Ibid.
92. Ibid.
93. Ibid.
94. Ibid.
95. Ibid.
96. Ibid.
97. Ibid.
98. David Picker, *Musts, Maybes, and Nevers* (CreateSpace Independent Publishing, 2013).
99. Stig Bjorkman, *Woody Allen on Woody Allen* (Faber & Faber, 2004).
100. Ralph Rosenblum, *When the Shooting Stops, the Cutting Begins. A Film Editor's Story* (Viking, 1980).
101. Louis Malle, *Malle on Malle* (Faber & Faber, 1993).
102. Hawk Koch, author interview.
103. Tom Chapin, author interview.
104. Ibid.
105. Ibid.
106. Ibid.
107. Ibid.
108. Ibid.
109. Ibid.
110. Ibid.
111. Ibid.
112. Ibid.
113. Ibid.
114. Robert Fuest, author interview 2011.
115. Ibid.
116. Ibid.
117. Ibid.
118. Ibid.
119. Ibid.
120. Ibid.
121. Ibid.
122. Ibid.
123. Ibid.
124. Ibid.
125. Ibid.
126. Ibid.
127. Ibid.
128. Patrick Wayne, author interview.
129. Ibid.
130. Ibid.
131. Ibid.
132. Ibid.
133. Harry Kümel, author interview.
134. Ibid.
135. Ibid.
136. Ibid.
137. Ibid.
138. Danielle Ouimet, author interview.
139. Ibid.
140. Ibid.
141. Ibid.
142. Ibid.
143. Harry Kümel, author interview.
144. Julian Holloway, author interview.
145. Ibid.
146. Ibid.
147. Ibid.
148. Ibid.
149. Ibid.
150. Ibid.
151. Ibid.
152. Ibid.
153. Ibid.
154. Ibid.
155. Ibid.
156. Sidney Lumet, *Making Movies* (Knopf Doubleday, 1996).
157. Ernest Borgnine, *The Autobiography* (Citadel Press, 2009).
158. *Shock Cinema*, No. 43, 2013.
159. Ralph S. Singleton, author interview.
160. Ibid.
161. Ibid.

162. Jane Fonda, *My Life So Far* (Random House, 2005).
163. Bob Thomas, *Golden Boy. The Untold Story of William Holden* (Penguin, 1984).
164. Julie Andrews, *Home Work. A Memoir of My Hollywood Years* (Hachette Books, 2019).
165. Peter Samuelson, author interview.
166. Ibid.
167. Ibid.
168. Ibid.
169. Derek Bell, author interview.
170. Ibid.
171. Ibid.
172. Peter Samuelson, author interview.
173. Derek Bell, author interview.
174. Peter Samuelson, author interview.
175. Derek Bell, author interview.
176. Peter Samuelson, author interview.
177. Derek Bell, author interview.
178. Ibid.
179. David Foster, author interview 2010.
180. Ibid.
181. Ibid.
182. Don Carmody, author interview.
183. Ibid.
184. Ibid.
185. Ibid.
186. Ibid.
187. Ibid.
188. Ibid.
189. Ibid.
190. Mel Stuart, author interview 2011.
191. Ibid.
192. Ibid.
193. Ibid.
194. Ibid.
195. Ibid.
196. Ibid.
197. Ibid.
198. Ibid.
199. Ibid.
200. Ibid.
201. Ibid.
202. Ibid.
203. Ibid.
204. Henry Jaglom, author interview 2010.
205. Michael Margotta, author interview.
206. Henry Jaglom, author interview 2010.
207. Michael Margotta, author interview.
208. Ibid.
209. Ibid.
210. Ibid.
211. Ibid.
212. Ibid.
213. Ibid.
214. Ibid.
215. Candice Bergen, *Knock Wood* (Hamish Hamilton, 1984).
216. Ann-Margret, *My Story* (Putnam, 1994).
217. Neal Peters, *Ann-Margret. A Photo Extravaganza and Memoir* (Delilah Books, 1981).
218. Anthony B. Richmond, author interview.
219. Ibid.
220. Peter Hannan, author interview.
221. Anthony B. Richmond, author interview.
222. Ibid.
223. Peter Hannan, author interview.
224. Ibid.
225. Anthony B. Richmond, author interview.
226. Ibid.
227. Ibid.
228. Ibid.
229. Ibid.
230. Ibid.
231. Elaine Dundy, *Finch, Bloody Finch* (Michael Joseph, 1980).
232. William J. Mann, *Edge of Midnight. The Life of John Schlesinger* (Random House, 2004).
233. Trader Faulkner, *Peter Finch. A Biography* (Angus & Robertson, 1979).
234. William J. Mann, *Edge of Midnight. The Life of John Schlesinger* (Random House, 2004).
235. Ibid.
236. Gene D. Phillips, *John Schlesinger* (Twayne Publishers, 1981).
237. John Bailey, author interview.
238. Ibid.
239. Ibid.
240. Ibid.
241. Ibid.
242. Ibid.

243. Ibid.
244. Ibid.
245. Ibid.
246. Ibid.
247. Ibid.
248. Ibid.
249. Jerry Schatzberg, author interview.
250. Ibid.
251. Ibid.
252. Ibid.
253. Ibid.
254. Ibid.
255. Ibid.
256. Ibid.
257. Ibid.
258. Ibid.
259. Ibid.
260. Ibid.
261. Piers Haggard, author interview.
262. Ibid.
263. Ibid.
264. Ibid.
265. Ibid.
266. Ibid.
267. Ibid.
268. Ibid.
269. Ibid.
270. Ibid.
271. Ibid.
272. Ibid.
273. Ibid.
274. Ibid.
275. Murray Melvin, author interview.
276. Barbara Windsor, *All of Me. My Extraordinary Life* (Headline, 2000).
277. Murray Melvin, author interview.
278. Ibid.
279. Ibid.
280. Ken Russell, author interview 2005.
281. Murray Melvin, author interview.
282. Ken Russell, author interview 2005.
283. Larry Ceplair, *Dalton Trumbo. Blacklisted Hollywood Radical* (University Press of Kentucky, 2015).
284. Hawk Koch, author interview.
285. Ibid.
286. Ibid.
287. Ibid.
288. Ibid.
289. Ibid.
290. *Psychotronic Video*, No. 7.
291. Vic Armstrong, author interview.
292. Joss Ackland, *My Better Half and Me* (Ebury Press, 2009).
293. Clive Francis, author interview.
294. Ibid.
295. Ibid.
296. Charlton Heston, *In the Arena* (Simon & Schuster, 1995).
297. Barth David Schwartz, *Pasolini Requiem* (Pantheon Books, 1992).
298. John D. Hancock, author interview.
299. Ibid.
300. Ibid.
301. Ibid.
302. Ibid.
303. Ibid.
304. Ibid.
305. Ibid.
306. Ibid.
307. Ibid.
308. Ibid.
309. Ibid.
310. Ingmar Bergman, *Images. My Life in Film* (Little, Brown, 1994).
311. *New Yorker*, November 2011.
312. Chris Nashawaty, *Roger Corman. King of the B Movie* (Abrams, 2013).
313. *Fangoria*, June 1985.
314. Sofia Moran, author interview.
315. Ibid.
316. Ibid.
317. Ibid.
318. Ibid.
319. *Guardian*, October 2015.
320. *Film Comment*, Sept/Oct 1974.
321. *Guardian*, March 1971.
322. Richard Gibson, author interview.
323. Ibid.
324. Ibid.
325. Ibid.
326. Ibid.
327. Ibid.
328. Ibid.
329. Ibid.
330. *Sight & Sound*, Winter 1972/73.
331. John Cleese, author interview 2003.
332. Eric Idle, author interview 2003.
333. David Muir, author interview.
334. John Cleese, author interview 2003.
335. Eric Idle, author interview 2003.
336. Ibid.
337. David Muir, author interview.

338. Ibid.
339. Ibid.
340. Terry Jones, author interview 2003.
341. Eric Idle, author interview 2003.
342. L.M. Kit Carson, author interview 2010.
343. *Guardian*, March 2008.
344. Tom Mankiewicz, author interview 2010.
345. L.M. Kit Carson, author interview 2010.
346. Deborah Winters, author interview.
347. Ibid.
348. Ibid.
349. Ibid.
350. Ralph S. Singleton, author interview.
351. Tony Lo Bianco, author interview.
352. Ibid.
353. Ralph S. Singleton, author interview.
354. Ibid.
355. Tony Lo Bianco, author interview.
356. Ibid.
357. Ralph S. Singleton, author interview.
358. Ibid.
359. Ibid.
360. Ibid.
361. Ibid.
362. Peter Hannan, author interview.
363. Ibid.
364. Ibid.
365. Ibid.
366. Ibid.
367. Ibid.
368. Ibid.

369. Joan Churchill, author interview.
370. Ibid.
371. Ibid.
372. pwatkins.mnsi.net.
373. Damien Thomas, author interview.
374. Ibid.
375. Ibid.
376. Judy Matheson, author interview.
377. Ibid.
378. Ibid.
379. Damien Thomas, author interview.
380. Ibid.
381. Ibid.
382. Ibid.
383. Vic Armstrong, author interview.
384. Ibid.
385. Peter Sasdy, author interview 2011.
386. Ibid.
387. Ibid.
388. Angharad Rees, author interview 2011.
389. Ibid.
390. Ibid.
391. Ibid.
392. Peter Sasdy, author interview 2011.
393. Iain Johnstone, *The Man with No Name. Clint Eastwood* (Plexus, 1981).
394. Donna Mills, author interview.
395. Ibid.
396. Ibid.
397. Ibid.
398. Ibid.
399. Ibid.
400. Ibid.
401. Ibid.

402. Ibid.
403. Ibid.
404. Brian Clemens, author interview 2011.
405. Ibid.
406. Ibid.
407. Ibid.
408. Ibid.
409. Ibid.
410. Ibid.
411. Ibid.
412. Ibid.
413. Ibid.
414. Valerie Leon, author interview.
415. Ibid.
416. Ibid.
417. Ibid.
418. Ibid.
419. Ibid.
420. Ibid.
421. Tony Palmer, author interview.
422. Ibid.
423. Ibid.
424. Ibid.
425. Ibid.
426. Ibid.
427. Ibid.
428. Ibid.
429. Ibid.
430. David Tomlinson, *Luckier Than Most. An Autobiography* (Hodder and Stoughton, 1990).
431. Kika Markham, author interview.
432. Ibid.
433. Ibid.
434. Ibid.
435. Ibid.
436. Ibid.
437. Ibid.
438. Ibid.
439. Ibid.

440. Katy Haber, author interview.
441. Steven H. Gale, *Harold Pinter. Critical Approaches* (Fairleigh Dickinson University Press, 1986).
442. Katy Haber, author interview.
443. Ibid.
444. Ibid.
445. Ibid.
446. Ibid.
447. Ibid.
448. Ibid.
449. Ibid.
450. Michael Feeney Callan, *Richard Harris. A Sporting Life* (Sidgwick & Jackson, 1990).
451. Michael Jayston, author interview 2011.
452. Ibid.
453. Ibid.
454. Ibid.
455. Ibid.
456. Ibid.
457. Ibid.
458. Ibid.
459. Ibid.
460. Ibid.
461. Ibid.
462. Ibid.
463. Ibid.
464. Ibid.
465. Ibid.
466. Ibid.
467. Anne Raitt, author interview.
468. Ibid.
469. Ibid.
470. Ibid.
471. Ibid.
472. Ibid.
473. Ibid.

474. Ibid.
475. Ibid.
476. Ibid.
477. *Jump Cut*, Nos 10–11, 1976.
478. Ibid.
479. Carolyn Seymour, author interview.
480. Ibid.
481. Shaun Considine, *Mad as Hell. The Life and Work of Paddy Chayefsky* (Random House, 1994).
482. Ibid.
483. Arthur Hiller, DGA website.
484. Timothy Burrill, author interview.
485. Ibid.
486. Ibid.
487. Ibid.
488. Ibid.
489. Ibid.
490. Ibid.
491. Ibid.
492. Michael Brandon, author interview.
493. Ibid.
494. Ibid.
495. Ibid.
496. Ibid.
497. Ibid.
498. Ibid.
499. Ibid.
500. Michael Tarn, author interview.
501. Ibid.
502. Ibid.
503. Ibid.
504. Ibid.
505. Ibid.
506. Ibid.
507. Ibid.
508. Ibid.
509. Ibid.
510. Ibid.

511. Ibid.
512. Ibid.
513. Ibid.
514. Ibid.
515. Ibid.
516. Clive Francis, author interview.
517. Ibid.
518. Ibid.
519. Ibid.
520. Nick Dawson, *Being Hal Ashby. Life of a Hollywood Rebel* (University Press of Kentucky, 2009).
521. Ellen Geer, author interview.
522. Ibid.
523. Ibid.
524. Ibid.
525. Ibid.
526. Ibid.
527. Hal B. Wallis, *Starmaker. The Autobiography of Hal Wallis* (Macmillan, 1980).
528. Ibid.
529. John Milius, author interview 2004.
530. Ibid.
531. Ibid.
532. Ibid.
533. Tom Mankiewicz, author interview 2010.
534. Ibid.
535. Bruce Glover, author interview.
536. Ibid.
537. Ibid.
538. Tom Mankiewicz, author interview 2010.
539. Ibid.

The Good, the Bad and the Weird: The Best of the Rest

1. Mark Lester, author interview.
2. Stanley Kramer, *A Mad, Mad, Mad, Mad World. A Life in Hollywood* (Harcourt Brace, 1997).
3. Beverly Todd, author interview.
4. Ibid.
5. Ibid.
6. Ibid.
7. *Shock Cinema*, Summer 2002.
8. Ibid.
9. Peter Sasdy, author interview 2011.
10. Ibid.
11. Ibid.
12. Judy Matheson, author interview.
13. Ibid.
14. Frank Langella, *Dropped Names* (HarperCollins, 2013).
15. Erika Blanc, author interview.
16. Ibid.
17. Ibid.
18. Christopher Sandford, author interview.
19. Ibid.
20. Ibid.
21. Ibid.
22. *Chiller Theatre*, No. 2 1995.
23. George Hamilton, *Don't Mind If I Do* (Simon & Schuster, 2008).
24. Leigh Montville, *The High-Flying Life of Evel Knievel* (Doubleday, 2011).
25. Hawk Koch, author interview.
26. John Baxter, *De Niro. A Biography* (HarperCollins, 2002).
27. Clive Francis, author interview.
28. Ibid.
29. Ibid.
30. Lee Server, *Robert Mitchum. Baby I Don't Care* (St Martin's Publishing Group, 2002).
31. Hawk Koch, author interview.
32. Ibid.
33. Julio Sempere, author interview.
34. Ibid.
35. Stephen Weeks, author interview.
36. Ibid.
37. Ibid.
38. Ibid.
39. Ibid.
40. *Interview* magazine, January 1976.
41. Michael Brandon, author interview.
42. Ibid.
43. Ibid.
44. Ibid.
45. Ilya Salkind, author interview.
46. Ibid.
47. Ibid.
48. Judy Matheson, author interview.
49. Ibid.
50. Hunter Allen, *Walter Matthau* (St Martin's Press, 1984).
51. Michael Winner, author interview 2010.
52. Ibid.
53. Ibid.
54. Ibid.
55. Ibid.
56. Diane Sherry Case, author interview.
57. Ibid.
58. Ibid.
59. Ibid.
60. Ibid.
61. Tom Marshall, author interview.
62. Ibid.
63. Ibid.
64. Ibid.
65. Henry Jaglom, author interview 2010.
66. Ibid.
67. Ibid.
68. Ibid.
69. Alvin Rakoff, author interview.
70. Ibid.
71. Ibid.
72. Ibid.
73. Ibid.
74. Norman Eshley, author interview.
75. Ibid.
76. Ibid.
77. Ibid.
78. Gerard Molyneaux, *Gregory Peck. A Bio-Bibliography* (Greenwood Press, 1995).
79. Julio Sempere, author interview.
80. Ibid.
81. Mike Higgins, author interview.

82. Ibid.
83. Ibid.
84. Ibid.
85. Carolyn Seymour,
    author interview.
86. Ibid.
87. Ibid.
88. Ibid.
89. Ibid.
90. Ibid.
91. Ibid.
92. Roger Corman, *How I
    Made A Hundred Movies
    In Hollywood And Never
    Lost A Dime* (Hachette,
    1998).
93. Debbie Reynolds,
    Unsinkable
    (HarperCollins, 2013).
94. Ibid.

SELECT BIBLIOGRAPHY

Baxter, John, *De Niro: A Biography* (HarperCollins, 2002).

Baxter, John, *Woody Allen: A Biography* (HarperCollins, 1998).

Bellos, David, *Jacques Tati: His Life and Art* (Harvill Press, 1999).

Biskind, Peter, *Easy Riders Raging Bulls* (Simon & Schuster, 1999).

Bosworth, Patricia, *Jane Fonda: The Private Life of a Public Woman* (Mariner Books, 2011).

Caute, David: *Joseph Losey: A Revenge on Life* (Oxford University Press, 1994).

Ceplair, Larry, *Dalton Trumbo: Blacklisted Hollywood Radical* (University Press of Kentucky, 2015).

Frayling, Christopher, *Sergio Leone: Something to Do with Death* (Faber & Faber, 2000).

Parks, Gordon, *Voices in the Mirror: An Autobiography* (Doubleday, 1990).

Perry, Jimmy, *A Stupid Boy* (Arrow, 2003).

Russo, Vita, *The Celluloid Closet: Homosexuality in the Movies* (HarperCollins, 1987).

Schwartz, Barth David, *Pasolini Requiem* (Pantheon Books, 1992).

Thomas, Bruce, *Bruce Lee: Fighting Spirit* (Frog Ltd, 1994).

INDEX